Absolutism and the eighteenth-century origins of compulsory schooling in Prussia and Austria

An Austrian parish school classroom (ca. 1750). Source: *Historisches Museum der Stadt Wien*.

Absolutism and the eighteenth-century origins of compulsory schooling in Prussia and Austria

James Van Horn Melton
Emory University

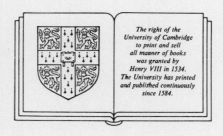

The right of the
University of Cambridge
to print and sell
all manner of books
was granted by
Henry VIII in 1534.
The University has printed
and published continuously
since 1584.

Cambridge University Press
Cambridge
New York   New Rochelle   Melbourne   Sydney

Published by the Press Syndicate of the University of Cambridge
The Pitt Building, Trumpington Street, Cambridge CB2 1RP
32 East 57th Street, New York, NY 10022, USA
10 Stamford Road, Oakleigh, Melbourne 3166, Australia

First published 1988

Printed in Canada

Library of Congress Cataloging-in-Publication Data
Melton, James Van Horn, 1952–
Absolutism and the eighteenth-century origins of compulsory
schooling in Prussia and Austria / James Van Horn Melton.
p. cm.
Revision of thesis (Ph. D.–University of Chicago, 1982)
originally presented under title: Pedagogues and princes.
Bibliography: p.
Includes index.
ISBN 0–521–34668–1
1. Education, Compulsory–Prussia (Germany)–History–18th
century. 2. Education, Compulsory–Austria–History–18th century.
3. Despotism–History–18th century. 4. Pietism–Prussia (Germany)–
History–18th century. 5. Catholic Church–Education–Austria–
History–18th century. I. Title. II. Title: Absolutism and the
18th-century origins of compulsory schooling in Prussia and Austria.
LC135.G32P785 1988
379'.23–dc19   87–33022

Contents

Tables

Abbreviations

A.B.   *Acta Borussica. Denkmäler der preussischen
Staatsverwaltung,* ed. Preussische Akademie der
Wissenschaften, Abt. I, vols. 5–12 (Berlin, 1894–1936)
AEO   *Archiv des Erzbischöflichen Ordinariats,* Vienna
AVA   *Allgemeines Verwaltungsarchiv,* Vienna
C.A.   *Codex Austriacus,* vols. I–VI (Vienna, 1704 ff.)
HFL   *Hausarchiv des regierenden Fürstens von Liechtenstein,*
Vienna
HHStA   *Haus-, Hof-, und Staatsarchiv,* Vienna
K.S.   Johann Ignaz Felbiger, *Kleine Schulschriften nebst einer
ausführlichen Nachricht von den Umständen und dem
Erfolge der Verbesserung der Katholischen Land- und Stadt-
Trivialschulen in Schlesien und Glatz* (Sagan, 1768)
PGStA   *Preussisches Geheimes Staatsarchiv,* West Berlin

Acknowledgments

This work has enjoyed the generous moral, intellectual, and financial support of numerous individuals and institutions. It is with pleasure that I acknowledge them.

At the University of Chicago, my dissertation committee offered an ideal blend of encouragement and criticism. I am especially indebted to my thesis director, Leonard Krieger, whose own work on absolutism helped spark my original interest in the subject. The other members of my committee, Keith Baker, John Boyer, John Craig, and Emile Karafiol, were equally generous in providing advice and criticism.

In its present form, this book has benefited immeasurably from the advice and encouragement of Marc Raeff. Professor Raeff was kind enough to read the manuscript in its entirety, and his support and encouragement have sustained me throughout. During extended stays in Vienna, Grete Klingenstein of the University of Graz rendered aid and comfort at every stage of my research and writing. The perspicacity of her criticism and the warmth of her hospitality place me deeply in her debt. I am likewise indebted to Edgar Melton, whose insights into the dynamics of peasant societies have served to inspire and temper my forays into agrarian history. To Charles Bolton, Thomas Kaiser, Howard Kaminsky, Eric Leed, Susan Mernitz, and Franz Szabo, all of whom read and commented on various chapters, I also express my thanks.

Coming at a time of progressively shrinking support for historical research, the financial assistance provided by a number of institutions places me all the more in their debt. In the summer of 1977, a grant from the Council of European Studies enabled me to conduct a preliminary inventory of libraries and archives in Austria and the German Democratic Republic. From 1978 to 1981, fellowships from the American Social Science Research Council in New York, the Fulbright Commission in

Vienna, and the University of Chicago supported further research in Europe. In 1984, subsequent grants from the American Council of Learned Societies and the American Philosophical Society gave me a semester off from teaching to complete much of the present manuscript.

I would also like to express my thanks to the staffs of the following libraries and archives: the Austrian National Library, the Vienna Municipal Library, the Vienna University Library, the State Library in Munich, the Wrocław University Library, the *Haus-, Hof, und Staatsarchiv* (Vienna), the *Hofkammerarchiv* (Vienna), the *Hausarchiv des regierenden Fürstens von Liechtenstein* (Vienna), the *Kriegsarchiv* (Vienna), and the *Archiv des österreichischen Bundesverlags* (Vienna). For his assistance, friendship, and irrepressible Viennese humor, I am particularly indebted to Dr. Lorenz Mikoletzky of the *Allgemeines Verwaltungsarchiv* in Vienna. On this side of the Atlantic, Virginia Wilbur of the Interlibrary Loan Staff, Florida International University, proved remarkably resourceful in tracking down material located elsewhere. The map was prepared by Rosellen Monter, to whom I am most grateful. My thanks go also to the University of Chicago Press for permission to reprint an earlier version of Chapter 3, which originally appeared in *The Journal of Modern History,* 58 (1986), 95–124. A shorter German version, "Von Versinnlichung zur Verinnerlichung. Bemerkungen zur Dialektik repräsentativer und plebejischer Öffentlichkeit," was published in Richard Plaschka and Grete Klingenstein, eds., *Österreich im Europa der Aufklärung,* 2 vols. (Vienna, 1985), 2:919–940.

Finally, I would like to thank William Melton and Barbara and Russell Valentine, all of whom have helped in ways they cannot imagine. Above all I owe thanks to my mother, Helen Melton, who has been an untiring supporter of my scholarly efforts ever since she taught me how to read, and to my father, Herman Melton, for communicating a love of history to his sons. As for my wife, Donna, I can only hope that our idyllic years in the Vienna Woods offer some recompense for the inconveniences she has suffered through her marriage to a professional historian. This book is dedicated to her.

Introduction

As the title suggests, this book does two things. First, it examines efforts in the eighteenth century to make schooling compulsory in the two leading states of Central Europe, Prussia and Austria. Second, it explores some of the distinctive features of absolutist social policy in those territories.

Compulsory education is widely held to be a creation of modern industrial society. Whether viewed positively or negatively, as a symbol of cultural democratization or bourgeois exploitation, compulsory schooling is customarily linked to the rise of industrialization, urbanization, and mass communications – all those processes and innovations that are held to distinguish industrial societies from their pre-industrial, rural predecessors.

In Central Europe, however, efforts on behalf of compulsory schooling began long before the industrial age.[1] Already in the sixteenth century, Protestant and Catholic princes, prelates, nobles, and magistrates had sought to make religious education compulsory for their subjects. By the seventeenth century, their efforts had produced an extensive network of parish schools throughout Central Europe. Although the pedagogical momentum of the Protestant and Catholic reformations had begun to sag by the mid-seventeenth century, the rise of Pietism in the late seventeenth century gave renewed impetus to the compulsory school movement. First established in the Prussian city of Halle, Pietist schools proved the single most powerful force behind the movement for compulsory schooling in eighteenth-century Central Europe. To be sure, attempts by rulers of the period to establish schools in accordance with Pietist models often fell short of their mark. Nonetheless, these efforts produced new institutions

---

[1]See Mary Jo Maynes, *Schooling in Western Europe: A Social History* (Albany, 1985), p. 60.

and pedagogical practices that decisively shaped public education not only in Central Europe, but throughout the West.

Visit any public school classroom and you will find visible evidence of the Pietist legacy. The teachers will have certificates attesting to their pedagogical competence. Pietist schools were the first to require formal training for elementary schoolmasters, and this gave rise to the first normal schools. The pupils you observe use only textbooks that have been approved by the state board of education. Pietist reformers, again, were pioneers in the standardization of elementary school textbooks. Pupils raise their hands when they have questions, another Pietist innovation. Most pupils are taught collectively rather than individually, a method uncommon in German elementary education until the Pietist pedagogue Johann Hecker helped popularize the practice in the 1740s.

This book is less concerned with the legacy of Pietist pedagogy, however, than with the reasons for its original appeal. How did Pietism become such a potent pedagogical force in the eighteenth century? Why did Pietist pedagogy find such resonance among rulers and reformers of the period? Why, in an age when many viewed popular literacy as unnecessary or even dangerous, did rulers begin to promote universal literacy on an unprecedented scale? How successful were efforts on behalf of compulsory schooling, and what were the obstacles to its implementation?

The present study addresses these questions through a comparative study of the compulsory school movement in Prussia and Austria. It focuses on the reigns of two of the most prominent rulers of the eighteenth century, Frederick the Great of Prussia (1740–86) and Maria Theresa of Austria (1740–80), each of whom attempted to make elementary education compulsory. Frederick's decrees of 1763 and 1765 and Maria Theresa's school edict of 1774 would both represent important milestones in the history of Central European education.

Chiefly concerned with schooling at the level of policy rather than practice, this book does not pretend to present a comprehensive picture of elementary education in these two states. Although I have attempted to describe some of the fundamental features of Central European education in the eighteenth century, I confess to having only scratched the surface. A host of questions remain to be addressed by historians of Central European schools, such as regional distribution, attendance rates, social composition, and impact on social mobility and literacy. Although this book suggests some answers to these questions, they are far from conclusive and must await confirmation in more detailed studies.

The above disclaimer is designed not simply to disarm potential critics, but to clarify from the start the aims of this study. Originating as a doctoral thesis at the University of Chicago,[2] this book arose not out of a concern with education per se, but rather with the problem of social control in early modern absolutism. Social control posed particular problems in the eighteenth century because of the radical discontinuities that marked the age. The century saw the scope of state authority expand, but also demands for greater freedom from that authority. It witnessed the emergence of enlightened ideals of personal autonomy, but also the persistence of feudal relations of dependence. It saw the rise of new forms of economic production, but also the preservation of serfdom. It presided over the expansion of agrarian capitalism, but also the retention of seigniorial paternalism. It fostered highly literate cultural forms, but also harbored a largely illiterate population. It witnessed the growth of pietistic forms of religious expression, but also the tenacious survival of the theatrical devotional forms we associate with baroque popular piety.

It was the existence of these antinomies in political, social, economic, and cultural life that made popular education such an object of concern for absolutist reformers of the eighteenth century. Insofar as these polarities served to disrupt existing relationships of authority, education provided an instrument for reconstituting those relationships. The very attempt to expand popular schooling in eighteenth-century Prussia and Austria suggests, although not conclusively, the existence of a *Legitimationskrise* in relationships of authority. Although the eighteenth century is customarily known as the Age of Enlightenment, its leading representatives were far from agreeing that education for *le menu peuple* was necessarily desirable.[3] Given the fear of educating the common people that prevailed even among the most enlightened figures of the century, attempts by rulers to make education compulsory were all the more extraordinary and require explanation. A study of the campaign for compulsory schooling offers a unique perspective for examining how shifting conceptions of authority manifested themselves at the most fundamental levels of society. Social transformation, or resistance to it, invariably

[2]James Van Horn Melton, "Pedagogues and Princes: Reform Absolutism, Popular Education, and the Dialectics of Authority in Eighteenth-Century Prussia and Austria," Ph.D. diss., University of Chicago, 1982.
[3]On the ambivalence of French *philosophes* toward popular education see Harry C. Payne, *The Philosophes and the People* (New Haven, 1976); and Harvey Chisick, *The Limits of Reform in the Enlightenment: Attitudes towards the Education of the Lower Classes in Eighteenth-Century France* (Princeton, 1981).

shows up in the way individuals define what the young should know and be. If absolutism in eighteenth-century Prussia and Austria was indeed characterized by an attempt to redefine the matrices of social and political authority, popular education should have played an important role in that endeavor. Given that such a redefinition took place, an analysis of the motives behind the absolutist promotion of compulsory schooling can help elucidate the broader social, economic, and cultural forces that produced a "crisis of *Herrschaft*" in these states. What changes in social, economic, and cultural life made it necessary to legitimate or exercise authority in a different fashion? Why had traditional modes of exacting obedience become ineffective or obsolete?

Until recently, two perspectives have dominated the study of Central European absolutism during this period. One, a product of the nineteenth-century statist tradition, stresses the evolution of bureaucratic institutions. Since the eighteenth century was the classic age of state building in Central Europe, this perspective has understandably focused on bureaucratization as the salient feature of early modern absolutism. This approach is typical of the massive source collections, such as the *Acta Borussica* for Prussia and Friedrich Walter's *Geschichte der österreichischen Zentralverwaltung* for Austria, that have proven so indispensable to historians of absolutism. Also tied to this genre are classics in the field of administrative history like Otto Hintze's comparative essays or Hans Rosenberg's pioneering analysis of the Prussian bureaucracy.[4]

The second perspective, sometimes combined with the first and also dating back to the nineteenth century, has viewed the evolution of eighteenth-century absolutism through the prism of enlightened absolutism. This category first entered Central European historiography in the nineteenth century, when the German historian and neomercantilist Wilhelm Roscher elevated enlightened absolutism to the status of a developmental stage in the history of the state.[5] Since Roscher, historians have commonly viewed enlightened absolutism as a form of monarchy particularly suited to the economic backwaters of Central and Eastern Europe, where rulers adopted innovative policies in order to catch up with their more advanced neighbors to the west. This view was particularly fashionable during the 1920s and 1930s, when the Soviet transformation of Russia,

[4]Felix Gilbert and Robert M. Berdahl, eds., *The Historical Essays of Otto Hintze* (New York, 1975); Hans Rosenberg, *Bureaucracy, Aristocracy, and Autocracy: The Prussian Experience* (Boston, 1958).
[5]Wilhelm Roscher, *System der Volkswirtschaft*, 10th ed., 2 vols. (Stuttgart, 1882), 2:392.

the rise of fascism in Italy and Germany, and the apparent demise of liberalism throughout Europe, all encouraged an emphasis on the dynamic role of the state. Singling out rulers such as Frederick the Great of Prussia, Joseph II of Austria, and Karl Frederick of Baden, historians of enlightened absolutism have been especially concerned with how the writings of Enlightenment theorists and publicists shaped and directed absolutist policy.[6]

These two perspectives have yielded valuable insights into the theory and practice of Central European absolutism. They often tend, however, to minimize or overlook the problem of social control in absolutist rule. Too narrow a concern with the evolution of state institutions risks imparting to eighteenth-century government the relative efficacy that bureaucracies enjoy today. Such an approach can easily lead historians to underestimate the practical obstacles that hindered the effectiveness of state institutions. At the same time, to be exclusively concerned with the exercise of authority through formal bureaucratic channels is to ignore the informal, noninstitutionalized paths of authority so prominent in societies of the Old Regime. Historians of absolutism often present a curiously one-dimensional view of their subject by reducing the content of eighteenth-century politics to the relatively narrow world of rulers and their bureaucracies. As Otto Brunner pointed out, the resulting distortions are further compounded by the dualism implicit in the post-Hobbesian political categories that inform modern historical thought. Church and state, state and society, sovereign and subject – these are dichotomies that can inhibit the historian's ability to understand the patterns of authority peculiar to the Old Regime.[7]

The category of enlightened absolutism, for its part, can also obscure the complexities of eighteenth-century administration through an excessive concern with the relationship between Enlightenment theory and absolutist practice. Without a sensitivity to the social and material constraints that circumscribed eighteenth-century rulers, the analysis of

[6]The literature on enlightened absolutism is too extensive to include here. Karl Otmar Freiherr von Aretin, "Der aufgeklärte Absolutismus als europäisches Problem," in *Der aufgeklärte Absolutismus* (Cologne, 1974), provides a useful historiographical survey, as does Leonard Krieger, *An Essay on the Theory of Enlightened Despotism* (Chicago, 1975). For more recent summaries see Charles Ingrao, "The Problem of 'Enlightened Absolutism' and the German States," and Eberhard Weis, "Enlightenment and Absolutism in the Holy Roman Empire," both of which appear in the *Journal of Modern History*, 58 (1986).

[7]Otto Brunner, "Das Problem einer europäischen Sozialgeschichte," in his *Neue Wege der Verfassungs- und Sozialgeschichte*, 2d ed. (Göttingen, 1968), pp. 81–84.

absolutist policy becomes a simple matter of establishing its literal connections with Enlightenment theory. The image conveyed is that of a ruler implementing policy much as a cook prepares dishes for his hosts: a dash of Physiocracy for agriculture, a touch of mercantilism for industry, a bit of natural law for the bureaucracy, a dose of Beccaria for the penal system, and voilà, enlightened absolutism! Such a mechanistic approach is inadequate not only because the imputed connections between Enlightenment principles and absolutist practice often dissolve upon closer scrutiny, but also because it reduces politics to the simple imposition of formal doctrines on passive and static societies.

This is not to deny the significance of such doctrines for eighteenth-century government, or to belittle the role of ideas in history. In the realm of politics, however, the relationship between ideas and action is highly complex. Reducing absolutist policy to the imposition of political formulas from above fails to capture the underlying interests and concerns that informed absolutist practice. This formalistic view of the relationship between political theory and practice ignores the social, economic, and cultural forces that helped shape absolutist policy in the eighteenth century. In other words, too great a concern with the absolutist practice of Enlightenment theory can obscure the theory immanent in absolutist practice. As an ideological phenomenon, absolutism encompassed more than the beliefs and attitudes of a particular ruler. Absolutist ideology was no more coterminous with the ideas of individual rulers than, say, the ideology of the New Deal was coterminous with the ideas of Franklin Roosevelt. Absolutist ideology was more than a set of political maxims; it was a mode of ruling, a leviathan of individuals, institutions, and procedures informed by patent or latent assumptions about the ends of power and the means of achieving them.[8]

If historians of absolutism sometimes overlook the less explicit and more diffuse mechanisms of control that operated in the early modern period, it is perhaps because we are ourselves products of societies with such advanced technologies of social discipline. One need not be a disciple of Foucault to recognize this. A major theme in the work of social theorists since the nineteenth century – Marx, Weber, Durkheim, and

---

[8]Along these lines, see William Sewell's plea for a broader conception of ideology, "one that treats ideology as anonymous, collective, and constitutive of social order," in his "Ideologies and Social Revolutions: Reflections on the French Case," *Journal of Modern History*, 57 (1985), p. 84.

Marcuse, to name just a few – has been the degree to which industrial societies are able to preserve social order through the use of highly internalized and invisible forms of control. As members of societies that have managed to control behavior with an unprecedented degree of efficiency, Western historians are apt to overlook the fact that the less industrialized and egalitarian states of early modern Europe faced problems of social control fundamentally different from those of today. Studies of absolutism that collapse the preservation of social order into formal bureaucratic structures or systems of thought ignore the degree to which rulers of the eighteenth century lacked those instruments of control over which governments today dispose, such as mass communications, the electronic media, mass consumerism, mechanized systems of transport, police and armed forces equipped with highly sophisticated technology, or mass education.

In probing into the reasons why schooling had become such a central concern to Frederickian and Theresian reformers, I have described a pattern of assumptions about the nature of authority that I believe characterized broad areas of absolutist social policy. Absolutist reformers in fields seemingly tangential to education – agrarian relations, manufacturing, popular piety, and the theater, for example – shared concerns strikingly similar to those held by reformers of popular education. What united these reformers was the conviction that the state, if it was to master social, economic, and cultural change, had to redefine the manner in which power was displayed and exercised. Whether seeking to commute labor services, restrict pilgrimages, foster industry, ban burlesques, or build schools, absolutist social policy in Prussia and Austria sought to strengthen moral pillars of authority by refining its exercise. Central to this refinement was a shift in the technology of social discipline, whereby the locus of coercion was to be transferred from outside to inside the individual. Implicit in this attempted transformation was the belief that the extraneous, visible, and objective forms through which authority had traditionally been exercised were no longer efficacious.

It is my contention that this search for more subjective and effective modes of coercion was a defining feature of absolutist social policy in eighteenth-century Prussia and Austria. To be sure, the attempt to reconstitute authority on a more subjective basis did not originate in the eighteenth century. Protestant reformers in the sixteenth century, for example, repeatedly stressed the difference between outward assent and inner conviction. This theme also characterized the Neostoic movement of the

late sixteenth and seventeenth century, a phenomenon whose importance
for Continental political thought has been demonstrated by the constitu-
tional historian Gerhard Oestreich.[9] But only in the eighteenth century
was this theme expressed so explicitly in absolutist theory and practice.

As a study of absolutist social policy, this book is by no means the first
to pursue the theme of social control. In an important essay on absolutism as an agent of social discipline, Oestreich considered the process of
Sozialdisziplinierung in the early modern period a phenomenon equal in
importance to the democratization of Western society in the nineteenth
century. Marc Raeff has also explored absolutist efforts at transforming
social behavior in a book of essays on "the well-ordered police state."
Comparing Russia and the Germanies in the early modern period, Raeff
argues that the apparatus of absolutism was instrumental in the development of an "active, productive, efficient, and rationalistic style of economic and cultural behavior." Cultural theorists, above all Norbert Elias
and Michel Foucault, have also stressed the role of absolutism in promoting social discipline. Elias and Foucault credit absolutism with having
fostered the shift from external coercion to self-discipline as mechanisms
for regulating social behavior, a transformation that both view as critical
to the development of "modernity" in the West.[10]

The insights of Oestreich, Raeff, Elias, and Foucault are profound and
illuminating, and my own debt to these authors should be obvious
throughout this book. Yet one must be careful not to exaggerate the
transformation they describe. The exercise of authority in any society,
whether "primitive" or "modern," always rests on a blend of "internal"

---

[9]See the essays in Part I of Gerhard Oestreich, *Neostoicism and the Early Modern State*,
ed. Brigitta Oestreich and H. G. Koenigsberger, and trans. David McLintock
(Cambridge, 1982).

[10]Gerhard Oestreich, "The Structure of the Absolute State," in *Neostoicism and the Early
Modern State;* Marc Raeff, *The Well-Ordered Police State: Social and Institutional
Change through Law in the Germanies and Russia, 1600–1800* (New Haven, 1983);
Norbert Elias, *Über den Prozess der Zivilisation. Soziogenetische und psychogenetische
Untersuchungen,* 2 vols. (Bern, 1969). The best example of Foucault's views on the
subject is his *Discipline and Punish: The Birth of the Prison,* trans. Alan Sheridan (New
York, 1977). For other analyses that focus on the theme of social discipline in the
eighteenth century see Joachim Gessinger, *Sprache und Bürgertum. Zur Sozialgeschichte
sprachlicher Verkehrsformen in Deutschland des 18. Jahrhunderts* (Stuttgart, 1980);
Mohammed Rassem, "Bemerkungen zur 'Sozialdisziplinierung' im frühmodernen Staat,"
Zeitschrift für Politik, 30 (1983); James Van Horn Melton, "Absolutism and 'Modernity' in Early Modern Central Europe," *German Studies Review,* 8 (1985), a review of the
issues raised in Raeff's work, and idem, "Arbeitsprobleme des aufgeklärten Absolutismus
in Preussen und Österreich," *Mitteilungen des Instituts für österreichische Geschichtsforschung,* 90 (1982).

and "external" controls.[11] It would be absurd to claim that, say, the behavior of medieval individuals was not also embedded in a complex matrix of internal controls. For instance, the penitential system developed by the Catholic church in the Middle Ages certainly carried with it internal modes of control, however much Luther may have dismissed that system for resting on little more than "gallows sorrow."[12]

Conversely, if self-discipline has assumed an increasingly important function in the regulation of human behavior since the early modern period, force and violence nonetheless remain central to the quotidian practice of ruling. In the case of eighteenth-century Prussia and Austria, the expansion of standing armies proved as important for the maintenance of domestic order as it did for the conduct of foreign policy. The development of standing armies in the early modern period enabled rulers to preserve social order in a way that had not been possible before. Johann Heinrich Gottlob von Justi, the eighteenth-century cameralist, was characteristically blunt in assessing the domestic role of standing armies in the eighteenth century: "In former times, before states had standing armies, mob rebellions were frequent. . . . But now that rulers have armies capable of imposing strict discipline and docility on the lower orders, religion and morality are sufficient for holding the mob in check. Since the common people know that the army can put down any popular disturbance, they rebel less frequently."[13] In a more recent work, Otto Büsch has carefully described the role of the army as an agent of socialization and control in eighteenth-century Prussia.[14]

Although standing armies provided eighteenth-century rulers with an important coercive weapon, however, more positive instruments of control became increasingly necessary. As the scope of state authority steadily expanded in the eighteenth century, and as changes in social, economic, and cultural life eroded existing relationships of authority, absolutist reformers and officials became more convinced that the

[11]See David Sabean's remarks on the nature of *Herrschaft* in his *Power in the Blood: Popular Culture and Village Discourse in Early Modern Germany* (Cambridge, 1984), pp. 20–27.
[12]See Thomas N. Tentler, *Sin and Confession on the Eve of the Reformation* (Princeton, 1977).
[13]Johann Heinrich Gottlob von Justi, *Politische und Finanzschriften über wichtige Gegenstände der Staatskunst, der Kriegswissenschaft, und des Cameral- und Finanzwesens*, 3 vols. (Copenhagen, 1764), 3:141–142.
[14]Otto Büsch, *Militärsystem und Sozialleben im alten Preussen, 1713-1807* (West Berlin, 1962).

efficacious exercise of authority depended on freely rendered rather than coerced obedience. What distinguished absolutist social discipline as it evolved in eighteenth-century Prussia and Austria was not just its internal character, but the moral autonomy it sought to cultivate. For absolutist reformers of the time, an enlightened subject was one who rendered obedience voluntarily and spontaneously; conversely, an enlightened ruler exacted the obedience of his subjects through love rather than force. Joseph Sonnenfels, the Austrian cameralist and *Aufklärer*, expressed this view in his *Man without Prejudice:* "Enlightened subjects are obedient because they wish to be, subjects blinded by prejudice because they are forced. A domesticated lion fondles his master, while a lion in fetters constantly seeks to break out of his chains. The lion in bondage will eventually free himself of his fetters, and turn on his master in fury."[15] Count Johann Anton Pergen, who would gain notoriety as chief of the Habsburg secret police under Joseph II, likewise argued in 1770 that rulers of "a state in which enlightened subjects acknowledge and fulfill their duties out of conviction . . . will face fewer uprisings and will need to issue fewer laws and commands."[16] Carl Abraham Freiherr von Zedlitz, one of Frederick II's chief ministers, told the Berlin Academy in 1777 that "an enlightened ruler prefers to govern subjects who serve and obey out of love and conviction, not those mired in the slavish habits of forced servitude."[17] Thomas Ignaz Freiherr von Pöck, an archducal administrator in Lower Austria, similarly observed that obedience must come from inner conviction rather than external force. In his introduction to the fifth volume of the *Codex Austriacus* (1777), he observed: "A wise ruler does not seek to win the obedience of his subjects through force . . . but appeals to their reason and moves their hearts. This he does so that they will obey his laws not only because he requires it, but also because their deep convictions and righteous sentiments motivate them to do so."[18]

In the eighteenth century, as I hope to demonstrate, schools became a central target of state policy precisely because they offered an instrument for exacting obedience in a less coercive fashion. Here the promotion of literacy was to be a crucial means of cultivating the moral autonomy of the

---

[15]Joseph Sonnenfels, *Der Mann ohne Vorurtheile*, 3 vols. (Vienna, 1785), 3:8.
[16]*Haus-, Hof-, und Staatsarchiv*, Vienna: Alte Kabinettsakten, Kart. 1, fol. 1126.
[17]Karl Abraham Freiherr von Zedlitz, *Über den Patriotismus als ein Gegenstand der Erziehung in monarchischen Staaten* (Berlin, 1777), p. 13.
[18]*Codex Austriacus*, 6 vols. (1704–77), 5:5.

subject. Part I, which describes the cultural and religious origins of the compulsory school movement, shows how Pietism and reform Catholicism relied heavily on popular education and literacy in their efforts to cultivate more inward forms of popular devotion. Pietist pedagogy, systematically formulated by August Hermann Francke in the early eighteenth century and later incorporated into reform Catholicism by the Silesian abbot Johann Ignaz Felbiger, provided both movements with a vehicle for reconstituting popular culture on a more literate basis. If I appear to have stressed the religious roots of absolutist reform at the expense of more "secular" sources, this reflects a deliberate attempt on my part to rectify the one-sided concern with Enlightenment thought that often characterizes studies of eighteenth-century reform.

Part II moves from the cultural and religious roots of pedagogical reform to the social and economic setting that gave it resonance. There I focus on the transitional forces at work in the Prussian and Austrian countryside, most notably the rapid expansion of the rural poor, the rise of rural industry, and changes in the relationship between peasant and seignior. From the standpoint of absolutist reformers, the concomitant disruption, or transformation, of social relations of production in the countryside necessitated a greater degree of moral autonomy in the peasant. Pietist pedagogy, with its stress on inner discipline and obedience, provided a means of fostering this autonomy.

Part III examines more narrowly the efforts to implement the Frederickian school decrees of 1763–65 and the Theresian edict of 1774. In evaluating the relative success or failure of those measures, I have tried to suggest some of the ways in which they helped lay the basis for mass public education. At the same time, these chapters examine in detail the obstacles and contradictions that seriously impeded the success of the compulsory school movement in these states. As in other fields of absolutist policy, a wide chasm separated royal edicts from their implementation. And as is so often the case with reform in general, school reform in eighteenth-century Prussia and Austria was to have consequences quite different from those envisioned by its original authors.

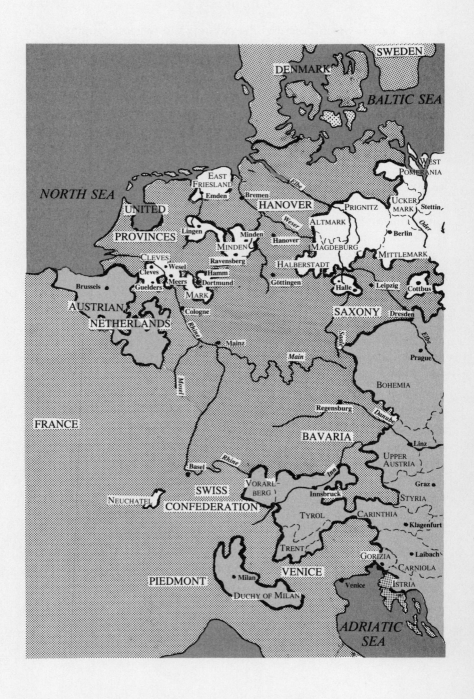

SWEDEN

DENMARK

BALTIC SEA

WEST
POMERANIA

NORTH SEA

EAST
FRIESLAND
Emden
Bremen
HANOVER
PRIGNITZ
UCKER
MARK
Stettin

UNITED
Lingen
Weser
ALTMARK
Berlin
Oder

PROVINCES
Minden
Hanover
MAGDEBURG
MITTLEMARK

MINDEN
Ravensberg
HALBERSTADT

CLEVES
Wesel
Hamm
Halle
Leipzig
Cottbus

Brussels
Cleves
Meers
Dortmund
Göttingen

Guelders
MARK
Dresden

AUSTRIAN
Cologne
SAXONY

NETHERLANDS
Rhine
Mainz

Elbe
Prague

Main
BOHEMIA

Mosel
Regensburg
Danube

FRANCE
BAVARIA
Linz

Rhine
UPPER
AUSTRIA

Basel
Inn
Graz

SWISS
VORARL-
BERG
Innsbruck
STYRIA

NEUCHATEL
CONFEDERATION
TYROL
CARINTHIA
Klagenfurt

TRENT
GORIZIA
Laibach

PIEDMONT
Milan
VENICE
CARNIOLA

DUCHY OF MILAN
Venice
ISTRIA

ADRIATIC
SEA

BALTIC SEA

RUSSIA

ADMINISTRATIVE DIVISIONS
OF THE HABSBURG AND
HOHENZOLLERN
MONARCHIES. 1780

——— National Borders
----- Provincial Borders
Habsburg Territories
Hohenzollern Territories

Niemen

Königsberg

Gumbinnen

LITHUANIA

EAST
POMERANIA

Danzig

EAST
PRUSSIA

WEST PRUSSIA

Marienwerder

NEU-
MARK

NETZE

Kulm

Netze

Vistula

Warsaw

POLAND

Glogau

Sagan

Breslau

SILESIA

Oppeln

Niesse

Oder

Glatz

SI-
LE-
SIA

Troppau

Beuthen

Lemberg

Olmütz

MORAVIA

Brünn

GALICIA

Dniester

LOWER
AUSTRIA

Vienna

Danube

HUNGARY

BUKOVINA

Buda

Pest

TRANSYLVANIA

Save

SLAVONIA

CROATIA

MILITARY

FRONTIER

BANAT

MILITARY

FRONTIER

Save

Danube

Danube

OTTOMAN EMPIRE

Part I

Cultural and religious forces

I

Popular schooling in early modern Prussia and Austria

Di quem oderunt, aut scribam aut ludimagistrum fecerunt.

Whom the gods despise, they make a scribe or a schoolmaster.

European proverb

The Reformation legacy

To understand the peculiarities of popular education in early modern Prussia and Austria, one must keep in mind that primary schooling, like the Old Regime itself, was not a coherent "system." Primary schooling consisted of a variety of discrete institutions, possessing little or no organizational relationship to each other or to higher educational institutions.[1] During the Middle Ages, relatively few options were available to those families desiring basic schooling for their children. To be sure, churches in larger towns and cities had begun to establish parish schools as early as the thirteenth century. But these served primarily to train future priests and sacristans, or to provide choral singing for festive and ceremonial occasions. Those who could afford it hired private tutors or sent their sons to a Latin school. Located in towns and cities, *Lateinschulen* (also called *Stadtschulen*) provided the Latin instruction necessary for university study and a clerical or legal career. As such, they served primarily the sons of respected and established burghers. Girls, if they received any education at all, were instructed by tutors or by nuns in a nearby convent.

By the second half of the fifteenth century, this picture had begun to change. The revival of trade, the growing importance of the vernacular,

---

[1] On the "patchwork" organization of schooling in the Old Regime, see François Furet and Jacques Ozouf, *Reading and Writing: Literacy in France from Calvin to Jules Ferry* (Cambridge, 1982), pp. 69–82.

3

and the advent of print helped generate a growing demand for basic literacy. Typifying this demand was the emergence of so-called *Deutsche Schulen* and *Schreib- und Rechenschulen*. Eschewing Latin study for basic German instruction in the three Rs, these schools catered to families whose aspirations were more utilitarian in nature. They imparted the basic literacy and mathematical skills deemed necessary for future artisans, shopkeepers, and merchants. While *Deutsche Schulen* were in some cases absorbed by Latin schools, most remained independent. By the sixteenth century, they existed in most towns and cities.[2]

With the outbreak of the Reformation, however, popular education ceased to be a purely parental or community matter. Whether the product of evangelical fervor or the need to inoculate subjects against radical sectarian movements, popular education now became an urgent concern of municipal elites and territorial princes.[3] Martin Luther considered popular education to be crucial to the success of the Reformation, and exhorted secular authorities to establish schools for their subjects. Ac-

[2]The above discussion is drawn largely from Heinrich Heppe, *Geschichte des deutschen Volksschulwesens*, 3 vols. (Gotha, 1858), 1:1–5, and Helmut Engelbrecht, *Geschichte des österreichischen Bildungswesens*, 3 vols. (Vienna, 1982–84), 1:226–252. For Europe as a whole, Philippe Ariès, *Centuries of Childhood: A Social History of Family Life*, trans. Robert Baldick (New York, 1962), pp. 286–314, is useful on the emergence of primary schools in the fifteenth and sixteenth centuries. Detailed accounts of the rise of *Deutsche Schulen* in northern Germany and Franconia can be found in the recent articles by Klaus Wriedt, "Schulen und bürgerliches Bildungswesen in Norddeutschland im Spätmittelalter," and Rudolf Endres, "Das Schulwesen in Franken im ausgehenden Mittelalter," in Bernd Moeller, Hans Patze, and Karl Stackmann, eds., *Studien zum städtischen Bildungswesen des späten Mittelalters und der frühen Neuzeit* (Göttingen, 1983).
[3]Gerald Strauss, *Luther's House of Learning: Indoctrination of the Young in the German Reformation* (Baltimore, 1978), has conclusively demonstrated the relationship between the Reformation and the expansion of parish schooling in sixteenth-century Germany. Protestantism also spurred the expansion of primary schooling in other parts of Europe. For France see Bernard Grosperin, *Les petites écoles sous l'Ancien Régime* (Rennes, 1984), pp. 12–14; and Furet and Ozouf, *Reading and Writing*, pp. 58–69. For Prussia see F. Wienecke, "Die Begründung der evangelischen Volksschule in der Kurmark und ihre Entwicklung bis zum Tode König Friedrichs I. 1540–1713," *Zeitschrift für die Geschichte der Erziehung und des Unterrichts*, 3 (1913), p. 16. While primarily concerned with the eighteenth century, the excellent study by Wolfgang Neugebauer, *Absolutistischer Staat und Schulwirklichkeit in Brandenburg-Preussen* (Berlin, 1985), contains a good analysis of the relationship between Prussian schooling and the Reformation. See particularly his remarks on the role of the *Stände* and the nobility, pp. 69–73, 235–236. For selected Austrian territories see Engelbrecht, *Geschichte des österreichischen Bildungswesens*, 2:122–134; Wincentz Ostrowski, *Wiejskie szkolnictwo parafialne na Śląsku w drugiej 17. Wieku* (Wrocław, 1971), p. 135; J. Hubel, "Das Schulwesen Niederösterreichs im Reformationszeitalter," *Jahrbuch für die Geschichte des Protestantismus in Österreich*, 51 (1930); Christian d'Elvert, *Geschichte der Studien-, Schul-, und Erziehungs-Anstalten in Mähren und österreichischen Schlesien* (Brünn, 1857), pp. xxvii–ix; Josef Hanzal, "K dějinám nižšiho školství před rokem 1775," *Acta Universitatis Carolinae-Historiae Universitatis Carolinae Pragensis*, 6 (1965); Johann Loserth, *Die protestantischen Schulen der Steiermark im sechzehnten Jahrhundert* (Berlin, 1916), pp. 182–188.

cordingly, Protestant territories and municipalities throughout the Holy Roman Empire issued a flood of school ordinances requiring religious and catechistic instruction for the young. Gerald Strauss calculates that more than one hundred such *Schulordnungen* were issued during the sixteenth century. These were promulgated not only in most major Protestant cities, but also in prominent territories like Hesse (1526, 1537, and 1566), Electoral Saxony (1528 and 1533), Pomerania (1535), Brandenburg (1573), Braunschweig (1543), and Württemberg (1559).[4] Protestant town councils transformed existing *Deutsche Schulen* and *Schreib- und Rechenschulen* from purely utilitarian institutions into centers of religious indoctrination. In the countryside, Protestant princes and their consistories required pastors and their sacristans to maintain parish schools. Here Brandenburg can serve as a typical example. The Ecclesiastical Constitution of 1573 required the sacristan (*Küster*) to provide religious instruction to parish youth on a regular basis. Following the disappointing church visitations of 1581, sacristans were threatened with a fine if they failed to hold school.[5] By 1600, so-called sacristan schools (*Küsterschulen*) were scattered throughout the province, and formed the prototype for elementary schools in the region. They were designed for girls and boys alike, although in some cases girls attended their own schools. By the late sixteenth century, schools for girls (known as *Jungfernschulen* or *Mädchenschulen*) could be found in every major town in the province.[6]

Shocked by the spread of Protestantism in their territories, Catholic princes followed suit. As confessional differences sharpened, Catholics too came to view schooling as crucial to the preservation of doctrinal purity and liturgical uniformity.[7] In Habsburg Austria, schools became a central battleground in efforts to roll back Protestantism. As Luther's teachings spread rapidly throughout the Habsburg domains, so did Protestant schools. Cardinal Khlesl fretted in 1587 that fifty-seven schools attached to Lutheran parishes had been established in Lower Austria alone, many at the instigation of Protestant nobles.[8] Thanks to the efforts

[4]Strauss, *Luther's House of Learning*, p. 13.
[5]Wienecke, "Begründung der evangelischen Volksschule," p. 24.
[6]In 1574 two *Jungfernschulen* existed in Berlin, two in Prenzlau, and one in Potsdam, Nauen, and Frankfurt an der Oder. Ibid., pp. 33–36.
[7]Here again, one can draw parallels with France. See Grosperin, *Les petites écoles*, pp. 15–16; Mireille Laget, "Petites écoles en Languedoc au XVIIIe siècle," *Annales*, 26 (1971), p. 1417; Furet and Ozouf, *Reading and Writing*, pp. 58–69.
[8]Gustav Strakosch-Grassmann, *Geschichte des österreichischen Unterrichtswesens* (Vienna, 1905), p. 44; Helmuth Feigl, *Die niederösterreichische Grundherrschaft* (Vienna, 1964), p. 270; Hubel, "Das Schulwesen Niederösterreichs," pp. 27–38.

An Austrian Mädchenschule (ca. 1750). Source: *Historisches Museum der Stadt Wien.*

of vigorous counter-reformers like Ferdinand II, the Protestant tide was soon turned. As archduke of Styria and later as emperor, Ferdinand vigorously promoted parish visitations to root out Protestant schoolmasters. Following his defeat of the Bohemian Protestants at White Mountain (1620), Ferdinand's energetic campaign against heresy succeeded in converting or exiling most Protestant schoolmasters by 1630.[9] The Catholic church quickly attempted to move into the resulting vacuum, basing parish school instruction on the catechism of the sixteenth-century Jesuit Peter Canisius.

In Prussia and Austria alike, the movement on behalf of popular schooling was clearly on the wane by the mid-seventeenth century. In areas ravaged by the marauding *Soldateska* of the Thirty Years War, rural and urban schools invariably suffered the consequences. Beyond outright physical destruction, many suffered from the demographic effects of the war. In those areas experiencing a sharp population loss,

[9]Strakosch-Grassmann, *Geschichte des österreichischen Unterrichtswesens*, pp. 20–21, 66–67; Andreas Stoll, *Geschichte der Lehrerbildung in Tirol* (Weinheim and Berlin, 1968), p. 27.

declining enrollments and fees imposed further hardships on school-masters already perched precariously on the subsistence threshold. Fur-thermore, as confessional tensions subsided after 1648, so did the impe-tus to establish or maintain parish schools. In Prussia the traditional instrument of enforcement, church visitations, declined in frequency dur-ing the latter part of the seventeenth century. Except in the Altmark, the western region of Brandenburg, no Prussian church visitations were con-ducted between 1601 and 1710.[10] The Hohenzollern conversion to the Calvinist faith in 1613 also impeded the expansion of Prussian parish education. The conversion strained relations between the dynasty and the Lutheran-dominated estates and consistories, thereby hampering any concerted promotion of parish education.[11]

In Austria, likewise, parish schooling expanded little during the sec-ond half of the seventeenth century. While formerly Protestant schools were placed in the hands of the Catholic parish clergy, many never re-opened owing to a shortage of confessionally reliable schoolmasters.[12] In the late seventeenth century, the existence of crypto-Protestantism in Upper Austria was blamed on the decline in the number and quality of Catholic parish schools.[13] The sponsorship of parish education in the Habsburg monarchy, as will be seen later, also tended to be subordinated to the more visual, theatrical, and nonliterary forms of proselytism typ-ical of Habsburg baroque piety.

Despite the apparent stagnation of popular schooling in the latter part of the seventeenth century, available statistics nevertheless point to an extensive network of parish schools in Prussia and Austria by the eigh-teenth century. By 1700 every parish seat in Brandenburg had a school, and schools could be found in two-thirds of all East Prussian parishes.[14] In Silesia, Catholic visitation reports from the 1660s revealed a total of seventy-four schools in the diocese of Liegnitz alone, instructing more than 1,200 pupils.[15] While seventeenth-century statistics for other

---

[10]Wienecke, "Begründung der evangelischen Volksschule," p. 30.

[11]Ibid., pp. 36–37.

[12]Loserth, *Die protestantischen Schulen*, p. 95; Alois Kross, *Geschichte der böhmischen Provinz der Gesellschaft Jesu*, 2 vols. (Vienna, 1910), 2:148–149; d'Elvert, *Erziehungs-Anstalten*, p. xxxxvi.

[13]See Rudolf Weiss, *Das Bistum Passau unter Kardinal Joseph Dominikus von Lamberg (1723–1761). Zugleich ein Beitrag zur Geschichte des Kryptoprotestantismus in Oberösterreich* (St. Ottilien, 1979), pp. 275–276.

[14]Gerhard Duesterhaus, *Das ländliche Schulwesen im Herzogthum Preussen im 16. und 17. Jahrhundert* (Bonn, 1975), p. 135; Wienecke, "Begründung der evangelischen Volks-chule," pp. 38–39.

[15]Ostrowski, *Wiejskie szkolnictwo parafialne*, pp. 31–37.

Habsburg territories are rare, estimates on the eve of the Theresian school reform of 1774 reveal a considerable number of parish schools. The consistory of the bishopric of Passau, whose jurisdiction included most of Upper and Lower Austria, reported in 1772 that virtually every parish in these provinces had a school, although the attendance rate among children of school age (ages five through twelve) averaged only 10–20 percent.[16] In Vienna and its suburbs, schools were equally plentiful and better attended. In 1770, 4,665 pupils – more than a third of all school-age children–attended a total of sixty-five parish or municipally franchised schools.[17]

Popular schooling and literacy

Although it is customary to equate schooling with the acquisition of literacy, one must be cautious in projecting that equation on the early modern period. Given their confessional origins, parish and community schools above all provided instruction in the articles of faith.[18] Such instruction, however, was often oral rather than literate in character. Based largely on the oral recitation and memorization of catechisms, education at a parish school did not necessarily include reading or writing instruction.

Particularly in Austria, the teaching of reading in parish schools was sporadic given the church's distrust of popular literacy and preference for nonliterate media of religious instruction.[19] What appears in Catholic visitation reports as a school sometimes signified little beyond oral catechistic instruction by the church sacristan.[20] Further testifying to the nonliterary function of Catholic parish schools was their heavy emphasis

---

[16]*Archiv des Erzbischöflichen Ordinariats*, Vienna: Schulakten, Mappe 120, Fasz. 3, 1772. This estimate is corroborated by a 1771 archducal investigation of Lower Austrian schools, which revealed that only 18,527 out of 114,105 school-age children (or 16 percent) actually attended school. See the table in the *Allgemeines Verwaltungsarchiv*, Vienna: Nachlass Pergen, 1771, "Tabellarisches Verzeichnis sämmtlicher von 5. bis 12. und 13. Jahren Schulfähigen im Erzherzogthum Unterösterreich."
[17]Ibid.
[18]Prior to the eighteenth century, most school ordinances were issued as integral parts of comprehensive ecclesiastical ordinances. See Strauss, *Luther's House of Learning*, p. 8.
[19]See Chapter 3, "The Non-literate Legacy of Habsburg Baroque Catholicism."
[20]On the frequent absence of reading and writing instruction in rural parish schools see the example of Styria in Peter Czimeg, "Die Entwicklung der Pfarrschulen im heutigen Schulbezirk Liezen," Ph.D. diss., University of Graz, 1965, p. 6; and Moravia in d'Elvert, *Erziehungs-Anstalten*, p. 141. In Lower Austria, visitations such as those conducted in Laa (1686), Simonsfeld (1704), and Hadersdorf (1756) suggest that parish school instruction was often limited to catechistic instruction on Sundays and religious holidays. *AEO:* Visitationen D. D. Dechanten (1664–1760), Passau.

on music. The parish school in the Silesian town of Ratibor, where two hours a day were devoted to choir singing in 1740, was far from atypical.[21] The English musicologist Charles Burney, a traveler through Bohemia in 1772, was struck by the dominant role of music instruction in Bohemian parish schools. Burney went so far as to attribute the flowering of musical culture in the Habsburg territories to the stress upon music in parish schools.[22] The role of music in the parish schools of the Habsburg monarchy was tied to the prominent role of processions, religious festivals, and similar manifestations of "baroque popular piety" in cultural life. Choir singing on such occasions was usually provided by the schoolmaster and his pupils. Baptisms, weddings, and funerals were other occasions that often called on the services of a school choir.

In a Protestant territory like Prussia, one might well expect a greater emphasis on reading. Historians have long stressed Protestantism's role in the diffusion of literacy by virtue of its alleged promotion of lay Bible reading. But as Richard Gawthrop and Gerald Strauss have recently argued, Protestant reformers of the sixteenth century were highly ambivalent about the wisdom of placing Bibles in the hands of the laity. Only after the emergence of Pietism in the late seventeenth century was lay Bible reading vigorously promoted in Prussia.[23] The spread of sectarianism in the 1520s had convinced many church leaders of the need to restrict and control lay Bible reading. Consistories instead relied on the catechism as a safer tool of popular education. As objects of memorization, catechisms inculcated the articles of faith in a more uniform manner, thereby minimizing the risk of independent or aberrant popular interpretation.[24]

Lending support to the interpretation of Gawthrop and Strauss is the fact that Prussian school ordinances did not emphasize the teaching of reading until after the mid-seventeenth century.[25] In the countryside

[21]Augustin Weltzel, *Geschichte der Stadt Ratibor* (Ratibor, 1861), p. 539.
[22]Charles Burney, *The Present State of Music in Germany, the Netherlands, and United Provinces,* ed. Percy A. Scholes (London, 1959), pp. 131–136. Burney also attributed the emphasis on music to the nobility, whose insatiable musical appetites created a demand for trained musicians. Burney observed that in Prague, for example, "The nobility were now out of town, but in winter they are said to have great concerts frequently at their hotels and palaces, chiefly performed by their own domestics and vassals, who have learned music at country schools" (p. 135).
[23]See Chapter 2, "Goals and Methods of Pietist Schooling."
[24]Richard Gawthrop and Gerald Strauss, "Protestantism and Literacy in Early Modern Germany," *Past and Present,* 104 (1984); Strauss, *Luther's House of Learning,* p. 17; Gessinger, *Sprache und Bürgertum,* pp. 35–44.
[25]Heppe, *Geschichte des deutschen Volksschulwesens,* pp. 15–16; Wienecke, "Begrün-

school instruction frequently amounted to little more than an hour or so on Sunday afternoons, when the sexton led the children in reciting the catechism and singing hymns. Even as late as 1764, the head of the provincial administration in Prussian Silesia reported that pupils in rural schools learned little more than prayers and hymns.[26] Often the rural parish schoolmaster himself was barely literate, as visitation reports in the seventeenth century often remarked. In such cases, of course, instruction was purely oral in nature.[27]

If literacy had been a primary aim in rural areas, one would expect a relatively high rate of literacy given the existing network of parish schools. Unfortunately, literacy rates in early modern Prussia and Austria have yet to be systematically examined. The limited evidence available, however, suggests extremely low rates of literacy even in areas where parish schools were available. Only 10 percent of the adult peasants in East Prussia could sign their names around the mid-eighteenth century, although some 1,500 parish schools existed in the countryside.[28] In Austria, Jesuit missionaries traveling through the village of Zell (Carinthia) reported in 1760 that only 4 of the 650 inhabitants could read.[29] Also illustrative of the low literacy rate in rural Austria was the census of 1787, when each peasant commune (*Gemeinde*) elected representatives to assist royal and archducal officials conducting the census. Peasant representatives in Upper Styrian parishes were rarely able to sign their names to the census reports. In the parishes of Weng and Lassing, for example, none of the fourteen peasant representatives could sign their names, even though they were the most respected members of their com-

---

dung der evangelischen Volksschule," pp. 38–39. See the example of Magdeburg, which was incorporated into Prussia in 1680, in Friedrich Danneil, *Geschichte des evangelischen Dorfschulwesens im Herzogthum Magdeburg* (Halle, 1876), p. 41, 55–57.
[26]Max Lehmann, ed., *Preussen und die katholische Kirche seit 1640*, 9 vols. (Leipzig, 1878–85), 3:182–185.
[27]Duesterhaus, *Das ländliche Schulwesen*, p. 65, 181; Reinhold Dorwart, *The Prussian Welfare State before 1740* (Cambridge, Mass., 1971), p. 153; Edmund Michael, "Die schlesische Dorfschule im 16. Jahrhundert," *Zeitschrift des Vereins für die Geschichte Schlesiens*, 63 (1929), p. 23.
[28]Rolf Engelsing, *Analphabetentum und Lektüre. Zur Sozialgeschichte des Lesens in Deutschland zwischen feudaler und industrieller Gesellschaft* (Stuttgart, 1973), p. 62. In Mecklenburg, another East Elbian territory, only one person in every six households was literate during the second half of the seventeenth century. See the excellent article by Jochen Richter, "Zur Schriftkundigkeit mecklenburgischer Bauern im 17. Jahrhundert," *Jahrbuch für Wirtschaftsgeschichte*, 3 (1981), p. 89.
[29]August Leidl, "Die religiöse und seelsorgerliche Situation zur Zeit Maria Theresias (1740–80) im Gebiet des heutigen Österreichs," *Ostbairische Grenzmarken*, N.F., 16 (1974), p. 169.

munities. Both parishes, moreover, had long been served by parish schools.[30]

The teaching of reading was more common in towns and cities, where forms of commerce and exchange placed literacy more at a premium. Still, one should not overestimate the extent of urban literacy. During the judicial investigation into a Berlin riot in 1615, 301 out of the 562 burghers who testified could not sign their names.[31] Since this sample did not include noncitizens, who were generally less affluent and thus even less likely to be literate, the illiterate proportion of the total municipal population was doubtless much higher.

Moreover, townspeople who acquired literacy frequently obtained it not because of parish and community schools, but in spite of them. Many parents preferred to send their children to so-called *Winkelschulen,* "backstreet schools," franchised neither by the church nor by municipal authorities.[32] Except in Austria, where backstreet schools often served as havens for crypto-Protestantism, instruction in these schools was strictly utilitarian. *Winkelschulen* subordinated religious instruction to the goal of imparting literacy to their pupils in the shortest time possible. Thus backstreet schools offered poorer families a more cost-effective means of acquiring literacy.[33] Attendance at a backstreet school was a less time-consuming affair, since its curricular focus was narrower. This was an important advantage for households that depended heavily on the labor of their children.

The steady stream of ordinances directed against the backstreet schools testifies to their enduring popularity. Franchised schoolmasters resented them as a threatening source of competition, while church authorities and conservative city fathers distrusted their neglect of religious instruction in favor of the 3 Rs.[34] Although they lacked corporate sanction, however, backstreet schools flourished in Central European cities.

[30]Czimeg, "Entwicklung der Pfarrschulen," pp. 3–5.
[31]Gerhard Krienke, "Das Berliner Elementarschulwesen von 1696 bis 1739," *Bär von Berlin,* 32 (1983), p. 7.
[32]In Scotland, which was renowned for its high literacy rate in the early modern period, these were called adventure schools. In parts of Scotland, they educated more pupils than did parochial schools. See Rab Houston, *Scottish Literacy and the Scottish Identity: Illiteracy and Society in Scotland and Northern England* (New York, 1986), p. 115.
[33]See Christopher R. Friedrichs, "Whose House of Learning? Some Thoughts on German Schools in Post-Reformation Germany," *History of Education Quarterly,* 22 (1982), pp. 374–375. A good discussion of Prussian *Winkelschulen* is provided by Neugebauer, *Schulwirklichkeit,* pp. 581–601.
[34]Friedrichs, "Whose House of Learning?" p. 373; Wienecke, "Begründung der evangelischen Volksschule," pp. 30–32.

In 1662 Halle had no less than eighteen, most of which were attended by children of laborers in the city's salt industry.[35] In 1716, Leipzig's thirty-nine backstreet schools were attended by more than 1,200 pupils, most of them children of soldiers and day laborers. Bremen had twenty-six *Winkelschulen* in 1638, while Braunschweig could boast thirty-nine in 1673.[36] Frankfurt an der Oder had thirty backstreet schools in 1713, while in 1768, seven *Winkelschulen* were located in Berlin's Jakobstrasse alone.[37] Even in Austria, where monarchical and ecclesiastical authorities bitterly condemned *Winkelschulen* as real or potential harbingers of heresy, they continued to lead a shadowy and elusive existence. Backstreet schools often served as underground Protestant cells, where children and adults alike received instruction in reading, writing, and Lutheran doctrine. Some were hidden away on the estates of unreconstructed Protestant nobles, as was the case in Styria and Lower Austria during the seventeenth century.[38] In Upper Austria and Styria, they were patronized by crypto-Protestant peasants seeking a Lutheran education for their children.[39] Backstreet schools were usually quite small and often amounted to little more than a tutor collectively employed by four or five families. Occasionally, however, they drew more pupils than their franchised competitors. In 1718, for example, Viennese municipal authorities closed down a *Winkelschule* serving more than 60 pupils.[40] This came at the instigation of a neighboring franchised schoolmaster, who had only 18 pupils. Despite efforts to eradicate them, a 1771 investigation in Vienna revealed the existence of fifty-nine backstreet schools instructing a total of 317 pupils.[41]

---

[35]Erich Neuss, "Entstehung und Entwicklung der Klasse der besitzlosen Lohnarbeiter in Halle," *Abhandlungen der Sachsischen Akademie der Wissenschaften zu Leipzig* (Philologisch-historische Klasse), 51 (1958), p. 148.

[36]Engelsing, *Analphabetentum und Lektüre*, p. 48; Friedrichs, "Whose House of Learning?" p. 373.

[37]Neugebauer, *Schulwirklichkeit*, p. 594; Dietrich Rittershausen, "Beiträge zur Geschichte des Berliner Elementarschulwesens von der Reformation bis 1836," *Märkische Forschungen*, 9 (1865), p. 267.

[38]Loserth, *Die protestantischen Schulen*, p. 124; Hubel, "Das Schulwesen Niederösterreichs," pp. 36–37.

[39]Weiss, *Bistum Passau*, p. 300; Johann Schmut, "Erstes Eingreifen des Staates zur Hebung des niederen Schulwesens in der Steiermark unter Maria Theresia," *Beiträge zur österreichischen Erziehungs- und Schulgeschichte*, 11 (1909), p. 152. See also the example of Austrian Silesia in Theodore Haase, "Das evangelische Schulwesen in Bielitz bis zum Toleranzpatent," *Jahrbuch für die Geschichte des Protestantismus in Österreich*, 53 (1932), p. 96.

[40]Albert Hübl, "Die Schulen," in Anton Mayer, ed., *Geschichte der Stadt Wien*, 6 vols. (Vienna, 1914), 5:360.

[41]*AVA:* Nachlass Pergen, "Tabellarisches Verzeichnis."

It is revealing that the *Winkelschule,* an institution so oriented toward instruction in the 3 Rs, belonged to the educational underground of early modern Central Europe. This suggests that in the corporately sanctioned primary schools of early modern Central Europe, literacy was a frequent but not always essential goal of "official" popular schooling.[42] Parish schools primarily sought to train good Christians, not necessarily literate ones.

Schoolmasters

As far as parish and community schools were concerned, no real teaching profession existed in early modern Central Europe.[43] In most cases teaching was not a professionalized, self-sufficient occupation, but an activity pursued on the side. Exceptions could be found in towns, cities, and larger parish seats, where franchised schoolmasters in larger schools could support themselves purely from teaching. Such schoolmasters were frequently highly educated, long-suffering theology graduates whose hopes for a pastoral appointment had yet to be fulfilled. In most rural schools, on the other hand, the schoolmaster was either the church sacristan or a village artisan, and teaching the children of the parish community was merely one of his chores. Here little or no formal preparation was required. Since a sacristan was expected to lead the church choir, play the organ, or sing hymns with his pupils at baptisms and burials, his musical talents were often valued more than teaching skills. That the titles *Cantor* and *Schulmeister* were interchangeable illustrates concretely

[42]Historians of popular education have become increasingly cautious about inferring literacy from the presence or absence of schools. On this point see Rab Houston, "Literacy and Society in the West, 1500–1850," *Social History,* 8 (1983), pp. 273–275, and the discussion of literacy in early-modern Scotland and northern England in idem, *Scottish Literacy,* pp. 101–102, 110–161. In the case of France, Michel Vovelle has cautioned that "il n'y a pas correlation méchanique entre alphabetisation et équipment scholaire." Vovelle, "Y a-t-il eu une revolution culturelle au XVIIIe siècle? A propos de l'education populaire en Provence," *Revue d'histoire moderne et contemporaine,* 22 (1975), p. 121, quoted in Houston, "Literacy and Society," p. 273. Furet and Ozouf, *Reading and Writing,* p. 68, similarly warn against "fetishizing the role of the school" by "subordinating the whole history of literacy to it." On this point see also Harvey Chisick, "School Attendance, Literacy, and Acculturation: *Petites écoles* and Popular Education in Eighteenth-Century France," *Europa,* 3 (1979), pp. 185–221.

[43]Although largely concerned with the nineteenth century, the opening chapter in Anthony J. La Vopa, *Prussian Schoolteachers: Profession and Office, 1763–1848* (Chapel Hill, 1980), pp. 11–24, provides a highly useful discussion of the occupational status of schoolmasters in eighteenth-century Prussia. On Prussian schoolmasters see also Neugebauer, *Schulwirklichkeit,* pp. 302–333.

the schoolmaster's musical function. In Magdeburg village schools, for example, schoolmasters were hired on the basis of a singing audition in front of the parish congregation.[44] Inhabitants of the Tyrolean village of Nonsthale clearly indicated their priorities in 1648, when they requested a schoolmaster "who is trained in music, can sing, play organ, and also teach."[45] Thus Johann Ignaz Felbiger did not exaggerate when he charged that "a man who applies to be a schoolmaster is considered qualified as long as he knows enough music to sing, lead a choir, play a little organ, and perhaps write a bit."[46]

Beyond his music duties, the schoolmaster-sacristan was often expected to fill in for the priest in case of illness. This could be a burdensome chore if the priest was old or chronically infirm, and was a frequent source of complaints by schoolmasters.[47] He was also responsible for keeping the church in good repair, assisting at burials, traveling between parishes to deliver messages to and from the archbishop or consistory, visiting the sick, or serving as the village scribe.[48] In fact, the term *Schulmeister* in the sixteenth and seventeenth centuries did not necessarily refer to the instruction of children. Rather, the term encompassed all of the duties rendered by the pastor's assistant, especially that of singing at religious services, and did not necessarily imply teaching.[49] This etymological ambiguity is suggestive of the parish schoolmaster's own ill-defined status.

The income that the schoolmaster earned from his school and parish work was not usually adequate for the support of himself and his family. Although the church or community usually provided his lodgings, his room sometimes amounted to little more than the stable of the parish church or a hut on the village common. Moreover, his accommodations

[44]Danneil, *Magdeburg,* pp. 60–61.
[45]"Geschichtlicher Abriss über die Schule zu 'Unsere liebe Frau im Walde' im Nonsthale," *Die katholische Volksschule,* 27 (1897), p. 393.
[46]Julius Scheveling, ed., *Johann Ignaz Felbiger. General-Landschulreglement. Eigenschaften, Wissenschaften, und Bezeigen rechtschaffener Schulleute* (Paderborn, 1958), p. 66.
[47]See, for example, the complaints from 1757 and 1762 by East Prussian schoolmasters in Nikolaiken, Drengfurt, and Rosenberg, in the *Preussisches Geheimes Staatsarchiv,* West Berlin: Staatsarchiv Königsberg, Étatsministerium (Königsberger Kammer), Tit. 39a/1, Bd. III, fol. 246–247, and Bd. IV, fol. 61–85.
[48]See the description of these duties in Johann Ignaz Felbiger, *Kleine Schulschriften nebst einer ausführlichen Nachricht von den Umstände und dem Erfolge der Verbesserung der Katholischen Land- und Stadt-Trivialschulen in Schlesien und Glatz* (Sagan, 1768), pp. 180–181.
[49]Duesterhaus, *Das ländliche Schulwesen,* p. 168.

usually had to serve as the schoolroom, which he and his pupils might share with a sheep or a cow.[50] He sometimes received a small garden plot from the church or the community, but he often had to pay a part of the yield as rent.[51] If he had a cow, he sometimes received a plot of pasture land, often the cemetery adjacent to the church, on which it could graze.

In addition to his dwelling and garden plot, the schoolmaster received a payment in cash or kind from the parents of his pupils. In 1765, Felbiger calculated that a schoolmaster needed an annual income of at least fifteen talers and thirty-two bushels of wheat in order to subsist.[52] Once the wheat is converted into a cash equivalent, Felbiger's proposed subsistence standard for schoolmasters equaled approximately twenty-one talers – an amount slightly less than what a peasant paid a farm servant in an average year.[53] In cities and market towns, where a franchised school might have as many as sixty pupils, a schoolmaster frequently earned or surpassed this minimum. In Berlin's Friedrichstadt district, for example, five parish schoolmasters each earned an average of forty-two talers per year.[54] Rural schoolmasters in East Prussia also fared reasonably well, averaging a combined grain and cash income equal to that prescribed by Felbiger.[55] Elsewhere, however, the yearly income of parish schoolmasters fell far below Felbiger's subsistence standard. Schoolmasters in Pomerania averaged only five talers in 1748.[56] As late as 1786, the cash income of a village schoolmaster in Upper Silesia averaged less than ten talers annually. This included his pay as sexton and village scribe, forcing him to supplement his income through spinning or woodcutting. In 1754, two schoolmasters in the Styrian village of Wildalpen and the Bohemian village of Annaberg earned sixty-four flo-

---

[50]R. Schmidt, *Volksschule und Volksschulbau von den Anfängen des niederen Schulwesens bis in die Gegenwart* (Dotzheim, 1967), pp. 20–22.

[51]Michael, "Schlesische Dorfschule," pp. 232–235.

[52]Felbiger, *K.S.*, p. 135.

[53]I have based my conversion on the average price of wheat on the Halle market between 1720 and 1750, as given in Neuss, "Lohnarbeiter," p. 169. The figure for farm wages is taken from Wolfgang Jacobeit and Heinz Nowak, "Zur Lebensweise und Kultur der werktätiger Dorfbevölkerung in der Zeit der Herausbildung des Kapitalismus in der Landwirtschaft vom Ende des 18. Jahrhunderts bis in die dreissiger/vierziger Jahre des 19. Jahrhunderts," in Hans-Jürgen Roch and Bernard Weissel, *Bauer und Landarbeiter im Kapitalismus in der Magdeburger Börde* (East Berlin, 1982), p. 17.

[54]Rittershausen, "Geschichte des Berliner Elementarschulwesens," p. 267.

[55]H. Notbohm, *Das evangelische Kirchen- und Schulwesen in Ostpreussen während der Regierung Friedrichs des Grossen* (Heidelberg, 1959), p. 37.

[56]*Acta Borussica. Denkmäler der preussischen Staatsverwaltung,* ed. Preussische Akademie der Wissenschaften, Abt. I, *Die Behördenorganisation,* ed. Gustav Schmoller et al., 15 vols. (Berlin, 1894ff.), 8:195.

rins – almost half the annual income of a day laborer in Vienna.[57] In fact, observers commonly compared the schoolmaster's economic position with that of a day laborer. A member of the Lutheran Consistory in Prussian Silesia reported in 1768 that a day laborer earned more in three months than a schoolmaster the entire year.[58] Felbiger, the school reformer, found it scandalous that in many villages "the income of a schoolmaster makes his position equal to that of a day laborer, or perhaps even lower."[59]

The seasonal rhythm of agriculture made the economic position of the schoolmaster even more precarious. The sharp drop in school attendance between April and November, when children worked in the fields, drastically reduced the schoolmaster's income. In the district of Neureppin in Brandenburg, for example, parish schools were empty between March and November.[60] The schoolmaster in the Styrian village of St. Georgen ob Murau had eight to ten pupils during the winter months, but he had none at all during the summer and early fall.[61] In the neighboring village of Fahndorf, the thirty pupils attending the village school during the winter fell to fifteen in the summer, while the twenty-five pupils in St. Georgen ob Judenberg fell to twelve.[62] In mountainous areas, attendance patterns were just the reverse. In the Tyrol, where weather and terrain limited access to schools in winter, attendance was much higher during the summer months.[63] The number of pupils could vary daily as well as seasonally: In Bohemia, parents often kept their children home on the day of the week when school fees were collected.[64]

---

[57]Czimeg, "Entwicklung der Pfarrschulen," p. 204; Franz Heisinger, *Zur Geschichte der deutschen Schulhalter in Eger und dem Egerlande* (Eger, 1897), p. 5; Johann Pezzl, *Skizze von Wien* (Vienna, 1786), p. 556.

[58]Ferdinand Vollmer, *Die preussische Volksschulpolitik unter Friedrich dem Grossen* (Berlin, 1918), pp. 120–121. An observer in eighteenth-century Lüneberg (Hanover) similarly noted that "in some areas the schoolmaster leaves town for the summer to work as a herdsman in nearby villages. During that summer, he earns more than he does the entire year as a schoolmaster." Quoted in Eno Fooken, *Die geistliche Schulaufsicht und ihre Kritiker im 18. Jahrhundert* (Dotzheim, 1967), p. 42.

[59]Scheveling, ed., *Johann Ignaz Felbiger*, p. 43.

[60]Visitation report from 1710 in *PGStA:* Provinz Brandenburg, Rep. 40 (Consistorium), Nr. 1773, fol. 140.

[61]Schmut, "Erstes Eingreifen," p. 149.

[62]Ibid., p. 148.

[63]Joseph Alexander Freiherr von Helfert, *Die Gründung der österreichischen Volksschule durch Maria Theresia* (Prague, 1860), pp. 59–60.

[64]Ferdinand Kindermann, *Nachricht von der Landschule zu Kaplitz* (Prague, 1774), republished in Josef Aigner, *Der Volks- und Industrieschulen-Reformator Bischof Ferdinand Kindermann* (Vienna, 1867), pp. 52–53. Cf. Rittershausen, "Geschichte des Berliner Elementarschulwesens," p. 199.

Since the schoolmaster's teaching income often fell well below his subsistence needs, moonlighting was an accepted part of the schoolmaster's life. An East Prussian ordinance from the reign of Frederick William I declared that "if the schoolmaster is an artisan, then he already possesses the means of supporting himself; if not, he is allowed to work for six weeks during the harvest as a day laborer."[65] A year later, a similar edict for Pomerania even forbade the hiring of schoolmasters outside of those "who can work and earn something beyond their teaching duties, so that they will not overburden the parish community."[66] Visitation reports from seventeenth- and eighteenth-century Silesia cite weaving, tailoring, and shoemaking as trades typically practiced by schoolmasters. During the 1750s, for example, the schoolmaster in the Silesian village of Strein was a smith, and in Seifersdorf he was a linen weaver.[67]

Tavern keeping was another occupation common among schoolmasters. In 1762, an administrator on the Liechtenstein estates in Rumburg (Bohemia) reported that although the schoolmaster in the village of Grund operated a tavern, his income was not sufficient for the support of his family.[68] In sixteenth- and seventeenth-century Prussia, it was considered the schoolmaster's privilege to operate a tavern in the village if he so wished. Responding to petitions from schoolmasters complaining of peasants and peddlers who operated competing taverns, the elector Georg Friedrich granted schoolmasters the sole privilege (aside from others already privileged) of operating a village tavern.[69] The results were not always edifying, at least from the standpoint of outraged Pietists who

[65] Quoted in Karl-Heinz Günther et al., *Geschichte der Erziehung* (East Berlin, 1960), p. 137.
[66] Eduard Reimann, "Über die Verbesserung des katholischen höheren Schulwesens in Schlesien durch Friedrich den Grossen," *Zeitschrift für die Geschichte Schlesiens,* 19 (1885), p. 319.
[67] Ostrowsky, *Wiejskie szkolnictwo parafialne,* p. 65; Carl Weigelt, "Die Volksschule in Schlesien nach der preussischen Besitzergreifung," *Zeitschrift für die Geschichte Schlesiens,* 24 (1890), p. 10; Richard Juhnke, *Wohlau: Geschichte des Fürstentums und des Kreises* (Würzburg, 1965), p. 176. See similar examples from East Prussia and Brandenburg in Notbohm, *Schulwesen in Ostpreussen,* p. 146, and Wienecke, "Begründung der evangelischen Volksschule," pp. 66–67. Wolfgang Neugebauer's survey of 432 rural schoolmasters in Brandenburg between 1668 and 1806 showed that over 60 percent also worked as tailors or weavers. See Neugebauer, *Schulwirklichkeit,* p. 322.
[68] *Hausarchiv des regierenden Fürstens von Liechtenstein,* Vienna: Kart. 650, May 12, 1762. Similar examples are found in *AEW,* Visitationen D. D. Dechanten (1664–1760), Passau, 1708; and Theodor Wiedemann, *Geschichte der Reformation und Gegenreformation im Lande unter der Enns,* 5 vols. (Prague, 1879–1882), 5:179.
[69] Duesterhaus, *Das ländliche Schulwesen,* pp. 78–81, 110.

first condemned the practice beginning in the late seventeenth century. In 1710, an inspection of the parish school in the village of Läsikow (Brandenburg) revealed that the schoolmaster not only instructed pupils in his tavern, but drank with the older ones.[70]

To ensure the schoolmaster's economic survival, parishes often allowed him a monopoly on the performance of odd jobs in the community. These included tasks like maintaining the village commons or repairing buildings and roads. When towns and villages began installing church tower clocks in the late sixteenth century, schoolmasters were usually paid for their upkeep. Ringing the parish church bell was another common source of income. Bell ringing not only beckoned village inhabitants to church, but was also intended to alter the weather. It was widely believed that a ringing bell could disperse clouds and hence end a violent storm.[71] Both Frederick II and Joseph II later denounced this practice as gross superstition. Although they outlawed the custom (Joseph even used military detachments to enforce the prohibition), they nevertheless insisted that the schoolmaster continue to receive payment for the service.[72] This action suggests that odd jobs like bell ringing could be a vital part of the schoolmaster's income.

Adding to the misery of impoverished schoolmasters was their low esteem in the community. A Prussian official in Silesia noted in 1768 that because of the rural schoolmaster's poverty, his prestige in the village community barely exceeded that of a cattle herdsman.[73] Even in towns, where schoolmasters were usually better paid and more highly educated, little prestige was attached to their occupation. Here the schoolmaster's low social status reflected the low reputation of parish and community schools among more propertied families. During the eighteenth century, as private tutors increasingly came into vogue in middle-class households, propertied families viewed "public schools" with disdain.[74] A 1770 report on schools in the Styrian city of Graz asserted that "only the worst sort of people send their children to these schools. Aristocrats,

[70]Wienecke, "Begründung der evangelischen Volksschule," p. 52. Cf. Danneil, *Magdeburg,* 80–81; and Duesterhaus, *Das ländliche Schulwesen,* p. 172.

[71]Karl Biedermann, *Deutschland im 18. Jahrhundert,* 2 vols, 2d ed. (Leipzig, 1880), 2:1099; Michael, "Schlesische Dorfschule," p. 259.

[72]Lehmann, *Preussen und die katholische Kirche,* 3:607; P. K. Jaksch, ed., *Gesetzeslexikon . . . für das Königreich Böhmen,* 5 vols. (Prague, 1828), 2:490; Walter Pietsch, *Die theresianische Schulreform in der Steiermark (1775–1805)* (Graz, 1977), p. 159.

[73]Vollmer, *Preussische Volksschulpolitik,* p. 121.

[74]Gustav Stephan, *Die häusliche Erziehung im 18. Jahrhundert* (Wiesbaden, 1891), pp. 62–64.

respectable burghers, even propertied artisans would deem it a disgrace to send their children to public schools."[75] Joseph Messmer, rector of the St. Stephan *Stadtschule* in Vienna, likewise noted that only "children of coachmen, servants, poorer artisans, and day laborers" attended Viennese parish and community schools.[76]

The poor reputation of parish and community schools was doubtless galling to those schoolmasters who were university trained. In the eighteenth century, highly educated schoolmasters were especially common in East Prussia, where a growing surplus of theology graduates was forced to seek refuge in parish schools.[77] University educated, yet often inferior to their fellow parishioners in income and prestige, many lived lives of bitter frustration. Some sought to compensate by assuming elevated titles, while others latinized their names to underline their educational credentials. Thus Heinrich Kotke, a Magdeburg schoolmaster who had pursued desultory studies at the University of Helmstedt, customarily signed his name "Henricus Codinus".[78] Many doubtlessly reconciled themselves to their lot in a spirit of Christian resignation. Others pinned their hopes on a vacant pastoral position, submitting petitions and letters of recommendation whenever a neighboring pastor died. The case of Michael Czwalina, a schoolmaster in the East Prussian village of Belslack, illustrates the problems facing university-trained schoolmasters. Czwalina had been a parish schoolmaster since 1753 and in 1762 he applied for a vacant pastoral position. A theology graduate of the University of Königsberg, he was highly praised by his former professors and was obviously a studious sort. Yet he received a meager income, which had been so reduced by the need to support his brother's widowed family that he could no longer afford wood to heat his room. Even worse, complained Czwalina, was the time-consuming tedium of his position. He had no time for reading or scholarship, and his poorly educated parish offered no outlet or esteem for his talents. He assured the consistory in Königsberg that his education could be put to better use as a pastor or a rector of a Latin school. The consistory apparently thought other-

[75]*AVA:* Akten der Studienhofkommission, Fasz. 70, fol. 110–111.
[76]Messmer, "Zustand der hiesigen gemeinen Schulen in und vor der Stadt," in *AVA:* Akten der Studienhofkommission, Fasz. 70, fol. 220.
[77]Notbohm, *Schulwesen in Ostpreussen,* p. 110. On this surplus see Henri Brunschwig, *Enlightenment and Romanticism in Eighteenth-Century Prussia,* trans. Frank Jellinek (Chicago, 1975), pp. 132–134.
[78]Danneil, *Magdeburg,* p. 59. Cf. Konrad Fischer, *Geschichte des deutschen Volksschullehrerstandes* (Hanover, 1898), p. 211.

wise, and as far as we know Czwalina never obtained his pastoral position.[79]

In the classroom, the schoolmaster was constantly plagued with disciplinary problems. The notorious absence of discipline in parish and community schools in part resulted from the prevailing practice of teaching pupils individually rather than as a group. Children of differing ages and abilities sat in the same classroom and were instructed one at a time. Ferdinand Kindermann, a Bohemian educational reformer and a critic of this practice, described its consequences: "The pupils, young and old, all talk at the same time, one asking for bread, another for milk. One child leaves the classroom while another enters. As one pupil reads, another talks with his friends, while another stutters the first few lines of the catechism."[80] Joseph Messmer, also a critic, similarly complained that "while the teacher works with one child, the others talk and joke with one another. If one calculates the actual time allotted to each child, it amounts at most to two minutes per day, twelve minutes per week, 48 minutes per month, and in an entire year . . . hardly ten full hours."[81]

The schoolmaster's ability to command the respect and obedience of his pupils was severely hampered by his low status in the community. Confronted with an unruly pupil, he often had only the rod to preserve his authority. Hence corporal punishment was a constant feature of school life. The schoolmaster's authority in the classroom, unbuttressed by the esteem of the community, had to be maintained through pure force.[82] But here the schoolmaster's position was virtually untenable. The resort to force was ultimately ineffective, since by punishing a child the schoolmaster risked the anger of the pupil's parents. In the Styrian village of Haus, the parish priest complained in 1752 that discipline in the parish school was poor because "the parents are very touchy and refuse to let the schoolmaster punish their children."[83] Ferdinand Kindermann, who operated a village school, wrote in 1774 that when a schoolmaster punished a pupil, "in no time at all the loving mother is there, loudly scolding the schoolmaster for being a brutal child-beater,

[79]*PGStA:* Staatsarchiv Königsberg, États-Ministerium (Königsberger Kammer), Tit. 39a/1, vol. 3, fol. 109ff.
[80]Kindermann, *Nachricht,* p. 13.
[81]Messmer, "Zustand der hiesigen gemeinen Schulen."
[82]On the frequency of corporal punishment see Jürgen Kuczynski, *Geschichte des Alltags des deutschen Volkes,* 5 vols. (Cologne, 1981), 2:200–201, and Heppe, *Geschichte des deutschen Volksschulwesens,* pp. 37–38.
[83]Schmut, "Erstes Eingreifen," p. 150.

although bodily punishment was probably the only thing the little beggar understands."[84] Such humiliating treatment at the hands of parents only further undermined the schoolmaster's authority. Felbiger noted in exasperation that parents too often "reinforce the willfulness and maliciousness of their children by speaking disrespectfully of the schoolmaster, insulting and cursing him behind his back, sometimes even storming into the classroom and scolding him in front of his pupils."[85]

A schoolmaster could ill afford to anger the parents of his pupils, since the town or village community customarily had a voice in the hiring and firing of schoolmasters.[86] Competition for pupils could be keen in towns with more than one school, and the plethora of backstreet schools only worsened matters. Franchised schoolmasters were often reluctant to punish unruly pupils, fearing their parents would transfer them to a *Winkelschule*. In the Styrian town of Marburg, for example, a parish priest lamented in 1752 that "the schoolmaster is unable to punish the children for their mischievous and spiteful behavior because he fears that a mother will barge into the schoolroom, scold him brazenly in front of his pupils, and then remove her child to a *Winkelschule*."[87]

The schoolmaster's relationship to his parish priest was also fraught with difficulties. The two by necessity worked closely with one another, which offered ample occasion for conflict. A priest could easily feel threatened by a popular or talented schoolmaster, while a highly educated schoolmaster who had been waiting years for a pastoral vacancy could understandably resent his superior. Feuds between priest and schoolmaster were commonplace and carried on in public view. In 1757 relations

---

[84]Kindermann, *Nachricht*, p. 49.
[85]Felbiger, *K.S.*, p. 182. Cf. the disciplinary problems facing English schoolmasters, described in Keith Thomas, *Rule and Misrule in the Schools of Early Modern England* (Reading, 1975), pp. 13–14.
[86]The right to appoint a schoolmaster (*Patronenrecht*) was formally shared by a variety of authorities. Prior to the reign of Frederick II, the hiring of Prussian schoolmasters on royal domains had been in the hands of the pastor and the community, and final approval rested with the provincial consistory. In towns and on noble domains, appointments were subject to the approval of the magistracy or nobility. In Austrian towns, schoolmasters in secular schools were customarily franchised by the magistracy, while parish schoolmasters were formally appointed by the priest or episcopal consistory. Nobles frequently held the *Patronenrecht* in the countryside, although many chose not to exercise it if the school was far removed from their residences. In such cases the *Patronenrecht* usually devolved to the parish priest and community. On the complexities of the *Patronenrecht* see Neugebauer, *Schulwirklichkeit*, pp. 134–167; Vollmer, *Preussische Volksschulpolitik*, pp. 19–22; Feigl, *Niederösterreichische Grundherrschaft*, pp. 108–121.
[87]Schmut, "Erstes Eingreifen," p. 222. Cf. Friedrichs, "Whose House of Learning?" p. 373.

between the pastor and schoolmaster in the village of Streckenthin (Brandenburg) deteriorated to the point where the priest berated the schoolmaster for drunkenness in full view of the congregation. The schoolmaster responded by threatening the pastor and calling his daughter a "drunken sow."[88] In 1755, money was the issue in a protracted feud between the pastor and schoolmaster in the Brandenburg village of Schmöllen. Here the pastor accused the schoolmaster of overcharging parents for school primers. As a result, he argued, households were less willing to pay the parish tax, and the pastor's income was threatened. The schoolmaster denied the accusation, charging instead that the pastor refused to remunerate him for his instruction of pauper children.[89]

Poverty, low social status, humiliations at the hands of parents, resentment toward his superior — these help account for the frequently unflattering references to the schoolmaster's character. One of the most common criticisms leveled at schoolmasters in visitation reports concerned habitual drunkenness.[90] Here boredom was doubtless a cause, especially among those who were highly educated. Frequent tavern work may have been another cause. In 1752, the Liechtenstein estate steward in the Rumburg region recommended a replacement for the schoolmaster, who apparently operated a tavern and could not resist his own wares.[91] For most alcoholic schoolmasters, however, it is just as likely that drink offered an escape from the low self-esteem fostered by their low status in the village community and constant humiliations at the hands of their pupils and pupils' parents. It was the often desperate position of the schoolmaster that led eighteenth-century reformers to focus their attention as much upon teacher as pupil.

[88]*PGStA:* Provinz Brandenburg, Rep. 40 (Consistorium), Nr. 1115, fol. 1–52.
[89]Ibid., Nr. 796, fol. 1–3. See Nr. 819, fol. 25–29, for other examples of conflict. See also the reference to tensions between pastors and schoolmasters in Lithuania in *PGStA:* Staatsarchiv Königsberg, États-Ministerium (Gumbinnen Kammer), Rep. 8, Abt. 6, Nr. 1, Bd. 3, fol. 17.
[90]See *PGStA:* Staatsarchiv Königsberg, États-Ministerium (Königsberger Kammer), Tit. 39a/1, Bd. 3, fol. 157–206; Ostrowski, *Wiejskie szkolnictwo parafialne*, p. 114; Felbiger, *Kleine Schulschriften*, pp. 180–181; *AEW:* Visitationen D. D. Dechanten (1724–60), Passau, reports on Erdberg (1756) and Gudransdorff (1768).
[91]*HFL,* Kart. 650, May 12, 1762.

2

The rise of Pietist pedagogy

We are not to be satisfied if the child exhibits an outer show of piety but at heart remains unchanged. . . . The purely external, no matter how fair its appearance, cannot stand before the omniscient eye of God without the power of Christ in one's heart.

August Hermann Francke, 1702

The late seventeenth century witnessed a revival of interest in popular schooling. What helped spark this revival was the reform movement within German Protestantism known as Pietism.

It is difficult to overestimate Pietism's impact on pedagogical theory and practice in eighteenth-century Central Europe. This applies not only to Protestant states like Prussia, but also to Catholic territories. The Pietist celebration of "inwardness" (*Innerlichkeit*) produced a renewed concern with the role of education in the shaping of personality. With schools the focus of their campaign for moral and spiritual regeneration, Pietist reformers introduced pedagogical innovations whose impact is still felt today. Stressing lay Bible reading, they promoted popular literacy on an unprecedented scale. As the first to establish schools for the formal training of schoolmasters, they played a key role in professionalizing teaching. With their pronounced work ethic and stress on "vocation" (*Beruf*), they laid the basis for the emergence of vocational education. Finally, they introduced or popularized many pedagogical techniques that survive today, such as hand raising (to ask a question) or the collective instruction of pupils in primary school classrooms.

Pietist pedagogy first emerged in Prussia, or to be more specific, the town of Halle. This chapter examines the rise of Pietist pedagogy, tracing its impact on the reform and expansion of Prussian popular schooling during the first half of the eighteenth century.

The emergence of Pietism

Pietism arose in Germany during the latter half of the seventeenth century. As a reform movement within Lutheranism, Pietism was fueled by the conviction that Protestantism had failed to fulfill the spiritual promise of the Reformation. The Pietists were not the first to raise doubts about the success of the Reformation. Already in the late sixteenth century, Lutheran reformers had begun to question the effectiveness of their efforts among the laity. Endless complaints of poor church and school attendance, ignorance of the catechism, and the sinful behavior of a recalcitrant laity inspired doubts as to whether Luther's reformation had genuinely taken root.[1] Further reflecting the belief that "official" Lutheranism had failed to bring about a true spiritual renewal was the revival of mysticism in the late sixteenth and seventeenth centuries. Demanding a more subjective and purified faith, Lutheran mystics like Jacob Böhme (1575–1624) and Johann Arndt (1555–1621) insisted that the spiritual promise of the Reformation remained unfulfilled.

The Thirty Years War only deepened this sense of failure and decay. Devout Lutherans like Duke Ernst the Pious of Saxony-Gotha attributed the war to divine punishment, retribution for spiritual disobedience, and corruption.[2] At midcentury, contemporaries found it difficult to contest the Duke's gloomy diagnosis. A century after the death of Luther, extensive areas of Germany lay ravaged by war. Orphans, widows, and vagabonds roamed its cities and towns. Lutheran princes, far from tending to the spiritual welfare of their subjects, increasingly indulged a taste for luxury and display in the style of Louis XIV. During the closing decades of the seventeenth century, the siege of Vienna in 1683 and the devastating impact of the wars of Louis XIV seemed to provide further evidence of divine disfavor. In seeking to explain the spiritual decline they saw around them, critics blamed the laity's ignorance of or indifference to the fundamental articles of faith. Condemning the sterility and rigidity of Lutheran scholasticism, they blamed the church establishment itself for the tepid state of religious faith among the laity. This charge, as Hans

---

[1] See Strauss, *Luther's House of Learning*, pp. 268–308; Hans Leube, *Orthodoxie und Pietismus* (Bielefeld, 1975), pp. 68–70. On the religious roots of Pietism see also Gerhard Kaiser, *Pietismus und Patriotismus im literarischen Deutschland* (Wiesbaden, 1961), pp. 1–14.

[2] August Beck, *Ernst der Fromme, Herzog zu Sachsen-Gotha* (Weimar, 1865), p. 65; Leube, *Orthodoxie und Pietismus*, pp. 71–72; Hartmut Lehmann, "Der Pietismus im alten Reich," *Historische Zeitschrift*, 214 (1972), pp. 70–72.

Leube has suggested, may well have exaggerated the failings of orthodox Lutheran theologians.[3] Whether such criticism was justified is beside the point. From the standpoint of countless contemporaries, the Lutheran faith faced a crisis of massive proportions.

It was in the context of this real or perceived crisis in German Lutheranism that the Pietist demand for a "Reformation within the Reformation" must be understood. The spiritual father of Pietism was the Alsatian-born theologian Phillip Jacob Spener (1635–1705). As a student at the University of Strassburg, Spener had read copiously in Arndtian mysticism and Puritan devotional literature. Particularly important for Spener's theological development was Lewis Bayly's *Practice of Piety*, one of the most popular devotional guides in seventeenth-century England.[4] Bayly's biblicism and stress upon the practical value of Scripture for daily life were to be central features of Pietism. Spener's views were also shaped by his friendship with Jean de Labadie (1610–74), the fiery Calvinist minister whom Spener had met during a visit to Geneva in 1660. Labadie, a French ex-Jesuit, was a determined church reformer whose Genevan sermons called for a "new reformation" in the city. Labadie's sermons on the decline of public morals – his condemnation of luxury, display, dancing, and the theater – had a profound impact on Spener.[5] Although Spener proved receptive to Calvinist influences, he carefully avoided straying beyond the acceptable bounds of Lutheran doctrine. After further study at the universities of Basel and Tübingen, Spener returned to Strassburg to receive his doctorate. Shortly thereafter he accepted a pastoral position in Frankfurt am Main.

In Frankfurt, Spener's moral rigorism and eschewal of theological subtleties attracted a wide following among those critical of public morals and dissatisfied with the contentious scholasticism of orthodox Lutheran theologians. In 1670 Spener and his followers formed the Collegium Pietatis, an informal study group devoted to fostering piety in the

---

[3]Leube, *Orthodoxie und Pietismus*, pp. 36–68.

[4]By 1735, Bayly's treatise had gone through fifty-nine editions. Bayly (1580–1631) was chaplain to Prince Henry when his handbook appeared, but distanced himself from the Puritan movement when his views brought him into disfavor at court. In 1616 he was appointed chaplain to James I, and later in the same year bishop of Bangor in north Wales. *The Practice of Piety* continued to be purchased and used in Puritan circles, and Bayly himself followed Calvin in everything but church organization. Spener used the Latin edition, *Praxis Pietatis*, published in Basel in 1628. On Spener's development during this period see Johannes Wallman, *Philipp Jakob Spener und die Anfänge des Pietismus* (Tübingen, 1970), pp. 50–81. On Bayly see Horton Davies, *Worship and Theology in England*, 5 vols. (Princeton, 1975), 2: 112–114.

[5]Wallman, *Spener*, pp. 140–143.

community. This lay conventicle met on Sunday and Wednesday evenings at Spener's home, where Bible readings were followed by discussion and prayer. The Collegium Pietatis soon attracted widespread attention both in Germany and abroad – William Penn paid a visit in 1674 – and is rightfully considered the first Pietist conventicle in Germany.

As a private circle with no formal ties to the church, the group soon aroused distrust among the more orthodox clergy and magistrates of Frankfurt. These suspicions were confirmed when a faction within the Collegium left the Lutheran Church altogether.[6] Spener's enemies seized upon the scandal to discredit him, and Spener finally left Frankfurt in 1686 to assume a position as pastor and confessor at the electoral court in Dresden.

There, too, Spener incurred the hostility of the Lutheran establishment, which accused him of undermining the church by encouraging private worship services and sectarian *Schwärmerei*. Moreover, tensions soon surfaced in his relationship with Johann Georg II, the Saxon elector, who grew to resent Spener's open disapproval of his drunkenness, dissipation, and prodigal taste for luxury.[7] Spener's final break with the elector in 1691 led him to the Prussian capital of Berlin, where he remained as a pastor and influential consistory advisor until his death in 1705.

Central to Spener's theology was the conviction that spiritual renewal from within was far more important than the purely passive, external observance of a rigid theological system. In his *Pia Desideria*, Spener described the inwardly directed, subjective faith of the Pietists:

The essence of our Christianity is to be found in the reflective, spiritually-reborn individual whose soul is possessed by faith and whose actions are the fruit of this faith. . . . Inward reflection must form the core of all worship and observance of the sacraments, for it is not enough that we hear the Word of God with our ears alone. We must let his Word penetrate our hearts. It is not enough to partake outwardly of the Eucharist, or to pray only with our lips, or to serve God outwardly in his temple. . . . The individual must serve God from deep within the temple of his very soul.[8]

[6] Many emigrated to Pennsylvania and joined the Quaker colony of William Penn. Francis Daniel Pastorius, who founded the Quaker settlement at Germantown, was one such émigré. See Carl Hinrichs, *Preussentum und Pietismus. Der Pietismus in Brandenburg-Preussen als religiös-soziale Reformbewegung* (Göttingen, 1971), p. 44. On the *Collegium Pietatis* see ibid., pp. 245–266, and P. Grünberg, *Phillip Jakob Spener*, 3 vols. (Göttingen, 1893–1906), 1:200–203.
[7] On Johann Georg II see Karl Biedermann, *Deutschland im 18. Jahrhundert*, 2 vols. (Leipzig, 1867–90), 2:58.
[8] Spener, *Pia Desideria*, ed. Kurt Aland (Berlin, 1955), p. 151.

The distinction between the external and the internal, between outward observance and inner conviction, was fundamental to Pietism. For the Pietists, the actual performance of one's Christian duties was less important than the spirit in which they were carried out. True Christians fulfilled their obligations voluntarily and through conviction, not mechanically or through coercion.

The distinction between inner conviction and external coercion, of course, was central to the Lutheran doctrine of justification. Luther had written in his preface to *Romans* that "God judges according to that which lay within the depths of your heart. Hence you fulfill His law not through works, but through the sincerity of your beliefs."[9] Yet the Pietists were critical of their church precisely because they believed it had lost sight of Luther's original message. "It is a disgrace to the Lutheran religion," wrote Spener, "that so many of its members believe they can be saved by observing the externals of the faith alone."[10] Pietists charged that Lutheran theologians bore much of the blame for the shallow faith of their flock. Their arid scholasticism and dogmatism had encouraged passive doctrinal conformity at the expense of inner piety.

Like the Puritans, furthermore, Pietists blamed the decline of inner spirituality on the excessive luxury and display of court and aristocratic life. To be sure, Pietists like Spener were more muted in their critique of baroque pomp and ostentation than their English counterparts. Spener conceded, for example, that social differences in dress were necessary "so that the subject will venerate his lord more deeply."[11] Yet he also warned that an excessive concern with the display of power and wealth corrupted society by breeding a taste for luxury among the common folk. Pietists generally condemned sensual display of any sort – dancing, the stage, opera, popular festivals – for diverting attention from the individual's inner spiritual state.[12] This suspicion of display extended to Lutheran public worship, which Pietists felt had become infected with the ostentation they condemned in other areas of cultural life. Veit Ludwig von Seckendorff (1626–92), the influential cameralist writer who had close ties to the Pietist movement, criticized the increasing reliance on pomp and theatricality in Lutheran services. "In place of this ostentatious

---

[9]*D. Martin Luthers Werke. Kritische Gesamtausgabe. Die deutsche Bibel,* 12 vols. (Weimar, 1906–1961), 7:4–5.
[10]Grünberg, *Spener,* 3:155.
[11]Spener, *Die evangelischen Lebenspflichten,* 3d ed., 2 pts. (Frankfurt am Main, 1715), 1:71.
[12]Ibid., p. 54; 2:175. See also Grünberg, *Spener,* 3:201–210.

pomp," wrote Seckendorff, "more emphasis should be placed on inner spirituality."[13]

Pietist inwardness was accompanied by a determined social activism. This at first seems paradoxical, for the Pietist emphasis upon spiritual renewal from within would seem to discount the efficacy or importance of worldly enterprise. Indeed, critics of Pietism, from seventeenth-century orthodox Lutherans who viewed Pietist social activism as a heretical abandonment of Lutheran solafideism, to modern historians who see in Pietist *Innerlichkeit* the roots of the "unpolitical German," have each stressed the incompatibility of the two attitudes.

Yet the relationship between the two positions was dialectical, not contradictory. For Pietists, it was precisely the individual's renewed faith and purified will that made good works possible; conversely, good works were evidence of spiritual renewal. As Spener wrote, "even faith . . . must be verified through action. This in the end is the highest proof of the power of faith."[14] Here the Pietists again followed Luther, who stressed the indivisibility of faith and works.[15] Pietism by no means held that human beings could justify themselves before God on the basis of good works. "Even when performing his best works," wrote Spener's disciple, August Hermann Francke, "man remains sinful to his very core."[16] Good works were not efficacious for salvation, but merely testimony to spiritual purification and renewal. As such, the Pietist concern with social reform was simply a further extension of their plans for a "second Reformation."

Hence Pietist inwardness, although seeming to minimize the value of worldly activity, actually encouraged it. Although this paradoxical blend of piety and action recalls similar features in Calvinism, the two movements differed in their rationale for worldly activity. The Calvinist concept of the "elect" was premised on the predestinarian conviction that only a small proportion of the human race is chosen for eternal grace. Far from inspiring passivity or resignation, however, Calvinism encouraged worldly activity as a means of dispelling the individual's religious doubts and providing the certainty of grace. The Calvinist promotion of worldly activity derived from the individual's uncertainty about his own state of

---

[13]Veit Ludwig von Seckendorff, *Christen-Stat* (Leipzig, 1685), p. 312.
[14]Spener, *Pia Desideria*, p. 42.
[15]Cf. Luther's preface to Romans in *D. Martin Luthers Werke, Kritische Ausgabe. Die deutsche Bibel,* 7:10ff.
[16]August Hermann Francke, *Catechismus-Predigten* (Halle, 1729), p. 213.

grace, so that the imperative to labor was more personal than social.[17] The Pietist justification for worldly activity, on the other hand, had broader social implications. Although Pietist criteria for the reception of grace were somewhat more rigorous, Pietism shared the Lutheran belief that grace was in principle available to all. Through repentance and conversion, every individual was eligible for divine grace. Consequently, every Christian was obliged not only to seek salvation for himself or herself, but also to help others do so. Thus worldly activity was not a sign of election, but a means of helping others acquire salvation.[18]

The Pietist rationale for social action provided the theological basis for the movement's renowned efforts on behalf of the poor. Yet the Pietist social ethos was in no way "socialist," as Carl Hinrichs suggested in his otherwise brilliant and indispensable study.[19] While stressing the Christian's duties to the poor, Pietism accepted the hierarchical social order of its day as divinely ordained. God created individuals of varying means and talents in order that each could serve God and others in his own way. Hence the vocation of an individual constituted the arena within which Christian duty was performed. The frivolous rejection or abandonment of one's *Beruf* was a violation of that duty. Using an organic analogy, Francke wrote that "the body of Christ consists of different members. Not every member can be a hand, foot, eye, or ear. Each member has its own task. . . . The foot should not desire to become an eye, nor the hand an ear."[20]

Here, of course, a tension existed between the energy and diligence that individuals were to invest in their vocation on the one hand, and the acceptance of their social position on the other. The former required initiative and hard work, the latter a recognition of the social parameters within which these virtues had to be contained. Yet Pietism was able to resolve this tension, as Anthony La Vopa has argued, through the dynamics of the "conversion experience" (*Bekehrung*).[21] For the Pietists,

[17]The classic treatment of this question, of course, is Max Weber, *The Protestant Ethic and the Spirit of Capitalism*, trans. Talcott Parsons (New York, 1958), pp. 95–183. However individualistic its theological premises relative to Pietism, Calvinist activism by no means precluded social activism. See Anthony La Vopa, "Vocations, Careers, and Talent: Lutheran Pietism and Sponsored Mobility in Eighteenth-Century Germany," *Comparative Studies in Society and History*, 28 (1986), pp. 277–278. See also Michael Walzer, *The Revolution of the Saints: A Study in the Origins of Radical Politics* (Cambridge, Mass., 1965), pp. 1–21.
[18]See Hinrichs, *Preussentum und Pietismus*, pp. 11–12.
[19]Ibid., p. 16.
[20]Quoted in Leube, *Orthodoxie und Pietismus*, p. 146.
[21]La Vopa, "Vocation, Careers, and Talent."

conversion did not take place immediately, but occurred in distinct stages and states of mind. The Pietist conversion experience was the product of an intense grappling with the self, an inner conflict that accompanied the "atonement struggle" (*Busskampf*). In the course of this struggle, individuals were to acquire the spiritual self-control that would later manifest itself in the work-discipline required for the exercise of their vocation. But the individual was able to resolve the atonement struggle only through a passive acceptance of God's grace, and the self-denying, passive trust in providence implied in this acceptance was designed to curb excessive ambition. In other words, the conversion experience fostered in individuals both the self-discipline required by their vocation and the calmness and passivity that enabled them to accept limits on their social mobility. In this way, estate and vocation, *Stand* and *Beruf*, were reconciled.

So however much the Pietists may have stressed individual initiative and social action, they nonetheless accepted social inequality as necessary and proper. Their social ethos aimed not at leveling the existing order, but rejuvenating it spiritually. Schooling was assigned a key role in this process of renewal.

Francke and his Halle schools

Although Spener had worked actively among the poor,[22] his primary contribution to Pietism was as a theologian. Pietism acquired its reputation as a social reform movement largely through the work of August Hermann Francke (1663–1727), who succeeded Spener as the leader of north German Pietism. Francke spent much of his childhood in Gotha, where his father served as a legal counselor to Duke Ernst the Pious. A stern Lutheran patriarch, Duke Ernst himself exhibited many of the traits later associated with Pietism.[23] He stood out among the territorial princes of his day for the austerity of his court and the modesty of his dress. Ernst shunned baroque ostentation, insisting that "a prince should not

[22]In Frankfurt, for example, Spener was instrumental in establishing the city's orphanage and workhouse (*Armen-, Waisen-, und Arbeitshaus*) in 1679. It formed the model for subsequent institutions of its type in Württemberg and Hesse-Kassel. Spener was later responsible for the creation of the Friedrichshospital, Berlin's largest poorhouse, in 1702. See Klaus Deppermann, *Der hallesche Pietismus und der preussische Staat unter Friedrich III. (I)* (Göttingen, 1961), pp. 58–61; and Krienke, "Berliner Elementarschulwesen," pp. 8–14.

[23]See Lowell C. Green, "Duke Ernst the Pious of Saxe-Gotha and His Relationship to Pietism," in H. Bornkamm, F. Heyer, and A. Schindler, eds., *Der Pietismus in Gestalten und Wirkungen* (Bielefeld, 1975).

burden his subjects with extravagant ceremonies, hunting parties, comedies, ballets, and fireworks displays."[24] Instead, he devoted his energies
to rebuilding his territory following its devastation during the Thirty
Years War. He focused special attention on the reform of public morals,
closing taverns on Sundays and establishing special courts to punish
drunkenness and brawling.

He devoted the bulk of his energies, however, to the promotion of
popular schooling. During his reign (1640–75), the small principality of
Saxony-Gotha became the center of educational innovation in the empire. While traditional in its stress on religious instruction, his compulsory school edict (1642) was the first in Germany to introduce the so-called
Realien – "practical" subjects like natural history, geography, and bota-
ny – into primary schools. Here Ernst drew largely on the pedagogical
realism of Jan Comenius, whom he knew personally, and Wolfgang
Ratke, who had once served as tutor to his mother. The educational
reforms of Ernst the Pious were also innovative in their concern with the
economic plight of the schoolmaster. Ernst attempted to raise the income
of village schoolmasters so that they could devote their full energies to
teaching. At the time of his death, Ernst was also drafting plans for a
teacher-training institute.[25] Francke later acknowledged the formative
influence of the Duke's educational reforms on his own pedagogy. The
rector of the *Gymnasium* where Francke was a pupil (1673–79), Andreas Reyher (1601–73), had himself authored the 1642 school edict.[26]
The introduction of the *Realien*, as well as the concern with the income
and training of the schoolmaster, were both to characterize Franckean
pedagogy.[27]

[24]Beck, *Ernst der Fromme*, p. 123.
[25]On the Gotha school reform see Hermann Böhne, *Die pädagogischen Bestrebungen Ernst
des Frommen von Gotha* (Gotha, 1888), pp. 96–186; Andreas Braem, *Der Gothaische
Schulmethodus. Untersuchung über die ersten Spuren des Pietismus in der Pädagogik*
(Berlin, 1897), pp. 11–19; K. A. Schmidt, *Geschichte der Erziehung,* 5 vols. (Stuttgart,
1896), 4/1:1–74.
[26]Schmidt, *Geschichte der Erziehung,* 4/1:50; Rudolph Heine, *Rector Andreas Reyher, der
Verfasser des Gothaischen Schulmethodus* (Holzminden, 1882), pp. 21–27.
[27]A seminal figure in the history of absolutist reform, Ernst the Pious deserves a modern
biography. His paternalistic style deeply influenced not only Francke, but early cameralist
writers. Veit Ludwig von Seckendorff's *Teutscher Fürstenstaat* (1655), destined to be
read by generations of cameralist students in the eighteenth century, was based largely on
the writer's experiences as advisor to the duke. See H. Kraemer, "Der deutsche Kleinstaat
des 17. Jahrhunderts im Spiegel von Seckendorffs 'Teutscher Fürstenstaat'," *Zeitschrift
für thüringische Geschichte,* 33 (1922). Both Seckendorff and Wilhelm von Schröder,
who helped introduce cameralistic science into the Habsburg monarchy, were raised at
the court of Ernst the Pious and attended the Gotha Gymnasium. See T. Kolde, "Veit

After leaving Gotha to matriculate at Erfurt and Kiel, Francke entered the University of Leipzig to finish his theological studies. There he experienced a profound religious conversion and became closely associated with a circle of Spenerian students at the university. In 1688 he visited Spener in Dresden and had become an ardent disciple by the time he returned to Leipzig in 1689 as a *Magister* in the theological faculty. Exhibiting all the enthusiasm and conviction of the converted, Francke soon attracted a student following as well as the hostility of the more conservative Leipzig theologians.

Leipzig was a bastion of orthodoxy, and Francke's insistence that the devotional study of Scripture was far more important than the subtleties of systematic theology raised eyebrows among those trained in the Lutheran scholastic tradition. Not without justification, his critics blamed Francke for the declining attendance at lectures on logic and metaphysics. The scandal worsened when it was learned that some students were selling or even burning their scholastic textbooks. Faced with the determined opposition of Johann Benedict Carpzov and other guardians of orthodoxy, Francke finally left Leipzig to accept a deaconate in Erfurt. Here he encountered similar opposition, and in less than a year conservative theologians had succeeded in engineering his dismissal.[28]

Francke ultimately found refuge in Prussia, arriving in 1691 with his Pietist companion J. J. Breithaupt. That Prussia proved such a Pietist haven was largely due to the patronage of the elector and his leading advisors. Frederick I was hardly a man of Pietist temperament. His lavish building projects and extravagant court epitomized everything the Pietists condemned. But Frederick's patronage of the Pietists was dictated by politics, not spiritual affinity. The Hohenzollerns were a Calvinist dynasty ruling a predominantly Lutheran population. Their much-celebrated promotion of religious toleration sought to attract colonists to their underpopulated territories, but it also reflected the dynasty's recognition of its own heterodoxical status within Prussia. It was in the interest of the dynasty to encourage a religious movement that stressed personal faith and compassion over theological controversy. Although the elector failed to secure Pietist backing for his ecumenical efforts to unify the two

Ludwig von Seckendorff," *Allgemeine Deutsche Bibliographie*, 33 (1891), pp. 519–520; and Erhard Dittrich, *Die deutschen und österreichischen Kameralisten* (Darmstadt, 1974), p. 63.

[28]My account of Francke's early career is taken from Ernest Stoeffler, *German Pietism during the Eighteenth Century* (Leiden, 1973), pp. 1–7; and Leube, *Orthodoxie und Pietismus*, pp. 174–206.

confessions of his realm, the Pietist advocacy of religious toleration clearly served the interests of a dynasty fearful of the political dangers of theological controversy.[29]

The Hohenzollern dynasty, moreover, had other reasons for supporting an institutional counterforce to Lutheran orthodoxy. The Lutheran church in Prussia was closely tied to the provincial nobility, whose rights of church patronage had been confirmed by the Brandenburg Recess of 1653. The nobility had traditionally controlled pastoral appointments and enjoyed those other privileges, properties, and incomes customarily associated with the *Patronenrecht*. The provincial nobility likewise dominated the provincial estates, which remained a potential source of opposition to Hohenzollern absolutism. This link between the established Lutheran church and the provincial estates helps further explain the partnership that ultimately developed between Hohenzollern absolutism and Prussian Pietism. The Pietists, confronted by orthodox opposition, were naturally inclined to support the monarchy against the estates. The monarchy, faced with potential opposition from the estates, was equally disposed to support the Pietists against their orthodox opponents. As Mary Fulbrook has recently argued, this peculiar constellation of political, social, and church relations helps explain why Pietism in Prussia, unlike Pietism in Württemberg or English Puritanism, ultimately developed into a state religion.[30]

Yet it was some time before Pietism gained a secure footing in Prussia. Following their arrival in Prussia, Spener and Francke were fortunate in obtaining the support of influential figures in the Prussian government. Eberhard von Danckelmann, a former tutor to the elector and now his leading advisor, proved a sympathetic and influential patron. Spener and Francke also gained a useful ally in Veit Ludwig von Seckendorff, who had also arrived in 1691 to assume the chancellorship of the newly established University of Halle. Seckendorff, a good friend and longtime correspondent of Spener, had published an edition of Spener's sermons in 1689 and publicly defended the movement in 1692.[31] As a cameralist

---

[29]Deppermann, *Der hallesche Pietismus*, p. 40ff.
[30]Mary Fulbrook, *Piety and Politics: Religion and the Rise of Absolutism in England, Württemberg, and Prussia* (New York, 1983), pp. 84–89.
[31]Seckendorff's edition of Spener's sermons was published in Frankfurt am Main in 1689 under the title *Capita doctrinae et praxis christianae*. His *Bericht und Erinnerung* (Halle, 1692) defended Spener against an anti-Pietist polemic written by Christian Albrecht Roth, a Halle archdeacon, entitled *Imago Pietismi* (Frankfurt am Main, 1691). See Grünberg, *Spener*, 1:276–277; and Kolde, "Seckendorff," pp. 519–520.

committed to state action as a means of mobilizing the resources of society, Seckendorff looked favorably upon the "social Gospel" of the Pietists. Largely through Seckendorff's intervention, Spener succeeded in securing the appointment of Francke and Breithaupt to the Halle faculty.[32]

Francke devoted most of his energies to his pastoral work rather than his university duties. Francke was pastor of a parish in Glaucha, a seedy slum on the outskirts of Halle. Halle's declining salt trade, the disruptive effects of the Thirty Years War, and the devastating plague of 1681–83 had brought economic depression to the entire region. Glaucha was particularly poor, adorned by little beyond a few slaughterhouses and a remarkable number of alehouses. Beer and schnapps had been the chief products of the town since the fifteenth century. The year Francke arrived in Glaucha, 37 of the 200 houses in the town were taverns. On weekends Glaucha became a raucous center of plebeian entertainment, attracting day laborers, the unemployed, and prostitutes in search of amusement and clients.[33]

Appalled by the drinking and whoring, the plebeian parroting of dandified aristocratic fashion, and the groggy appearance of his parishioners on Sunday mornings, Francke embarked on a vigorous campaign of moral and religious reform. He revived an ordinance prohibiting dancing and tavern keeping on Sundays and railed against the desecration of religious holidays with profane popular celebrations and festivals.[34] Francke resorted to strict sanctions in his efforts to reform his parishioners, including withholding communion to those who refused to heed his call for reform.

Francke soon grew convinced, however, that the only effective antidote to the moral depravity he found among the poor was education. In 1695, he established in Halle the first of a series of schools destined to establish his reputation as one of the most influential reformers of the eighteenth century. This school was originally a charitable institution for the children of beggars and similarly destitute parents. School was held daily from 7:00 to 3:00. Early morning was devoted to prayer, the sing-

---

[32]Deppermann, *Der hallesche Pietismus,* pp. 66–74.

[33]My description of Glaucha is based on Neuss, "Lohnarbeiter in Halle," pp. 116–117, 146–153.

[34]Francke, *Glauchisches Gedenck-Buchlein, oder einfältiger Unterricht für die christliche Gemeinde zu Glaucha an Halle* (Leipzig and Halle, 1693), pp. 122–124, republished in A. H. Francke, *Schriften über Erziehung und Unterricht,* ed. Karl Richter (Berlin, 1871), pp. 122–125, 131–147.

ing of hymns, and the reading of a passage from the Scriptures. This was followed by catechism drills, two hours of reading instruction, an hour of writing, and an hour of arithmetic. The schoolmaster also led the pupils on daily walks, which provided physical exercise as well as an opportunity for lessons in natural history. On Sundays, the pupils accompanied the schoolmaster to worship service and Sunday school.[35]

Francke's school soon gained such a reputation for piety and orderliness that artisans and middle-class parents began enrolling their children as well. As enrollment grew, the institution split up into more specialized schools. A separate elementary school was established for the children of more prosperous families, to which a Latin school was later added. In 1701 Francke acquired a separate building for the housing of orphan children. By 1710 Francke's orphanage (Waisenhaus) had expanded so rapidly that another building was constructed to house the girls in the orphanage. Francke's educational complex was crowned by the Pädagogium, an elite boarding school for "the children of rank and means." The Pädagogium was a secondary school preparing the children of nobles and prosperous Bürger for the university or bureaucracy.[36]

Francke owed his success in part to his fund-raising and entrepreneurial talents. He acquired many of the necessary supplies for his schools through charitable contributions.[37] In 1698 he received additional help from the elector, who exempted all materials purchased for the schools from excise taxes.[38] Far more important for the financial future of the schools, however, was the fact that the elector gave Francke permission to establish a bookstore and apothecary shop. Although the bookstore alone annually netted 2,000 – 3,500 talers between 1700 and 1725,[39] its profits paled in comparison with those of the pharmacy. Supervised by the physician Christian Friedrich Richter, head of the orphanage's infirmary, the pharmacy marketed highly popular remedies for

[35] A detailed description of Francke's schools is found in the editor's introduction to ibid., pp. 218–255.

[36] August Hermann Francke, Ordnung und Lehrart, wie Selbige in dem Paedagogio zu Glaucha an Halle eingeführt ist (Halle, 1702), republished in Francke, Pädagogische Schriften, ed. Hermann Lorenzen (Paderborn, 1957), pp. 89–101.

[37] Contributors to the Halle orphanage included Cotton Mather of Harvard College. Mather corresponded with Francke and was a great admirer of Halle Pietism. He donated a number of Francke's works to the Harvard library, and his diary is full of references to "the incomparable Dr. Franckius" and "our invaluable friends at Halle." See the entries from May 20, 1711, and May 10, 1718, in The Diary of Cotton Mather, 2 vols. (New York, 1957), 2:74, 534.

[38] See Francke, Schriften, p. 368.

[39] Ibid., p. 375.

Table 1   *Profits of the Pietist pharmacy in Halle, 1710–70*

Decade	Average annual profit (talers)
1710–20	8,968
1720–30	15,065
1730–40	20,512
1740–50	23,993
1750–60	27,807
1760–70	30,445

Source: A. H. Francke, *Schriften über Erziehung und Unterreicht*, ed. Karl Richter (Berlin, 1871), pp. 377–78.

gout, toothache, scurvy, menstrual cramps, and insomnia. By the second decade of the eighteenth century, Pietist medicines were being sold throughout Europe and Russia.[40] Originally conceived as a humanitarian undertaking, the pharmacy proved so profitable (see Table 1) that it was able to subsidize most of the subsequent expansion of Francke's schools.

Beyond money, of course, Francke's schools required trained teachers. In 1696 Francke established the *Seminarium selectum praeceptorum,* the first pedagogical institute in Central Europe. Most of the candidates were needy theology students who received meals at the orphanage in exchange for teaching in one of the schools. Francke believed that if schools were to be instruments of moral and spiritual reform, they required teachers who were both technically proficient and morally exemplary. Francke directly supervised his candidates, seeking to provide them with the methodological training and moral education necessary for their occupation. Those who successfully completed their apprenticeship received a permanent position at one of the Halle schools.[41]

By 1727, the year of Francke's death, his Halle schools contained more than 2,000 pupils and 175 teachers. The *Pädagogium* had become an elite establishment preparing its pupils for positions in the Prussian army and civil service. The *Waisenhaus,* for its part, became the pro-

[40]Ibid., pp. 376–377; Hinrichs, *Preussentum und Pietismus,* p. 68.
[41]Francke, *Die bisherige Einrichtung des Seminarii selecti Praeceptorum* (Halle, 1708), pp. 101–102, as published in *Pädagogische Schriften,* pp. 101–106; Elisabeth Gloria, *Der Pietismus als Förderer der Volksbildung und sein Einfluss auf die preussische Volksschule* (Osterwieck, 1933), pp. 60–63.

totype for the Central European orphanage of the eighteenth century. The *Seminarium selectum praeceptorum* proved equally influential, serving as the basic model for teacher training in the eighteenth century. Its graduates went on to play leading roles in the reform of popular schooling throughout Central Europe, helping further to popularize Pietist pedagogy.

Francke was not lacking in opponents. From the very beginning, Francke had antagonized important religious and economic groups in Halle. By scolding orthodox pastors for granting communion to those "unreformed" parishioners he had excommunicated from his own parish, Francke became embroiled in bitter controversies with the native Lutheran establishment. Francke also antagonized local guilds by obtaining from the crown certificates of honor allowing orphan children of unknown parentage to acquire guild apprenticeships. The privileges and exemptions granted to Pietist enterprises also aroused the resentment of local guilds and merchants.[42]

Only the continued support of the Prussian court protected Francke and his institutions from his opponents. After Eberhard von Dankelmann's dismissal as minister in 1697, the Pietists found an equally influential patron in Paul von Fuchs. As a privy councillor and supervisor of ecclesiastical and school affairs, Von Fuchs helped the Pietists further consolidate their position within the Lutheran Church. In 1702, for example, preceptors at the *Pädagogium* were given preference in all pastoral and school appointments.[43] Royal patronage made possible the establishment of additional schools on the Pietist model, including an orphanage (1701) and a *Gymnasium* (1703) in Königsberg.[44]

Following the death of Fuchs in 1704, the enemies of Pietism within the Lutheran and Calvinist clergy sought to reverse the tide. Their hopes were aroused by the well-known hostility of the young crown prince, Frederick William, toward the Pietists. Frederick William had blamed the mental collapse of his stepmother, Sophie Luise, on her Pietist leanings. Even worse, the young martinet suspected the Pietists of pacifism. But Gen. Dubislav von Natzmer, a friend of the crown prince and a Pietist sympathizer, was soon able to dispel this distrust. The alliance that ulti-

---

[42]For a summary of these and other antagonisms see Fulbrook, *Piety and Politics,* pp. 154–160.

[43]Hinrichs, *Preussentum und Pietismus,* pp. 28, 88–90.

[44]The *Gymnasium* became the famed *Friedrichs-Collegium,* whose graduates would include Immanuel Kant. See Walther Hubatsch, *Geschichte der evangelischen Kirche Ostpreussens,* 3 vols. (Göttingen, 1968), 1:177–178.

mately developed between Frederick William and the Pietists was a natural one. Both shared a puritanical distaste for ostentation and disapproved of the extravagance of the court. Pietists applauded the austerity measures imposed on the court by Frederick William following his accession in 1713, even if they were uncomfortable with the new mood of militarism. The practical-minded king, for his part, was delighted with the mixture of piety and utility he found during his tour of the Halle orphanage in 1713.[45]

Frederick William now enthusiastically embraced the Pietist movement, installing Francke as rector at Halle and appointing Heinrich Lysius, also a Pietist, as court chaplain. He subsequently required that every pastoral candidate study at least four semesters at Halle or Königsberg. Since Pietists were occupying virtually every theological chair at these universities by the 1730s, Frederick's requirement gave them *de facto* control over admission to the Lutheran pastorate.[46] As Mary Fulbrook concludes, "Pietism had become established as the new orthodoxy of Brandenburg-Prussia."[47]

Goals and methods of Pietist schooling

Francke's pedagogical aims were inseparable from his Pietism. Pietist schooling sought to cultivate an inner spirituality whose depth of conviction far exceeded the mere outward observance of Christian doctrine. Francke reminded his schoolmasters that "we are not to be satisfied if the child exhibits an outer show of piety but at heart remains unchanged. . . . The purely external, no matter how fair its appearance, cannot stand before the omniscient eye of God without the power of Christ in one's heart."[48]

The systematic promotion of popular literacy in Pietist schools was intimately tied to the cult of inwardness. Spener and Francke insisted that the cultivation of inner piety required a genuine knowledge of Christ and his teachings, which could be obtained only by reading the Scriptures. They held that the reading of Scripture transformed individuals spiritually and psychologically, filling them with the spirit of God and deep-

[45]Hinrichs, *Preussentum und Pietismus*, pp. 91–101.
[46]Notbohm, *Schulwesen in Ostpreussen*, pp. 15–17; and Danneil, *Magdeburg*, pp. 90–95.
[47]Fulbrook, *Politics and Piety*, p. 169.
[48]Francke, *Paedagogio zu Glaucha*, p. 94.

ening their faith.[49] Hence both insisted that the cultivation of inner piety depended on the ability to read the Scriptures. Pietism, in every sense, was a religion of the word. That Spener and Francke first expounded their ideas in Frankfurt and Leipzig, the two leading centers of German book production, is itself suggestive of the movement's "literate" roots.[50]

As mentioned in the previous chapter, Luther and his successors had never entirely overcome their ambivalence toward lay Bible reading. In this respect, Pietism's unequivocal promotion of Bible reading represented an important milestone within German Lutheranism.[51] Pietists were unrestrained in their advocacy of Bible reading among the laity. During his brief pastoral tenure in Erfurt, for example, Francke distributed over 900 Bibles and New Testaments to his parishioners.[52] In Glaucha he required every household to have a Bible, while his Halle schools provided every pupil with a copy.[53] To be sure, instruction in the catechism preceded Bible reading. Catechistic instruction in Francke's schools was rigorous and demanded more than rote memorization. As the child recited the catechism, the schoolmaster interrupted with questions designed to test the child's understanding.[54] But once pupils had mastered the catechism and the rudiments of reading, two periods a day were devoted to the reading of Scripture.

The establishment of a Pietist printing press in Halle was further testimony to the Pietist promotion of lay Bible reading. The press was established by Carl Hildebrand von Canstein, the leader of the Berlin Pietist community. Although his press had no formal links to Francke's educational complex, Canstein was in fact an untiring co-worker of Francke. Canstein's press printed not only the textbooks for Francke's schools, but also inexpensive editions of the Bible and New Testament. Within a year of its establishment in 1712, the Canstein Bible House had printed 10,000 inexpensive copies of the New Testament. By 1727, it had

[49]Spener told his Dresden parishioners that the reading of Scripture "profoundly moves the spirit and will of the believer, touching his heart and arousing his benevolence." Spener, *Evangelische Lebenspflichten*, p. 154.
[50]This point is stressed by Wallmann, *Spener*, pp. 195–196.
[51]Cf. Gawthrop and Strauss, "Protestantism and Literacy," pp. 43–44.
[52]Kurt Aland, "Bibel und Bibeltext bei August Hermann Francke und Johann Albrecht Bengel," in *Pietismus und Bibel* (Witten-Ruhr, 1970), p. 90.
[53]Francke, *Glauchisches Gedenck-Buchlein*, p. 137, and *Schriften*, p. 219.
[54]Francke, *Kurzer und einfältiger Unterricht, wie d: Kinder zur wahren Gottseligkeit und christlicher Klugheit anzuführen sind* (Halle, 1702), pp. 22, as republished in Francke, *Pädagogische Schriften*, pp. 13–66. On Pietist methods of catechistic instruction see Gessinger, *Sprache und Bürgertum*, pp. 42–43.

become one of the world's leading distribution centers of religious literature. By then, more than 400,000 Bibles and New Testaments had been
published. At the end of the century, the total had risen to 2.5 million.[55]

Pietist pedagogy, like Pietist theology, blended devotional inwardness
with an emphasis on the individual's social obligations. One of the most
important of these duties was obedience to authority. Here Franckean
pedagogy reflected the close ties between Pietism and Hohenzollern absolutism. Francke held that mere outward obedience, like outward piety,
was insufficient. The subject of a lord or a ruler had to obey voluntarily
and from inner conviction, even in the face of an unjust master or ruler.
In a sermon from 1701 celebrating the Hohenzollern acquisition of the
royal title, Francke reminded the pupils of the Halle orphanage that
"genuine obedience is not merely outward, but comes from deep within
the soul. It is not rendered out of coercion but with a willing heart."[56]

A strong work ethic also characterized Pietist schooling. The Pietist
work ethic stemmed from the Protestant notion of work as a "calling," a
Beruf whose duties God has entrusted the individual to perform.[57] As
Max Weber suggested, the idea of work as a duty imposed by the Divine
Will implicitly infused labor with a moral and religious significance.
Work became not merely a means of meeting subsistence needs or fulfilling a contractual obligation, but a spiritual duty.[58] False Christians,
wrote Spener, "work purely out of necessity, so that they can have bread
on the table," whereas true Christians labor "because they know they are
fulfilling God's will."[59]

The importance of vocation in Pietist schooling is seen in Francke's
attempt to tailor the education of children to their future trade or profession. Imbued with the realism that had marked Francke's own education
in Saxony-Gotha, the Halle schools sought to prepare pupils for their
future vocations. In the orphanage, lower-class pupils learned to sew or
spin wool. Pupils in the more exclusive primary and Latin schools learned
skills useful to the future merchant or clerk, like orthography or the
writing of letters and receipts. Future statesmen and officials in the elite
Pädagogium studied history, geography, and modern languages, while
those embarking on military careers studied geometry, mechanics, and

---

[55]Oschliess, *Arbeits- und Berufspädagogik,* pp. 30–31.
[56]Quoted in Deppermann, *Der hallesche Pietismus,* p. 141. See also Spener, *Evangelische Lebenspflichten,* 1:213–214.
[57]See Oschliess, *Arbeits- und Berufspädagogik,* passim.
[58]Weber, *Protestant Ethic,* pp. 84–85.
[59]Spener, *Evangelische Lebenspflichten,* 1:176.

engineering. To ensure that its noble pupils learned to manage their estates efficiently, the *Pädagogium* also provided instruction in agronomy.[60]

Condemning idleness as sinful, Pietist schooling encouraged diligence by cultivating an acute sense of time in its pupils. The hourglasses that Francke had installed in every classroom reminded pupils that work was an omnipresent duty, with time the currency in which performance of that duty was measured. In a manner worthy of Benjamin Franklin, Francke exhorted pupils of the Halle orphanage to "make proper use of your time. Take advantage of every possible moment to perform your duties. Consider time the way a merchant at a market eyes an article of merchandise. Knowing that he can purchase and resell that article at a great profit, he wastes no time. He knows that at any moment someone else may purchase the article instead, and that he may never in his life-time be confronted with another such opportunity."[61] In Francke's schools, every hour of the pupil's day was consigned to a prescribed activity. To be sure, pupils were given free time. Twice a day, they were led into the courtyard for recess. As Wolfgang Nahrstedt has pointed out, Francke himself was the first to adopt "free time" as a pedagogical category.[62] But the assignment of free time in Francke's schools, para-doxically, reflected the Pietist conception of work as a moral imperative. By establishing a period of time free from the normal demands of work, Francke's schools also created a period that was to be devoted to nothing but work. Francke's bifurcation of time merely accentuated the Pietist labor imperative, reinforcing rather than attenuating the obligation to work. In this respect, Francke's innovation anticipated the polarization of work and leisure so characteristic of industrial societies.

As with any duty, Francke's schools enjoined their pupils to perform their tasks freely, spontaneously, and out of conviction. Francke insisted that pupils work "not as if you were performing compulsory labor [*Fron*], but faithfully, diligently, and with relish."[63] Pupils were exhorted

---

[60]Oschliess, *Arbeits- und Berufspädagogik,* pp. 63–84; Hinrichs, *Preussentum und Pietismus,* pp. 17–25; Francke, *Paedagogio zu Glaucha,* pp. 90–100.

[61]Francke, *Der rechte Gebrauch der Zeit* (Halle, 1713), p. 12.

[62]Wolfgang Nahrstedt, *Die Entstehung der Freizeit. Ein Beitrag zur Strukturgeschichte und zur strukturgeschichtlichen Grundlegung der Freizeitpädagogik* (Göttingen, 1972), pp. 32–33. See also Rolf Engelsing, "Die Arbeitszeit und Freizeit von Schülern," in Gerhard Huck, ed., *Sozialgeschichte der Freizeit. Untersuchungen zum Wandel der Alltagskultur in Deutschland* (Wuppertal, 1980).

[63]Francke, *Ordnung und Lehrart, wie selbige in denen zum Waisenhaus gehörige Schulen eingeführt ist* (Halle, 1702), p. 79, republished in Francke, *Pädagogische Schriften,* pp. 67–88.

to work "not out of coercion, but a love of God."[64] They were to perform their tasks "not with the hands alone, but in and with the spirit of God."[65] The work ethic found in Francke's schools offers yet another example of the Pietist distinction between outward compliance and inner conviction. Whether seeking to cultivate piety, obedience, or diligence, Francke's schools were based upon the principle that external assent was not enough; these virtues had to penetrate the depth of the pupil's being, internalized to the point where he acted in accordance with them of his own free will.

This principle also characterized the Pietist approach to discipline. Discipline in Francke's schools was comparatively mild for its day. Francke's theory of punishment reflected the Pietist effort to subjectify coercion, transferring its locus from outside to inside the individual. Pupils were to learn to obey their teachers just as they were to obey their rulers: out of love rather than compulsion. Warning that excessive severity risked embittering or estranging the pupil, Francke beseeched his teaching candidates to "strive to be a father, not a disciplinarian."[66] As an instrument of pedagogical control, argued Francke, affection was a far more effective instrument than corporal punishment. In Bourdieuean terms, Francke advocated the use of "gentle" rather than "open" violence.[67] A schoolmaster was to administer the rod only to punish a pupil's misbehavior, never his mental failings. Even then, the teacher was to give three warnings before administering the punishment. Francke recommended an interlude between the announcement of the punishment and its execution. Delaying the punishment allowed the teacher to regain his self-control; more important, it gave pupils time to examine their consciences and reflect upon their sinfulness.[68] Pietist schooling placed great stock in introspection as a tool for developing self-discipline. Francke's schools encouraged pupils to keep diaries, for example, as a way to promote self-examination and reflection.[69]

[64]Quoted in Oschliess, *Arbeits- und Berufspädagogik,* p. 166.
[65]Francke, *Sonn-, Fest-, und Apostel-Tags-Predigten* (Halle, 1715), p. 157.
[66]Francke, *Bisherige Einrichtung des Seminarii selecti Praeceptorum,* p. 102.
[67]See Pierre Bourdieu and Jean-Claude Passeron, *Reproduction in Education, Society, and Culture,* trans. Richard Nice (London and Beverly Hills, 1977), p. 17: "To overwhelm one's pupils with affection . . . by the use of diminutives and affectionate qualifiers, by insistent appeal to an affective understanding, etc., is to gain possession of that subtle instrument of repression, the withdrawal of affection, a pedagogical technique which is no less arbitrary . . . than corporate punishment or disgrace."
[68]Francke, *Schriften,* pp. 248–250.
[69]Deppermann, *Der hallesche Pietismus,* p. 93. Numerous commentators have stressed the

Yet here Pietist schooling rested on a fundamental paradox. The very attempt to cultivate free and voluntary assent was predicated on the negation of the child's freedom and will. Francke's schools operated on the assumption that in order to transform the child's will into a compliant instrument, it first had to be broken. As Francke wrote, "the formation of the child's character involves the will as well as the understanding. . . . Above all, it is necessary to break the natural willfulness of the child. While the schoolmaster who seeks to make the child more learned is to be commended for cultivating the child's understanding, he has not done enough. He has forgotten his most important task, namely that of making the will obedient."[70] As with the Pietist attempt to combine individual initiative with an acceptance of social hierarchy, the apparent paradox implicit in cultivating voluntarism by destroying the will was resolved through the conversion experience. Pietist schooling aimed at nothing if not conversion, and conversion required the passivity and self-abnegation through which the individual could become the instrument of God's will. By helping to break the child's natural will, the schoolmaster contributed to this transformation.

One way the will of the child was to be broken was by intensifying the institutional control of the school. The precondition for such control, argued Francke, was compulsory attendance. Francke was the first to stress the importance of taking roll as a means of monitoring the child's attendance and behavior. Teachers were required to record the names and occupations of their pupils' parents, as well as a daily evaluation of the progress and character of each child.[71] Once the pupil was in school, control was further tightened by an uninterrupted vigilance over the child's activities. At the end of each lesson, the schoolmaster remained with his pupils until the arrival of a replacement or the beginning of the next lesson. As Francke explained, "youth do not know how to regulate their lives, and are naturally inclined toward idle or sinful behavior when left to their own devices. For this reason, it is a rule in this institution that a pupil never be allowed out of the presence of a supervisor. The supervisor's presence will stifle the pupil's inclination to sinful behavior, and slowly weaken his willfulness."[72]

role of Pietist introspection in the development of German autobiography. See, for example, Koppel S. Pinson, *Pietism as a Factor in the Rise of German Nationalism* (New York, 1934), pp. 69–71.

[70]Francke, *Kurzer und einfältiger Unterricht*, p. 15.

[71]Ibid., p. 67; Gloria, *Pietismus als Förderer der Volksbildung*, p. 42.

[72]Francke, *Paedagogio zu Glaucha*, p. 94.

Francke's goal of perpetual supervision was most easily accomplished in his boarding schools. "Wherever pupils may be," Francke told the director of the orphanage, "whether sitting in class, playing in the schoolyard, eating in the dining hall, sleeping in their alcoves, or changing their clothes, they must never remain unsupervised."[73] Francke's schools sought to create a completely regulated and self-enclosed environment, neutralizing the impact of the outside environment and thus ridding pupils of any bad habits they might have developed outside the institution. Hence the *Pädagogium,* for example, vehemently discouraged frequent trips home by the students or visits from the parents. In the orphanage and *Pädagogium,* even letters to and from the pupils were subject to inspection.

The school reforms of Frederick William I

By the end of the reign of Frederick I, Pietists were pressing for a general reform of popular schooling in the Prussian monarchy. In 1710, at the urging of Pietists like Francke, the king ordered the first general visitation of Brandenburg schools and churches since 1601. This visitation betrayed the influence of Pietism through its concern with popular literacy: Inspectors were to inquire "whether the village schoolmaster provides instruction in reading, writing, and the catechism."[74] The visitation also brought to light the usual problems afflicting rural schools. Distance made it impossible for many peasant children to attend, while the economic position of schoolmasters and their families was often desperate.

The efforts of Frederick I to alleviate these problems were generally ineffective. When he instructed officials on crown domains to contribute stone and wood for the construction of additional schools in 1711, they protested that such a measure would devastate royal forests. Frederick modified the order, stipulating that the crown would only subsidize the transportation of construction materials.[75] Equally unsuccessful was his attempt to establish a pension fund for the widows and orphans of schoolmasters. To be eligible for such a pension, the schoolmaster had to pay a hundred talers into the fund. Since it was not uncommon for many schoolmasters to earn less than twenty talers annually, the pension plan proved highly unrealistic and was abandoned.[76]

---

[73]Francke, *Waisenhause,* p. 98.
[74]Quoted in Ferdinand Vollmer, *Friedrich Wilhelm I. und die Volksschule* (Göttingen, 1909), p. 11; see also Wienecke, "Begründung der evangelischen Volksschule," pp. 51–52.
[75]Vollmer, *Friedrich Wilhelm I. und die Volksschule,* p. 9.
[76]Ibid., p. 10.

Initially, Frederick William I's efforts on behalf of school reform proved no more successful. Frederick's attempts to expand popular schooling were directly tied to his so-called restoration (*Rétablissement*) in East Prussia. Between 1709 and 1711, a plague spread by the marauding armies of the Northern War had devastated the province. The East Prussian population fell from 600,000 to 360,000 – a decline of 40 percent – and more than 11,000 peasant holdings now stood vacant.[77] Although the primary purpose of the *Rétablissement* was to resettle the province with Protestant refugees from the archbishopric of Salzburg, the deaths of countless parish priests and schoolmasters made schools a target as well.

From the standpoint of religion, the 1714 visitation of East Prussian churches and schools exposed problems far more serious than vacant pastoral positions. Consistorial inspectors encountered regions where Christian doctrine had made few inroads among the population. Especially in the northeastern reaches of the province, where a Lithuanian population was concentrated, inspectors found widespread ignorance of even the most basic propositions of Christianity. One observer noted in 1724 that Lithuanian peasants "have absolutely no acquaintance with the Divine Word. Indeed, very few know even the most common prayers, or have the slightest familiarity with Christian doctrine."[78] At first sight, the historian is inclined to attribute such judgments to a lack of familiarity or sympathy with Lithuanian language and customs. In this case, however, the observer was Matthaeus Praetorius, a native of Memel who spoke Lithuanian, was familiar with Lithuanian customs, and authored one of the earliest ethnographic studies of Lithuanian culture.[79] Given the notoriously thin ecclesiastical infrastructure existing in the region, there is no reason to doubt the accuracy of Praetorius's comment. Some Lithuanian parishes served as many as eighty villages. Few pastors in the region knew Lithuanian, which doubtless discouraged attendance and hampered pastoral effectiveness. The church had yet to translate the Bible and devotional literature into Lithuanian, while there was no standardized Lithuanian catechism.[80]

These revelations prompted the king to issue a series of ordinances

[77]Fritz Terveen, *Gesamtstaat und Rétablissement. Der Wiederaufbau des nördlichen Ostpreussens unter Friedrich Wilhelm I. 1714–1740* (Göttingen, 1954), pp. 17–19; Hubatsch, *Geschichte der evangelischen Kirche Ostpreussens*, 1:182.
[78]Quoted in Terveen, *Gesamtstaat und Rétablissement*, p. 16.
[79]On Praetorius see Hubatsch, *Geschichte der evangelischen Kirche Ostpreussens*, 1:160.
[80]Terveen, *Gesamtstaat und Rétablissement*, pp. 84–92, 132; Vollmer, *Friedrich Wilhelm I. und die Volksschule*, pp. 23–24.

that culminated in his famous school edict of 1717. Nineteenth-century
historians of the Prussian school exaggerated the importance of this
edict, calling it the first in Europe to establish the principle of universal
compulsory schooling. But as Ferdinand Vollmer later demonstrated, the
edict contained little that was new and was never enforced.[81] Far from
introducing universal compulsory schooling, as Treitschke and Droysen
were to claim, the edict only required that "in those places where schools
exist, parents, under threat of fine, be compelled to send their children to
school."[82] It is even questionable whether the edict was ever published in
some regions.[83] The school edict of 1717 was little more than an exercise
in wishful thinking, since it contained no workable provisions for financing school construction or hiring schoolmasters. As the visitation of 1736
was to reveal, the edict was simply never enforced.[84] All in all, it did
nothing but recapitulate earlier *Kirchen- und Schulordnungen*.

Still, school reform remained on the royal agenda. Following an inspection tour of Lithuania in 1718, Frederick William I enlisted his Pietist
favorites in the cause of reform. He appointed Lysius, his Pietist court
pastor, to develop a plan for the improvement of Lithuanian schools. In
collaboration with Francke in Halle, Lysius created a Lithuanian seminary in Königsberg for the training of pastors and schoolmasters. Exhibiting a Pietist dedication to the diffusion of literacy, he sponsored the
publication of a Lithuanian-German catechism in 1721 (a Lithuanian
translation of the Bible would appear in 1735). Lysius also required every
Lithuanian parish to report annually on the number of children who had
learned to read and write during the past year.[85]

As regards school reform itself, Lysius was less successful. In an attempt to raise the income of rural schoolmasters, Lysius required villages
to set aside a plot of land for their subsistence. The plan backfired: Many
villages were too poor to comply, and in those that did, schoolmasters
tended to devote more time to their gardens than their pupils.[86] With few

---

[81]Vollmer, *Friedrich Wilhelm I. und die Volksschule*, pp. 30–40. For a more recent confirmation of Vollmer's conclusions see Wolfgang Neugebauer, "Bemerkungen zum
preussischen Schuledikt von 1717," *Jahrbuch für die Geschichte Mittel- und Ostdeutsch-
lands*, 31 (1982).
[82]Quoted in Dorwart, *Prussian Welfare State*, p. 183.
[83]Neugebauer, "Bemerkungen," p. 171.
[84]Dorwart, *Prussian Welfare State*, p. 184.
[85]*PGStA*, Staatsarchiv Königsberg, États-Ministerium (Gumbinnen Kammer), Rep. 8, Abt.
6, Nr. 1/Bd. 111, fol. 7–21, 197; Hubatsch, *Geschichte der evangelischen Kirche Ostpreussens*, 1:182–186; Terveen, *Gesamtstaat und Rétablissement*, pp. 87, 133–135. A
Polish seminary for the training of priests on the Polish border was established in 1728.
[86]Terveen, *Gesamtstaat und Rétablissement*, p. 95.

funds at his disposal, Lysius was unable to finance the construction of schools or the hiring of new schoolmasters. Local clergy and their noble patrons often resented his interference in parish affairs, and faced with their obstructionist tactics, Lysius achieved little. His enemies, who included representatives of the orthodox Lutheran clergy, were finally able to engineer his dismissal in 1722.

However, in 1728 the king once again entrusted the task of school reform to his Pietist theologians. Abraham Wolf from Königsberg and Georg Friedrich Rogall from Halle submitted a plan to require schooling for all children beginning at the age of six. No pupil was to be allowed to leave school, and no adult was to be admitted to confession who could not read or write. Although the king approved the plan, finances again proved a stumbling block. The Königsberg War and Domains Chamber, one of the two seats of royal administration in East Prussia, protested that the weekly tuition fee of two groschen was simply too high for poorer rural families. Moreover, sheer distance made school attendance impossible for many peasant children, and impoverished parishes simply lacked the resources to build additional schools.[87] It was obvious, in short, that the system of parish education bequeathed by the Reformation had reached the limits of its expansion. As long as parishes alone shouldered the financial responsibility for schoolmasters and school construction, further expansion was impossible.

The king himself reached this conclusion toward the end of his reign. This is clear from his Principia Regulativa of 1736, which established guidelines for Prussian elementary schools. On one level, the Principia Regulativa merely codified existing practice. It required each parish to pay its schoolmaster four talers annually, along with additional payments in kind, (e.g., free use of the village common for his livestock, two-thirds of an acre for his garden plot). Moreover, the edict required the parents of each child between the ages of five and twelve to pay the schoolmaster fifteen groschen annually. The schoolmaster could also supplement his income by practicing a craft or performing field work during the harvest.[88]

Again, these provisions were hardly innovative. Yet the Principia Regulativa and its subsequent implementation represented a historic achieve-

[87]Ibid., pp. 96–98; Hubatsch, *Geschichte der evangelischen Kirche Ostpreussens,* 1:84–85.
[88]The provisions of the *Principia Regulativa* are summarized in Dorwart, *Prussian Welfare State,* pp. 187–188.

ment in the history of Prussian schooling. For the first time, state funds were used to subsidize the construction of schools and the salaries of teachers. The crown now supplied free timber and firewood to build and heat schools in villages where no schools had existed.[89] Far more significant, however, was the creation of the Mons Pietatis in 1736. This was a royal endowment of 50,000 talers, the interest from which (4 percent) went to hire and pay schoolmasters in villages too poor to support them.[90] In addition, the king twice levied a parish tax that raised an additional ten thousand talers for the establishment of East Prussian parish schools.[91]

Crown subsidies now made it possible both to build schools and to hire the necessary schoolmasters. These subsidies, it is true, were confined to East Prussian schools, so that the Principia Regulativa had little effect on other Prussian provinces. Still, the impact on East Prussia itself was indeed dramatic. In the Königsberg War and Domains Chamber, 384 rural schools existed in 1736. Six years after the creation of the Mons Pietatis, royal subsidies had helped establish an additional 572 schools. In the Gumbinnen War and Domains Chamber, whose jurisdiction included the Lithuanian minority, a mere 70 schools existed in 1736. By 1742, the number of rural schools had increased by 312. Thus in all of East Prussia, the reforms of Frederick William I established a total of 884 rural schools between 1736 and 1742.[92]

This impressive achievement owed much to the Pietist movement. Throughout the reign of Frederick William I, Pietists like Francke, Lysius, Wolf, and Rogall worked closely with the king in efforts to expand popular schooling. The Pietist movement did not merely contribute to the expansion of schooling; the Pietist stress on lay Bible reading made universal literacy an explicit goal of educational reform. In 1739, for example, Frederick William I paid for the distribution of thousands of Bibles in East Prussian schools "so that the Word of God will be known to all my subjects."[93]

Given the paucity of sources, it is difficult to gauge the impact of the reforms on school life. Visitation reports, the major source of information on schools during this period, focused mainly on the physical condi-

[89]Ibid., p. 187.
[90]Terveen, *Gesamtstaat und Rétablissement*, pp. 110–111.
[91]Vollmer, *Friedrich Wilhelm I. und die Volksschule*, p. 75.
[92]Statistics taken from Vollmer, *Die preussische Volksschulpolitik*, p. 11.
[93]Terveen, *Gesamtstaat und Rétablissement*, p. 140.

tion of the church, the piety (or lack of it) of parishioners, and pastoral effectiveness. To the extent that consistory inspectors mentioned schools, they usually commented only briefly and formulaically on the condition of the school and the moral character of the schoolmaster. While the reforms doubtless alleviated the financial distress of many East Prussian schoolmasters, it is questionable whether they had any significant impact on pedagogical practice in the 1730s and 1740s. Few institutes existed for the training of schoolmasters. In 1732 Johann Christoph Schienmeyer, a Halle theology graduate and a disciple of Francke, added a pedagogical institute to his school for the poor in Stettin. Schienmeyer's institute received subsidies from the king to train Pomeranian schoolmasters in accordance with the principles of Franckean pedagogy. But bickering between Schienmeyer and the local clergy led to his resignation in 1737, and enrollment at the institute fell dramatically.[94] More successful was the Pietist institute at Kloster Berg, near Magdeburg. Established in 1736 by Johann Adam Steinmetz, a Magdeburg consistory official and graduate of Francke's *Seminarium selectum praeceptorum*, the Kloster Berg institute provided pedagogical training as well as instruction in silkworm cultivation. The goal was to train village schoolmasters capable of spreading silkworking techniques throughout the neighboring villages.[95]

Although the institutes in Halle, Königsberg, Stettin, and Kloster Berg worked to instill Pietist ideals, they affected only a small proportion of Prussian schoolmasters. In my own perusal of schoolmasters' vitae from the 1730s and 1740s, few showed evidence of attendance at a Pietist pedagogical institute. Those schoolmasters who did enroll did not necessarily become schoolmasters, and some may have attended purely for the free meals they received. Furthermore, because Pietist theology graduates received preference in pastoral appointments, many who attended the Halle and Königsberg institutes entered the pastorate without ever teaching in a rural school. J. J. Hecker (see the next section), who carried on the Pietist pedagogical tradition after Francke, went directly into the pastorate after receiving pedagogical training and experience in the Halle

---

[94] On Schienmeyer and the Stettin seminary see Heppe, *Geschichte des deutschen Volksschulwesens*, 3:10–15; Neugebauer, *Absolutistischer Staat und Schulwirklichkeit*, pp. 376–377.

[95] See Gustav Schmoller and Otto Hintze, *Die preussische Seidenindustrie im 18. Jahrhundert und ihre Begründung durch Friedrich den Grossen*, 2 vols. (Berlin, 1892), 1:283. On the early Pietist teaching seminaries see Gloria, *Pietismus als Förderer der Volksbildung*, pp. 64–70.

Seminarium and *Pädagogium*. Ironically, then, the very success with which Pietist theology graduates were able to obtain pastoral appointments may well have drained rural schools of trained schoolmasters. Beyond the minority of university-trained schoolmasters who taught in schools located in parish seats, teaching remained a part-time, auxiliary duty of the sacristan.

Thus the substantive impact of the reforms of Frederick William I was limited. Confined to East Prussia, they had little or no effect on other Prussian provinces. Still, the reign of Frederick William I represented an important watershed in the history of Prussian schools. Literacy had become an explicit goal of popular schooling, while the monarchy had begun to assume an active role in school financing. Testifying to the growing importance of popular schooling in Prussian absolutist policy was the fact that unlike earlier school edicts, which comprised merely one part of comprehensive ecclesiastical ordinances, the edicts of 1717 and 1736 were strictly concerned with schools. Schools, in other words, had become a discrete object of state action.[96] In the process, the reign of Frederick William I had set the stage for the further expansion of popular schooling.

Pietist pedagogy after Francke

The most significant figure in the second generation of Pietist educational reformers was Johann Julius Hecker (1707–68). Like many theology students, Hecker found himself without a job after completing his studies in 1729 at the University of Halle. While waiting for a pastoral opening, Hecker accepted a teaching post at the *Pädagogium* – a prudent career move, since *Pädagogium* instructors received preference in appointments to the ministry. As an instructor, Hecker also underwent pedagogical training at the *Seminarium selectum praeceptorum*.[97]

With his impeccable Pietist credentials, Hecker was able to obtain his first pastoral appointment in 1735 as chaplain in the Potsdam Military Orphanage. Frederick William I had established the orphanage in 1722

[96]On this point see the excellent study by Achim Leschinsky and Peter Roeder, *Schule im historischen Prozess. Zum Wechselverhältnis von institutioneller Erziehung und gesellschaftlicher Entwicklung* (Stuttgart, 1976), p. 40.
[97]For Hecker's biography see Hugo Bloth, "Johann Julius Hecker (1707–1768). Seine 'Universalschule' und seine Stellung zum Pietismus und Absolutismus," *Jahrbuch des Vereins für westfälische Kirchengeschichte*, 61 (1968).

for the orphaned children of soldiers. The rigorous daily schedule of the orphanage, like that of its Halle prototype, combined study, discipline, and manual labor. Contracted by the Berlin wool manufacturer Daum, children in the orphanage combed, carded, and spun wool. In the following decades, the Military Orphanage farmed out its inmates with increasing frequency to work in trades and domestic service in the towns and in agriculture and cottage industry throughout the countryside.[98]

Following his appointment in 1739 to the pastorate of Trinity Church in Berlin, Hecker drew on his Potsdam experience to establish a school for the poor.[99] The school proved so successful that Hecker went on to establish an entire network of "pauper schools" in his Berlin parish. Raising money through charitable contributions and lotteries, Hecker was able to establish a total of seven schools. He subsequently consolidated these into four, two for beginning pupils and two for the more advanced.

Hecker's pupils were primarily the children of soldiers, who accounted for more than 20 percent of the Berlin population.[100] The upbringing of these children had become a source of deep concern to civil authorities and Pietist reformers. The atmosphere of the barracks, after all, was hardly conducive to child rearing. A girl could lose her virginity early in such an environment, and barracks were a notorious breeding ground for prostitution. Relatively free from adult supervision, boys joined the ranks of the juvenile beggars, pickpockets, and pilferers so prevalent in eighteenth-century cities.[101] Furthermore, since many of the pupils were illegitimate, their integration into society proved difficult at a time when legitimate parentage was an important prerequisite for guild apprenticeships.

---

[98] By 1786, almost half of the 2,714 children affiliated with the orphanage were being farmed out to work in outside occupations. See Friedrich Nicolai, *Beschreibung der Königlichen Residenzstädte Berlin und Potsdam*, 3d ed., 3 vols. (Berlin, 1786), 3:1293. On the Military Orphanage see also Hinrichs, *Preussentum und Pietismus*, pp. 311–315; and Kurt Hinze, *Die Arbeiterfrage in Brandenburg-Preussen zu Beginn des modernen Kapitalismus* (Berlin, 1927), p. 168.

[99] Unless otherwise cited, the following description of Hecker's schools is based on Bloth, "Hecker;" J. H. Schulz, *Die königliche Realschule in Berlin* (Essen, 1844); and Detlef Müller, *Sozialstruktur und Schulsystem. Aspekte zum Strukturwandel des Schulwesens im 19. Jahrhundert* (Göttingen, 1977), pp. 111–122.

[100] See Horst Krüger, *Zur Geschichte der Manüfakturen und der Manufakturarbeiter in Preussen. Die mittleren Provinzen in der zweiten Hälfte des 18. Jahrhunderts* (East Berlin, 1958), p. 411.

[101] On soldier children in eighteenth-century Berlin, see ibid., pp. 246–249; and Kuczynski, *Geschichte des Alltags*, 2:355–356.

As in the Pietist orphanages of Halle and Potsdam, Hecker's school sought to socialize its lower-class pupils through both religious and vocational training. Pupils learned not only the four Rs — reading, writing, arithmetic, and religion — but also spinning, sewing, and knitting. Since these were tasks that lay beyond guild control, they served to integrate a socially marginal group into the work force. They also sought to provide the daughters of soldiers with an occupational alternative to prostitution or begging.

Like Francke, Hecker sought to provide his schoolmasters with the moral and methodological training necessary for their occupation. Complaining that "when a tailor, cobbler, or day laborer can no longer make a living from his work, he becomes a schoolmaster,"[102] Hecker established a pedagogical institute along the lines of Francke's *Seminarium selectum praeceptorum*.[103] Hecker's seminar became a state institution in 1753, when the Supreme Consistory (to which Hecker had been appointed in 1750) began subsidizing the institute with an annual grant of 600 talers.[104]

Hecker's institute not only popularized Franckean pedagogical techniques, but it also introduced one of the most important and lasting innovations in eighteenth-century elementary schooling. This was the practice of teaching children collectively as a group, rather than individually. As mentioned earlier, elementary schools had traditionally operated on the principle of what today might be termed the open classroom: Schoolmasters instructed pupils one at a time. Hecker and other critics charged that this practice wasted valuable instruction time and produced disorder and chaos in the classroom. By grouping pupils according to proficiency, Hecker's schools enabled the schoolmasters to instruct a class of pupils simultaneously rather than individually. Hecker was not the first to advocate this method, which was originally introduced in seventeenth-century French schools by Jean-Baptiste de la Salle and the Brothers of the Christian Schools,[105] but he was the first to introduce collective instruction into German common schools.

[102]Quoted in E. Clausnitzer, "Zur Geschichte der preussischen Volksschule unter Friedrich den Grossen," *Die deutsche Schule*, 5 (1901), p. 352.
[103]Hecker's seminar was one of several such institutes established in Königsberg, Stettin, and Kloster Berg (Magdeburg) in the 1730s and 1740s. All were founded by graduates of the *Seminarium selectum praeceptorum* in Halle. See Gloria, *Pietismus als Förderer der Volksbildung*, pp. 64–70.
[104]Clausnitzer, "Geschichte der preussischen Volksschule," p. 347.
[105]François Lebrun, Marc Venard, and Jean Queniant, *Histoire générale de l'enseignement*

Group instruction, or what Hecker somewhat pedantically termed the *Zusammenunterrichtsmethode,* was a tremendously important innovation. By making it possible to educate more pupils in less time, this technique became a cornerstone of modern mass education. Collective instruction also gave the schoolmaster more control over the classroom. Praising its disciplinary advantages, Hecker boasted that pupils in his school "have less opportunity to misbehave than soldiers on a parade ground."[106] In seeking tightened control over the classroom and the more efficient use of class time, Hecker's innovation was merely a further extension of Franckean pedagogical principles. By involving the entire class in the lesson, Hecker sought to ensure that pupils never withdrew their attention or remained unsupervised. His more economical use of class time betrayed the acute consciousness of time so characteristic of Pietism. In accordance with the aims of Pietist pedagogy, Hecker sought to intensify classroom learning, thereby inculcating the subject matter more profoundly in the pupil.

Another innovation that Hecker introduced into his elementary schools was the so-called tabular-literal method (*Tabular- und Buchstabiermethode*). The actual inventor of this method was Johann Friedrich Hähn, an administrator at Hecker's *Realschule* who became head of the Kloster Berg institute in 1757. Hähn designed the tabular-literal method as a mnemonic tool enabling children to learn the catechism quickly and effectively. Under this method, the schoolmaster organized the catechism into an outline on the blackboard. Roman numerals indicated the main articles of the catechism, while letters designated the elaborations on those articles. The pupils then learned the outline by memorizing the first letter of each entry. Proponents of the method argued that it eased the burdens of memory work, since pupils memorized a series of letters rather than entire sentences. Furthermore, they believed that the method trained the faculty of reason by visually illustrating the relationship of parts to the whole. They argued that pupils who studied the catechism in accordance with the method learned a coherent doctrine

---

et de l'éducation en France, 3 vols. (Paris, 1981), 2:440–442; Furet and Ozouf, *Reading and Writing,* p. 80; Mary Jo Maynes, *Schooling for the People: Comparative Local Studies of Schooling History in France and Germany, 1750–1850* (New York, 1985), pp. 78–79.
106Quoted in Clausnitzer, "Geschichte der preussischen Volksschule," p. 352.

instead of a set of discrete, seemingly unrelated propositions. The tabular-literal method was something of a fad and fell completely out of
fashion by the 1780s. Still, like group instruction, it illustrates efforts by
early proponents of mass education to develop quicker, more economical
instruments of literacy and indoctrination.[107]

Hecker did not confine his pedagogical efforts to plebeian pupils. Like
Francke, he also established a school for the children of more prosperous
families. This institution initially consisted of both an elementary and a
Latin school. In another important innovation, however, Hecker added
the so-called *Realschule* to this complex in 1747. Like its successor in the
nineteenth century, Hecker's *Realschule* was technically and vocationally
oriented. In Hecker's words, this school was designed for those "who do
not intend to be scholars, but desire to become competent clerks, merchants, estate administrators, craftsmen, and manufacturers."[108] Pupils
could study a wide variety of vocational subjects, including bookkeeping,
mining, engineering, architecture, printing, silkworm cultivation (practiced in the botanical garden of the *Realschule*), letter writing, and manufacturing. Attached to the school was a scientific laboratory, a thou-
sand-volume library, and a printing press.

The *Realschule* marked the culmination of efforts in eighteenth-century Germany to develop a secondary school serving middle- and lower-
middle-class vocational interests. Secondary education had not apprecia-
bly changed since the sixteenth century. Whether Protestant or Catholic,
the curricula of Latin schools and *Gymnasien* were humanist to the core
and stressed Latin.[109] They provided no specialized technical, clerical, or
commercial training. Hecker's *Realschule* was the first successful attempt
to offer an alternative to bourgeois and artisan families who did not want
to send their sons to the university, but were dissatisfied with the absence
of vocational training in Latin schools and *Gymnasien*.

Hecker's emphasis on vocational subjects also reflected growing dissatisfaction with the apprentice system.[110] At issue was a fundamental
clash between the economic aims of pedagogical reformers and absolutist

---

[107]On the tabular-literal method see Schmidt, *Geschichte der Erziehung,* 4/1:88–90.
[108]Quoted in Günther, *Geschichte der Erziehung,* p. 139.
[109]The curricular similarity of Catholic and Lutheran *Gymnasien* is clear from the detailed
    descriptions in Johann Christian Kundmann, *Die hohen und niederen Schulen Teutsch-
    enlandes* (Breslau, 1741).
[110]The above analysis is based on the valuable study by Karl Wilhelm Stratmann, *Die Krise
    der Berufserziehung im 18. Jahrhundert als Ursprungsfeld pädagogisches Denkens*
    (Ratingen, 1967).

officials on the one hand, and corporate guild values on the other. For guilds, vocational ability was only one of a host of considerations that went into the hiring of an apprentice. The "honor" of the guild, for example, required that the apprentice be of legitimate and respectable parentage. Most guilds excluded those children unable to present a proper birth certificate, as well as those whose parents were employed in "dishonorable" occupations (e.g., shepherds, knackers, and executioners). Guilds also tended to exclude children of the very poor, since masters normally required apprentice fees (*Lehrgeld*).

Mercantilist officials attacked this system on both utilitarian and moral grounds. While arguing that the exclusion of illegitimate, dishonorable (*unehrliche*), and poor children deprived society of potential laborers, they also charged that guild masters were failing to fulfill their pedagogical and moral responsibilities toward their apprentices. Critics of guilds maintained that apprentices were often little more than household servants who instead of learning a trade, merely performed chores and ran errands for the master and his wife.[111] Guild custom had prescribed that a master keep no more than one apprentice. But in practice, the growing economic pressures on eighteenth-century guild masters sometimes led them to employ as many as twenty apprentices. By reducing apprentices to the status of mere employees, this practice served further to undermine the moral foundations of the apprentice system. If apprentices did receive training, critics charged, it was one that subordinated moral education and technical proficiency to the corporate, particularistic values and norms of the guild. Apprentices received no proficiency examination at the end of their training, which further convinced critics that guilds had abdicated their pedagogical responsibilities. Some suspected that the failure of masters to train their apprentices adequately was deliberate: by ensuring that apprentices never acquired the technical expertise necessary to become journeymen, masters were able to curb competition within their trades.

During the 1730s, the Prussian monarchy's broad intervention in guild affairs sought to remedy these abuses. Guilds were now forbidden to exclude sons whose fathers practiced dishonorable occupations. Pro-

[111]In 1700 Johann Dietz, a Halle barber, summarized his apprenticeship: "I had to help the serving girl fetch water, carry and cut wood, keep the fire going, and perform similar household chores." Quoted in Andreas Griessinger, *Das symbolische Kapital der Ehre. Streikbewegungen und kollektives Bewusstsein deutscher Handwerksgesellen im 18. Jahrhundert* (Frankfurt am Main, 1981), p. 59.

cedures for certifying legitimate birth were simplified and standardized, while pupils in the Halle and Potsdam orphanages were exempted from providing such proof altogether. In addition, orphans were no longer required to pay apprentice fees to their masters.[112]

The ultimate effect of this attack on the apprentice system was to enhance further the importance of primary schooling. The charge that guild masters were not adequately training their apprentices provided yet another justification for the vigorous promotion of elementary education. If guilds had indeed abdicated their pedagogical responsibilities, as critics claimed, then it was incumbent on the school to fill the vacuum. Hence the guild reforms of 1734–36 also forbade any child from assuming an apprenticeship who could not read, write, and recite the five articles of the catechism. The fact that the Principia Regulativa (1736) followed on the heels of guild reform further suggests the relationship between school reform and efforts to reform the apprentice system. Institutions like the *Realschule* must be seen as another in a series of responses to what Karl Wilhelm Stratmann has called the "crisis of vocational training" in the eighteenth century. By providing specialized vocational training, the *Realschule* sought to move into the pedagogical vacuum left by a decaying guild system.

Hecker's plan to crown his Berlin educational complex with an elite *Pädagogium* was not fulfilled until several years after his death. The Berlin *Pädagogium,* later to become the prestigious Friedrich-Wilhelm-Gymnasium, was a boarding school preparing its pupils for the university or state service. In addition to traditional academic subjects like Latin, Greek, and Hebrew, pupils studied modern languages, mathematics, history, and geography.

Like its Halle predecessor, the Berlin *Pädagogium* attracted substantial numbers of noble pupils. Despite earlier opposition, Pietism had developed a considerable following among the Prussian nobility. Eighteenth-century graduates of the Halle and Berlin *Pädagogia* included names like Von Arnim, Von Bismarck, Von Schlabrendorff, Von Stein, and Von Wartensleben.[113] Although Pietism's appeal to Prussian nobles has never been entirely explained, it may perhaps lie in the peculiar social composition of the Prussian nobility. Lacking a stratum of great magnates, the Junkers during the first half of the eighteenth century were a

[112]Stratmann, *Krise,* pp. 43–47.
[113]Hinrichs, *Preussentum und Pietismus,* pp. 154–155.

relatively homogeneous class possessing small or medium-sized estates. When not engaged in official duties, most were directly involved in the economic administration of their estates.[114] Thus the Pietist stress on work and duty easily found resonance among a class of landowners actively involved in the organization of production. Furthermore, Pietist austerity had a natural appeal among a noble class whose members generally lacked huge fortunes and were often indebted.[115]

The attraction of nobles to Pietist educational institutions also reflected a rising noble demand for career training. This demand had accompanied the evolution of the Prussian nobility into a service class, a process that had begun under the Great Elector. During the reign of Frederick William I, when competition for civil posts with university-trained bourgeois aspirants became especially keen, noble demand for practical career training increased even further. Although his successor, Frederick II, personally preferred noble to bourgeois servitors, the numerical ratio between nobles and commoners within the Prussian bureaucracy did not significantly change during his reign.[116] Nobles continued to find the kind of education provided by the Berlin and Halle *Pädagogia* a valuable credential for bureaucratic advancement. By cultivating an internalized sense of duty and a strong work ethic, Pietist education helped instill those virtues expected of a state servant.

Pietist reformers like Francke and Hecker directed their efforts at a broad social spectrum. They established boarding schools for the elite, vocational schools for the middle class, asylums for the orphaned, elementary schools for the poor, and institutes for teachers. The educational efforts of Francke and Hecker reflected a belief that it was necessary to educate all individuals, regardless of their social position, to serve God, their rulers, and society.

The universality and versatility of Pietist schooling does much to explain its appeal to absolutist rulers in eighteenth-century Prussia and Austria. Pietist education offered the absolutist state a potential instru-

---

[114]This would change during the latter half of the century, when the leasing of estates became increasingly common among noble landowners. See Chapter 6, "The Crisis of Seigniorial Authority in Eighteenth-Century Prussia and Austria."

[115]On the structure of the Prussian nobility see the concise analysis in Perry Anderson, *Lineages of the Absolutist State* (London, 1974), pp. 262–263. See also Hinrichs, *Preussentum und Pietismus*, pp. 174–216.

[116]See the classic study by Hans Rosenberg, *Bureaucracy, Aristocracy, and Autocracy: The Prussian Experience, 1660–1815* (Cambridge, Mass., 1958), pp. 67–70.

ment of control appropriate for every social milieu. In the realm of popular education, Pietist schooling provided a means of integrating recalcitrant or anomalous social groups into changing patterns of economic production. Francke and Hecker had both attempted to integrate into the production process those orphans and soldier children who had been excluded from guild membership. As will be seen in Chapter 5, Prussian and Austrian absolutism faced a similar task. The rapid expansion of rural industry in these territories encouraged the rise of production forms no longer organized on a guild basis. Like Hecker and Francke, absolutist educational policy would be concerned with educating future laborers in spheres of production divorced from corporate organization and regulation. Here it is no accident that both sexes were the target of absolutist educational policy. Women, while generally excluded from guild membership, were an integral part of rural textile production. With the growth of rural industry in the eighteenth century, women played an increasingly important role in household production for the market.[117] In the process, their importance as objects of absolutist educational policy was also enhanced.

At a different level, Pietist pedagogy was to find resonance in eighteenth-century Central Europe precisely because of the paradoxical nature of its enterprise. Pietism's simultaneous use and eschewal of coercion, and its desire to cultivate the self-discipline and autonomy of individuals while preserving control over them – these were the antinomies that were to characterize absolutist policy in eighteenth-century Prussia and Austria. At issue, as Marc Raeff has argued, was the fundamental tension between regulation and the promotion of autonomy characteristic of the Central European "well-ordered police state."[118] This tension was heightened as the scope of state activity expanded in the course of the eighteenth century. While Frederick II and Maria Theresa fully embraced the *étatiste* assumptions of their cameralist advisers, they also recognized that their goals could not be accomplished through regulation alone. On the one hand, they continued to rely on coercion to achieve their domestic aims; on the other hand, they also pursued policies that sought to reduce the need for coercion. Both shared the cameralist belief in the efficacy of state intervention in economic life; yet both sought to foster a work ethic in their subjects in order to make such intervention

[117]See Jean H. Quataert, "The Shaping of Women's Work in Manufacturing: Guilds, Households, and the State in Central Europe," *American Historical Review*, 90 (1985), pp. 1125–1135.
[118]Raeff, *The Well-Ordered Police State*.

unnecessary. Both preserved an agrarian structure in which extra-economic coercion – serfdom – governed the relationship between lord and peasant; yet both attempted to maintain the stability of that structure through policies aimed at modifying its coercive character.

The function of Pietist schooling in eighteenth-century Prussia and Austria was to mediate between these conflicting demands of social discipline and individual autonomy. The appeal of Pietist pedagogy to absolutist reformers lay in its simultaneous promotion of submission and autonomy. Pietism provided a pedagogy that encouraged both activity and passivity, entrepreneurial enterprise and an acceptance of existing social and political structures. It represented, in short, a pedagogical compromise between the demands of state-building and a hierarchical social and political order.

Habsburg Austria was, of course, a Catholic monarchy in which Protestantism was not officially tolerated until 1781. What, then, was the appeal of Pietist pedagogy in a monarchy traditionally dedicated to the preservation of Catholic orthodoxy? The answer lies in the movement on behalf of cultural and religious reform that emerged during the reign of Maria Theresa. Although this movement was as dedicated to the survival of Catholicism as the Pietists were to the preservation of Protestantism, both shared similar goals. The next chapter examines the nature and significance of Theresian cultural and religious reform.

3

From image to word: cultural reform and the rise of literate culture in Theresian Austria

It would be preferable if the peasantry were not able to read and write, for then they would be unable to read heretical books together.

A parish priest from the Styrian village of Unzmarkt, 1752

Every common man should have a copy of the Bible.

Decree of Joseph II, 1781

In 1752, local Austrian officials conducted an investigation into rural parishes in the provinces of Styria, Carinthia, and Upper Austria. Maria Theresa, the Austrian ruler, had been alarmed by the persistence of widespread crypto-Protestantism among the peasantry of these regions. Like her Habsburg predecessors, Maria Theresa was dedicated to the preservation of Catholicism and the extirpation of heresy in her domains.

To halt the further spread of Protestantism, numerous parish priests and higher ecclesiastical officials proposed a simple countermeasure: Parish schools in the countryside were to be eliminated. The parish priest from Unzmarkt cited at the beginning of the chapter was convinced that the abolition of parish schools would prevent the spread of literacy and, presumably, Lutheranism. The bishop of Graz-Seckau assured that the abolition of rural schools would deprive young peasants of the opportunity to read and write and thereby "dry up the fountain of poisonous heresy."[1] A parish priest in Troifach related with horror how, after

[1] Karl Klamminger, "Leopold III. Ernst Graf Firmian," in Karl Amon, ed., *Die Bischöfe von Graz-Seckau 1218-1968* (Graz, 1969), p. 350. On the investigation into crypto-Protestantism during this period see Rudolf Weiss, *Das Bistum Passau unter Kardinal Joseph Dominikus von Lamberg (1723–1761). Zugleich ein Beitrag zur Geschichte des Kryptoprotestantismus in Oberösterreich* (St. Ottilien, 1979), pp. 369–401; and Paul Dedic, *Der Geheimprotestantismus in den Vikariaten Schladming und Kulm-Ramsau in den Jahren 1753-60* (Vienna, 1941), pp. 60–97. See also the published sources in Johann Schmut, "Erstes Eingreifen des Staates zur Hebung des niederen Schulwesens in der Steiermark unter Maria Theresia," *Beiträge zur österreichischen Erziehungs- und Schulgeschichte*, 11 (1909).

scolding a peasant for expounding Lutheran ideas, the peasant replied: "But I read it in a book! It says so right there! Would a man go to the trouble of printing a book if it wasn't good?"[2]

Although Maria Theresa did not follow their advice, the episode reveals the relative distrust of popular literacy that characterized post-Tridentine Catholicism in the Habsburg monarchy.[3] In Austria, a center of the Catholic counteroffensive since the early seventeenth century, secular and ecclesiastical authorities condemned lay Bible reading as a source of Protestantism well into the eighteenth century.[4] Their attitude found papal support in the Bull Unigenitus (1713), which condemned Pasquier Quesnel's proposition that "the reading of scripture is for all."

Yet in 1774, the Austrian monarchy undertook the most ambitious reform of elementary education on the European continent. Maria Theresa's General School Ordinance (Allgemeine Schulordnung) required that every child between the ages of six and thirteen learn how to read and write. Those who worked to implement the reform included not only the empress and her officials, but also prominent figures in the Habsburg ecclesiastical hierarchy. What explains this transformation in elite attitudes toward literacy? Why, given their traditional ambivalence toward the diffusion of the printed word, did state and ecclesiastical authorities come to view popular literacy as desirable and even necessary?

As we saw in the previous chapter, Pietists viewed popular literacy as not only desirable but necessary. For them, devotional inwardness and Christian conviction required direct contact with the Word of God. Consequently, once Pietism had gained preeminence in the Protestant churches and universities of Prussia, the path was paved for the vigorous promotion of literate culture. By comparison, the acceptance of literate culture in Austria proved far more problematic. It was first during the reign of Maria Theresa – more than a half-century after the emergence of Pietism – that the Habsburg monarchy and Catholic church lent their unqualified approval to the idea of universal literacy.

[2]Schmut, "Erstes Eingreifen," p. 197. Similar sentiments were expressed by priests in the Styrian villages of Bruck, St. Dionysen, and Kammern. See Czimeg, "Entwicklung der Pfarrschulen," pp. 43–44.
[3]On the prevalence of this distrust throughout Catholic Europe see Elizabeth Eisenstein, The Printing Press as an Agent of Change, 2 vols. (Cambridge, 1979), 1:329–450; and James Curran, "Communications, Power, and Social Order," in Michael Gurevitch et al., eds., Culture, Society, and the Media (London, 1982), pp. 216–220.
[4]See Grete Klingenstein, Staatsverwaltung und kirchliche Autorität im 18. Jahrhundert. Das Problem der Zensur in der theresianischen Reform (Munich, 1970), pp. 23–26; Czimeg, "Entwicklung der Pfarrschulen," p. 43.

Given the belated promotion of popular literacy in the Habsburg
monarchy, the rise of literate culture in eighteenth-century Austria begs
analysis. Why did elites come to view popular literacy as a positive good?
The answer lies in efforts to reform popular culture during the reign of
Maria Theresa. This chapter focuses specifically on the attempt to reform
popular religion and the popular stage. Admittedly, these are areas seemingly tangential to popular education. Yet efforts to reconstitute popular
piety and reform the plebeian stage help illustrate the shift in attitudes
toward literate culture that characterized the Theresian era. At the root
of this shift was a transformation of the media through which the leading
institutions of Austrian society – namely the monarchy and the Catholic
church – sought to regulate popular culture. This chapter describes the
growing dependence upon literate media to preserve the dominion of
these institutions at the popular level. Conversely, I also attempt to show
how theatrical, ritualistic, and nonliterate media came to be viewed with
varying degrees of distrust. This change, I believe, was one of the most
significant developments in eighteenth-century Austrian culture. The resulting shift away from "image culture" toward "word culture," to borrow Lawrence Stone's dichotomy, would be an important prerequisite
for the establishment of Austrian compulsory schooling.[5]

The nonliterate legacy of Habsburg baroque
Catholicism

Habsburg baroque Catholicism was characterized by an unquenchable
drive toward self-representation and display. The symbiotic relationship
between the House of Habsburg and the Catholic church, forged in the
course of the Counter Reformation in a struggle against heretics at home
and abroad, found expression in a monarchical ideology propagated in a
visual, nonliterary fashion. Hermeneutical starvation will surely afflict

---

[5]Lawrence Stone, "Literacy and Education in England, 1640–1900," *Past and Present*, 42
(1969), p. 278. In her critique of Stone's use of this dichotomy, Eisenstein rightly notes
that the two cultures are not mutually exclusive; indeed, printing facilitated the diffusion
of "images" as much as it did "words." See her *Printing Press as an Agent of Change*,
1:67–70. Similarly, R. W. Scribner's *For the Sake of the Simple Folk: Popular Propaganda
for the German Reformation* (New York, 1981) illustrates how visual culture could be
enhanced, not replaced, by the printing press. I have deliberately employed Stone's distinction, however, to underscore the importance that literate culture had begun to acquire in
eighteenth-century Austria. I in no way imply that it replaced nonliterate culture. To the
contrary – as Carl Schorske has demonstrated – the idea of a literate culture remained
problematic for Austrian intellectuals well into the twentieth century. See Carl Schorske,
Fin-de-siècle Vienna: Politics and Culture (New York, 1980).

those historians of political theory who, dependent upon contemporaneous texts for the exercise of their craft, seek to understand how Habsburg rulers demonstrated the divine source of their authority. That God inspired and guided the dynasty was demonstrated less through political tracts than through the ruler's demonstrative observance of the Sacraments, participation in pilgrimages and processions, and sponsorship of cults of the Virgin and the Saints. To express its identification with the Virgin Mary, the House of Habsburg patronized art and sculpture or participated in pilgrimages, such as the one to Mariazell, held in her honor. To symbolize the dynasty's commitment to the preservation of true doctrine in the face of heresy, Habsburg rulers promoted the cult of the Eucharist. Their annual participation in the Corpus Christi procession, which culminated in their public celebration of the Eucharist, visually and theatrically demonstrated this commitment.[6]

The visual and ritualistic representation of authority, of course, was hardly specific to the Habsburg monarchy. As Norbert Elias and Jürgen Habermas have shown, theatricality and display were central components of political representation in early modern Europe.[7] Nonliterary forms of propaganda were aptly suited to societies in which the level of literacy was relatively low. In the Habsburg monarchy, however, the tendency to represent authority in a nonliterary fashion was even more pronounced given the dynasty's intense identification with Catholicism and the Counter Reformation.[8] The frequent equation of lay Bible read-

[6]A valuable glimpse into the world of Habsburg baroque Catholicism is found in the *Wienerisches Andachtsbüchl, oder Festcalender vor das Jahr 1715* (Vienna, 1715). This devotional calendar for Vienna vividly illustrates the dynasty's dutiful participation in an endless succession of pilgrimages, processions, and ceremonies. For a good, concise treatment of Habsburg baroque Catholicism see Anna Coreth, *Pietas Austriaca. Ursprung and Entwicklung barocker Frömmigkeit in Österreich* (Vienna, 1959). On the Habsburg patronage of religious cults see also Gerhardt Kapner, *Barocker Heiligenkult in Wien und seine Träger* (Munich, 1978), pp. 13–22; and Theodor Wiedemann, *Geschichte der Reformation und Gegenreformation im Lande unter der Enns,* 5 vols. (Prague, 1879–82), 5:185–261. On Habsburg baroque Catholicism see also the extraordinary work of erudition by R. J. W. Evans, *The Making of the Habsburg Monarchy, 1550–1700: An Interpretation* (Oxford, 1979), especially pp. 100–116, 189–191, 223–232.
[7]Norbert Elias, *Die höfische Gesellschaft. Eine Untersuchung zur Soziologie des Königtums und der höfischen Aristokratie* (Neuwied, 1969), pp. 79–201; Jürgen Habermas, *Strukturwandel der Öffentlichkeit. Untersuchung zu einer Kategorie der bürgerlichen Gesellschaft* (Darmstadt, 1962), pp. 17–28. On the role of theatricality and display in baroque culture see also Richard Allewyn, *Das grosse Welttheater. Die Epoche der höfischen Feste in Dokument und Deutung* (Hamburg, 1959); and more recently Jürgen Freiherr von Kruedener, *Die Rolle des Hofes im Absolutismus* (Stuttgart, 1973).
[8]This point is not adequately stressed in Hubert Christian Ehalt, *Ausdrucksformen absolutistischer Herrschaft. Der Weiner Hof im 17. und 18. Jahrhundert* (Vienna, 1980).

ing with Protestantism, and Protestantism with political disloyalty, encouraged the nonliterary propagation of Habsburg baroque Catholicism.

As seen earlier, parish schools did exist where villagers and townspeople learned to read and write. The Catholic church and the Habsburg dynasty, obviously, could not entirely dispense with the written word. No matter how remote the parish, someone was needed to read royal decrees and ecclesiastical directives, as a parish priest from Riegersburg (Styria) pointed out in 1752. Although he favored abolishing parish schools, he recommended that at least one pupil from each village learn to read and write so that "the inhabitants of a village don't have to run far and wide to find someone who can read a printed ordinance."[9] Outside of larger towns and cities, however, as we saw in Chapter 1, instruction in parish schools was often limited to the oral recitation of the catechism. Parish schooling in early modern Austria was, to a considerable degree, nonliterary in character.

Moreover, parish schooling was only one of a number of instruments used by the church to propagate Catholic doctrine among the laity. The church – and the Jesuits in particular – relied heavily upon iconography and spectacle in their proselytizing efforts. The catechistic mission, quite common in seventeenth- and eighteenth-century Austria, is a striking example of the use of nonliterary methods of religious instruction. A 1695 account from Graz related how the Jesuits provided catechistic instruction by setting up three stages in the Jesuit church. On each stage there were pictures depicting Moses receiving the Ten Commandments. Moving from picture to picture, the children acted out the story in front of their adult audience. Later reports show that this kind of instruction was still common in Graz in the 1760s. Often the catechistic mission took the form of a procession in which the participants carried pictorial representations of the Scriptures and the Sacraments.[10]

A similar theatricality characterized the Jesuit popular mission *(Volksmission)*. Borrowed from Italy, the popular mission reached the height of its popularity in Austria between 1700 and 1740. It appears to have been particularly common in regions like the Tyrol, where access to parish

[9]Schmut, "Erstes Eingreifen," p. 208.
[10]B. Duhr, *Geschichte der Jesuiten in den Ländern deutscher Zunge*, 4 vols. (Freiburg im Breisgau, 1907–28), 3:215, 615; 4 (pt. 1): 215, 354, 389–390. On the promotion of the catechistic procession in Vienna see Albert Hübl, "Die Schulen," in Anton Mayer, ed., *Geschichte der Stadt Wien*, 6 vols. (Vienna, 1914), 5:358–359.

churches was difficult because of the mountainous terrain. The Jesuit popular mission served as a traveling parish school that educated the laity in the basic articles of faith. In other instances, the popular mission was a response to rural disorder. The decision of the Jesuit college in Graz to send popular missions throughout Styria and Carinthia in 1734 was motivated by an outbreak of peasant uprisings in those provinces.[11] Jesuit organizers of a popular mission customarily entered a town or village, erected a stage in the square, and proceeded to preach to their audience for a period lasting from eight to fourteen days. The *via purgativa* and the *via illuminata et unitativa* constituted the two phases of the ritual. In a typical example of the former, a Jesuit, bound with rope, appeared on a stage strewn with bones or pictures of hell. To illustrate the tortures of hellfire, he laid his hand on a red-hot coal or displayed a skull while preaching to his audience. If the *via purgativa* was a lesson in damnation, the *via illuminata et unitativa* illustrated redemption through the Eucharist. Here the Jesuits administered general communion to adults or first communion to children.[12]

The quintessentially theatrical and nonliterary medium of religious proselytization was the Jesuit school drama. The cultural influence of the Jesuits in the seventeenth and eighteenth centuries, seen in their control of the monarchy's universities and most of its *Gymnasien,* extended to the theater. Emerging in the late sixteenth century, the Jesuit school drama enjoyed wide popularity well into the reign of Maria Theresa. School dramas were an integral part of the life and curricula of Jesuit universities and *Gymnasien.* When the Jesuits established or took over a university or *Gymnasium,* a large hall that was to serve as a theater was generally included in the building plan or added to the existing structure. Dramas were usually written and produced by the professor of rhetoric, although frequently he did little more than adapt the plays of renowned Jesuit dramatists such as Niccolo Avancini or Johann Baptist Adolf.[13]

[11]Ibid., pp. 389–410; 4 (pt. 2): 190–259.
[12]Ibid., p. 237; L. A. Veit and L. Lenhart, *Kirche und Volksfrömmigkeit im Zeitalter des Barock* (Freiburg im Breisgau, 1956), pp. 91–92.
[13]Willi Flemming, *Geschichte des Jesuitentheaters in den Ländern deutscher Zunge* (Berlin, 1923), pp. 32, 121–122. In composing a drama, the Jesuit professor of rhetoric had at his disposal a number of theoretical manuals that prescribed thematic, aesthetic, and technical criteria. Augmenting the uniformity that these manuals gave to the Jesuit school drama was the career mobility of Jesuit professors. At the Jesuit *Gymnasium* in Klagenfurt, for example, the professor of rhetoric rarely taught more than two years before moving on to another school. See Kurt Drozd, *Schul- und Ordenstheater am Collegium S.J. Klagenfurt (1604–1773)* (Klagenfurt, 1965), pp. 40–58.

School plays were acted out by the students. Normally the conclusion of the school year provided the occasion for a dramatic production, and each class put on its own production. At other times school dramas commemorated the accession of a king, the conclusion of a treaty, or the end of a religious festival or procession.[14] As a pageant celebrating the close of the school year, it served as a kind of final examination that required students to demonstrate their declamatory skills in Latin. More important, the school drama taught aristocratic comportment. Pupils learned how to make entrances, exits, and a strong overall impression on their audience. The school theater had become a forum for noble self-representation as a result of the Jesuits' prominent role in aristocratic education. The Jesuit *Gymnasium* and university in the seventeenth and early eighteenth centuries were virtually the sole educational institutions serving the Habsburg nobility.[15] Often the performances were directly subsidized by the nobility, as was the case with the Klagenfurt school theater. The nobles in the Carinthian estates, viewing the theater as an arena for aristocratic self-representation, regularly made financial contributions to support the purchase of costumes and stage decor.[16]

However, the pedagogical mission of the school drama was not directed at the students alone. Apart from the socially exclusive premier performances, the dramas sought to reach all classes of society by offering repeat performances to the general public. The number of such performances varied, but in cities such as Prague or Vienna a drama was performed as many as five or six times.[17] The themes treated in the dramas reflected the synthesis of classical humanism and baroque Catholicism so characteristic of the Jesuit *Ratio Studiorum*. Plays depicting the lives of the Saints – Johannes Nepomuk or Teresa of Ávila, for

---

[14]Kurt Adel, *Das Wiener Jesuitentheater und die europäische Barockdramatik* (Vienna, 1960), p. 54; Flemming, *Geschichte des Jesuitentheaters*, p. 181.

[15]Only around the 1730s did this begin to change, when the upper nobility began attending German Protestant universities and the lower nobility started establishing academies of their own. See Grete Klingenstein, *Der Aufstieg des Hauses Kaunitz* (Göttingen, 1975), pp. 159–219; idem, "Vorstufen der theresianischen Studienreformen in der Regierungszeit Karls VI," *Mitteilungen des Instituts für österreichische Geschichtsforschung*, 76 (1968), pp. 319–331. On the institutional origins of the noble academy in Central Europe, see also Norbert Conrads, *Ritterakademien der frühen Neuzeit. Bildung als Standesprivileg im 16. und 17. Jahrhundert* (Göttingen, 1982).

[16]Drozd, *Schul- und Ordenstheater*, p. 191.

[17]Flemming, *Geschichte des Jesuitentheaters*, pp. 263; Alexander von Weilen, "Das Theater," in Mayer, *Geschichte der Stadt Wien*, 6:333–368.

example – or stories from the Old Testament were frequent dramatic subjects. Toward the end of the seventeenth century, themes drawn from Greek and Roman history and mythology grew increasingly popular.[18] The Jesuit drama, of course, treated classical antiquity in an allegorical rather than historical fashion. The classical heroes and heroines appearing on the Jesuit stage dressed not as Greeks or Romans, but as seventeenth- and eighteenth-century cavaliers and ladies.[19] The distribution of acting roles reinforced this reification of an aristocratic world from Greek and Roman antiquity. Jesuit theorists of the school drama insisted that the pupil's role on stage correspond to his social position. Thus the theoretician Franciscus Lang argued that the scion of a noble family was never to appear in a role that was low or vulgar. Conversely, the son of an artisan or merchant was never to be cast in the role of a king or nobleman.[20]

Greek and Roman historical and mythological subjects also served as a vehicle for political expression. By focusing the dramatic action on the affairs of classical rulers and states, the Jesuit drama visually glorified the Habsburg dynasty. The frequent use of court scenes, depicting the ruler in all his splendor, further exalted the monarchy. The popularity of battle scenes and the glorification of war also conveyed a clear political message, while countless scenes depicting executions or the pronouncement of verdicts were visual reminders of the punishments awaiting the disobedient.

The *Kaiserspiel,* a variant of the Jesuit school drama, was the most overt form of dynastic propaganda. The *Kaiserspiel* glorified the House of Habsburg as the defender of Catholicism and the scourge of heresy. A typical example of this genre was "Austria Exclusit Iugo Orientis Ungariam" (1686), a drama performed at the Jesuit *Gymnasium* in Steyr that celebrated the imperial victory over the Turks in 1683. In the Steyr performance of "Maxiamus Austriacus" (1748), Emperor Maximilian

---

[18]This is seen in the case of the Jesuit *Gymnasium* in Krems, where typical performances included *Zeno* (1697), *P. Scipio Iurans* (1731), *M. Tullius Cicero* (1732), *Paris* (1743), and *Brutus* (1751). See the list of performances at the Jesuit *Gymnasium* in Herman Wlczek, "Das Schuldrama der Jesuiten zu Krems (1616-1763)," Ph.D. diss., University of Vienna, 1952, pp. 176ff.

[19]See Walter Benjamin, *Der Ursprung des deutschen Trauerspiels* (Frankfurt am Main, 1978), pp. 69–72.

[20]Franciscus Lang, *Dissertatio de actione scenica* (Munich, 1727), p. 68.

loses his way in the mountains at night. He is ultimately saved, however, when an angel administers him the Holy Eucharist.[21]

Up to the mid-eighteenth century, Latin was used exclusively on the Jesuit stage. In order to reach its popular audience, most of whom could not understand Latin, the Jesuit school drama relied extensively upon visual effect. Stage machinery and special effects compensated for the inability of much of the audience to understand the dialogue.[22] School theaters with especially elaborate machinery could depict angels in flight or Christ on a cloud. In others, fireworks conjured up the burning bush, while smoke machines graphically depicted the burning of a martyr. The Jesuit *Gymnasium* in Glatz won renown for its thunder machine, and the theater at the University of Vienna for its simulated earthquakes, storms, and shipwrecks. The audience of one performance in Graz was awed when an effigy of Jezabel, filled with raw meat, blood, and bones prior to the performance, was torn to pieces by a pack of dogs before its very eyes.[23]

The Jesuit school drama, in short, was paradigmatic of the forms through which the Catholic and aristocratic values of Habsburg baroque Catholicism were mediated at the popular level. The stage, an integral part not only of Jesuit drama but of cultural and religious life in general, epitomized the manner in which these values were visibly communicated. How effective were these forms of religious proselytization, dynastic glorification, and aristocratic self-representation? The dominant role of processions, pilgrimages, and similar forms of piety in eighteenth-century Austrian popular culture would suggest that such media were very effective. A closer analysis nonetheless reveals that these expressions of ostensible cultural hegemony could be appropriated and transformed into autonomous forms of plebeian self-expression, notably the Viennese popular comedy of the first half of the eighteenth century.

[21]Josef Fröhler, "Von der Klosterschule zum Gymnasium. Das höhere Schulwesen in Steyr von 1500 bis 1773," in Manfred Brandl, ed., *500 Jahre Dominikaner und Jesuiten in Steyr 1478–1978* (Steyr, 1978), pp. 23–24.

[22]The nonliterary quality of Jesuit drama is evidenced by the rarity of their publication. They survive today, if at all, only in manuscript. The Jesuit dramatist Avancini, whose lavish productions at the Habsburg court heavily influenced school drama, testified to the nonliterary character of his medium when he explained: "I have written plays that I believed would perhaps please a theater audience, but the creation of pleasure for the reader was never my intent." Avancini, *Poesis dramatica*, 5 vols. (Vienna, 1655), 1:preface.

[23]For these and similar examples see Adel, *Das Wiener Jesuitentheater*, pp. 128–131; and Flemming, *Geschichte des Jesuitentheaters*, pp. 152–171.

Popular comedy and popular piety: toward plebeian autonomy

The Viennese popular stage found a permanent home with the establishment of the Kärtnertor Theater in 1710.[24] The flowering of the Viennese popular comedy in the early eighteenth century reflected Vienna's rapid development as a court and administrative center following the expulsion of the Turks in 1683. Imperial Vienna lured not only the aristocracy, but also its entourage of servants.[25] These were the chambermaids and footmen who would come to dominate the stage and audience of the Kärtnertor.

The Viennese popular comedy emerged out of the theatrical milieu of Habsburg baroque culture. Joseph Stranitzky (1676–1726), Gottfried Prehauser (1699–1769), and Joseph Felix Kurz (1718–78), the leading actors of the Viennese stage during the first half of the eighteenth century, were deeply influenced by Jesuit dramaturgy. A footman's son from Graz who earned his living partly as a tooth extractor, Stranitzky began his theatrical career as the owner of a marionette theater. In the booth of his puppet show he reproduced the characters and themes that appeared on the Jesuit stage of his day – kings and tyrants, aristocratic heroes, politics and intrigue. Stranitzky later achieved resounding success on the stage of the Kärtnertor for his portrayal of Hanswurst, the eternal servant of peasant stock with a perennial green hat and beard. Stranitzky's comedies contained all the pomp and splendor of their Jesuit prototypes. The bombastic language, the allegorizing use of the double title, the courtly settings and costumes – all these elements reveal an affinity with Jesuit drama.[26] Prehauser, Stranitzky's successor as Hanswurst, and

---

[24]Two considerations appear to have motivated the Viennese municipal government and Lower Austrian provincial government to establish the Kärtnertor. One was the threat of fire in the houses where wandering troupes had previously performed. The other was the need to raise money for Vienna's workhouse. The management of the Kärtnertor had to promise to turn over a portion of its profits to the administration of the workhouse. See Eleonore Schenk, "Die Anfänge des Wiener Kärtnertortheaters 1710-1749," Ph.D. diss., University of Vienna, 1969, pp. 19–20.

[25]Elizabeth Lichtenberger, "Von der mittelälterlichen Bürgerstadt zur City," in Heimold Helczmanovszky, ed., *Beiträge zur Bevölkerungs- und Sozialgeschichte Österreichs* (Vienna, 1973), pp. 308–315.

[26]According to Friedrich Nicolai, *Beschreibung einer Reise durch Deutschland und die Schweiz im Jahre 1781*, 4 vols. (Berlin, 1783), 3:566–567, Stranitzky became interested in acting after attending Jesuit school performances in Breslau. On Stranitzky and his plays see R. M. Werner, ed., *Der Wiener Hanswurst. Stranitzky und seine Nachfolger.*

Kurz, whose popular magic burlesques and machine comedies dominated the stage of the Kärtnertor during the 1750s, both relied heavily upon Jesuit theatrical forms. Kurz's father had himself been the leader of a wandering theatrical troupe in Bohemia and Moravia. In Brünn, Olmütz, and Prague, he frequently attended Jesuit school performances and subsequently adapted their themes and stage techniques in the performances of his own troupe. When his son took over the troupe, he developed even more elaborate machinery and stage devices.[27]

Yet the actors of the Viennese popular stage broke with the Jesuit stage in one important respect: Interwoven with and often overshadowing the actions of the great was the servant Hanswurst. Ridden with scatological and sexual humor, the antics of Hanswurst acquired within the plot a significance that rivaled and eventually overshadowed the heroic actions of his masters. Unlike his aristocratic counterparts, who strove ceaselessly for fame and glory, Stranitzky's Hanswurst was motivated purely by the satisfaction of his physical appetites. In "The Magnanimous Conflict between Friendship, Love, and Honor, or Scipio in Spain with Hanswurst the Generous Slave," Hanswurst's master tells him that "it is better to die than to soil one's honor through cowardice." To which Hanswurst replies: "You can have your honor but I'll keep my head. . . . As soon as my courage faces death, it falls straight down into my pants. . . . I would rather sit down with a jug of wine and be happy."[28] Here Hanswurst (whom Mozartians will recognize as the prototype of Papageno in *The Magic Flute*) represented the antithesis of the baroque hero. What motivated Hanswurst was not the aristocratic, self-

Ausgewählte Schriften, 2 vols. (Vienna, 1908), 1:iv–xl; Rudolf Payer von Thurn, ed., *Wiener Haupt- und Staatsaktionen,* 2 vols. (Vienna, 1908), 1:preface; Otto Rommel, *Alt-Wiener Volkskomödie* (Vienna, 1952), pp. 177–206. There is also a brief but good discussion of Stranitzky in Ernst Wangermann, *The Austrian Achievement, 1700-1800* (London, 1973), pp. 42–44. As a comical figure, Hanswurst was not unique to Vienna. Luther had frequently used the term to ridicule his theological opponents, while the figure of Hanswurst appeared in the performances of theatrical troupes throughout Central Europe. It was Stranitzky, however, who first placed Hanswurst in a specifically Austrian context. He dressed and spoke like a Salzburg peasant, while his routines were filled with Viennese allusions. See Rommel, *Die Alt-Wiener Volkskomödie,* p. 215.

[27]Fritz Raab, *Johann Joseph Kurz genannt Bernardon. Ein Beitrag zur Geschichte des deutschen Theaters im 18. Jahrhundert* (Frankfurt am Main, 1899), pp. 3–4; Max Pirker, ed., *Teutsche Arien, welche auf dem Kayserlich-priviligirten Wienerischen Theatro in unterschiedlich producirten Comoedien . . . gesungen worden,* 2 vols. (Vienna, 1929), 1:preface; Moritz Enzinger, *Die Entwicklung des Wiener Theaters vom 16. zum 19. Jahrhundert,* 2 vols. (Berlin, 1918), 2:21ff.

[28]Thurn, *Weiner Haupt- und Staatsaktionen,* 2:166–172.

representational world of his masters, but his own drive for self-preservation and the satisfaction of his physical appetites.

Reinforcing the autonomy of the plebeian figure was the extemporaneous character of Stranitzky's comedy, which allowed Hanswurst to comment freely and spontaneously on the actions of his masters. He judged the world of his superiors without text, without prompters. Although he by no means questioned the existing social order, he constantly sought to legitimate an identity separate from and undefined by the masters whom he served.

By the time the comedies of Kurz and Prehauser began appearing in the 1730s and 1740s, the plebeian figures had appropriated the world of the baroque stage in its entirety. They transformed this world into a universe centered completely around their own needs and interests. True, the gods, heroes, and allegorical figures who had dominated the Jesuit stage still appeared from time to time; but in comparison with the chambermaids, coachmen, common soldiers, peasants, and other plebeian figures who now monopolized the stage, such illustrious figures played only a secondary role. Prehauser's Hanswurst had himself become a calculating and worldly servant who knew how to pursue his self-interest. Although he did not reject the hierarchical social order of his day, he reserved the right, within the limits of his social position, to pursue his economic interests in the same fashion as his master. In an aria from "The Braggart," Hanswurst sings:

> I serve with obedience and with discretion,
> But should I find something, I'll call it my own.
> Oh sure, my master will get what's his,
> But I'll keep an eye on that what's mine,
> And so I'll get by one step at a time.[29]

Here Hanswurst did not openly challenge the master–servant relationship. Yet in his insistence upon the right to "keep an eye on that what's mine," the servant established a realm of autonomy from which he could pursue his self-interest. Material needs, not the gods or the pious

[29]Pirker, *Teutsche Arien,* 1:39. Kurz and Prehauser incorporated music into their performances beginning in the 1740s. With the exception of Kurz's published collection of machine comedies located in the Vienna *Stadtbibliothek* (sig. A22200), the arias are practically all that has survived from the Kurz-Prehauser performances. Kurz's original manuscript of these arias was subsequently edited and published in Pirker, *Teutsche Arien.*

Übermenschen of the Jesuit drama, governed his world. "Love begins in the pocketbook," he asserts. The chambermaid Colombine cries, "Geld! Geld! Geld! Bleibt die Quint-Essenz der Welt" – money makes the world go 'round – and proceeds to swindle a rich old man out of his fortune.[30]

In the comedies of Stranitzky, Kurz, and Prehauser, the appropriation of Jesuit theatrical forms itself reinforced the autonomy of the plebeian figure, while debasing forms of aristocratic self-representation. Stranitzky's Hanswurst adopted the bombastic, pompous language of his masters in a fashion bordering on parody, as in his frequent references to himself as a "highly-born descendent of a distinguished line of Salzburg pork butchers."[31] The use of elaborate stage machinery, which in the Jesuit theater had served to display the power of the divine forces at work in the universe, made a mockery out of the allegorical and supernatural. Thus in "The Merchant's Daughter Idolized," for example, Hanswurst floats through the air while speaking with the Devil.[32] Lady Mary Wortley Montague, a visitor to the Kärntnertor in 1716, saw a Stranitzky comedy that "began with Jupiter's falling in love out of a peep hole in the clouds and ended with the birth of Hercules."[33] The theater reformer Joseph Sonnenfels, a bitter critic of the Viennese popular stage, described with indignation a machine comedy in which a live donkey suspended from ropes "flew" across the stage of the Kärntnertor Theater.[34]

The use of disguises, also a common device in Jesuit drama, was another technique that simultaneously appropriated and debased the symbols of courtly self-representation. A Hanswurst in noble dress created a dissonance between sign and referent, placing in question the correspondence of appearance to reality. In Stranitzky's dramas a kind of proto-Brechtian *Verfremdungseffekt* sharpened this symbolic dissonance. Contemporaries noted how Stranitzky frequently made asides to the audience, commenting upon the actions of himself or the other players. Thus when Stranitzky/Hanswurst once appeared on the stage dis-

---

[30]"Hanswurst the Love-Stricken Court Chamberlain," and "A Silent Love," in Pirker, *Teutsche Arien*, 1:39, 67–68.

[31]"Die lüstige Reiss-Beschreibung aus Salzburg in verschiedenen Länder," in Werner, *Wiener Hanswurst*, 2:127.

[32]Vienna *Stadtbibliothek*, sig. A22200.

[33]Quoted in R. Halsband, ed., *The Complete Letters of Lady Mary Wortley Montague*, 2 vols. (Oxford, 1965), 1:264. Lady Montague thoroughly enjoyed her evening at the Kärntnertor, although she dutifully confessed to being shocked by the obscenity and horrified when one actor took off his pants.

[34]Sonnenfels, *Briefe über die wienerische Schaubühne*, 2 vols. (Gesammelte Schriften, vols. 5–6, Vienna, 1784), 1:281–282.

guised as an aristocrat, he confessed to the audience that he had to return the gown to the cloakroom attendant after the performance.[35] Such a dramatic device destroyed the illusion that the stage referred to anything outside of itself. In so doing, it negated the allegorical function performed by the stage in baroque drama.

The Viennese popular comedy thus arose dialectically out of the visual and nonliterary media of Habsburg baroque culture. These media, as we have seen, were appropriated and defined in a manner entirely independent of their original sponsors. In this respect the emergence of the Viennese popular comedy brings to mind the phenomenon described by Eugene Genovese and E. P. Thompson, whereby institutions or practices originally serving the interests of dominant groups could be dialectically transformed into instruments providing subordinate groups a measure of cultural autonomy.[36]

Was this process of plebeian assimilation and transformation also to be found in other realms of Austrian popular culture? Let us turn now to popular religion. Whether or not "officially" sanctioned forms of popular devotion were indeed transformed at the popular level, this much is certain: By the mid-eighteenth century, lay and ecclesiastical critics alike were questioning the degree to which popular devotional forms actually corresponded to Catholic doctrine. Instrumental in sparking the reexamination of prevailing pastoral practice was the discovery of widespread crypto-Protestantism beginning in the 1730s. Investigations showed that the mountainous regions of Styria, Carinthia, and Upper Austria were infested with thousands of "secret Protestants" *(Geheimprotestanten)* who feigned Catholic belief while privately adhering to the Lutheran faith.[37]

[35]Rommel, *Alt-Wiener Volkskomödie*, p. 334.
[36]See Genovese's analysis of the relationship between slavery and religion in the antebellum South in *Roll, Jordan, Roll: The World the Slaves Made* (New York, 1972), pp. 161–284. Thompson examines the interdependence of patrician and plebeian modes of self-expression in "Patrician Society, Plebeian Culture," *Journal of Social History,* 7 (1974), pp. 383–405. On the relationship between elite and popular culture see Peter Burke, *Popular Culture in Early Modern Europe* (New York, 1978), pp. 23–29. For France see Roger Chartier, "Culture as Appropriation: Popular Culture Uses in Early Modern France," in Steven Kaplan, ed., *Understanding Popular Culture: Europe from the Middle Ages to the Nineteenth Century* (The Hague, 1984), pp. 229–253.
[37]In 1732, authorities estimated the number of Styrian and Carinthian crypto-Protestants at more than 25,000. See Hans von Zwiedineck-Südenhorst, *Dorfleben im achtzehnten Jahrhundert. Culturhistorische Skizzen aus Innerösterreich* (Vienna, 1877), p. 13. See also Weiss, *Bistum Passau,* pp. 311–335; Adam Wandruszka, "Geheimprotestantismus, Josephinismus, and Volksliturgie in Österreich," *Zeitschrift für Kirchengeschichte,* 78 (1967); Ernst Wangermann, "Reform Catholicism and Political Radicalism in the Austrian Enlightenment," in Roy Porter and Mikuláš Teich, eds., *The Enlightenment in National Context* (Cambridge, 1981), p. 128.

Jesuit missions, house searches, the confiscation of Lutheran Bibles and prayerbooks, deportations to Transylvania – none of these counter-measures proved effective. Protestant peasants in these regions proved remarkably clever in concealing their heresy. Exasperated investigators into Styrian crypto-Protestantism complained in 1754 that these peasants "behave outwardly like good Catholics, while their hearts remain stubbornly Lutheran."[38] To deflect suspicion in the event of house searches, some hung pictures of saints in their huts, or conspicuously displayed basins of holy water. Father Manzador, a Barnabite whose 1755 memorandum urged far-reaching reforms in parish organization, noted that a pamphlet confiscated from crypto-Protestant households "describes how one can outwardly profess the Catholic faith, visibly observing its requirements, while inwardly retaining the Lutheran faith."[39] It was not simply the existence of Protestantism that alarmed Catholic and monarchical authorities, but the subterfuge through which it survived. By its very nature, crypto-Protestant dissemblance seemed to subvert the outwardly directed pastoral practice on which Habsburg Catholicism was based.

Beyond the apparent impotence of prevailing pastoral practice in the face of creeping crypto-Protestantism, reformers were growing increasingly concerned about the integrity of popular Catholicism. As they examined pastoral practice more closely, they came to perceive many of the theatrical, outward forms of devotion as a danger to the coherence and purity of the Catholic faith. Underlying their arguments was the fear that theatrical and iconographic forms of popular devotion – the processions, pilgrimages, and cults outwardly Catholic in character – had now acquired a life of their own independent of their religious function. These critics were convinced that a dissonance had developed between devotional form and confessional content, between representational symbol on the one hand, and doctrinal referent on the other.

Typifying this fear was the 1751 ordinance banning performances of a number of popular religious celebrations, such as the "Drama of the Three Kings" (Dreikönigspiel), on the grounds that they led to "scandal rather than spiritual uplift."[40] Similarly, a royal ordinance for Vienna required

[38] Quoted in Dedic, *Geheimprotestantismus*, p. 8. See also August Leidl, "Die religiöse und seelsorgerliche Situation zur Zeit Maria Theresias (1740–80) im Gebiet des heutigen Österreichs," *Ostbairische Grenzmarken*, N.F., 16 (1974), p. 169.
[39] "Kurzer Unterricht von dermaligen Zustand deren Religionsangelegenheiten in denen böhmischen und österreichischen Erbländer," *AV: Alte Kultus*, 68 in genere, Nr. 66, 1755.
[40] *Codex Austriacus*, 5 vols. (Vienna, 1704–77), 5:598.

that the spring celebration in honor of St. Johannes Nepomuk end by 9:00 p.m. The ordinance claimed that especially in suburban districts, where the poorest classes in Vienna resided, the Nepomuk celebrations were a source of drunken and riotous behavior.[41] The intermingling of the sacred and profane in popular religion provoked one critic in the early 1780s to complain indignantly of the manger scenes displayed in the Viennese marketplace at Christmas. Surrounding the cribs, charged the indignant observer, were not only the figures of Mary, Joseph, and the Three Kings, but also Hanswurst and Colombine![42]

To a considerable degree, economic motives lay behind the reduction in the number of religious holidays in 1754 and 1771.[43] Yet here, too, one finds a concern with the apparent discrepancy between devotional form and content. "Those very days that were to be devoted to God and the Saints," fumed the 1754 abolition ordinance, "are desecrated rather than sanctified because of extravagant celebrations and profane behavior. . . . They are no longer an occasion for Christian devotion, but pernicious sin."[44] Joannis Korziska, a missionary in rural Moravia, claimed that most villagers spent these holidays dancing and gambling in their local taverns. Card playing and dice throwing often led to quarreling, brawling, or sometimes even murder. Equally insidious, lamented Korziska, was the effect on village youth. Such holidays served as social occasions, during which young people danced and carried on courtships at local taverns. Korziska noted that in the week preceding a religious holiday, children in parish schools talked of nothing except the upcoming dance. Some children even stole from their parents or masters in order to pay the musicians' fees. At fault, charged Korziska, was the parish school's inordinate stress on music at the expense of religious instruction.[45]

[41]Ibid., p. 419. The Habsburg dynasty had vigorously promoted the cult of the martyred Nepomuk, the Archbishop of Prague drowned by King Wenceslas IV in 1393, ever since the defeat of Bohemian Protestantism in 1620. Heavy wine consumption and popular theatrical presentations customarily accompanied the Nepomuk celebration. Stranitzky, for example, was known to have performed a version of his life. See Gustav Gugitz, *Das Jahr und seine Feste im Volksbrauch Österreichs*, 2 vols. (Vienna, 1949–1950), 1:267–268; Freiherr von Reinsberg-Düringsfeld, *Fest-Kalender aus Böhmen. Ein Beitrag zur Kenntnis des Volkslebens und Volksglaubens in Böhmen* (Prague, 1861), pp. 239–245; Rommel, *Alt-Wiener Volkskömodie*, p. 109.

[42]J. Richter, *Bildergalerie katholischer Missbräuche* (Frankfurt, 1784), p. 34.

[43]See James Van Horn Melton, "Arbeitsprobleme des aufgeklärten Absolutismus in Preussen und Österreich," *Mitteilungen des Instituts für österreichische Geschichtsforschung*, 90 (1982).

[44]*Codex Austriacus*, 5:837.

[45]*AV: Alte Kultus*, 68, Cassa Salis, 1772.

That the devotional forms sponsored by the church frequently assumed a life of their own at the popular level is demonstrated by the fact
that even after their abolition, they often continued to be celebrated –
albeit in a fashion not envisioned by their original sponsors. In 1773 the
prince-bishop of Gurk in Carinthia reported that attempts to reduce the
number of religious holidays in his diocese had failed. The populace of
his diocese continued to spend the abolished holidays "in idleness –
drinking, dancing, and indulging in all manner of lewd behavior."[46]

The rise of reform Catholicism

During the reign of Maria Theresa (1740–80), much of the campaign to
reform popular culture centered around the attempt to reconstitute popular religion. Underlying this effort was the fear that popular devotional
forms had begun to veer dangerously into profanity or superstition.
What was new about the Theresian reform of popular religion was its
reliance upon literate media. Whereas political and ecclesiastical authorities had earlier viewed lay Bible reading with distrust, reformers
now came to view it as crucial to preserving the doctrinal purity and
devotional efficacy of Catholicism. Conversely, many of the visual and
theatrical elements of Catholic baroque culture now came under attack.

The rise of Austrian reform Catholicism during the second half of the
eighteenth century epitomized this reversal in attitudes. The key figure in
the development of Austrian reform Catholicism was Ludovico Antonio
Muratori (1672–1760). Muratori is best remembered today as a historian, but it was his frontal assault on baroque popular piety that was
responsible for his widespread influence in Austrian ecclesiastical circles.
During his seventeen years as a parish priest in Modena, Muratori had
grown convinced of the need for a thoroughgoing reform of popular
religion.[47] His *On the Proper Devotion of the Christian* (Della regolata
divozione de' Christiani), originally published in Venice in 1747, sharply
condemned the innumerable processions, pilgrimages, cults, festivals,
and religious holidays so rooted in popular religious life. Central to his
critique was the charge that profane and superstitious practices had thoroughly debased the rituals and practices of popular devotion. Holy days

---

[46]*Haus-, Hof-, und Staatsarchiv*, Vienna: Kaiser Franz Akten, Alt 75c, fol. 30–31.
[47]On Muratori and popular piety in Modena see Pietro Stella, "Preludi della 'Regolata
divozione de' Christiani'," in *Atti del convegno internationale di studi Muratoriani*, 2
vols. (Florence, 1975), 1:258–265.

were spent "watching comedies, dancing, and playing games." "Frivolous theatrical spectacles arouse laughter and scandal rather than piety." Visualization was carried to profane extremes — "even pictures of the Holy Virgin are used as signs outside of taverns, where all manner of sin is commonly committed."[48]

In place of baroque theatricality and sensuality, Muratori called for a more inward religion in which piety originated inside rather than outside the individual. "Each must recognize that the core of Christian devotion originates deep within the heart of the individual."[49] Suggestive of Muratori's devotional inwardness was his view of the relationship between the interior of the church and outside world. Muratori believed that Catholic devotional forms should find expression as much as possible within the spatial confines of the church itself. So while stressing the centrality of the mass, he favored curtailing those forms of worship, such as pilgrimages, processions, and religious festivals, that took place primarily outside the church. Conversely, if religious life was to be moved inside the church to preserve the spiritual integrity of devotional symbols and rituals, the purity of the church as a place of worship was to be upheld by purging profane activities from the worship service. Thus he criticized the performance of plays in the church for their bad effect on the laity. Beggars, who Muratori complained "even follow you up to the confessional booth," were to be forbidden from plying their trade inside the church.[50] Parishioners were not to be allowed to bring farm animals or dogs into the church: "The temple of God was not built to serve as a showplace for cattle, but for the assembly of devout Christians." He complained of roaming dogs in the church who disrupted the service by "barking and biting, not to mention worse things."[51]

For Muratori, the shift from external to internal forms of devotion in turn required that the individual's attachment to the faith derive from an understanding of a coherent set of doctrinal principles. This in turn necessitated a return to written texts — in this case the Bible, the works of the church fathers, and the decrees of the councils. By returning to the written sources of the faith, the church could eliminate liturgical and devotional aberrations and reinforce its authority. Hence Muratori

---

[48]Cited here is the Vienna edition of Muratori's treatise, published in 1762 under the title *Die wahre Andacht des Christen,* pp. 210, 275, 253.
[49]Ibid. p. 271.
[50]Ibid., p. 90.
[51]Ibid., p. 93.

stressed the devotional importance of texts over iconographic or ritualistic representation. In this respect, his historical interests were intimately tied to his critique of popular piety. Purity of doctrine, rooted in
the written sources of the faith, required methods of historical-critical
exegesis. Muratori's historical training had indeed followed in the
Maurist tradition of Jean Mabillon and Bernard de Montfaucon, the
seventeenth-century French Benedictine scholars whose textual criticism
had attempted to place Catholic doctrine on a more solid footing.[52] If
On the Proper Devotion of the Christian attempted to prune popular
devotion of its profanity, much of Muratori's historical and textual criticism sought ultimately to reconstitute popular devotion by rooting it
firmly in the written sources of the faith.

Muratori did not go so far as to advocate lay Bible reading. The laity's
contact with the textual sources of the faith was to be indirect, mediated
through the church hierarchy. Hence Muratori's reform proposals
focused on raising the cultural level of the clergy through the creation of
seminaries and the reform of monastic education. By requiring the study
of biblical languages, history, and the moral teachings of the Scriptures,
these reforms were to bring the clergy into closer contact with the textual
sources of the faith.

Here Muratori remained firmly within the Tridentine tradition, and in
fact justified many of his proposals with citations from Charles Borromeo and the decrees of the council. Trent had, after all, represented the
last and most thoroughgoing attempt to consolidate the popular influence of the Catholic church. Through frequent references to Trent,
Muratori implied that the crisis now confronting the Catholic church
required measures as energetic as those undertaken in the wake of the
Reformation. True, Muratori attacked many of the devotional practices
associated with the post-Tridentine church, but for him these practices
were a distortion, not a realization, of the aims of Tridentine reformers.

In the Habsburg monarchy, Muratori's demand for more inward
forms of religious life struck a responsive chord among those concerned
with profane or superstitious tendencies in popular religion.[53] The

[52]See Sergio Bertelli, Eruditione e storia in Ludovico Antonio Muratori (Naples, 1960), pp.
30–99.
[53]As quantitative analyses of Benedictine, Cistercian, and Augustinian libraries have
shown, Muratori's On the Proper Devotion of the Christian circulated widely among the
Austrian monastic clergy. See Eleanore Zlabinger, Ludovico Antonio Muratori und Österreich (Innsbruck, 1970), pp. 66, 178, 217. Out of the twenty German editions published between 1751 and 1795, eight appeared in Vienna. In 1777, Muratori's treatise
was introduced as a textbook in pastoral theology at the University of Vienna.

urgency of his tone, his appeals to the Tridentine tradition, served to legitimate remedies that would ultimately supercede that tradition. Any analysis of the attempted reform of popular culture during the reign of Maria Theresa must take into account the reform movement within the Catholic ecclesiastical hierarchy.

Few historians still maintain, as did Ferdinand Maass in the 1950s, that the far-reaching educational, liturgical, and monastic reforms of the Theresian period were forced upon a recalcitrant church hierarchy.[54] Rather, recent scholarship has emphasized the support that these measures enjoyed within the Habsburg episcopacy.[55] True, the reform of cultural and educational institutions under Maria Theresa was generally marked by an expansion of state control over their administration. One by one, Maria Theresa declared institutions previously administered by ecclesiastical corporations – censorship, university faculties, secondary schools, and primary schools – to be a *politicum,* a realm of activity in which the state had a legitimate interest and thus the authority to intervene. But to reduce this process to a church–state conflict distorts the picture. The Catholic church had not acquired its preponderant position in Austrian culture without the tacit support of the Habsburg dynasty; by the same token, when the monarchy began to intervene in areas previously under church control, it did so with the support of influential circles within the ecclesiastical hierarchy. Hence the cultural and ecclesiastical reforms of the Theresian era signified not a church–state conflict, but an attempt by absolutist and ecclesiastical reformers alike to consolidate the authority of their respective institutions within society.

One of the earliest centers of Catholic reform was Salzburg, where a Muratorian circle emerged in the late 1730s. The leader of the circle was Johann Baptist di Gaspari, a Benedictine at the archbishop's court who later became a professor of history at Vienna and a member of the Commission for Education (*Studienhofkommission*).[56] Gaspari had befriended Muratori while in Venice and was primarily interested in the historical and exegetical work of the Italian scholar. Out of the group of young clerics and students who belonged to the Gaspari circle emerged

[54]Ferdinand Maass, *Der Frühjosephinismus* (Vienna, 1969).

[55]See the historiographical and thematic survey in Bernard Plongeron, "Was ist katholische Aufklärung?," in Elisabeth Kovács, ed., *Katholische Aufklärung und Josephinismus* (Vienna, 1979), pp. 1–35. For an excellent example of the revisionist approach see Klingenstein, *Staatsverwaltung und kirchliche Autorität,* especially pp. 88–130.

[56]Zlabinger, *Muratori und Österreich,* pp. 26–27; Klingenstein, *Staatsverwaltung und kirchliche Autorität,* pp. 104–105; Peter Hersche, *Der Spätjansenismus in Österreich* (Vienna, 1977), p. 51.

some of the leading representatives of Austrian reform Catholicism, including Johann Joseph von Trautson, archbishop of Vienna from 1750 to 1757, Johann Karl von Herberstein, bishop of Laibach from 1772 to 1787, and Joseph Maria von Thun, bishop of Passau from 1761 to 1763. In 1740, the archbishop suppressed the Gaspari circle in response to complaints by the local clergy. Apparently confusing the name "Muratori" with the term "Freimauerei," several priests had grown convinced that the archbishop was unknowingly harboring freemasons in his bosom.[57]

But if the Muratorian circle in Salzburg proved short-lived, others soon emerged in Innsbruck and Olmütz. Both the Academia Taxiana in Innsbruck and the Societas eruditorum incognitorum in Olmütz were drawn to the exegetical studies of Muratori, with whom both groups had personal contact. The Olmütz society was especially concerned with the reform and promotion of the German language. Its corresponding members included Johann Gottfried Gottsched, the north German dramatist, critic, and reformer of the German language.[58] Gottsched's importance for Austrian cultural reform is discussed later. The point to stress here is that Gottsched's correspondence with the Olmütz society was a sign of the growing importance of literate culture in Austrian reform circles, as well as increased cultural contacts with Protestant Germany. The same was true of the Benedictine abbey at Kremsmünster, which became an important center of Austrian reform Catholicism during the 1750s. The abbot of Kremsmünster, Placidus Fixlmüllner, introduced biblical exegesis into his 1752 reform of the abbey's *Gymnasium*. Under Fixlmüllner's leadership, Kremsmünster also became one of the first Austrian *Gymnasien* to give instruction in German. Fixlmüllner himself became renowned for his attempt to reconcile Wolffian philosophy with Catholic theology.[59] Elsewhere, other Benedictine abbots like Gottfried Bessel at Göttweig, Bernhard and Hieronymous Pez at Melk, and Martin Gerbert at St. Blasien, showed a similar interest in biblical exegesis and textual criticism.[60]

[57]Zlabinger, *Muratori und Österreich*, p. 27.

[58]Werner Rieck, "Gottsched und die 'Societas incognitorum' in Olmütz," *Forschungen und Fortschritte*, 40 (1973), pp. 83–85.

[59]Hans Sturmberger, "Studien zur Geschichte der Aufklärung des 18. Jahrhunderts in Kremsmünster," *Mitteilungen des Instituts für österreichische Geschichtsforschung*, 53 (1939), pp. 453–460. Notker Hammerstein, *Aufklärung und katholisches Reich. Untersuchung zur Universitätsreform und Politik in den katholischen Territorien des Heiligen Römischen Reiches der deutschen Nation im 18. Jahrhundert* (West Berlin, 1977), has examined the diffusion of Wolffian philosophy in the Catholic universities of the Holy Roman Empire.

[60]Anna Coreth, *Österreichische Geschichtsforschung in der Barockzeit* (Vienna, 1950), pp. 113–120.

Still, these were isolated individuals who hardly constituted a well-established Catholic reform movement. Not until 1750, when Johann Joseph Trautson was elected archbishop of Vienna, did Austrian reform Catholicism find a secure foothold. Formerly a member of the Salzburg Muratorian circle, Trautson had corresponded with Muratori while in the service of the prince bishop of Passau.[61] Two years after assuming his duties as archbishop, Trautson issued a pastoral letter that sharply criticized prevailing practices of popular piety.[62] Following Muratori, Trautson's letter condemned those priests who relied upon images, cults, relics, and processions for the propagation of Christian doctrine. These misguided clerics "speak to the laity of saints, rosaries, images, and processions . . . but preach not one word about Christ and the doctrines of the faith." They "shamelessly turn the pulpit into a stage," and their preoccupation with the externals of faith was responsible for misleading a large segment of the laity, "whose understanding of the basic articles of faith is false and completely unrelated to Christian doctrine."[63]

Trautson supported the reduction of religious holidays in 1754. He also showed himself generally hostile to the Jesuits. Given their popular influence and sponsorship of "debased" forms of devotion, it was only natural that the Jesuits became the target of Catholic reformers. Trautson worked hand in hand with monarchical officials to dismantle the Jesuit monopoly of censorship and education.[64] Christoph Anton Migazzi, who in 1757 succeeded Trautson as archbishop, shared his Muratorian views. Migazzi himself wrote a laudatory preface to the 1762 Viennese edition of Muratori's On the Proper Devotion of the Christian.[65] A year earlier, his pamphlet On the Veneration of Images had warned against an excessive reliance upon "visual aids" in popular devotion.[66] Under Migazzi, the theatricality and emotionalism of the traditional Jesuit Volksmission gave way to the more disciplined and restrained missionary methods of Ignaz Parhammer, while in 1768 Jesuit school dramas were forbidden altogether.[67] Although later known for his opposition to the

---

[61]Zlabinger, Muratori und Österreich, p. 27.

[62]Trautson's letter has recently been republished in Peter Hersche, ed., Der aufgeklärte Reformkatholizismus in Österreich (Bern, 1976), pp. 9–15.

[63]Ibid., pp. 10, 14.

[64]See Klingenstein, Staatsverwaltung und kirchliche Autorität, pp. 158–202.

[65]Published in ibid., pp. 207–208.

[66]Christoph Anton Migazzi, Unterricht über die Verehrung der Bilder (Nuremberg, 1761).

[67]For an example of the disciplined, almost martial quality of Parhammer's methods, see the eyewitness account in Rudolf Graf Khevenhüller-Metsch and Hanns Schlitter, Aus der Zeit Maria Theresias: Tagebuch des Fürsten Khevenhüller-Metsch, 7 vols. (Vienna, 1910), 3:245. See also Duhr, Geschichte der Jesuiten, 4 (pt. 2):238–242. On the aboli-

ecclesiastical reforms of Joseph II, Migazzi proved a conscientious if cautious reformer throughout the 1750s and much of the 1760s. One of his first acts as archbishop in 1757 was to establish in Vienna a seminary where candidates for the priesthood studied the Scriptures and patristic literature. Migazzi's seminary soon became a hotbed of reform Catholicism and a breeding ground for aspiring young reformers.[68]

Like Muratori, neither Trautson nor Migazzi advocated lay Bible reading. Their overriding concern was to create an ecclesiastical infrastructure capable of reforming existing pastoral practice. By the mid-eighteenth century, however, none other than Pope Benedict XIV had opened the door to the diffusion of the Bible. Benedict's 1757 revision of Unigenitus, which had condemned lay Bible reading, sanctioned translations of biblical passages for the laity. Benedict required only that an authorized commentary accompany passages that were theologically controversial or ambiguous.[69]

By the 1760s, leading members of the Habsburg episcopacy had begun to promote Bible reading in their dioceses. Joseph Maria Count Thun, the energetic prince bishop of Passau from 1761 to 1763, recommended in his 1762 pastoral letter that the laity themselves read the Bible. Accordingly, he commissioned a German translation of the Gospels. He was also the first bishop of his diocese to issue pastoral letters in German, a gesture symbolic of his desire to communicate directly with the laity through the printed word.[70] Thun's successor in Passau, Leopold Ernst Count Firmian, was also committed to the spread of literacy among the laity. This had not been the case in the 1750s, when, as Bishop of Graz-

tion of the Jesuit school drama see the decree for Bohemia in P. K. Jaksch, ed., *Gesetzeslexikon . . . für das Königreich Böhmen von 1601 bis 1800,* 5 vols. (Prague, 1828), 3:564.

[68]Hersche, *Spätjansenismus,* p. 68. Historians have yet to explain Migazzi's evolution from Catholic reformer into a leading opponent of Theresian and Josephinian ecclesiastical policy. His nineteenth-century biographer, Coelestin Wolfsgruber, viewed Migazzi's turnabout as a principled response to the radicalization of the monarchy's church policy toward the end of the reign of Maria Theresa. See Wolfsgruber, *Christoph Anton Migazzi* (Saulgau, 1890), pp. 132–133. For an alternative view see Johann Friedel, *Briefe aus Wien* (Leipzig, 1783), pp. 264–266. Friedel, the Austrian actor and *Aufklärer* of the Josephinian period, claimed that Migazzi's motives were opportunistic, the product of frustrated ambition resulting from Maria Theresa's failure to appoint him primate of Hungary in 1776. Friedel's verdict is too harsh. Migazzi's disenchantment with the monarchy's ecclesiastical reforms was apparent long before 1776. The motives of Migazzi, who awaits his modern biographer, remain unclear.

[69]E. Appolis, *Entre jansenistes et zelanti. Le "tiers parti" catholique au XVIIIe. siècle* (Paris, 1960), pp. 349–350.

[70]On Thun see Hersche, *Spätjansenismus,* pp. 51–53.

Seckau, Firmian had proposed the abolition of parish schools to combat the spread of Protestantism. By the late 1760s, however, his anxiety over the spread of Protestantism and unbelief in his diocese had convinced him that Catholicism had to be defended by literary means. His urgent memorandum to the empress in 1769, "On the Value of Good Schools for the State and the Holy Religion," would set the reform of Austrian primary education in motion.[71]

Ecclesiastical reformers frequently contrasted the devotional efficacy of Bible reading with the harmfulness of traditional devotional forms. Emmanuel Count Waldstein, bishop of Leitmeritz in Bohemia, blamed the outbreak of peasant unrest in Bohemia on the superficial, purely external forms of devotion sponsored by the Jesuits. The laity, argued Waldstein, had to be brought into closer contact with the Bible in order to educate them in the proper duties of the Christian subject.[72] The archbishop of Salzburg, Hieronymus Count Colloredo, likewise asserted that popular contact with the Word should be stressed over the purely external exercise of piety. While recommending daily Bible reading to the laity, Colloredo exhorted his clergy to "clear from the house of our solemn, majestic God . . . all indecent, ambiguous, and often ridiculous images, dramas, ornaments, and all else which hinders rather than furthers the worship of God in Spirit and in truth."[73]

Reform Catholicism, then, emphasized the positive role of texts in promoting the uniformity of doctrine and its more effective internalization by the laity. In this regard, the movement occupied a position within Austrian Catholicism closely analogous to that of the Pietist movement in the Lutheran church.[74] Both called for a "second reformation," the Pietists hearkening back to Luther and reform Catholics to Borromeo. Both preached a more introspective devotional style purged of excessive pomp and theatricality. In their advocacy of lay Bible reading, both prepared the ground for the promotion of compulsory schooling in their respective states.

[71]Joseph Alexander Freiherr von Helfert, *Die Gründung der österreichischen Volksschule durch Maria Theresia* (Prague, 1860), pp. 122–123.
[72]See Hersche, *Spätjansenismus*, p. 58.
[73]Colloredo's pastoral letter is published in Hersche, *Der aufgeklärte Reformkatholizismus*, pp. 71–75.
[74]Historians have not adequately studied the parallels between Pietism and reform Catholicism. Two who have noted similarities between the movements are T. C. W. Blanning, *Reform and Revolution in Mainz, 1743–1803* (Cambridge, 1974), pp. 27–32; and Hartmut Lehmann, "Der Pietismus im alten Reich," *Historische Zeitschrift*, 214 (1972), pp. 92–93.

Gottschedian dramaturgy and literate theater

A similar belief in the moral utility of literate culture characterized Austrian theater reform. The reform of the Viennese popular stage was based largely on the aesthetic ideas of Johann Christoph Gottsched (1700–66), the North German critic and a key figure in the German Enlightenment. Reformer of language, creator of the German bourgeois theater, Gottsched viewed the function of art as preeminently moral and didactic. Trained in the utilitarian moralism of Christian Wolff, Gottsched held that literature and drama must contribute to the moral education and enlightenment of their audience.

Gottsched emphasized the importance of language as the medium for this moral mission. The moral and cultural level of a people, he maintained, was only as high as the purity of its language. For language to perform its moral function, its primary components – words – had to be clearly defined and their use standardized. Consequently, much of Gottsched's work was devoted to the proper definition of words and their usage.[75]

This concern with language was central to Gottsched's proposals for the reform of the stage. In Leipzig, Gottsched succeeded in transforming the harlequin comedies and extemporaneous routines of the resident theatrical group into a fixed repertoire of French tragedy and comedy performed in German.[76] Gottsched's adaptation of French models did not contradict his commitment to the reform of the German language. In the future, assured Gottsched, Germany would have its own Racine or Molière. In the meantime, however, neither the decorative, bombastic language of German baroque drama nor the vulgar humor of the popular stage were worthy of the theater's didactic mission. Only when cultivated

---

[75] A typical example was his *Beobachtungen über den Gebrauch und Missbrauch vieler deutschen Wörter und Redensarten* (Strassburg, 1758). Here he listed words in the German language that had been commonly misused. "Many who are lacking in learning or proper moral insight have unclear or capricious definitions of the words they use." (p. 4) In the preface to his translation of Pierre Bayle's *Dictionnaire historique et critique*, Gottsched likewise asserted that "the common man and the half-educated . . . often use words whose meanings are not at all clear." *Historisches und kritisches Wörterbuch*, 4 vols. (Leipzig, 1741), 1:preface.

[76] On Gottsched's Leipzig reforms see the fine studies by Hilde Haider-Pregler, *Des sittlichen Bürgers Abendschule. Bildungsanspruch und Bildungsauftrag des Berufstheaters im 18. Jahrhundert* (Vienna, 1980), pp. 137–145, 393–394; and Werner Rieck, *Johann Christoph Gottsched: Eine kritische Würdigung seines Werkes* (East Berlin, 1972), pp. 131–145.

men of letters in Germany began writing for the stage could the German theater dispense with French models.[77]

The essence of Gottsched's theater reform was his subordination of theater to literature.[78] He eliminated extemporaneity by establishing a fixed repertoire performed in strict conformity with the prescribed texts. He thereby subordinated the role of the actor to that of the author. Gottsched's abandonment of the exaggerated gestures and exotic special effects of German baroque drama further reinforced the literary quality of his stage. His austere dramas hardly merit staging, as the performance adds virtually nothing to the text. Most important, however, the creation of a literate stage facilitated the censorship of theatrical performances. With the elimination of spontaneity and extemporaneity, the stage became far more susceptible to censorship. With the text at his disposal, the censor did not even need to be present at performances.[79]

Gottsched's ideas took root in Austria at a time when his influence was waning in Protestant North Germany. Their belated arrival in Austria is significant: It points above all to the late emergence of a German literary culture in Catholic Austria as compared with Protestant Germany. In 1740, when Gottsched was at the height of his popularity in Protestant Germany, Vienna ranked forty-sixth among German cities in German book production. In fact, Viennese editions never even appeared in the catalogues of North German book fairs until after the Seven Years War. By 1765, the high-water mark of Gottschedian influence in Austrian literary circles, Vienna had become the third largest producer of German books. Already in 1764, the Viennese publishing firm of Tratt-

---

[77]For Gottsched's critique of German baroque and popular theater see his *Versuch einer critischen Dichtkunst vor die Teutscher*, 3d ed. (Leipzig, 1742), pp. 724–734.

[78]Similar tendencies toward a "literacization" of the theater characterized the English stage during the second half of the seventeenth century. See Julie Stone Peters, "Print-World Ideology and the Double-Natured Stage: Towards an Alliance 1660–1700," *Publishing History*, 19 (1986). Peters argues that the closing of theaters following the outbreak of the English Civil War in 1642 helped to shift the locus of popular entertainment from the stage to print media. The effect was to bring about "the end of the theater as the only secular mass-medium." D. F. McKenzie, *The London Book Trade in the Later Seventeenth-Century* (Cambridge, 1976), p. 2, as quoted in Peters, "Print-World Ideology." Even though theaters reopened in 1660, the growth of the book trade during the intervening years resulted in a gradual alliance between publishing and the theater. As a consequence, dramatists like Congreve now wrote increasingly for readers, not just a theater audience. The effect of the alliance between print and the stage, Peters concludes, was to produce dramatic characters more prone to introspection and self-observation.

[79]In the preface to the first volume of his *Deutsche Schaubühne nach den Regeln der alten Griechen und Römer eingerichtet* (Leipzig, 1740), Gottsched noted with approval how a literate theater subjected the stage to the supervision of an "upright moral censor."

ner listed twenty-four editions in North German catalogues; a year later the number had more than tripled to seventy-six.[80]

The Austrian Gottschedians inherited from their mentor a belief in the importance of literary culture. Their literary societies and moral weeklies of the 1760s aimed specifically at promoting such a culture in Austria. A refined literary language, as Joseph Sonnenfels told the Vienna German Society in 1761, "educates the father to be a loyal citizen and the mother to be a worthy, loving wife."[81] Loyal supporters of absolutism, they also stressed the political value of a refined vernacular. Karl Heinrich Seibt, the first professor to lecture in German at the University of Prague, argued that written language had emerged historically as a result of the sovereign's need to render laws perpetual and binding. Printing, according to Seibt, allowed rulers to extend their influence to isolated and remote regions.[82] Here the sensitivity of Seibt and the Austrian Gottschedians to the political significance of printed discourse reflected the massive growth of written correspondence that accompanied the proliferation of administrative agencies in the Theresian period.[83] Viewed in this light, their concern with the purity of language was political as well as aesthetic. Administrative efficiency demanded a simpler style, one pruned of the luxuriant prolixity and turgidity of baroque prose. In line with this goal, Joseph II would appoint Sonnenfels to a "chair of administrative writing" *(Lehrstuhl für Geschäftsstil)* at the University of Vienna in 1780. One of Sonnenfels's duties in this capacity was to make concrete proposals on how style could be simplified in bureaucratic correspondence.[84]

Like Gottsched in Leipzig, the Austrian Gottschedians directed their missionary zeal toward the popular stage. Maria Theresa had tried to ban the performances of Kurz and Prehauser as early as 1752. The attempt to replace them with French classical dramas failed. Attendance at

[80]See Leslie Bodi, *Tauwetter in Wien: Zur Prosa der österreichischen Aufklärung 1781–87* (Frankfurt am Main, 1977), pp. 82–87.
[81]Sonnenfels, *Ankündigung einer deutschen Gesellschaft in Wien, in der ersten feyerlichen Versammlung des 2. Jäner, 1761* (Vienna, 1761), pp. 10–11.
[82]Karl Heinrich Seibt, *Von dem Unterschiede des zierlichen, des Hof- und Curialstyles* (Prague, 1768), published in Karl Wotke, "Karl Heinrich Seibt. Der erste Universitätsprofessor der deutschen Sprache in Prag, ein Schüler Gellerts und Gottscheds. Ein Beitrag zur Geschichte des Deutschunterrichts in Österreich," *Beiträge zur österreichischen Erziehungs- und Schulgeschichte*, 9 (1907), pp. 93–95.
[83]See K. H. Osterloh, *Joseph von Sonnenfels und die österreichische Reformbewegung im Zeitalter des aufgeklärten Absolutismus. Eine Studie zum Zusammenhang von Kameralwissenschaft und Verwaltungspraxis* (Lübeck, 1970), pp. 234–231. See also the general comments in Raeff, *The Well-Ordered Police State*, pp. 43–56.
[84]Osterloh, *Sonnelfels*, pp. 234–231.

the Kärtnertor dropped, the house fell into arrears, and by 1754 Kurz and Prehauser were back on the stage.[85] The Austrian Gottschedians took up the battle once again in 1760 when a pamphlet by Joseph Heinrich von Engelschall, a Gottschedian professor of rhetoric at the Savoy Noble Academy in Vienna, branded the Viennese popular stage immoral and socially subversive. The servants who appeared on the stage, charged Engelschall, set examples of dishonesty, deception, and disloyalty. He went so far as to claim that "the behavior of servants outside of the theater is all too often patterned on that of the servant on the stage."[86] "The more depraved their characters, the more applause they win, and by the end of the play one has viewed neither the praise of virtue nor the reproval of vice."[87] Engelschall found an ally in Christian Gottlob Klemm, whose moral weeklies *The World* (1761–63) and *The Patriot* (1764–66) propagated Gottschedian ideas. At the Hanswurst performances, charged Klemm, "the riff-raff learns every kind of vice, obscenity, and prodigality."[88] Attacks on the popular stage grew even more bitter when Joseph Sonnenfels, professor of cameralistics at the University of Vienna, assumed leadership of the anti-Hanswurst campaign. His invective against Hanswurst in *The Man without Prejudice* (1765–67) and his *Letters on the Viennese Stage* (1767–69) finally provoked Prehauser and his troupe at the Kärtnertor to perform a parody on Sonnenfels.[89] Prehauser's half-disguised portrayal depicted Sonnenfels as a humorless, arrogant pedant. To add to the ridicule, Prehauser wore masks and adopted a nasal tone of voice.

Sonnenfels's assertions to the contrary, the parody was a rousing success. His efforts to reform the Viennese stage had nevertheless won him friends in high political circles. Tobias Phillipp von Gebler, a powerful state councillor, used his influence with the empress to push for the suppression of extemporaneous performances. These pieces, he warned the empress in a 1770 memorandum, "contain highly immoral plots in which sons and daughters betray their fathers, wives deceive their hus-

[85]The royal ordinance charged that the performances of Kurz and Prehauser promoted "public scandal instead of public morality." See Raab, *Kurz*, p. 75, and Gustav Zechmeister, *Die Wiener Theater nächst der Burg und nächst dem Kärtnertor von 1747 bis 1776* (Vienna, 1971), pp. 35–36.

[86]Joseph Heinrich von Engelschall, *Zufällige Gedanken über die deutsche Schaubühne* (Vienna, 1760), p. 27.

[87]Ibid., p. 16.

[88]*Die Welt*, 3 (1761), p. 28.

[89]"Der auf dem Parnass versetzte Grüne Hut," published in Werner, *Wiener Hanswurst*, 4:20–55.

bands, servants betray their masters, and the lowest class of rogues practice their shameful arts. And worse, it is precisely the vulgarity and obscenity of the words and gestures that attract the rabble to these performances."[90]

Like their mentor, the Austrian Gottschedians wanted to transform the plebeian stage into literate theater, suppressing extemporaneity and tying each performance to its text. In the words of Engelschall, "Not one word should be spoken on the stage which cannot also be found in the text submitted to the censor."[91] Since the theater, insisted Sonnenfels, must be a "school for morals," a censor was needed to police the stage; but "censorship is impossible if the entire dialogue is not written down beforehand and subjected to the eye of the censor."[92] In order to serve its moral function, argued the Austrian Gottschedians, the stage had to be subordinated to the text.

In 1770, the Gottschedians achieved a major triumph with the appointment of Sonnenfels as Viennese theater censor. Sonnenfels promptly banned all extemporaneous performances in the city. Before a play could be performed, its text had to be submitted to the censor at least a month before the scheduled performance.[93] Predictably, the first victim of the crackdown was Kurz, who was fired as director of the Kärntnertor for producing two plays that had incurred the displeasure of Sonnenfels. "Four Mismatched Marriages" portrayed the intrigues of a servant girl who, through lies and deceit, was able to trick her noble master into marrying her. The second play, "The Mosquito Islands," revolved around the efforts of two girls to win paternal permission to marry their lovers. When their fathers refused to approve the marriages, the girls hired Bernardon, a servant, as their factotum. In the subsequent action the fathers were repeatedly chased, beaten, and imprisoned until they agreed to the marriages. Sonnenfels banned both plays because of their extemporaneous dialogue, "shameful gestures," and "double mean-

[90]Quoted in Zechmeister, *Wiener Theater*, p. 54. Accounts of the anti-Hanswurst campaign can be found in Robert Kann, *A Study in Austrian Intellectual History: Late Baroque to Romanticism* (London, 1960), pp. 208–224; Karl von Görner, *Der Hans-Wurst Streit in Wien* (Vienna, 1884); C. Glossy, "Zur Geschichte der Wiener Theaterzensur," *Jahrbuch der Grillparzergesellschaft*, 7 (1897), p. 249–270.
[91]Engelschall, *Zufällige Gedanken*, pp. 46–47.
[92]Sonnenfels, *Der Mann ohne Vorurtheile*, 2 (1765), p. 757. See also his *Sätze aus den Polizey-, Handlungs-, und Finanzwissenschaften* (Vienna, 1765), pp. 76–82.
[93]Sonnenfels's ordinance is published in Glossy, "Zur Geschichte der Wiener Theaterzensur," pp. 258–261.

ings." Such plays, warned Sonnenfels, undermined the social order by encouraging marriage above one's station and disobedience to parents.[94]

Sonnenfels's triumph was short-lived. For reasons still obscure, Sonnenfels was dismissed as censor only seven months after his initial appointment.[95] Nevertheless, his successor, Franz Karl Hägelin, was as convinced a Gottschedian as Sonnenfels. During his tenure as theater censor under Joseph II, the extemporaneous comedy remained forbidden.[96]

The creation of a literate Viennese theater had a significance beyond the stage. It symbolized a radical transformation of the forms through which popular culture was to be shaped. As a propagandistic medium, the stage had earlier played a far more important role than printed discourse. Now, however, the relationship between the two forms of expression was reversed: Texts were employed to preserve control over the stage. Texts, safeguarded through censorship, now appeared more susceptible to control than the illiterate stage. The theater censor Hägelin actually argued that theater censorship had to be far stricter than the censorship of printed material: "The book censor can correct the errors of a book or restrict it to specified readers. The theater, however, is open to individuals of every station, class, and age."[97] In contrasting theater with printed discourse, the Gottschedian Engelschall had similarly observed that "an actor can spread more immorality in half a day than can be found in ten scurrilous books."[98]

In eighteenth-century Prussia and Austria, as we have seen, cultural and religious reform movements succeeded in overcoming major obstacles to the diffusion of popular literacy. Through their stress on the value of literate culture as an instrument of moral and religious reform, these movements helped to shed any fears of popular literacy left over from the Protestant and Catholic reformations, and stressed instead the value of literate culture as a tool of moral and religious reform. As a result, the

---

[94]Sonnenfels's memorandum is published in Zechmeister, *Wiener Theater,* pp. 57–62.
[95]One possible explanation for his dismissal was his considerable unpopularity among the Viennese theater public. Eva König, the daughter of a Viennese merchant and the future wife of Lessing, wrote to Lessing that "all of Vienna rejoices when Herr Sonnenfels is ill." Quoted in Glossy, "Zur Geschichte der Wiener Theaterzensur," p. 266.
[96]Ibid., pp. 270–273.
[97]Ibid., pp. 301–302.
[98]Engelschall, *Zufällige Gedanken,* p. 46.

promotion of literacy was to become the central goal of compulsory schooling in these states.

But just as the acceptance of popular literacy came later in Austria than in Prussia, so did the pedagogical efforts to implement it. Whereas Prussian Pietism had produced two generations of pedagogical theorists during the first half of the eighteenth century, pedagogical innovation was conspicuously absent in the Catholic territories of Central Europe. Johann Ignaz Felbiger, whose efforts on behalf of popular schooling date from the 1760s, was the first Catholic school reformer of any note in eighteenth-century Central Europe. Felbiger and the birth of Catholic school reform in Silesia are the subject of Chapter 4.

4

The Catholic appropriation of Pietist
pedagogy: Johann Ignaz Felbiger

Early life and career

Neither Felbiger nor his biographers say much about his childhood, background, or education.[1] Felbiger was born in 1724 in the Lower Silesian town of Gross-Glogau. His grandfather, Heinrich Felbiger, had spent most of his life as a municipal clerk in the neighboring town of Guhrau. His father, Ignaz Anton, left Guhrau for Gross-Glogau, where he pursued a career in the imperial postal service. Ignaz Anton enjoyed considerable success in his marriage and career. His wife, Anna Katherina Schackin von Schonfeldt, was of petty noble origins, her father having been a minor official in the service of the elector of Bavaria. Through his loyal bureaucratic service, Ignaz Anton was knighted by Charles VI in 1733, but the prestige that Ignaz acquired through his marriage and subsequent ennoblement apparently did not translate into wealth, for he left Johann Ignaz, his only son, no property at his death.[2]

Felbiger, like the sons of most respectable families, never attended a

---

[1] The most detailed biographical treatments of Felbiger are Franz Volkmer, *Johann Ignaz Felbiger und seine Schulreform. Ein Beitrag zur Geschichte der Pädagogik des 18. Jahrhunderts* (Habelschwerdt, 1890), pp. 8–17; the editor's introduction in Panholzer, *Felbigers Methodenbuch*, pp. 3–7; Ulrich Kromer, *Johann Ignaz Felbiger. Leben und Werk* (Freiburg im Breisgau, 1966), pp. 21–25; and Josef Stanzel, *Die Schulaufsicht im Reformwerk des J. I. von Felbiger (1724–1788). Schule, Kirche, und Staat in Recht und Praxis des aufgeklärten Absolutismus* (Paderborn, 1976), pp. 60–62.

[2] Ignaz Anton's elevation into the Bohemian *Ritterstand* (Silesia was at that time a part of the Bohemian crown) reflected the inflation of titles then occurring throughout the Habsburg monarchy. In 1733, the year in which Ignaz was ennobled, more titles of nobility were issued in the Habsburg territories than in any previous year of the century. Bureaucratic service was at that time the most common path to ennoblement in the monarchy: Out of the 927 individuals ennobled between 1701 and 1739, 479 were civil officials. See P. Mahringer, "Österreichischer Wirtschaftsadel von 1701–1740," Ph.D. diss., University of Vienna, 1969, p. 128.

parish or community school.[3] He most likely studied with a private tutor and attended the Latin school in Gross-Glogau. His educational career then followed a Jesuit path leading from the Jesuit *Gymnasium* in Gross-Glogau to the Jesuit-dominated University of Breslau. By this time, as mentioned earlier, the Jesuits had succeeded in establishing a near monopoly over higher education in Catholic Central Europe. Their missionary zeal, as well as their political skill in winning the favor and patronage of Catholic princes, partly accounts for their educational success. But their pedagogical prowess also played a role. A well-defined curriculum, embodied in the *Ratio Studiorum,* facilitated their diffusion of a relatively centralized, uniform network of *Gymnasien* and universities. The *Ratio Studiorum* not only fixed the course of study from the *Gymnasium* through the university, but also prescribed hours of study, textbooks, disciplinary procedures, and housing of students. The Jesuits' political and pedagogical persistence enabled them to gain control over the philosophical and theological faculties of every Habsburg university, as well as most *Gymnasien.*[4] The University of Breslau, created in 1702, proved no exception. In 1739, the year Felbiger entered the university, the rector and every one of the sixteen professors in the faculties of philosophy and theology belonged to the Society of Jesus.[5]

At Breslau, Felbiger embarked upon an Aristotelian course of study in the philosophical faculty consisting of logic, metaphysics, physics, mathematics, and natural science. This curriculum, known as the *studia superiora,* was normally completed in three years, but Felbiger took five.[6] The outbreak of the first Silesian war in 1740 disrupted university life and may well have prolonged Felbiger's studies.[7]

Although educated by the Jesuits, Felbiger never embraced their cul-

[3]See Felbiger, "Ausführliche Nachricht von der erst zu Sagan, denn aber in ganz Schlesien und in der Grafschaft Glatz unternommenen Verbesserung der katholischen Schulen," in *K.S.,* p. 429.

[4]Grete Klingenstein, "Vorstufen der theresianischen Studienreform in der Regierungszeit Karls VI.," *Mitteilungen des Instituts für österreichische Geschichtsforschung,* 76 (1968), p. 429.

[5]See the description of the Breslau faculty in Ernst Ludewig Rathlef, *Geschichte jetzlebender Gelehrten,* 3 vols. (Zelle, 1741), 2:502–504.

[6]On the Breslau curriculum at this time see Kundmann, *Die hohen und niederen Schulen Teutschenlandes,* pp. 181–182; and Hermann Hoffmann, "Zur Vorgeschichte der Breslauer Jesuiten-Universität," *Zeitschrift des Vereins für die Geschichte Schlesiens,* 68 (1934), p. 113.

[7]In 1741 the Prussians occupied Breslau and for a time used the main hall of the university as a hospital for their wounded. See R. Haass, *Die geistige Haltung der katholischen Universitäten Deutschlands im 18. Jahrhundert* (Freiburg im Breisgau, 1952), p. 152.

tural and intellectual *Weltanschauung*. Indeed, his later references to the University of Breslau were entirely derogatory. The faculty at Breslau was singularly undistinguished: Of the professors with whom Felbiger could have studied at the university, only the mathematician and astronomer Johann Lewald and the theologian Timothy Raisky are listed in eighteenth-century scholarly lexicons.[8] Writing some twenty-five years later, Felbiger condemned the "irrelevance" of the Jesuit curriculum, its failure to keep pace with new discoveries in the natural sciences, its neglect of the German language, and the plodding scholasticism of Jesuit professors. Learning at the Jesuit university, charged Felbiger, was not cumulative: What was learned in an earlier class was not elaborated and expanded in a later one. Each class formed a closed unit, and the student had no freedom to choose either his classes or professors. Felbiger criticized the professors for their lack of specialization, which resulted from the mobility of Jesuit professors within and between universities. The Jesuit professor was expected to teach everything, and he seldom taught a subject for more than a year at a time.[9] Felbiger's disparaging comments on the Jesuits were not atypical. These were stock criticisms circulated widely in anti-Jesuit circles of the period, and reflected growing dissatisfaction with a Jesuit curriculum that appeared increasingly rigid and arcane.[10]

The peculiar cultural and religious history of Silesia also helps explain why Felbiger, despite his education, never remained within the Jesuit orbit. Unlike most regions of the Habsburg monarchy, where Counter-Reformation policies helped create a relatively homogeneous elite culture,

---

[8]On Lewald see Duhr, *Geschichte der Jesuiten*, 4 (pt. 1):425. Lewald and Raisky were the only Breslau faculty listed in Johann Georg Meusel, *Lexikon der vom Jahr 1750 bis 1800 verstorbenen teutschen Schriftsteller* (Leipzig, 1802); or Christian Gottlieb Jocher, *Algemeines Gelehrten-Lexikon* (Leipzig, 1751). Raisky subsequently left Breslau to become rector at the University of Prague. In 1760 he came into conflict with Cardinal Migazzi and the Commission for Education over his opposition to the appointment of Dominicans and Augustinians to the theological faculty. *HHStA:* Alte Kabinettsakten, Studiensachen, Kart. 1, fol. 457.

[9]For Felbiger's critique of Jesuit education see his 1769 memorandum published in Lehmann, *Preussen und die katholische Kirche*, 4:350–353. See also his letter from 1772 to his fellow Augustinian Franz Töpsl in Bavaria, published in Richard van Dülmen, "Die Prälaten Franz Töpsl aus Polling und Johann Ignaz von Felbiger aus Sagan. Zwei Repräsentanten der katholischen Aufklärung," *Zeitschrift für bayerische Landesgeschichte*, 30 (1967), p. 805.

[10]On the growing opposition to Jesuit educational methods in the Habsburg monarchy see Grete Klingenstein, "Bildungskrise. Gymnasium und Universitäten im Spannungsfeld theresianischer Aufklärung," in Walther Koschatzky, ed., *Maria Theresia und ihre Zeit* (Salzburg, 1979).

Silesia was able to preserve a remarkable degree of cultural and religious pluralism. Political vicissitudes in part explain Silesia's anomalous position. During the sixteenth century, 90 percent of Silesia's population had embraced Luther's doctrines. Like their confessional brethren in Bohemia, Silesian Protestants were able to obtain from Rudolf II a letter of majesty that guaranteed their freedom of worship; unlike the Bohemians, however, Silesian Protestants never openly revolted against the Habsburg monarchy. Their political loyalty paid dividends, for Ferdinand II never waged the strong Catholicization campaign in Silesia that he pursued in Bohemia. Silesia's Protestants were also aided by Johann Georg, the Saxon elector, who in 1621 won a guarantee from the emperor that Silesian Lutherans would continue to enjoy freedom of worship. Silesian Protestantism suffered a setback under Leopold I (1658–1705), who exiled thousands of Protestants and vigorously promoted the Catholicization of the province.[11] Through the Convention of Altranstadt (1709), however, Silesian Protestants once again won a reprieve. Confronted by Swedes in the north, rebellious Hungarians in the south, the French in the west, and Turks in the East, the Emperor Joseph I was forced to grant Silesian Protestants limited toleration.[12] As a consequence, the Pietist movement spread rapidly in Silesia during the following decades.[13] After Frederick II seized the province in 1740, Protestants gained complete freedom of worship. By this time, almost 50 percent of the population was Protestant.[14]

Further contributing to Silesia's cultural and religious diversity was its geographic position. Silesia was an entrepôt linking northern and southern Germany as well as eastern and western Europe. As Herbert Schöffler argued, Silesia's role as a cultural mediator also rested on the fact that the province did not have a university before the eighteenth century.[15] Until the Habsburgs threw caution to the wind and began pursuing a vigorous

[11]On Silesia during the Reformation and Counter-Reformation see Ludwig Petrÿ and Joachim Menzel, *Geschichte Schlesiens*, 2 vols. (Darmstadt, 1973), 1:1–135; and Joachim Köhler, *Das Ringen um die tridentinischen Erneuerung im Bistum Breslau* (Cologne, 1973), pp. 55–201.

[12]The treaty returned 125 churches to the Lutherans and allowed them to build additional churches in specified areas. See Norbert Conrads, *Die Durchführung der Altranstädter Konvention in Schlesien, 1707–1709* (Cologne, 1971), p. 125.

[13]See the anti-Pietist edicts from the 1720s published in *Silesia Diplomatica. Oder Verzeichnis deren gedruckten schlesischen Diplomatum, Privilegiorum, und Landesgesetze*, ed. Anton Balthasar Walther, 2 vols. (Breslau, 1741–42), 1:59–61.

[14]Colmar Grünhagen, *Schlesien unter Friedrich dem Grossen*, 2 vols. (Breslau, 1890–92), 1:32.

[15]Herbert Schöffler, *Deutsches Geistesleben zwischen Reformation und Aufklärung. Von Martin Opitz zu Christian Wolff*, 2d ed. (Frankfurt am Main, 1956).

Catholicization policy in the late seventeenth century, neither Catholics nor Protestants in Silesia were inclined to upset the religious status quo by establishing a university. Thus, Silesians who wanted to attend a university had to go abroad. They studied medicine at Leyden or Padua, law at Bologna, Protestant theology at Wittenberg or Leipzig, and Catholic theology at Vienna or Prague. As a result of this intellectual migration, Silesia became a mediator between widely disparate cultures. Italian, Dutch, and German humanism, Dutch Calvinism, Melanchthonian Lutheranism, Böhmean mysticism, Pietism, the Italian and Austrian baroque, Leyden Cartesianism and physiology – all of these cultural currents met in Silesia. Hence it is not surprising that the three leading writers of the German baroque – Martin Opitz, Andreas Gryphius, and Angelius Silesius – were all Silesians. Opitz, Gryphius, and Silesius epitomized the cultural pluralism of their native province. Opitz, poet and reformer of the German language, pursued a scholarly career that took him from Breslau to Heidelberg, Leyden, Transylvania, Paris, and Danzig. Although Gryphius attended the Calvinist University of Leyden, he incorporated elements of the Jesuit school drama into his allegorical plays. The confessional vacillations of the melancholy Angelius Silesius – who began his life as a Lutheran, came heavily under the influence of Böhmean mysticism, and finally lived out his days as an orthodox Catholic – symbolize Silesian cultural diversity.[16]

In a province with a long tradition of cultural syncretism, Felbiger would be exposed to an array of religious, intellectual, and scientific currents not found in most Catholic territories. Although Jesuits dominated the University of Breslau, they were by no means the main cultural force in Silesia. Protestants, once grudgingly tolerated on a limited basis by the Habsburgs, now enjoyed complete freedom of worship under a Prussian king. Silesia was a province in which the Catholic south met the Protestant north; it was a territory in which one could visit a bookseller and purchase a Jesuit edition of Aristotle's *Physics,* a volume of Christian Wolff's *Natural Theology,* a Catholic devotional guide, or a Pietist chapbook. It was no accident, then, that the pedagogical union of Prussian Pietism and reform Catholicism epitomized by Felbiger was consummated in Silesia.

When Felbiger completed his studies in 1744, his career choices were

---

[16]On Opitz, Gryphius, and Silesius as examples of Silesian cultural syncretism, see Petrÿ and Menzel, *Geschichte Schlesiens,* 2:181–229; and Schöffler, *Deutsches Geistesleben,* pp. 81–84.

limited. His deceased parents had left him no inheritance, and his Jesuit education had prepared him for little outside a career in the church. Like many university graduates with no immediate career prospects, Felbiger took a position as a private tutor. His charges were the children of a Von Langenickel, an estate steward on the domains of the bishop of Breslau in Preichau (Lower Silesia).[17]

In 1746, two years after leaving the university, Felbiger decided to resign his tutorial post and embark on a monastic career. Indicative of Felbiger's disenchantment with the Jesuits was his decision to join the Augustinian Order. Not only did the Jesuits and the Augustinians have their theological differences, but they were also bitter rivals for influence within the Catholic church. The Augustinians envied the privileged position attained by the Jesuits and resented their virtual monopoly on secondary and university education. Hence it is no accident that many of the leaders of reform Catholicism in Central Europe – among them, Felbiger, Franz Töpsl in Bavaria, and Ignaz Müller in Vienna—were Augustinians.[18]

In 1746 Felbiger entered the Augustinian cloister in Sagan, a town of roughly 2,800 inhabitants on the Saxon border of Lower Silesia.[19] Felbiger completed his novitiate in two years and became one of the thirty monks living in the monastery. Here he devoted his spare time to studying the church fathers, Roman classics, meteorology, and mathematics. He also claimed to have become an avid reader of French religious literature at this time, although he never mentioned specific writers. The literature was quite possibly Jansenist in tone, which would have reinforced Felbiger's anti-Jesuit, reform Catholic sensibilities. Whatever the

---

[17]Panholzer, *Felbigers Methodenbuch*, p. 3.

[18]On Töpsl see Dülmen, "Die Prälaten"; Müller: Ferdinand Miksch, "Der Augustinerorden und die Wiener Universität," *Augustiniana*, 16 (1966). On the role of Augustinians in the rise of reform Catholicism see also Hersche, *Spätjansenismus*, pp. 103–108.

[19]Population figures taken from Friedrich Albert Zimmermann, *Beyträge zur Beschreibung von Schlesien*, 13 vols. (Brieg, 1783–96), 7:77. A duchy before its annexation by Prussia in 1740, Sagan had once been a part of the vast domains belonging to Wallenstein, the great condottiere of the Thirty Years War. Wallenstein had planned a university for Sagan before his assassination, and his astrologer Johannes Kepler spent the last years of his life there writing the second part of his *Ephemeriden*. See Johann Gottlob von Worbs, *Geschichte des Herzogthums Sagan* (Weimar, 1795), pp. 327–348. The Augustinian cloister in Sagan had a stormy history. Beginning in the early sixteenth century, when the Wittenberg-educated abbot of the cloister sold its silver and gold and reformed the mass, the cloister had been an object of contention between Lutherans and Catholics. During the course of the seventeenth century, Catholicism gained ground in Sagan, with the Jesuits founding a college in 1629. From this time on the existence of the Augustinian cloister was secured.

case, Felbiger rapidly distinguished himself as a studious and conscientious monk. When the health of the aging Abbot Gottfried Ignaz Kanur began to deteriorate in 1758, Felbiger was appointed his secretary. In effect, administration of the cloister now lay in Felbiger's hands, and when the abbot died at the end of 1758, Felbiger was a leading candidate to succeed him.[20]

However, Frederick II, not the Augustinian fathers, had the final say over who was to be abbot. To win Silesia from the Austrians, Frederick had fought two wars with a Catholic ruler and was now in the midst of a third. He had never trusted the Silesian Catholic clergy, and his discovery in 1757 that the bishop of Breslau, Philipp Gotthard von Schaffgotsch, was an Austrian agent did little to ease his suspicions.[21] Hence Frederick was not about to leave appointments to higher ecclesiastical positions completely in clerical hands. Although he allowed the Augustinians in Sagan to nominate three candidates for the vacant abbacy, he reserved for himself the final choice among the three.[22] Felbiger, who had been placed in charge of administering the cloister after the Abbot Kanur's death, was one of the three candidates. Frederick ordered Ernst Wilhelm von Schlabrendorff, the head of the Prussian administration in Silesia, to investigate the qualifications and loyalty of each. A month later Schlabrendorff wrote to Frederick and recommended Felbiger for the position. In September 1758, at the age of thirty-four, Felbiger became abbot of the Augustinian cloister.[23]

As abbot, Felbiger devoted much of his time to his scientific interests. After entering the monastery, he had begun to read widely in the fields of astronomy and meteorology. Although science was little more than a hobby for Felbiger, he subsequently acquired a modest scientific reputation for his treatises on the aurora borealis, trigonometry, and electricity.[24] The breadth of Felbiger's scientific interests is seen in his 1770–74 correspondence with Johann Heinrich Lambert, the Berlin mathematician and astronomer. Here Felbiger showed a familiarity with Kepler's

---

[20]Volkmer, *Felbiger*, p. 5.
[21]Frederick's strained relations with his Catholic subjects in Silesia are discussed in Chapter 7, "The Origins of Catholic School Reform."
[22]Lehmann, *Preussen und die katholische Kirche*, 3:580.
[23]Volkmer, *Felbiger*, p. 6.
[24]Felbiger, *Vorschläge, wie Nordlichter zu beobachten* (Sagan, 1771); *Versuch, die Höhe des Riesengebirges zu bestimmen* (Breslau, 1769); *Die Kunst, Thürme oder andere Gebäude vor den schädlichen Wirkungen des Blitzes durch Ableitungen zu bewahren* (Breslau, 1771). The latter work was based on Benjamin Franklin's treatise published in the *Transactions of the American Philosophical Society* in Philadelphia.

astronomy, Boscowitz's physics, Franklin's electrical experiments, and Euler's mathematics.[25] The need to improve the economic state of the cloister, which had suffered severe damage during the Seven Years War, also led Felbiger into the field of agronomy. He introduced flax cultivation on monastic lands and wrote a treatise on soil types that went through two editions.[26] Felbiger's efforts on behalf of agriculture later led to his appointment as director of the Silesian Economic-Patriotic Society.[27]

The reform of Sagan parish schools

Felbiger's duties as abbot extended beyond the cloister. He was charged with supervising not only the personnel and property of the cloister, but also six parish churches in the surrounding countryside. Felbiger periodically dispatched his prior, Benedict Strauch, to ensure that services and festivals were properly observed, church property was maintained, and parish youth were educated in the faith.

In 1761 Strauch, a close friend and former classmate of Felbiger, submitted a report to him on the condition of those parish churches lying within the monastery's jurisdiction.[28] Strauch singled out parish education as the area most in need of improvement and was particularly disturbed by poor school attendance. Felbiger, who was preoccupied with cloister finances, simply instructed parish schoolmasters to perform their teaching duties more diligently. After conducting a closer investigation several months later, Strauch became even more alarmed. He discovered that parish school attendance was low because Catholic parents were sending their children to neighboring Lutheran schools.[29]

The Sagan region was overwhelmingly Protestant. In the town itself, 850 Protestants and 133 Catholics enjoyed the right of citizenship in 1758.[30] Thus it is not surprising that Catholic families were sending their

[25]Johann Bernoulli, ed., *Johann Heinrich Lamberts deutscher gelehrten Briefwechsel*, 4 vols. (Berlin, 1781–84).

[26]Kromer, *Felbiger*, p. 16; Felbiger, *Erkenntnis und Anwendung der verschiedenen Erdarten zur Verbesserung des Ackerbaues*, 1st ed. (Leipzig, 1770); 2d ed. (Sorau, 1772).

[27]This society was created in 1763 through the initiative of Johann Heinrich Casimir von Carmer, then a Prussian judicial official in Breslau. Its charter is published in Johann Heinrich Ludwig Bergius, ed., *Sammlung auserlesener teutschen Landesgesetze welche das Policey- und Cameralwesen zum Gegenstand haben*, 7 vols. (Frankfurt am Main, 1780–85), 2:364–367.

[28]Felbiger, "Ausführliche Nachricht," p. 429. On Strauch see Carl Conrad Streit, *Alphabetisches Verzeichnis aller 1774 in Schlesien lebenden Schriftsteller* (Breslau, 1776), pp. 131–132.

[29]Felbiger, "Ausführliche Nachricht," pp. 429–430.

[30]Gottfried Münch, "Jugend und Aufstieg Anton Michael Zeplichals. Ein Beitrag zur Geschichte der schlesischen Jesuitenprovinz im 18. Jahrhundert," in Bernard Stasiewski, ed., *Beiträge zur schlesischen Kirchengeschichte* (Cologne, 1969), p. 392.

children to Protestant schools, since Protestants doubtless had more of them. The apparent disarray of Catholic education noted by Strauch may also have stemmed from the financial crisis afflicting Catholic parishes in Silesia at this time. Up until the Seven Years War, Frederick II had scrupulously observed the religious clauses of the Treaty of Berlin (1742). This treaty, while granting full religious toleration, still required Silesian Protestants to pay the Catholic tithe (*taxa stola*). However, when the Schaffgotsch scandal of 1757 confirmed Frederick's suspicion of wide-spread Catholic disloyalty, he retaliated by exempting districts with Protestant majorities from all Catholic tithes.[31] This exemption was a serious financial blow to Catholic parish churches and schools like those under Felbiger's jurisdiction, which were located in predominantly Protestant areas.

Yet there was another reason why Felbiger's parish schools were so poorly attended. Felbiger, deeply disturbed by the fact that Catholic children were attending Protestant schools, summoned several par-ishioners to the cloister and demanded an explanation. They replied, somewhat sheepishly, that although they had tried sending their children to Catholic schools, they withdrew them when they found their children were not learning to read and write. Lutheran schoolmasters were better trained, they assured Felbiger, and taught reading and writing to their children. Felbiger investigated further, visiting a Protestant bookseller in Sagan to learn which teaching manuals Protestant schoolmasters were using. The bookseller lifted two Pietist pamphlets from his shelves: a teaching manual written by Hecker for use in his Berlin schools, and a report by Johann Arnold Zwicke on the reform of parish schools in Braunschweig-Wolffenbüttel.[32] Zwicke, like Hecker, was a graduate of Francke's teaching institute in Halle. In 1750, Duke Karl I had appointed him to supervise the reform of parish schools in the town of Braun-schweig. His subsequent account of the reform was widely circulated in German pedagogical circles.[33]

One is tempted to conclude on the basis of the above incident that Lutheran parish schools had taken the lead over their Catholic counter-

[31]Hanus, *Church and State in Silesia*, p. 559.
[32]Felbiger, "Ausführliche Nachricht," p. 430.
[33]I have not been able to locate Hecker's manual, entitled *Des Berlinischen neu eingerichteten Schulbuches 3. Teil, welcher die Lehrart, wornach die im 1. und 2. Teil befindlichen Sachen der Jugend beizubringen sind, enthält* (Berlin, 1758). Zwicke's report, "Vorläufige Nachricht von jetziger Einrichtung der kleiner Schulen in der Stadt Braun-schweig," has been republished in Friedrich Koldeway, ed., *Schulordnungen des Herzogthums Braunschweig vom Jahre 1248–1826* (Berlin, 1890), pp. 259–268.

parts in the promotion of literacy. Although this may well have been the case, far more evidence is needed to substantiate such a sweeping claim. Moreover, variables other than religion determined the extent to which literacy was promoted in a particular locale. In western Germany along the Middle Rhine, for example, the high literacy rates that prevailed among Protestants and Catholics alike were clearly a product of the region's relatively urbanized character.[34] In the Sagan region, as mentioned above, the alleged superiority of Lutheran over Catholic schooling may well have resulted from Protestant preponderance in the area.

These qualifications aside, the incident does illustrate the extent to which Pietist pedagogical writings were being diffused by the middle of the eighteenth century. Pietist educational writings were no longer confined to a pedagogical elite, but had begun to trickle down to the level of the parish schoolmaster; and at least from the standpoint of parents in Felbiger's parishes, the effect of these writings had been salutary.

After studying the manuals of Hecker and Zwicke, Felbiger resolved to visit Hecker in Berlin to observe "whether the impressive principles of his book are actually followed." In the meantime he called another meeting with Catholic parish schoolmasters in November 1761, and circulated excerpts from Hecker's textbook. Felbiger spoke enthusiastically of Hecker's methods and warned that poor school attendance would continue until Catholic schoolmasters had mastered Pietist educational methods.[35]

In May of 1762, with the Seven Years War still in progress, Felbiger journeyed to Berlin. It was highly irregular for a Catholic abbot to visit a Protestant school in Protestant Berlin, and Felbiger's flirtation with Pietist pedagogy had already aroused the suspicion of the Jesuits in Sagan. To avoid a scandal, Felbiger traveled to Berlin under an assumed name in the guise of a Silesian nobleman.[36] After his arrival in Berlin, Felbiger spent the next month visiting with Hecker, observing classes, and studying Pietist educational writings. Since parish education was his main concern, Felbiger spent most of his time in Hecker's schools for the poor. There he saw pupils divided according to ability and receiving instruction collectively. Felbiger was particularly impressed by the discipline and order he

[34]See Etienne François, "Die Volksbildung am Mittelrhein im ausgehenden 18. Jahrhundert. Eine Untersuchung über den vermeintlichen 'Bildungsrückstand' der katholischen Bevölkerung Deutschlands im Ancien Régime," *Jahrbuch für westdeutsche Landesgeschichte*, 3 (1977).
[35]Felbiger, "Anrede an die saganischen Schulbediente," in *K.S.*, pp. 275–279.
[36]Felbiger, "Ausführliche Nachricht," pp. 432–433.

found and also by Hähn's tabular-literal method, the mnemonic device that organized each lesson into outline form. Felbiger paid a personal visit to Hähn in Kloster Berg, where Hähn had become director of the noted *Gymnasium* and teaching institute. The abbot was particularly attracted to the method as a tool for teaching the catechism.[37]

Felbiger spent the rest of his Prussian visit in Hecker's teaching institute. He now realized that if he was to reform his parish schools in Sagan, he would need a core of trained teachers. Upon returning to Sagan in July of 1762, Felbiger dispatched to Berlin two young acquaintances, Anton Wende and Johann Coccius, who were to spend a year at Hecker's institute. Still fearful of arousing Catholic distrust, Felbiger kept their journey a secret. He had deliberately chosen Wende and Coccius, neither of whom lived in Sagan, so that no one in the town would learn of his Berlin connections.[38] When Wende and Coccius returned to Sagan in June of 1763, Felbiger apprenticed them as schoolmasters in a local parish school to observe whether they had mastered the essentials of Hecker's pedagogy.

Fully satisfied with their performance, Felbiger now began reforming the parish schools under his jurisdiction. He started with the *Stadtschule* in Sagan, which was a combination of parish and Latin school. Since Felbiger, as abbot, possessed the right of patronage over the *Stadtschule*, he had the authority to hire or dismiss its personnel. Accordingly, he called a meeting with the rector and co-rector of the school and announced – doubtless to the surprise of both – their retirement with pension. He appointed Wende and Coccius as their replacements and named Joseph Sucher, who had accompanied Felbiger to Berlin and was the former catechism instructor at the *Stadtschule,* chief inspector of the school.[39] On the same day he issued a circular publicizing these changes and describing in detail his projected reform.[40]

Felbiger's circular sought to disarm those Catholics who might have objected to his adoption of Pietist methods: "We remind those individuals that in the most pristine days of the Church . . . Christians did not hesitate to visit the schools of the heathen. We ask them to remember that Basil the Great, John Chrysostom and Gregory of Nazianzus ac-

[37]Ibid., 433–434.
[38]Ibid., pp. 434–436.
[39]Felbiger, "Anrede an die neuen Schulbedienten," pp. 279–288.
[40]Felbiger, "Vorläufige Anzeige von besserer Einrichtung der öffentlichen Trivialschulen," in *K.S.,* pp. 16–32.

quired much of their learning from heathen schools."[41] Felbiger then
described the subjects to be taught in the beginning classes (reading,
writing, and the catechism), the method of instruction (children were
now to be taught as a group rather than individually), and the general
aims of his reforms. Felbiger's debt to Pietist pedagogy is clear from his
stated goals: to educate not only good Catholics, but also loyal subjects
and useful members of society; not only "creatures of God, instruments
of His holy will, and good members of the Church," but also "honest
subjects of their ruler, useful members of the state . . . and vessels of
earthly happiness."[42] Felbiger had earlier admonished his teachers to
help create "good Christians, upright servants of the common good, and
useful members of society."[43] These were sentiments inspired not by the
baroque popular piety of the south, but the moral utilitarianism of the
north.

Pietist echoes could also be heard in Felbiger's insistence that the
training of the child's memory was only the first step in the training of his
faculties. To ensure that children acted in accordance with what they had
learned, it was also necessary to develop their faculties of understanding,
judgment, and will. "Not only should the schoolmaster train the memory
of his pupils, as has been emphasized in the past, but also their faculties
of understanding and judgment. Above all, he should cultivate in his
pupils the will to act in accordance with these faculties, so that they will
be of practical value in daily life."[44] Moral and religious principles had
to penetrate deep enough so that children, independently exercising their
reason and judgment, would learn to act in accordance with these
principles.

Like Hecker, Felbiger divided pupils into two classes, one for begin-
ners and the other for the more advanced. Exams were held twice a year
to determine which pupils were ready to advance from the lower to the
higher class. Once pupils had been grouped according to their ability,
they were taught as a group. Under this system, of course, no more than
one class could be taught in a classroom during a given period. Up to
then, it had been customary in the larger schools for several teachers to
instruct their pupils in the same classroom at the same time. Thomas
Platter, the sixteenth-century Swiss humanist, had attended a Breslau

[41]Ibid., pp. 28–29.
[42]Ibid., p. 17.
[43]Felbiger, "Anrede an die neuen Schulbedienten," p. 284.
[44]Felbiger, "Vorläufige Anzeige," p. 22.

school in which nine schoolmasters gave their lessons at the same hour in the same classroom.[45] In the early eighteenth century, three teachers in a parish school in Wiener Neustadt held their classes simultaneously in a room with six benches and three tables.[46] Hecker and Felbiger broke with this practice by placing the beginning and advanced classes in separate buildings.

Not surprisingly, Felbiger's school placed heavy emphasis on religious instruction. The school day began with attendance at mass, and instruction in the catechism was an important part of the curriculum. Yet Felbiger believed that the catechism alone was not sufficient for the child's religious training. He especially favored the teaching of biblical history as a way of instilling principles of Christian piety and morality. Felbiger's historical methodology was pragmatic: The religious instructor was to use events and individuals from biblical times to illustrate good and evil actions.

Felbiger's reorganization of the Sagan *Stadtschule* established a model for the reform of his parish schools. In November 1763, Felbiger extended his reform to parish schools in the villages of Briessnitz, Klopscher, Quilitz, Schönbrun, Gräffenheyn, and Kalckreut. Attendance was now compulsory for all boys and girls in these parishes between the ages of six and thirteen. To ensure that all pupils were attending, schoolmasters took roll on the basis of parish baptismal records. The parish priest was assigned the weekly task of observing the schoolmaster and visiting parents of truant children. Since peasant parents needed their children in the summer and early fall to help with farmwork, school was held only a half-day during peak agricultural periods. Benedict Strauch, whom Felbiger had appointed as catechism instructor, traveled from village to village, giving catechism lessons twice a week to each school. After each Sunday Mass, pupils appeared before the parish priest to recite what they had learned.[47]

Each schoolmaster also compiled a "diligence catalogue" *(Fleisskatalog)* rating the effort and performance of each pupil. Felbiger ordered his parish schoolmasters never to allow a moment's idleness during class time. Group instruction was designed to achieve this goal by de-

---

[45]Ariès, *Centuries of Childhood*, p. 185.

[46]Strakosch-Grassmann, *Geschichte des österreichischen Unterrichtswesens*, p. 78.

[47]Felbiger, "Ausführliche Nachricht," pp. 436–437; "Verordnung nach welcher die Schulen der zum Saganischen Stifte gehörigen Dörfer eingerichtet und verbessert werden sollen," in *K.S.*, pp. 32–54.

manding the full attention and participation of each pupil. As Felbiger explained, "each child can at any time be called upon to answer a question."[48] Felbiger sent the schools hourglasses with which they could mark the beginning and end of each class period. This helped foster a consciousness of time as an object to be used with the utmost economy and efficiency. Class time, and thus work time, was concretely defined as a period in which a task was begun, pursued without interruption, and completed.

Felbiger's parish school reform also took steps to alleviate the economic distress of the village schoolmaster. It required the parents of pupils to pay a fixed tuition fee, which along with a garden plot provided by the parish, was to guarantee the schoolmaster's subsistence and obviate any need for an outside job. Parents were also asked to help heat the schoolroom during the winter by sending each child to school with an armful of wood every Monday. Felbiger had noted that schoolmasters tended to neglect their teaching during the summer to work in their gardens. Knowing how crucial the garden plot was to the schoolmaster's subsistence, Felbiger canceled school during July to allow the schoolmaster to work in his garden.

Felbiger's new program was a success and established his reputation as an educational reformer. His reform represented a compromise between the ambitious aims of Pietist schooling and the realities of rural society. On the one hand, Felbiger attempted to promote Pietist virtues like hard work, obedience, and inner piety. On the other hand, he was forced to accept the limitations imposed by local conditions. When group instruction was introduced, for example, beginning and advanced pupils still had to share the same room because additional classroom space was not available.[49] Discipline was difficult to maintain with one group waiting while the other received instruction. As noted earlier, Felbiger also had to adapt his reform to the seasonal rhythm of rural labor and the subsistence needs of the schoolmaster. This compromise with local realities presaged the tension that was to mark his subsequent efforts on behalf of compulsory schooling. Given the limited administrative and financial resources that states had at their disposal, local conditions invariably diluted any ambitious effort at reform. If this was the case in six Silesian parishes, it was to be all the more true for entire provinces.

[48]Ibid., p. 42.
[49]Ibid., pp. 42–43.

As a result of his encounter with Pietism, Felbiger's fundamental pedagogical goals and methods had already taken shape by 1763. Silesia's anomalous cultural and religious history in part explains Felbiger's adoption of Pietist pedagogy, but to fully understand how a Catholic abbot could have "gone to the schools of the heathen," one must also consider the political, cultural, and psychological state of the Catholic church in Central Europe around the middle of the eighteenth century. The year 1740 had not only brought two dynamic monarchs, Frederick II of Prussia and Maria Theresa of Austria, to power; it had also seen the accession of a reform pope, Benedict XIV. Between the time Felbiger entered the University of Breslau up until his appointment as abbot, a pope ruled who removed Galileo's *Dialogue* from the papal *Index,* knew and corresponded with Voltaire and Muratori, and abolished a large number of religious holidays.

Even more significant was the sense of crisis pervading the Catholic church at this time. The defeat suffered by the Catholic Habsburgs at the hands of the Protestant Hohenzollerns in the Silesian wars helped foster a deep sense of political inadequacy among Catholic rulers. Similarly, many Catholic scholars could not escape a sense of shame that the two most distinguished universities in the Empire, Göttingen and Halle, were Protestant institutions. Catholic rulers, prelates, and scholars began to suspect that the Catholic territories of the empire were lagging far behind their Protestant counterparts. Catholic uneasiness, fueled by complaints about widespread irreligion, immorality, and crypto-Protestantism, bred doubts about the efficacy of traditional pastoral practice.

This sense of crisis within the Catholic church helps explain why a Catholic like Felbiger could adopt Protestant educational ideas, not to mention work closely with a Protestant ruler to carry them out. By the 1770s, Catholic rulers and prelates throughout the empire had come to view the reform of parish schooling as an urgent necessity. Major reforms of popular schooling were subsequently introduced not only in Austria, but also in smaller Catholic territories like Bavaria, Mainz, and Bamberg-Würzburg. These reforms were based to a large degree on the synthesis of reform Catholicism and Pietism forged by Felbiger, the foremost Catholic pedagogue in eighteenth-century Central Europe.

Part II

Social and economic forces

Mastering the masterless: cameralism, rural industry, and popular education

The reason for the shortage of labor lies not in inadequate wages, but the laziness of the people.

Joachim Georg Darjes, 1768

Pupils must learn to earn their livelihood. If a plot of land is too small to support a family, children must be able to supplement the family income in other ways.

Ferdinand Kindermann, 1775

Although in many respects innovative, the educational reform movement in eighteenth-century Prussia and Austria hearkened back to older traditions. Both Pietism and reform Catholicism, the religious mainstays of this movement, marked the culmination of the Protestant and Catholic reformations of the sixteenth century. Their pastoral and pedagogical methods were different, but Pietists and reform Catholics alike were dedicated to completing the work begun by early Lutheran and Tridentine reformers. Thus they stressed the importance of popular schooling as an instrument of spiritual, moral, and social renewal, and worked to devise more effective methods of indoctrinating the laity.[1]

By the same token, the Prussian and Austrian rulers who promoted the pedagogical aims of Pietism and reform Catholicism often used language more redolent of sixteenth-century "confessional absolutism" than eighteenth-century "enlightened despotism." Hajo Holborn's reminder that Frederick William I "resembled more the Lutheran princes of the sixteenth century than his crowned cousins of the eighteenth" applies in particular to his educational policies.[2] The confessional concerns that

---

[1]Jean Delumeau, *Catholicism between Luther and Voltaire* (London, 1977); and Gawthrop and Strauss, "Protestantism and Literacy," stress the continuity between the reform movements of the sixteenth and eighteenth centuries.
[2]Hajo Holborn, *A History of Modern Germany 1648–1840* (New York, 1971), p. 192.

underlay his promotion of popular education place Frederick William
squarely in the patriarchal tradition of the Lutheran *Hausvater*. The
voice of the *Hausvater* is unmistakable in his famous remark, "Wenn ich
baue und bessere, und mache keine Christen, so hilft es mir nit" (What
do I gain if I build and reform, yet produce not one Christian?).[3]

This link with earlier absolutist traditions is even more striking in the
case of Maria Theresa. For all her innovative cultural and religious policies, her own religious *Weltanschauung* remained strongly rooted in the
Counter Reformation. Summing up the motives behind her promotion of
popular schooling, Ernst Wangermann aptly notes that "for all the vigorous applause which this drew from adherents of the Enlightenment, it
is perfectly clear that she was most concerned with arresting the decline
of Christian morality and Catholic orthodoxy which she believed to be
evident in her territories."[4] Indeed, it was a 1769 memorandum to the
empress from the prince bishop of Passau warning of growing heresy and
unbelief that sparked the empress to summon proposals for the reform of
parish schooling.[5]

Although the promotion of popular schooling in the eighteenth century continued to reflect traditional concerns, its focus had changed.
While still emphasizing the importance of schooling for religion, reformers drew more and more on economic arguments to justify the expansion
of popular education. Above all, they stressed that popular education
would help create and preserve a disciplined labor force. Their arguments
were rooted in a pronounced work ethic, one that aimed at eliminating
mendicancy, discouraging idleness, and fostering work discipline.

Cameralism and popular education

In part, this work ethic reflected the profound impact of Pietism. The
Pietist condemnation of idleness, its stress upon labor as an omnipresent
moral obligation, its acute awareness of time as the currency in which
this obligation was to be fulfilled – all profoundly influenced pedagogical
theory and practice in eighteenth-century Prussia and Austria. These
values were articulated not only by Pietists, but also by absolutist officials, many of whom were themselves the product of Pietist schooling.

---

[3]Quoted in Otto Hintze, *Die Hohenzollern und ihr Werk*, 2d ed. (Berlin, 1915), p. 305.
[4]Wangermann, *The Austrian Achievement*, p. 76.
[5]See Chapter 8, "The Creation of the Vienna Normal School."

Although the impact of Pietism on the Austrian bureaucracy was less direct, the growing tendency among prospective Habsburg officials to attend Protestant German universities opened the door to Pietist influences.[6] In Prussia, at least one or two semesters at Halle had become de rigeuer for most state servants. This helps explain how the Pietist work ethic became such an integral part of the Prussian bureaucratic ethos.

Ludwig Wilhelm Count von Münchow, minister of Prussian Silesia from 1741 to 1753, expressed his support of this work ethic when he exhorted his subordinates to "find real satisfaction in performing our daily tasks to the best of our ability, making sure that not a day – not even an hour – passes in which we have not served the king in some way."[7] When Friedrich Anton von Heynitz, the Prussian mining administrator, was assigned administrative responsibilities beyond an already onerous work load, he noted stoically in his journal:

It is the will of God that I be kept busy and I must therefore look upon this task as a service to God: to contribute to God's honor and to the true interests of my fellow men. In this I have the king as an example, for there are few like him. He is industrious, prefers duty to pleasure, gives priority to his responsibilities and has been endowed by God with the most superior gifts. There is nobody like him among his peers, nobody with his abstemiousness, his singlemindedness, his ability to occupy his time fruitfully.[8]

Frederick II, who received a Pietist upbringing on the orders of his father, wrote from his regiment in Rheinsberg while still crown prince: "Every day I become more economical with time. I begrudge its loss and hold myself accountable for its use."[9] Frederick's daily regimen reflected this Pietist submission to the rule of time: up at daybreak, at his desk until late afternoon with only a brief pause for a hurried midday meal, riding, reading, or writing in the evening, and then retiring regularly at ten o'clock.

But Pietism was not the only source of this bureaucratic work ethic. The emergence of cameralism as a science of politics also explains the

[6] On this tendency see Grete Klingenstein, *Der Aufstieg des Hauses Kaunitz: Studien zur Herkunft und Bildung des Staatskanzlers Wenzel Anton Kaunitz* (Göttingen, 1975), pp. 159–219.
[7] Quoted in Walther Hubatsch, *Frederick the Great: Absolutism and Administration* (London, 1973), p. 78.
[8] Ibid., p. 88.
[9] Ibid., p. 23. On Pietist influences in the early education of Frederick II see the recent biography by the late Theodor Schieder, *Friedrich der Grosse: ein Königtum der Widersprüche* (Frankfurt am Main, 1983), pp. 20–23.

preoccupation with labor in eighteenth-century school reform. Cameralism, like Pietism, had emerged in the decades following the Thirty Years War. Its stress on the need for state intervention in virtually every realm of social and economic life reflected the rise of territorial absolutism in Central Europe after 1648. By 1727, when Frederick William I established chairs of cameralism at Halle and Frankfurt an der Oder, cameralism had developed into a full-fledged theory of society and politics. Although cameralism was not formally institutionalized in the Habsburg monarchy until 1749, when Maria Theresa established a cameralistics chair at the *Collegium Theresianum,* cameralist doctrines had long enjoyed widespread currency in the bureaucracy through the writings of Johann Joachim Becher (1635–82) and Wilhelm von Schröder (1640–88).[10]

Cameralism closely resembled Pietism in its emphasis upon social action. Given the personal and institutional links between the two movements in their early stages, the similarity was not fortuitous. As noted earlier, one can find prototypes for both movements in the patriarchical absolutism of Ernst the Pious of Saxony Gotha. Seckendorff, who profoundly influenced eighteenth-century cameralist theory, had been a close ally of the Pietists, and both movements had grown to maturity under the institutional aegis of the University of Halle.

After the 1720s, it is true, cameralist social doctrine drew heavily on the moral utilitarianism of Christian Wolff. Wolff had taught at Halle from 1706 to 1723, when Pietist theologians forced his expulsion on charges of atheism. This incident, while customarily cited by historians as evidence of Pietist antipathy to the early German Enlightenment, can easily blind one to the important similarities between the two. In the first place, the conflict between Wolffians and Pietists ultimately gave way to efforts at a synthesis of the two positions by moderates in both camps. As Carl Hinrichs has argued, the resulting attempts to incorporate Pietist theology into Wolffian philosophy does much to explain why the German Enlightenment never acquired the overtly antireligious overtones that it did in France.[11] Moreover, the Pietists and Wolff were alike in their passionate belief in the importance of social action. Both stressed

---

[10]A brief but useful survey of cameralism is found in Erhard Dittrich, *Die deutschen und österreichischen Kameralisten* (Darmstadt, 1974). The older study by Luise Sommer, *Die österreichischen Kameralisten in dogmengeschichtlicher Entwicklung,* 2 vols. (Vienna, 1920), is particularly good on the intellectual origins of the movement. Mack Walker, *German Home Towns: Community, Estate, and General Estate, 1648–1871* (Ithaca, 1971), especially pp. 145–184, also provides a good analysis of cameralist doctrine.
[11]Hinrichs, *Preussentum und Pietismus,* p. 441.

the social duties of the individual, although they justified those duties on different grounds. For Pietists, service to society was a spiritual duty grounded in the individual's responsibility for assisting others in the attainment of salvation. Wolff's was a secularized social ethic, arising out of the reciprocal relationship between the individual's natural rights and duties. Wolff believed that individuals formed the state not only to protect themselves from foreign invasion and domestic disorder, but also to secure "whatever is required for life – that is, an abundance of the things which serve the necessities, the comforts, and the pleasures of life and an abundance of the means of felicity."[12] The sovereign was thus contractually obligated to promote the wealth and prosperity of society. The effect was to add to the ruler's obligations a host of welfare activities that now became legitimate objects of state regulation and action.

Rooted both in Pietist social activism and Wolffian interventionism, cameralism defined the individual and corporate components of society functionally, that is, in terms of their service to the whole.[13] Becher divided society into seven classes, each defined according to its social and economic contribution.[14] Justi defined even the most basic corporation, the family, in functional terms, insisting that "in all the affairs of the country, the attempt must be made to put the welfare of the separate families in the most accurate combination and interdependence with the collective best, or the happiness of the whole state."[15] This functional classification of social groups at the same time enabled the cameralists to legitimate their own social position. The cameralists were largely representatives of the bourgeois stratum of officials that had expanded with the rise of territorial absolutism. This stratum had no connection with older urban and bourgeois corporate groups, such as guild or mercantile associations, and thus constituted a foreign body within the traditional corporate order.[16] By defining a social group in terms of its contribution

---

[12]Christian Wolff, *Institutions du Droit de la Nature et des Gens* (Leyden, 1772, first Latin ed., 1750), 2:142, as quoted in Leonard Krieger, *The German Idea of Freedom* (Chicago, 1957), p. 68. Krieger presents an excellent analysis of Wolff's social and political thought.

[13]On the functionalist aspects of cameralism see Mack Walker, "Rights and Functions: The Social Categories of Eighteenth-Century German Jurists and Cameralists," *Journal of Modern History,* 50 (1978), pp. 234–251.

[14]Johann Joachim Becher, *Politische Diskurs,* 2d ed. (Frankfurt am Main, 1673), pp. 4–11.

[15]Johann Heinrich Gottlob von Justi, *Der Grundriss einer guten Regierung* (Frankfurt am Main, 1759), p. 51, as quoted in Leonard Krieger, *An Essay on the Theory of Enlightened Despotism* (Chicago, 1975), p. 60.

[16]This point is emphasized in Rudolf Vierhaus, "Deutschland im 18. Jahrhundert: soziales Gefüge, politische Verfassung, geistige Bewegung," in Franklin Kopitzsch, ed., *Aufklärung, Absolutismus, und Bürgertum in Deutschland* (Munich, 1976), p. 180.

to the whole, the cameralists thereby legitimated their own anomalous position as "servants of the common good."

The strong pedagogical undercurrent found in cameralism was a corollary of this mechanistic and functional definition of the social order. The cameralist social vision abhorred autonomy and had no place for those who failed to contribute to the social whole. Becher thus left no room for "idlers, thieves, murderers, rebels, and beggars, who stand outside of civil society" and "weaken society by performing no useful labor."[17] The purpose of schooling was to ensure that each subject developed into a productive member of society. Accordingly, cameralists since Seckendorff had viewed education as the responsibility of the state.[18] Becher organized the administration of the state into five departments, one of which was devoted entirely to public education.[19] Justi warned that if the state did not concern itself with the education of its subjects, they would grow up to become nothing but "beggars and good-for-nothings," "thistles and thorns in a garden, unwanted by all because they threaten those plants that are healthy."[20] Sonnenfels admitted that "the education of children is to be sure a parental duty." "But because education is so important to the common good," argued Sonnenfels, "the state cannot afford to leave it solely in the hands of the family." If parents neglected the education of their children, the state had the authority to remove them from parental supervision and place them in educational institutions controlled by the state.[21]

Although the state was responsible for educating its subjects, not everyone was to receive the same kind of education. Cameralists, like most absolutist reformers of the eighteenth century, insisted that education must be *standesmässig*, that is, compatible with the subject's role in the organization of production. In terms of the lower orders, this meant providing just enough schooling to inculcate obedience and diligence without encouraging further study. While the Prussian cameralist Jakob Friedrich Freiherr von Bielfeld favored compulsory primary schooling, he also argued that "the education of a child must conform with the occupation to which he is destined by birth. The education of the common

---

[17]Becher, *Politische Diskurs*, p. 310.
[18]See Seckendorff, *Christen-Stat*, pp. 227–230.
[19]Becher, *Politische Diskurs*, p. 55.
[20]Johann Heinrich Gottlob von Justi, *Politische und Finanzschriften über wichtige Gegenstände der Staatskunst, der Kriegswissenschaften, und des Cameral- und Finanzwesens*, 3 vols. (Copenhagen, 1761–64), 1:395.
[21]Joseph von Sonnenfels, *Sätze aus der Policey-, Handlungs-, und Finanzwissenschaft* (Vienna, 1765), p. 67.

people must instill a capacity for manual labor, simplicity in manners, docility in conduct, and acceptance of their existing social position."[22] Frederick II likewise admonished schoolmasters to be "especially careful that the common people remain attached to religion and do not steal or murder. . . . Otherwise, in the countryside it is enough if they learn a little reading and writing. If they learn more than this, they will flee to the cities and want to become clerks. In the countryside one must teach peasants what they need to know, but in such a manner that they will remain contentedly at their work."[23]

Thus, although cameralists (as well as most educational reformers) favored expanding primary schooling for the lower classes, they also insisted on curtailing plebeian access to secondary schools and universities. Their treatises were filled with dire warnings of a rising academic proletariat, of overeducated plebeians unfit for manual labor who would become parasitic on society. Already in 1713 Christian Thomasius, professor of law at Halle and a prominent figure in the German Enlightenment, complained that large numbers of plebeian university students deprived the state of laborers and were a corrupting influence on their more "upright and honest" colleagues.[24] Justi warned that if plebeian access to higher education were not limited, "The world will soon swarm with half-educated dilettantes, lawyers, and doctors . . . as well as candidates for the priesthood who spend their lives eking out a miserable existence as private tutors or teachers. Half of the scholars living today are utterly dispensable parasites."[25] Similarly, the Prussian cameralist Joachim Georg Darjes maintained that "while it is useful to establish more lower schools, it would be unwise to increase the number of universities."[26] Sonnenfels concurred, and proposed strict standards of university admission to stem the further growth of an academic proletariat.[27]

[22]Baron de Bielfeld, *Institutions politiques*, 2 vols. (The Hague, 1760), 1:36–37.
[23]Justus Bona-Meyer, ed., *Friedrichs des Grossen pädagogische Schriften und Abhandlungen* (Langensalza, 1885), p. 170.
[24]See Hans-Georg Herrlitz, *Studium als Standesprivileg. Die Entstehung des Maturitätsproblems im 18. Jahrhundert* (Frankfurt am Main, 1973), p. 36.
[25]Justi, *Politische und Finanzschriften*, 1:60.
[26]Joachim Georg Darjes, *Erste Gründe der Kameralwissenschaft*, 2d ed. (Leipzig, 1768), p. 398.
[27]Sonnenfels's proposals are examined in Grete Klingenstein, "Akademikerüberschuss als soziales Problem im aufgeklärten Absolutismus. Bemerkungen über eine Rede Joseph von Sonnenfels aus dem Jahre 1771," in *Bildung, Politik, und Gesellschaft. Studien zur Geschichte des europäischen Bildungswesens vom 16. bis zum 20. Jahrhundert* (Vienna, 1978). In France, *philosophes* such as Voltaire, Diderot, and Montesquieu advanced similar arguments in favor of limiting plebeian educational advancement. See Payne, *The Philosophes and the People*; and Chisick, *The Limits of Reform*. On the general trend

Available statistics on university enrollments in eighteenth-century
Central Europe suggest that cameralist fears were greatly exaggerated.
Indeed, matriculation at German universities actually declined in the
eighteenth century: In 1700 approximately 9,000 students were attending the twenty-eight universities then existing in Germany, but by the
1760s this number had fallen to 7,000. By the end of the eighteenth
century, university enrollments had dropped to some 6,000 students.[28]
This decline is all the more striking given the demographic expansion of
Central Europe during the eighteenth century. Relative to the Central
European population, the percentage of students at German universities
actually fell by two-thirds.[29]

Hence the almost hysterical invocation of an academic proletariat that
characterized cameralist writings did not mirror existing conditions. It
instead reflected the culmination of efforts, originating in the early eighteenth century, designed to transform secondary schools and universities
into more socially exclusive institutions. Central European universities
had always provided a haven for poor students. Figures from the fifteenth and sixteenth centuries, for example, show that the number of
students who matriculated as *pauperes* constituted 15–25 percent of
university enrollments.[30] In the spirit of medieval *caritas,* poorer students
generally paid no matriculation fee, while many of those too poor to
afford food and lodging were accommodated in inexpensive housing and
student soup kitchens (the so-called *Freitische*). Moreover, the renewed
emphasis on education that arose out of the Protestant and Catholic
Reformations had increased the number of stipends endowed by territorial rulers, ecclesiastical corporations, and individual donors. Then,
as now, university study offered an avenue of social mobility to poor but
ambitious students. In particular, a degree in theology, which held the
promise of a post as a Protestant or Catholic clergyman, offered the hope
of social advancement for lower-class students.[31] University study could

toward educational exclusivity in the eighteenth century, see Ariès, *Centuries of Childhood,* pp. 309–314.
[28]Charles E. McClelland, *State, Society, and University in Germany, 1700–1914*
(Cambridge, 1980), p. 28.
[29]Willem Frijhoff, "Surplus ou déficit? Hypotheses sur le nombre réel des étudiants en
Allemagne a l'époque moderne," *Francia,* 7 (1979), pp. 212–213.
[30]James H. Oberfeld, "Nobles and Paupers at German Universities to 1600," *Societas,* 4
(1974), pp. 200–201; Friedrich Schulze, *Das deutsche Studententum von den ältesten
Zeiten bis zur Gegenwart* (Munich, 1932), pp. 65–66.
[31]On the study of theology as an avenue of social mobility in eighteenth-century Germany
see Hans Gerth, *Bürgerliche Intelligenz um 1800. Zur Soziologie des deutschen
Frühliberalismus* (Göttingen, 1976), pp. 31–60.

bring other rewards as well. Even in a militaristic state like Prussia, university students were exempted from military service. In other instances, university study brought a release from seigniorial obligations. A Silesian peasant who obtained a degree in theology automatically gained his freedom, while his Bohemian counterpart needed only to graduate from a Jesuit *Gymnasium*.[32]

By the early eighteenth century, however, Prussian and Austrian rulers had begun to take steps to exclude poorer students from the university. In Prussia, the earliest attempt to stem the influx of plebeian students into universities was the Matriculation Patent of 1708.[33] Subsequent patents in 1718 and 1735 introduced proficiency examinations into theology faculties, thereby placing additional obstacles in the path of plebeian students. Although meritocratic on the surface, these examinations in effect introduced a two-class system into Prussian universities. Only holders of stipends were required to sit for the examinations, whereas students who could afford to study without a stipend were exempt. Hence the proficiency examinations were little more than stipend competitions for poorer students. Standards of merit allowed the state to restrict plebeian access without endangering the educational prospects of the propertied. In other words, by exempting the propertied from the examinations, the state ensured that merit did not interfere with privilege.[34]

---

[32]Johannes Ziekursch, *100 Jahre schlesischer Agrargeschichte* (Breslau, 1927), p. 104; Karl Grünberg, *Die Bauernbefreiung und die Auflösung des gutsherrlich-bäuerlichen Verhältnisses in Böhmen, Mähren, und Schlesien*, 2 vols. (Leipzig, 1893), 1:24.

[33]The patent declared that "every university faculty has fallen into disrepute because everyone, including artisans and peasants, wants their son to study at a university, regardless of whether he possesses sufficient talent. It would be far more beneficial to the public and to the common good if those possessing no academic talent earned their living through trade, manufacturing, agriculture, or the army, depending upon their present status and natural inclination." Quoted in Herrlitz, *Studium als Standesprivileg*, p. 36.

[34]Subsequent measures reinforced this two-class system. By 1791, the plebeian university aspirant faced two hurdles on his path to university advancement. The first was the introduction in 1788 of the *Abitur,* the examination required of secondary school graduates. The *Abitur* was not yet a formal requirement for university admission, but was required only of "holders of stipends and those dependent upon charity." Thus it applied not to those who could afford to study, but only to the unpropertied. The second hurdle was a military one. Since university students were exempt from military service, the Prussian state took steps to prevent the university from becoming a haven from the recruiting officer. Beginning in 1784, those desiring to attend a university who were not otherwise exempt from military service – primarily peasants, artisans, and day laborers – had first to report to their regiments. The regimental officer was then to determine whether the aspirant possessed the requisite talent and financial means for university study. See Paul Schwartz, *Die Gelehrtenschulen Preussens unter dem Oberschulkollegium (1787–1806) und das Abiturienten-Examen*, 3 vols. (Berlin, 1910–12), 1:122; and Manfred Heinemann, *Schule im Vorfeld der Verwaltung. Die Entwicklung der preussischen Unterrichtsverwaltung 1771–1800* (Göttingen, 1974), p. 300.

In Austria, efforts to make higher education the preserve of the propertied began under Charles VI. In 1735, the emperor issued a decree forbidding the sons of peasants and artisans from entering *Gymnasien* and universities unless they showed extraordinary talent.[35] Maria Theresa followed suit, issuing similar decrees in 1761, 1766, and 1767. The 1766 edict declared that "not all children should be admitted to Latin schools, but only those of exceptional talent whose parents are sufficiently propertied to support them."[36] These ordinances were apparently ineffective, for efforts to curtail *Gymnasium* and university enrollment continued into the 1770s.[37] The commission charged with educational reorganization following the abolition of the Jesuit order in 1773 proposed tighter restrictions upon *Gymnasium* and university admission.[38] Its proposals were incorporated into the *Gymnasium* reform of 1776, which attempted to establish effective controls over university admission by restricting access to *Gymnasien*.[39] As in Prussia, the target of these restrictions was the plebeian aspirant. Indigent students with no means of support were to be excluded from the *Gymnasium* in order to eliminate "idlers and beggar students."[40] The children of nobles, royal officials, and royal secretaries, on the other hand, were to be automatically admitted.[41]

Exclusionary measures in Prussian and Austrian higher education re-

---

[35]The 1735 decree is published in Karl Wotke, *Das österreichische Gymnasium im Zeitalter Maria Theresias* (Berlin, 1905), pp. 1–2.

[36]Ibid., p. 25.

[37]In 1770 Count Pergen, later to be chief of the Habsburg secret police, submitted to the Council of State detailed proposals for a thoroughgoing reform of the monarchy's educational institutions. These proposals advocated curtailing plebeian advancement beyond primary school. Pergen's proposals are located in *AV*, Vienna: Nachlass Pergen, and are discussed in Chapter 8, "The Pergen Plan."

[38]*HHStA*, Vienna: Alte Kabinettsakten, Fasz. 1, fol. 601ff.

[39]Published in Wotke, *Das österreichische Gymnasium*, pp. 255ff.

[40]Ibid., p. 257.

[41]Ibid., p. 271: "Her Majesty desires that the diligence and talent of the aspiring pupil be scrupulously examined. At the same time however, the children of noble persons, councillors, and secretaries are to be admitted even if they possess only mediocre talent and little proficiency in the necessary subjects. Children from the lower orders, however, are to be admitted only if they possess superior talent." In 1784, Joseph II placed further restrictions on plebeian university admission. He abolished all stipends for poor but qualified students in order, as the edict stated, "to prevent a horde of useless creatures from burdening society." Those unable to pay the annual tuition fee were to leave school immediately. This edict, combined with Joseph's closing of numerous *Gymnasien,* led to a 25 percent decline in *Gymnasium* enrollment – a drop of more than 2,200 pupils – in the following school year. A comparable trend toward social exclusivity is found in eighteenth-century Bavarian school reform. See Rainer A. Müller, "Sozialstatus und Studienchancen in Bayern im Zeitalter des Absolutismus," *Historisches Jahrbuch,* 95 (1975), pp. 120–141.

flected the mechanistic vision of the social order shared by cameralists. This vision was obsessed with maintaining *Gleichgewicht,* balance, among the various classes, corporations, and professions in society. Here parallels can be found with other aspects of eighteenth-century absolutism. On the diplomatic scene, for example, the state strove to achieve a balance of power favorable to its international position. In the realm of commerce, the state's policies were designed to secure a favorable balance of trade. As for absolutist educational policy, the aim was to produce a balance of productive forces.[42] Education was to achieve this balance by schooling individuals for work in the occupations in which they were born, thereby contributing to the social whole. Schools were to be organized in such a way as to eliminate imbalances in the social order, whether these took the form of idle beggars loitering in the streets or plebeian students lingering in universities.

The expansion of textile manufacturing

An exclusionary trend characterized higher education in much of Europe in the eighteenth century. Although a variety of causes underlay this trend, in Austria and Prussia it was closely tied to absolutist economic policy. Efforts to expand primary schooling while restricting plebeian educational advancement, reflected the cameralist drive to maintain a plentiful and productive supply of labor. On the one hand, by promoting schooling at the primary level, the state sought to inculcate diligence and work discipline. On the other hand, exclusionary policies at the secondary and university level were designed to prevent potential laborers from leaving their occupations in the pursuit of educational advancement and social mobility.

This concern with labor supply was a consequence of the rapid expansion of manufacturing in eighteenth-century Prussia and Austria. Although not without basis, the fashionable distinction between a dynamic Western European "core" and a backward Central and Eastern European "periphery" has obscured the degree to which regions of Austria

---

[42]See Grete Klingenstein's analysis of the concept of balance in Sonnenfels's social theory, in "Akademikerüberschuss," pp. 183–192. The absolutist quest for balance in the social realm found its most elegant expression in Frederickian social policy. The attempt by Frederick II to maintain a state of social equilibrium was epitomized in his attempts to prevent the bourgeois purchase of noble estates, the noble expropriation of peasant holdings, peasant migration to the city, and noble entry into bourgeois professions.

and Prussia had already experienced a structural shift away from agriculture by the middle of the eighteenth century.[43] By far the most important manifestation of this shift was the expansion of textile production.
Organized on a domestic basis, textile production in Prussia and Austria
had all the features normally associated with "proto-industry." Although
it involved a greater degree of economic specialization than the hand-
icraft system, proto-industrial production was less centralized than the
factory system.[44] Even the largest manufacturing enterprises – such as
the Berlin wool warehouse (*Lagerhaus*), the Linz woolens factory, and
the Schwechat cotton concern outside Vienna – put out the raw materials
to spinners and weavers before dyeing and fulling the woven cloth in the
factory. Thus much of the production in important textile centers like
Berlin and Prague involved rural producers with continued ties to agriculture. Hence the agrarian complexion of Prussia and Austria should
not blind the historian to the importance of nonagricultural commodity
production in these states.

In Prussia, the demand for woolens occasioned by the dramatic expansion of the army under Frederick William I did much to spur textile
production. Between 1722 and 1738, the production of woolen cloth
rose in weight from 1,086,708 to 1,830,052 pounds.[45] Under Frederick
II, who doubled the size of the army, the demand for woolen cloth
continued to rise. Far more important for the expansion of Prussian
textile production, however, was the acquisition of Silesia. When Frederick II occupied the former Austrian province in 1740, he doubled the
population of his realm and acquired one of the most important manufacturing centers in Central Europe. Located between the Sudeten
mountains and the Polish Jura, Silesia was an economic entrepôt linked
to Hamburg and Stettin in the north, Moravia in the south, Bohemia and
Saxony in the west, and Poland to the east. The Silesian linen industry
had grown steadily since the mid-seventeenth century, and while cotton

[43]For an example of this view see Immanuel Wallerstein, *The Modern World-System.
Capitalist Agriculture and the Origins of the European World-Economy in the Sixteenth
Century* (New York, 1974).
[44]To date, the most thorough elaboration of the concept of proto-industry is found in Peter
Kriedte, Hans Medick, and Jürgen Schlumbohm, *Industrialization before Industrialization: Rural Industry in the Genesis of Capitalism,* trans. Beate Schempp (Cambridge,
1981).
[45]Carl Hinrichs, *Die Wollindustrie in Preussen unter Friedrich Wilhelm I.* (Berlin, 1933), p.
262. The expansion of the Russian army under Peter I also benefited the Prussian wool
industry. Its annual export of finished cloth to Russia averaged 500,000 pounds during
the reign of Frederick William I. Ibid., pp. 211–231.

Table 2   *Flax, cotton, and wool spinners in Bohemia, 1768–79*

Fiber	1768	1776	1779
Flax	79,520	100,454	229,400
Cotton	7,267	6,451	6,410
Wool	22,590	30,996	37,943

Source: *Hofkammerarchiv*, Vienna: Kommerz Böhmen, Nr. 794, fol. 41–43.

began to absorb many of its markets after 1750, exports of Silesian linen continued to rise throughout Frederick's reign and helped Prussia become a major exporter of linen cloth for the first time. Production rose from 85,000 to 125,000 pieces between 1755 and 1775,[46] and the number of looms increased from 19,810 in 1748 to 28,704 in 1790, by which time more than 50,000 were employed in the industry.[47] The Silesian wool industry also expanded during this period. The number of spinners increased from 21,830 in 1748 to 32,830 in 1764, and woolen cloth production rose from 33,507 to 123,649 pieces between 1755 and 1788.[48]

The growth of the textile industry was equally dramatic in the Habsburg monarchy.[49] Much of this growth was centered in Bohemia, where an influx of English merchant capital in the late seventeenth century had provided an important boost to the production of linen. Although the loss of Silesia dealt a serious blow to Habsburg economic strength, it proved a positive benefit to Bohemia. Increased dependence on Bohemian manufactures within the monarchy spurred linen and wool production in the province, as witnessed by the rise in the number of spinners (see Table 2) between 1768 and 1779. Because Bohemian linen merchants feared the loss of spinners, cotton production was not vigorously promoted until the

[46]W. O. Henderson, *Studies in the Economic Policy of Frederick the Great* (London, 1963), p. 114.
[47]Herbert Kisch, "The Textile Industries in Silesia and the Rhineland: A Comparative Study in Industrialization (with a postscriptum)," in Kriedte et al., *Industrialization before Industrialization*, p. 181.
[48]Friedrich Freiherr von Schrötter, "Die schlesische Wollindustrie im 18. Jahrhundert," *Forschungen zur brandenburgischen und preussischen Geschichte*, 11 (1898), pp. 182–184; Herman Fechner, *Wirtschaftsgeschichte der Provinz Schlesien in der Zeit ihrer provinziellen Selbständigkeit 1741–1806* (Breslau, 1907), pp. 685–686.
[49]For a revisionist appraisal of "economic backwardness" in the Habsburg monarchy during this period see David F. Good, *The Economic Rise of the Habsburg Empire 1750–1914* (Berkeley, 1984), pp. 20ff.

1780s. Wool and linen manufacturing, however, grew rapidly during the Theresian era. The number of workers in the Bohemian woolen goods industry doubled between 1731 and 1775, when the ratio of wool weavers to the entire population was 1:480. By Joseph's reign, the ratio had increased to 1:350.[50] Much of this expansion was due to the investment and entrepreneurship of nobles. Prominent Bohemian families like the Waldsteins and the Kinskys promoted textile manufacturing on their estates, drawing on the labor of their rural subjects. By 1774, for example, the Waldstein woolen mill in Oberleutensdorf boasted 208 spinning wheels, 27 looms, 31 work benches, and 14 dyeing vats.[51] On the domains of Count Josef Kinsky in northern Bohemia, every village formed a part of his wool manufactory. After the wool was spun, it was sent to one of several weaving sheds on his estate to be woven into cloth.[52]

Other regions of the monarchy, particularly Upper and Lower Austria, also participated in this proto-industrial expansion. The Linz wool factory in Upper Austria was one of the largest industrial enterprises on the Continent. In 1754, its work force included 350 weavers and 9,000 spinners.[53] In Lower Austria, the number of those employed in manufacturing rose from 19,733 in 1762 to 94,094 in 1783.[54] Cotton manufacturing accounted for much of the growth: between 1768 and 1772, employment in the cotton industry grew by 30,637.[55] In the Schwechat

---

[50]Herman Freudenberger, "The Woolen Goods Industry of the Habsburg Monarchy in the Eighteenth Century," *Journal of Economic History*, 20 (1960), p. 384. See also Jaroslav Půrs, "Struktur und Dynamik der industriellen Entwicklung in Böhmen im letzten Viertel des 18. Jahrhunderts," *Jahrbuch für Wirtschaftsgeschichte*, 2 (1965); Arnošt Klíma, "The Role of Rural Domestic Industry in Bohemia in the 18th Century," *Economic History Review*, 27 (1974); and idem, "Industrial Development in Bohemia, 1648–1781," *Past and Present*, 11 (1957).

[51]Herman Freudenberger, *The Waldstein Woolen Mill: Noble Entrepreneurship in Eighteenth-Century Bohemia* (Boston, 1963), p. 82; L. Schlesinger, "Zur Geschichte der Industrie in Oberleutensdorf," *Mitteilungen des Vereins für die Geschichte der Deutschen in Böhmen*, 3 (1865), pp. 138–142.

[52]Klíma, "Rural Domestic Industry in Bohemia," p. 54. On noble entrepreneurship in Bohemian textile manufacturing see also Ralph Melville, "Zu den Anfängen der Industrialisierung in den böhmischen Ländern im Zeitalter des Merkantilismus," in Helmuth Feigl and Andreas Kusternig, eds., *Die Anfänge der Industrialisierung Niederösterreichs* (Vienna, 1982).

[53]Herman Freudenberger, "Zur Linzer Wollzeugfabrik," in Herbert Knittler, ed., *Wirtschafts- und Sozialhistorische Beiträge. Festschrift für Alfred Hoffman zum 75. Geburtstag* (Vienna, 1979), p. 230.

[54]Herbert Hassinger, "Der Stand der Manufakturen in den deutschen Erbländern der Habsburgermonarchie am Ende des 18. Jahrhunderts," in Friedrich Lütge, ed., *Die wirtschaftliche Situation in Deutschland und Österreich um die Wende vom 18. zum 19. Jahrhundert* (Stuttgart, 1964), p. 147.

[55]V. Hoffmann, "Die Anfänge der österreichischen Baumwollwarenindustrie in den österreichischen Alpenländern im 18. Jahrhundert," *Archiv für österreichische Geschichte*, 110 (1926), p. 589.

cotton concern in Lower Austria, the number of spinners, weavers, and dyers increased from 6,246 in 1752 to 31,350 in 1788.[56]

The labor force

The expansion of textile manufacturing, of course, increased the demand for labor. In response to this demand, as we saw earlier, absolutist rulers had attempted to undermine the guild monopoly on labor supply by prohibiting exclusion on the basis of birth, granting the use of non-guilded labor to privileged manufacturers, and selectively exempting from guild control those occupations producing for extralocal markets.[57] Such policies had important consequences for Berlin, where less than a third of the 15,371 textile workers (excluding spinners) belonged to a guild.[58] Guild restrictions had never applied to spinning. In cities like Breslau and Vienna, spinners were recruited from the urban proletariat, sometimes freely, sometimes by force. The wool industry in Berlin and Potsdam was distinguished by its reliance on soldiers and their families, who constituted the bulk of the proletariat in those cities.[59] Urban manufacturers also recruited spinners from workhouses (*Zucht- und Arbeitshäuser*), which could be found in most major towns and cities by the mid-eighteenth century. With their frequently large and concentrated labor force, workhouses were one of the earliest models of centralized production in Central Europe. Able to accommodate as many as 3,000 inmates in the course of a year, the spacious *Zucht- und Arbeitshaus* in Prague (1739) produced yarn for Bohemian wool manufacturers.[60] In 1781, the Brieg workhouse in Silesia owned fifty spinning wheels operated by 132 inmates.[61]

For the most part, however, proto-industrial production was centered in the countryside, where the absence of guilds made for a more elastic labor market. Moreover, seasonal fluctuations in the agricultural labor

---

[56]Ibid., p. 590.
[57]For details on these policies see Krüger, *Zur Geschichte der Manufakturen*, p. 215ff.; Herman Freudenberger, "Economic Progress during the Reign of Charles VI," in Jürgen Schneider, ed., *Wirtschaftskräfte in der europäischen Expansion. Festschrift für Hermann Kellenbenz* (Bamberg, 1978), p. 636.
[58]Krüger, *Zur Geschichte der Manufakturen*, p. 273.
[59]Ibid., pp. 278–284; Hinrichs, *Wollindustrie*, pp. 14–15.
[60]*HHStA*, Alte Kabinettsakten, Fasz. 74, fol. 256.
[61]H. W. Wagnitz, *Historische Nachrichten und Bemerkungen über die merkwürdigsten Zuchthäuser in Deutschland*, 2 vols. (Halle, 1791), 1:289ff. By the late eighteenth century, some workhouses were operating at a modest profit. The Halle workhouse earned a profit of 114 talers in 1788, while its Magdeburg counterpart netted 467. Ibid., 2:250.

Table 3 *Adult-male peasants, cotters, gardeners, and lodgers in selected Prussian and Austrian provinces, 1787*

Province	Full peasants	Cotters, gardeners, and lodgers
Brandenburg[a]	18,452	54,494
Prussian Silesia	41,344	123,329
Moravia	89,009	230,937
Bohemia	121,953	436,916
Lower Austria	62,865	166,246
Upper Austria	37,701	118,223
Styria	57,571	130,713
Carinthia	28,783	43,713

[a]Figures for Brandenburg are from 1770.
Source: HHStA, Nachlass Zinzendorf, vol. 30b, fol. 986–7. Figures for Prussian Silesia are taken from Tadeusz Ladagórski, *Generalne Tabele Statystyczne Śląska 1787 Roky* (Wrocław, 1954), p. 307, and those for Brandenburg are from Hans-Heinrich Müller, *Märkische Landwirtschaft vor den Agrarreformen von 1807* (Potsdam, 1967), p. 215.

market left the rural population free to spin or weave during much of the year. Rural labor was also cheaper: The cost of living was lower in the countryside, and because many rural laborers still derived a part of their income from agriculture, the entrepreneur could pay lower wages than would have been required had the laborers depended on industry alone for their subsistence.[62]

The labor force in rural manufacturing consisted largely of land-poor households dependent upon nonagricultural pursuits for their subsistence. The number of these households grew steadily in eighteenth-century Prussia and Austria and constituted most of the rural population.[63] Some were so-called lodgers (*Einlieger* or *Inleute*), who roomed with and were subject to the authority of more prosperous rural households. Most were gardeners (*Gärtner*) and cotters (*Häusler*) who owned little or no land and lived on the physical and social fringes of the village communi-

[62]On this point see Hans Medick, "The Proto-Industrial Family Economy," in Kriedte et al., *Industrialization before Industrialization*, p. 51.
[63]On the rural poor in Central Europe during this period see Jerome Blum, *The End of the Old Order in Rural Europe* (Princeton, 1978), pp. 96–115; Willi Boelke, "Wandlungen in der dörflichen Sozialstruktur während Mittelalter und Neuzeit," in *Wege und Forschungen der Agrargeschichte* (Frankfurt am Main, 1967); Jan Peters, "Ostelbische Landarmut – Sozioökonomisches über landarme und landlose Agrarproduzenten im Spätfeudalismus," *Jahrbuch für Wirtschaftsgeschichte*, 3 (1967).

ty. In Brandenburg, 52.5 percent of all rural households owned no land in 1743, whereas in 1750 70 percent of all East Prussian households were landless.[64] Table 3 shows the preponderance of land-poor households in other Prussian and Austrian provinces. The role of this "proto-proletariat" in rural industry can be seen in the district of Grünberg, a center of Silesian wool production. Here spinners belonged to a propertyless rural class that worked in the vineyards in the summer while spinning wool in the winter.[65] In the linen-producing districts of Bunzlau and Goldberg, similarly, the spinners and weavers were chiefly those whose plots were too small or barren to provide their subsistence.[66] Linen weavers in the Silesian village of Petersdorf owned no land, and generally lodged with peasant or cotter families;[67] and in Bohemia half of the 100,000 flax spinners in 1772 were landless.[68]

Drawing on the labor of this subpeasant stratum, rural industry in turn accelerated its growth. Since proto-industrial households were less dependent on agriculture for their livelihood, land inheritance became less of a precondition for marriage. Rural industry thus served to lower the average age of marriage, thereby spurring population growth.[69] Rural manufacturing further hastened the growth of a subpeasant stratum by encouraging peasant displacement (*Bauernlegen*). In the eighteenth century, peasant displacement was most common in regions like Bohemia, Silesia, and East Prussia, where labor services were the predominant form of seigniorial rent. Peasant displacement had been rare as long as peasants had few sources of income outside of agriculture. After all, the use of peasant labor on seigniorial demesne was possible only as long as the peasant household could subsist off its own holding. This placed objective limits on the size of the lord's demesne relative to the

---

[64]H. Tröger, *Die kurmärkischen Spinnerdörfer* (Leipzig, 1936), p. 8; and R. Stein, *Die Umwandlung der Agrarverfassung Ostpreussens durch die Reform des 19. Jahrhunderts*, 3 vols. (Jena, 1918–34), 1:98.

[65]Zimmermann, *Beyträge zur Beschreibung von Schlesien*, 10:312.

[66]Tadeusz Ladagórski, *Die Bevölkerung Schlesiens und ihre soziale Struktur in der 2. Hälfte des 18. Jahrhunderts* (Marburg, 1952), p. 11.

[67]Curt Liebich, *Wenden und Wachsen von Petersdorf in Riesengebirge. Siedlungskundliche und volkswirtschaftliche Untersuchung eines schlesischen Waldhufendorfes von der Gründung bis zum Jahre 1945* (Würzburg, 1961), pp. 91–92.

[68]Klíma, "Rural Domestic Industry," p. 50.

[69]See the pathbreaking study by Lutz Karl Berkner, "Family, Social Structure, and Rural Industry: A Comparative Study of the Waldviertel and the Pays de Caux in the Eighteenth Century," Ph.D. diss., Harvard University, 1973, especially pp. 63–87. Comparing family structure in Lower Austria and Normandy, Berkner demonstrates a high rate of early marriage among households dependent on spinning for their subsistence.

amount of land under peasant cultivation and thus discouraged the lord
from expropriating peasant land. However, with the expansion of rural
industry in the eighteenth century and the new sources of income this
provided, more people were able to subsist on less land. Consequently,
noble landlords now found it feasible to add peasant holdings to their
demesnes.[70] Already in the 1730s, Bohemian nobles were settling cotters
and their cattle on peasant holdings in order to obtain labor for their
manufactures.[71] Despite a 1751 decree forbidding peasant displacement
in Bohemia, nobles expropriated 215,669 *Strich* (approximately 155,000
acres) of peasant land during the following two decades.[72] Between 1723
and 1756, Silesian nobles added 1,635 peasant and cotter plots to their
holdings.[73] In Brandenburg, similarly, the number of peasant holdings
declined by 630 between 1725 and 1801, whereas the cotter population
increased by 11,859 during the same period.[74]

The labor shortage

In eighteenth-century Prussia and Austria, then, expanding textile production drew increasingly on a labor force whose position within existing
forms of production was in many ways anomalous. In large urban centers like Berlin and Vienna, more and more manufacturers employed
laborers with no connection to traditional guild organizations. In the
countryside, similarly, the textile industry drew on the labor of a subpeasant stratum existing on the margins of village society.

Despite these new sources of labor in cities and in the countryside, the
Prussian and Austrian textile industry experienced a persistent shortage
of labor in the eighteenth century. Since spinning machines were not
introduced in Prussia and Austria until the late eighteenth century, the
textile industry continued to depend on an extensive network of spinners
in the towns and countryside. The shortage of spinners was the single
most disruptive feature of the Prussian and Austrian textile industry. In

[70]On this point see the cogent analysis by W. Rusiński, "Das Bauernlegen in Mitteleuropa
im 16.–18. Jahrhundert," *Studia Historiae Oeconomicae*, 11 (1976).
[71]Grünberg, *Bauernbefreiung*, 2:28.
[72]This figure is cited by Prince Karl Egon von Fürstenberg, the Governor of Bohemia, in
HHStA, Nachlass Zinzendorf, vol. 158, fol. 371–372. On peasant displacement in
Bohemia during this period see also Josef Petran, "Der Höhepunkt der Bewegungen der
untertänigen Bauern in Böhmen," in Winfried Schulze, ed., *Europäische Bauernrevolten
der frühen Neuzeit* (Frankfurt am Main, 1982), p. 342.
[73]Ziekursch, *100 Jahre schlesischer Agrargeschichte*, p. 161.
[74]Krüger, *Zur Geschichte der Manufakturen*, p. 49.

his *Testament Politique* of 1752, Frederick II cited the spinner shortage as the prime impediment to textile production.[75] In Austria, similarly, manufacturers complained repeatedly of production bottlenecks resulting from yarn shortages.[76] In Bohemia, competition for spinners was so intense that the state had to ration spinners by allotting spinning regions to competing manufacturers.[77] The problem remained, however: In 1766 an official report claimed that chronic yarn shortages were turning Bohemian weavers into beggars.[78]

Cameralist writers and officials, frustrated in their efforts to expand production, blamed labor shortages on the sloth and lethargy of the labor force. Joachim Georg Darjes, professor of law at the University of Frankfurt an der Oder, insisted that "the reason for the shortage of labor lies not in inadequate wages, but the laziness of the people."[79] His fellow cameralist, Jakob Friedrich Freiherr von Bielfeld, agreed that "this penchant for idleness is certainly a cause for the failure of many manufacturing establishments."[80] Spinners and weavers alike, charged their cameralist critics, were subsistence-oriented and lacked drive or ambition. Once they had earned enough to support themselves and their families, they no longer wanted to work. Anticipating later theorists of the "moral economy" in pre-industrial societies,[81] cameralist officials attributed labor shortages to the weakness of the profit motive in laboring households. In Brandenburg, for example, Prussian officials repeatedly complained that spinning households worked only as long and as hard as was required for their subsistence.[82] In 1723 Severin Schindler, director of the

[75]*A.B.*, 1/9:349. See also Schrötter, "Schlesische Wollindustrie," pp. 453–454.
[76]See the 1754 report on the Linz Woolens Enterprise, the largest in the monarchy, in *HKA, Kommerz Niederösterreichisch,* Rot Nr. 207, Fasz. 85, fol. 1189. On similar problems in the Schwechat cotton concern outside Vienna see Hoffmann, "Baumwollwarenindustrie," pp. 585–586.
[77]Arnošt Klíma, "The Domestic Industry and the Putting-Out System (Verlags-System) in the Period of Transition from Feudalism to Capitalism," *Deuxième Conférence Internationale d'Histoire Économique, Aix-En-Provence,* 1962 (Paris, 1965), pp. 480–481.
[78]*HKA,* Kommerz Böhmen, Rot Nr. 794, fol. 630.
[79]Darjes, *Erste Gründe der Kameralwissenschaften,* 2d ed. (Leipzig, 1768), p. 420.
[80]Baron de Bielfeld, *Institutions politiques,* 2 vols. (The Hague, 1760), 1:146.
[81]The classic study by Werner Sombart, *Der moderne Kapitalismus,* 4th ed., 3 vols. (Munich, 1921–1928), stressed the subsistence orientation of precapitalist households. A more rigorous, less romanticized description of this orientation among peasant households is found in A. V. Chayanov, *Peasant Farm Organization,* in D. Thorner et al., eds., *A. V. Chayanov on the Theory of the Peasant Economy* (Homewood, Ill., 1966). For a more recent study in this vein see James C. Scott, *The Moral Economy of the Peasant: Rebellion and Subsistence in Southeast Asia* (New Haven, 1976). This question is also discussed in Medick, "Proto-Industrial Family Economy," pp. 64–66.
[82]Tröger, *Spinnerdörfer,* pp. 62–64.

largest wool manufactory in Berlin, used this argument to justify his opposition to higher wages in the wool industry. Schindler warned that because laborers worked only as long as was required for their subsistence, higher wages would merely encourage them to work less.[83] Darjes complained that the rural poor "would rather work less than earn more by working harder."[84] A 1768 report noted that the rural laborer in Bohemia "is satisfied if he produces enough to cover his livelihood and the payment of his dues."[85] A 1771 report on social conditions in Lower Austria similarly asserted that "the diligence of rural laborers seldom exceeds what is necessary to secure their households needs."[86] Johann Wiegand, a member of the Lower Austrian Economic Society, charged that rural day laborers found work in a town or village, worked for a few days, and then loafed until their earnings were spent.[87]

A further obstacle to labor productivity, according to cameralist officials, was the excessive number of religious holidays and celebrations. In the Habsburg monarchy, thirty-four religious holidays (excluding Sundays) were universally celebrated by the Catholic population. Added to those were locally celebrated holidays, which could number as many as thirty depending on the region, as well as a host of religious processions and celebrations that often broke up the work day.[88] Sonnenfels reckoned that a country of seven million inhabitants celebrating thirty religious holidays lost nine million florins.[89] Bielfeld estimated that if religious holidays and festivals were eliminated, production in rural industry would rise by a third.[90] According to a Prussian provincial administrator in Breslau, ten holidays and two pilgrimages cost the Silesian linen industry more than five million pieces of cloth.[91] In Upper Silesia, complained another Prussian official, "so many religious festivals are faithfully celebrated that many looms produce no more than two hundred pieces of cloth in a single year."[92] Such arguments, combined

---

[83]Hinrichs, _Wollindustrie_, p. 172.
[84]Darjes, _Erste Gründe_, p. 240.
[85]_HHStA_, Alte Kabinettsakten, Kart. 74, fol. 38.
[86]_Kriegsarchiv_, Vienna: Hofkriegsrat 98/737, fol. 77.
[87]Johann Wiegand, _Versuch den Fleiss unter dem Landvolk einzuführen_ (Vienna, 1772), p. 136. Cf. C.A., 5:1132, 6:741.
[88]See the disappointing treatment of a promising subject in J. Mössner, _Sonn- und Feiertage in Österreich, Preussen, und Bayern im Zeitalter der Aufklärung_ (Berlin, 1915).
[89]Joseph von Sonnenfels, _Sätze aus der Polizey-, Handlungs-, und Finanzwissenschaft_ (Vienna, 1765), p. 333.
[90]Bielfeld, _Institutions politiques_, 1:152.
[91]Kurt Hinze, _Die Arbeiterfrage in Brandenburg-Preussen zu Beginn des modernen Kapitalismus_ (Berlin, 1927), p. 44.
[92]Schrötter, "Schlesische Wollindustrie," p. 453.

with those condemning popular religious celebrations on devotional grounds, led Maria Theresa to approve holiday reductions in 1754 and 1771. In Prussian Silesia Frederick II, who normally insisted on maintaining his royal prerogatives in matters concerning his Catholic subjects, graciously endorsed the 1754 papal bull sanctioning a reduction in holidays. In the process he abolished a number of Protestant holidays as well, dismissing them as "solely an excuse for idleness and laziness in the performance of one's work and household duties."[93]

Reinforcing this jaundiced view of laborers was the existence of widespread mendicancy and vagabondage. During the seventeenth century, chronic warfare throughout Central Europe had helped foster an "underclass" of orphans, widows, ex-soldiers, and homeless peasants. War continued to be a major cause of mendicancy in the eighteenth century, although it was probably the demobilization of troops following a peace treaty, rather than the ravages of war per se, that drove mendicancy to inordinately high levels.[94] Adding to the mendicancy problem was the expanding class of rural poor described earlier. Often lacking the protection provided by landlords and the peasant *Gemeinde,* this nontenant class was cut off from the communal safety net that traditionally helped buffer the tenant population from economic disaster.[95] Perched precariously on the threshold of subsistence, the rural poor often had no choice beyond begging.[96] Although it remains to be proven whether mendicancy and vagabondage actually increased during the eighteenth century, efforts to combat the phenomenon certainly intensified under Frederick II and Maria Theresa.[97] Cameralist officials seized upon the

[93]Lehmann, *Preussen und die katholische Kirche,* 3:500–501.
[94]Begging and vagrancy tended to rise sharply after the conclusion of a major peace treaty (e.g., 1714, 1742, 1744, and 1763), when discharged soldiers flooded the cities and countryside. A useful introduction to the problem of vagabondage in eighteenth-century Central Europe can be found in Rudolf Endres, "Das Armenproblem im Zeitalter des Absolutismus," in Kopitzsch, *Aufklärung, Absolutismus und Bürgertum in Deutschland,* and more recently Carsten Küther, *Menschen auf der Strasse. Vagierende Unterschichten in Bayern, Franken, und Schwaben in der zweiten Hälfte des 18. Jahrhunderts* (Göttingen, 1984). See also Paul Frauenstadt, "Das Bettel- und Vagabundenwesen in Schlesien vom 16.–18. Jahrhundert," *Preussische Jahrbücher,* 89 (1897).
[95]Blum, *Rural Europe,* pp. 113–114; Stein, *Umwandlung,* 3:435; Herman Rebel, *Peasant Classes: The Bureaucratization of Property and Family Relations under Early Habsburg Absolutism 1511–1636* (Princeton, 1983), pp. 144–145.
[96]In 1727, for example, an investigation into rural mendicancy in Upper Austria found over 25,000 persons in need of assistance. Rebel, *Peasant Classes,* p. 145.
[97]The twenty-four patents issued against Silesian vagabondage between 1740 and 1763 illustrate how seriously Prussian officials took the problem. A typical edict from 1747 complained that "beggars are found everywhere, in towns, villages, and on public roads." *Kornsche Sammlung aller in dem souveränen Herzogthum Schlesien . . . ergangenen Ordnungen, Edikte, und Mandate,* 6 vols. (Breslau, 1765), 6:540. Austrian patents show a

fact that beggars lined the highways while manufacturers complained of labor shortages, and thus found confirmation for their belief that sloth was at the root of the labor problem.

The image of laborers presented in cameralist treatises and administrative reports should be viewed with caution. The repeated denunciations of laziness and lethargy on the part of textile laborers have led historians like Carl Hinrichs to draw the familiar contrast between "modern" economic rationality (represented by cameralist officials) and "traditional" social and economic behavior (embodied in laborers of the period).[98] The problem with this contrast is that it ignores the degree to which labor shortages, the major source of cameralist dissatisfaction with laborers, were related to the very structure of proto-industrial production. In the countryside, chronic labor shortages were inevitable given the seasonal basis of the textile industry. Yarn production fell sharply during peak agricultural periods, when fieldwork absorbed much of the rural labor force. In Prussia, where textile centers like Berlin and Potsdam depended so heavily on the labor of soldiers and their families, fluctuations in the garrison population could further destabilize yarn production. When soldiers left for battle or were discharged, as in 1756 and 1763, the resulting yarn shortages could precipitate depression in the industry.[99] Moreover, those chastised in cameralist treatises and absolutist ordinances as "vagabonds" were often migratory workers who "streamed out of their villages and fell in with the bands from other villages to seek work in distant places."[100]

Finally, a variety of motives other than laziness may have governed popular participation in religious holidays and festivals. For some households, these occasions provided an opportunity for arranging favorable marriages; in others, they may have allowed villagers to engage in forms of "conspicuous consumption" that might later have translated into credit or influence in the local community.[101] In short, until more is

---

similar preoccupation with mendicancy and vagabondage: "Now, more than ever, countless beggars are to be found throughout the land" (1749); "everywhere swarms of vagabonds and brigands" (1759); "disorderly public begging is growing rampant" (1767). *C.A.*, 5:449; 6:19, 1046. Under Maria Theresa, efforts to eliminate mendicancy included prohibiting vagabonds from marrying (1754), building workhouses (1765 and 1769), drafting them into the army (1741 and 1756), and transporting them to the Banat (1763–1770). *C.A.*, 5:840, 21; Sonja Jordan, *Die kaiserliche Wirtschaftspolitik im Banat im 18. Jahrhundert* (Munich, 1967), p. 92; *HKA*, Kommerz Niederösterreich, Abt. 24, fol. 32.
[98]Hinrichs, *Wollindustrie*, pp. 171–172.
[99]Ibid., p. 304.
[100]Blum, *Rural Europe*, p. 111; Küther, *Menschen auf der Strasse*, p. 10.
[101]Here Pierre Bourdieu's notion of "symbolic capital" – acquired prestige that can subse-

known about popular culture in eighteenth-century Central Europe, the image of laborers projected in cameralist tracts and absolutist decrees cannot be taken at face value.

The rise of child labor

This image was nonetheless important, for it had a decisive impact on absolutist educational policy. The cameralist preoccupation with labor shortages and their causes served to shift pedagogical discourse in a different direction, toward the view that the central aim of elementary schooling should be to create a disciplined labor force. Eighteenth-century cameralist writers repeatedly stressed the relationship between primary schooling and the productive capacities of the state. "One can observe," wrote Justi, "how in those countries where commerce and manufacturing thrive, children in their earliest years are spurred to industry and diligence."[102] How was it possible, asked Darjes, to travel through an area rich in natural resources and find lazy inhabitants? His answer was "the education of the young, who are not taught diligence sufficiently early."[103] Karl Heinrich Seibt, professor of ethics at the University of Prague, argued that laws, force, even high wages would never produce diligence "so long as the subject of the state is not habituated from youth on to a love of work and enterprise."[104]

This emphasis upon the economic value of primary education coincided with the vigorous promotion of child labor by Prussian and Austrian absolutism. During the eighteenth century, manufacturers and officials turned increasingly to child labor as a means of overcoming labor shortages in the textile industry.[105] The use of child labor was justified

quently be converted into "real" capital – is a useful corrective to overly economistic conceptions of economic rationality. See his *Entwurf einer Theorie der Praxis,* trans. Cordula Pialoux and Bernd Schwibs (Frankfurt am Main, 1976), pp. 335–357. On the significance of religious celebrations as occasions for the arrangement of marriages, see the example of Bavaria in Hermann Hörger, *Kirche, Dorfreligion, und bäuerliche Gesellschaft. Strukturanalysen zur gesellschaftsgebundenen Religiosität ländlicher Unterschichten des 17. bis. 19. Jahrhunderts, aufgezeigt an bayerischen Beispielen* (Munich, 1978), pp. 107–109.

[102] Justi, *Manufakturen,* 1:181.

[103] Darjes, *Erste Gründe,* p. 14.

[104] Karl Heinrich Seibt, *Von dem Einflusse der Erziehung auf die Glückseligkeit des Staates* (Prague, 1771), p. 21.

[105] On the growing importance of child labor during this period, see Arno Herzig, "Kinderarbeit in Deutschland in Manufaktur und Protofabrik," *Archiv für Sozialgeschichte,* 23 (1983).

on both economic and pedagogical grounds: It not only eased work shortages in manufacturing, but instilled a work ethic in children of those social groups customarily disposed to idleness. Frederick II expressed this view in a 1775 letter to Christoph Friedrich von Derschau, head of the provincial administration of Brandenburg:

For my subjects to be happy, they must grow accustomed to diligence and hard work. In the Electoral Mark these virtues are particularly rare among my rural subjects. . . . While children of eight or nine years can do little in the way of strenuous work, they can at least spin during the evenings when they have nothing better to do. In this way they could earn their keep and grow into disciplined laborers, instead of growing accustomed from youth onwards to a life of idleness. I would view it most favorably if you would see to it that children in the countryside who are presently idle devoted their free time to spinning. Our wool merchants presently complain so much about the lack of spinners: yet if these children were put to work, this shortage could be eased and our subjects could supplement their incomes.[106]

Maria Theresa shared Frederick's belief in the economic and pedagogical value of child labor. In 1761 she decreed that children of the poor "should grow accustomed to hard work. . . . Our manufacturers are in great need of spinners, and they would gladly employ children for this purpose."[107]

The evolution of the Prussian and Austrian orphanage into an entrepreneurial enterprise illustrates the growing emphasis on child labor during this period. Inmates of the Halle orphanage had always spun yarn or worked at other tasks. Francke, however, had attempted to subordinate the orphans' work regimen to their moral and religious training. He was not always successful. In 1705, a "strike" occurred when orphans openly resisted attempts to increase their work quotas. Francke, embarrassed by the incident and determined to dispel any suspicion that he was exploiting his charges for profit, strictly prohibited the use of orphan labor for production beyond the needs of the institution.[108] Although the Halle orphanage eschewed exacting "surplus value" from orphan labor, its institutional offspring were not so scrupulous. In 1725, Berlin wool manufacturers contracted sixty orphans from the Potsdam military orphanage for employment as spinners.[109] By 1740, the orphanage was

---

[106]Quoted in Jürgen Kuczynski and Ruth Hoppe, *Geschichte der Kinderarbeit in Deutschland 1750–1939*, 2 vols. (East Berlin, 1958), 1:92.
[107]C.A., 6:206.
[108]Oschliess, *Arbeits- und Berufspädagogik*, pp. 65–69.
[109]Hinze, *Arbeiterfrage*, p. 168.

regularly farming out its inmates to work in agriculture and manufacturing. By 1786, almost half of the 2,714 orphans were being used for this purpose.[110] The Du Vigneau orphanage for girls in Berlin provides another example of the evolution from charitable institution to proto-factory. The orphanage was originally established in 1743 by the widowed Mlle. Du Vigneau. In 1749 it was taken over by the mercantile firm of Ephraigm and Sons, which by 1763 was employing 360 orphan girls in the production of lace.[111]

The first Austrian orphanage was established in 1724 as a wing of the Vienna workhouse (*Zucht- und Arbeitshaus*). By the 1730s, labor from the orphanage was being used to spin wool and cotton supplied by the Oriental Company.[112] In 1742 the Viennese silk merchant Michael Kienmayr donated a building on the Rennweg, the center of silk production in the city, to house orphan inmates of the workhouse. Kienmayr used orphan labor in his own business, and in 1747 added a silk manufactory to the orphanage.[113] In 1759 Ignaz Parhammer, the Jesuit confessor to Maria Theresa's husband Franz Stephen, became director of the Rennweg orphanage. While retaining its economic function under Parhammer's leadership, the orphanage also gained notoriety for its strict military regimen. Children wore blue uniforms, were assigned military ranks, and marched in unison to church, classes, and meals.[114] In the countryside, noble entrepreneurs were quick to recognize the potential of orphan labor. Here the Waldstein family, as usual, were pioneers. At the orphanage established in 1754 on the Waldstein estates in Oberleutensdorf, boys and girls spun yarn for the count's woolen mill.[115] Orphans also provided the labor for the Waldstein stocking manufactory established in 1767 in Weisswasser.[116]

---

[110]Figures cited in Nicolai, *Beschreibung der königlichen Residenzstädte*, 3:1293.

[111]Hinze, *Arbeiterfrage*, p. 168.

[112]C.A., 6:138–139; Anton Reichsritter von Geusau, *Geschichte der Stiftungen, Erziehungs-, und Unterrichtsanstalten in Wien* (Vienna, 1803), pp. 480–482.

[113]Ignaz Parhammer, *Vollkommener Bericht von den Zustände des Waisenhauses . . . auf dem Rennweg* (Vienna, 1776), p. 33.

[114]On the regime of the Parhammer orphanage see Gernot Heiss, "Erziehung der Waisen zur Manufakturarbeit. Pädagogische Zielvorstellungen und ökonomische Interessen der maria-theresianischen Verwaltung," *Mitteilungen des Instituts für österreichische Geschichtsforschung*, 85 (1977). Incidentally, Mozart's popular "Orphanage Mass" was composed for the festive dedication of the orphanage chapel. The performance took place on December 7, 1768, in the presence of the empress and four of her children.

[115]Schlesinger, "Industrie in Oberleutensdorf," 2:144.

[116]Adolf Demuth, "Das Manufakturhaus in Weisswasser," *Mitteilungen des Vereins für die Geschichte der Deutschen in Böhmen*, 28 (1890): 31.

From spinning bee to spinning school

Orphans were not the only children used to alleviate labor shortages in the textile industry. In the course of the eighteenth century, households of the urban and rural poor became the targets for the recruitment of child labor. A striking example of this was the development of the so-called spinning bee (*Spinnstube*), which in Prussia and Austria followed a pattern strikingly similar to that of the orphanage. In both cases, the function of the institution grew progressively economic in character. The Central European *Spinnstube* had originated in the countryside during the late Middle Ages as a center of village social life.[117] Spinning as such had initially played a secondary role in the *Spinnstube,* which served more as a meeting place for young people from the village and its environs. On winter evenings boys and girls gathered in spinning bees to spin, tell stories, dance, and often court. By the sixteenth century the latter activity had begun to provoke criticism from Catholic and Protestant reformers, who attacked the *Spinnstube* as a source of sexual license. Territorial rulers followed suit, issuing edicts that attempted – usually unsuccessfully – to eradicate the institution.

Beginning in the eighteenth century, however, the expansion of rural industry transformed the *Spinnstube* from a target of condemnation into an object of praise. In northwestern Germany and parts of Saxony, Silesia, and Bohemia, economic activity came increasingly to dominate the *Spinnstube.* During the winter, men, women, and children gathered in the *Spinnstube* to spin and supplement their incomes. In 1728, for example, a *Spinnstube* on the Bohemian estates of Count Waldstein in Grossleutersdorf was indistinguishable from a manufactory.[118] In the region around Sloup in Northern Bohemia, similarly, village spinning parlors were fully integrated into the Kinsky wool manufactory by the 1750s.[119] In 1764, 382 children on the Lower Austrian estates of Freiherr von Grechtler learned to spin in spinning parlors. To foster a spirit of initiative among the children, Von Grechtler introduced a reward system for high-quality work.[120] By the middle of the eighteenth

117My description is based on Hans Medick, "Spinnstuben auf dem Dorf. Jugendliche Sexualkultur und Feierabendbrauch in der ländlichen Gesellschaft," in Gerhard Huck, ed., *Sozialgeschichte der Freizeit* (Wuppertal, 1980).
118An engraving of the *Spinnstube* (reproduced in Medick, "Spinnstuben," p. 34) portrays an overseer distributing raw wool to a group of spinners, with an orderly row of spinning wheels in the background.
119Klíma, "Rural Domestic Industry," p. 54.
120Hoffmann, "Baumwollwarenindustrie," p. 583.

century, the term *Spinnstube* no longer had exclusively rural connotations. It now referred also to urban spinning mills producing yarn for textile merchants. The spinners sometimes lived in the *Spinnstuben* and were usually children and young adults from families too poor to support them. The reputation of urban *Spinnstuben* was unsavory: In Berlin they sometimes doubled as bordellos, the spinning master (usually a woman) serving as procuress. In an attempt to end this practice, a Prussian edict from 1747 forbade girls living in *Spinnstuben* from going out at night.[121]

In the 1760s, the absolutist state in Prussia and Austria began to promote the establishment of *Spinnstuben*. These were now called "spinning schools" (*Spinnschulen*), reflecting the blend of economic and pedagogical motives that accompanied the promotion of child labor. In Silesia, the Prussian Minister von Schlabrendorff announced in 1763 that every village had to provide evening spinning instruction to local youth during the winter. In towns and cities, mendicant children and the children of soldiers were required to attend.[122] By 1766, 218 villages had complied with the decree, as well as towns and cities like Breslau, Ohlau, Brieg, and Namslau. Classes were often held in the parish school, and each was to begin with a prayer and a Bible reading.[123] Maria Theresa issued a similar edict in 1765. Aimed specifically at children from poor rural households, this edict required that instruction in spinning be provided in parish schools between October and March. Children between the ages of seven and fifteen were to attend for at least four weeks.[124] The government contributed a limited amount of support to the schools, but most of the initiative came from nobles themselves. Spinning schools on the Auersperg estates in Nassaberg and Setsel (Lower Austria) trained 700 cotton spinners in 1765, while the one on the Kinsky estates in Sikowitz (Bohemia) taught 108 children how to spin wool.[125] In Count Harttig's spinning school in Giesshübel, 57 children produced a profit of eighty florins in twenty-eight months. Similar examples could be found

---

[121]See Krüger, *Manufakturen*, p. 289.
[122]Schlabrendorff's edict is published in Johann Heinrich Ludwig Bergius, ed., *Sammlung auserlesener teutschen Landesgesetze welche das Policey- und Cameralwesen zum Gegenstand haben*, 7 vols. (Frankfurt am Main, 1780–1787), 2:319–330.
[123]Fechner, *Wirtschaftsgeschichte der Provinz Schlesien*, pp. 62–67; Schrötter, "Schlesische Wollindustrie," pp. 94–103.
[124]C.A., 6:763–764; Arnošt Klíma, "Probleme der Proto-Industrie in Böhmen zur Zeit Maria Theresias," in Richard Georg Plaschka and Grete Klingenstein, *Österreich im Europa der Aufklärung. Kontinuität und Zäsur in Europa zur Zeit Maria Theresias und Josephs II.*, 2 vols. (Vienna, 1985), 1:191–192.
[125]HKA, Kommerz Niederösterreich (Spinnerei und deren Emporbringung, 1742–1812), fol. 623–628; Kommerz Böhmen, fol. 176–259.

on the Buquoi estates in Sadlesdorf, the Sternberg estates in Jasmuck, the Trautson estates in Zechtnitz, and the Lobkowitz estates in Balien.[126]

However, with the exception of Hecker's schools for the poor in Berlin, efforts to integrate child labor into elementary school classrooms had been confined to orphanages. The first to introduce child labor into popular education on a significant scale was Ferdinand Kindermann, the Bohemian parish priest and school reformer. The son of a poor Bohemian cotter, Kindermann had himself spun wool as a child in order to supplement the family income. Because his family lived close to a parish school, Kindermann had been able to learn reading and writing from a sympathetic schoolmaster. Kindermann continued his education as a choir boy in a cloister, and subsequently entered the University of Prague.[127]

In Prague, Kindermann became interested in pedagogical questions through his studies with the moral philosopher Karl Heinrich Seibt.[128] The pedagogical views of Seibt, like those of Felbiger, were rooted in the culture of Protestant Germany. Seibt had studied at Leipzig in the 1740s with two of the leading figures of the German *Aufklärung*, Johann Christoph Gottsched and Christian Fürchtegott Gellert.[129] From Gottsched, Seibt gained an appreciation for language as a vehicle for moral and cultural reform.[130] Seibt's views were further shaped by Gellert's moral philosophy, which incorporated the then fashionable sentimen-

---

[126]Ibid., fol. 603–624.

[127]Kindermann's biographers disagree on the location of the cloister. According to Adelbert Schiel, *Ignaz von Felbiger und Ferdinand Kindermann* (Halle, 1902), p. 49, Kindermann attended a Premonstrant *Gymnasium* in Neuzelle (Bohemia). Josef Tibitanzl, *Die Bedeutung Ferdinand Kindermanns für das Schulwesen* (Munich, 1905), places him in a Cistercian monastery in Rauden (Upper Silesia). Anton Weiss, "Ferdinand Kindermann und die Landschule zu Kaplitz," *Beiträge zur österreichischen Erziehungs- und Schulgeschichte*, 6 (1905), pp. 46–47, accepts neither of these versions, maintaining that Kindermann attended the Augustinian *Gymnasium* in Sagan. The Weiss version is certainly incorrect, since there was no Augustinian *Gymnasium* in Sagan.

[128]Kindermann's relationship with Seibt is noted in Janet Wolf Berk, "The Elementary School Reforms of Maria Theresa and Joseph II in Bohemia," Ph.D. diss., Columbia University, 1970, p. 57.

[129]A key figure in the Austrian Enlightenment, Seibt deserves a detailed study. To my knowledge, the only treatment of his life and work is found in Karl Wotke, "Karl Heinrich Seibt. Der erste Universitätsprofessor der deutschen Sprache in Prag, ein Schüler Gellerts und Gottscheds. Ein Beitrag zur Geschichte des Deutschunterrichts in Österreich," *Beiträge zur österreichischen Erziehungs- und Schulgeschichte*, 9 (1907).

[130]For an example of Seibt's stress on the cultural and political significance of language see his *Von dem Unterschiede des zierlichen, des Hof- und Curialstyles* (Prague, 1768), published as an appendix in Wotke, "Seibt," pp. 91–121. It is significant in this regard that Seibt was the first to lecture in German at a Habsburg university. Ibid., p. 17.

talism of Francis Hutcheson and Christian Crusius into a deeply Pietist concern with moral and social reform.[131] For Gellert, a love for others (*Nächstenliebe*) was the essence of morality. His sentimentalism, with its stress on feeling and emotion as the mainsprings of moral action, further accentuated the Pietist contrast between inner conviction and outer coercion. Anticipating the Kantian distinction between legality and morality, Gellert believed an act was moral only insofar as it arose spontaneously out of the individual's feelings and sentiments. For Gellert, the purpose of education was to refine sentiment so as to harness it to serve morality. Following Gellert, Seibt stressed the importance of education for the internalization of social duty. As Seibt told his Prague students in 1771:

> If laws are to be faithfully observed, the subject of the state must obey them freely and willingly. Laws are as powerless in fostering diligence, industry, and thriftiness . . . as they are in deterring debauchery, dissolution, and prodigality. Force cannot inspire virtue and piety. These qualities lie beyond the range of external coercion, in a realm forever resistant to force. They wither away as soon as they are no longer freely rendered. The enlightened state which educates each subject in the duties of his profession, a state whose subjects fulfill their duties willingly and out of love – this is a powerful, invincible, and blessed state.[132]

For Seibt, as for Francke, education served to mediate between obedience and freedom. Kindermann would also stress the role of education in the subjectification of coercion.

After Kindermann completed his theological studies in 1766, he worked in Prague as a parish schoolmaster and waited for a vacant pastoral position. Kindermann finally obtained it in 1771 through the patronage of Count Johann Buquoi, a progressive young Bohemian landowner who had also belonged to the Seibt circle at the university. Buquoi was an energetic estate manager who commuted peasant labor services in order to promote linen and wool production on his estates. He also founded the Association for Christian Charity, a lay brotherhood established to care for the rural poor in Bohemia.[133] Buquoi appointed Kindermann to a vacant parish on his southern Bohemian estates in Kaplitz, specifically entrusting to Kindermann the reform of parish schools in the region.

[131]On Gellert see Hans M. Wolff, *Die Weltanschauung der deutschen Aufklärung in geschichtlicher Entwicklung*, 2d ed. (Bern and Munich, 1963), pp. 160–171.

[132]Seibt, *Von dem Einflusse der Erziehung*, pp. 17–18.

[133]For a description of this association see Bernard Spazierer, *Zuverlässige und ausführliche Nachrichten von dem Armeninstitute, welches auf den gräflichen Buquoischen Herrschaften in Boheim im Jahr 1779 errichtet worden* (Vienna, 1783).

Kindermann, himself a former schoolmaster, immediately turned his attention to the Kaplitz parish school. He was already familiar with Pietist pedagogical ideas, having made an earlier journey to the Halle orphanage and *Pädagogium*. He now traveled to Sagan to consult with Felbiger, whose reforms in Silesia had by this time won him renown in Central European pedagogical circles. In Sagan, Kindermann attended Felbiger's teaching seminar, established in 1764 along the lines of Hecker's institute. When Kindermann returned, Buquoi hired an additional schoolmaster, repaired the school building, bought new desks, and paid for the schoolbooks.[134]

The population of Kaplitz was dominated by poor cotters and gardeners. The poverty of the region was compounded by the devastating famine of 1771–72, when thousands died of starvation in the province. Kindermann and Buquoi were convinced that only the promotion of spinning could alleviate the poverty of the local population. Kindermann proposed using the parish school for this purpose and thereby hoped to provide land-poor families with an additional trade. As Kindermann argued, "Pupils must learn to earn their livelihood. If a plot of land is too small to support a family, children must be able to supplement the family income in other ways."[135] To accomplish this goal, Kindermann hired the wife of the parish schoolmaster to instruct the children in spinning.

At the same time, Kindermann's school stressed moral and religious instruction. "As long as the poor lack a moral sense and a virtuous heart," he maintained, "even the best proposals for improving their condition will have no effect."[136] Thus, children spun wool in the afternoon, but they learned reading, writing, arithmetic, and religion in the morning. Kindermann's pedagogical rejection of coercion and emphasis on self-discipline bore the unmistakable stamp of Seibt and Felbiger. In an account of his Kaplitz school reform, Kindermann wrote:

I wanted as far as possible to avoid all coercive measures [*Zwangsmittel*]. Seldom does coercion enlighten the understanding; even more rarely does it purify the heart. The will is moved of its own accord and cannot be coerced. Experience teaches that while a school that relies on force can produce hypocrites or machines, it can never create moral individuals.[137]

[134]Kindermann, *Nachricht von der Landschule zu Kaplitz*, p. 9.
[135]Quoted in Panholzer, ed., *Methodenbuch*, p. 101.
[136]Ferdinand Kindermann, *Von dem Einflusse der niederen Schulen auf das gemeine Leben, und auf die mittlern und hohen Schulen* (Prague, 1776), p. 10.
[137]Kindermann, *Nachricht von der Landschule zu Kaplitz*, p. 67.

"The pupils who submits himself to the will of his teacher out of love," assured Kindermann, "will later find it easier to accept the authority of others."[138] Rejecting coercion, Kindermann refused to impose fines on parents who kept their children at home. Instead, he hoped to encourage attendance by allowing children to keep the income derived from the sale of their homespuns. Kindermann was convinced that once their acquisitive instincts were aroused, parents would willingly send their children to school.

At the same time, Kindermann attempted to encourage attendance by incorporating features of the spinning bee into afternoon spinning classes. The time allotted to spinning was occupied by relaxed conversation and storytelling. In the school that Kindermann subsequently established in the village of Prachatitz, the schoolmaster's wife read fables to the pupils while they spun. She then explained the moral behind the tale and encouraged pupils to express their own opinions on the subject.[139] This combination of spinning and storytelling, according to Kindermann, educated children to be diligent and virtuous without resorting to coercion: "It is an excellent way of subtly inclining the children toward a virtuous life. They learn moral truths effortlessly, without coercion and in a pleasant fashion."[140]

The reputation of Kindermann's school quickly spread throughout Bohemia, and it was visited by state officials, clergymen, and nobles. In 1775 Maria Theresa appointed him supervisor of Bohemian parish education, and Kindermann succeeded in incorporating spinning classes into elementary schools throughout the province. Noble landlords readily provided the raw wool, cotton, or flax, which they then purchased from the schools after it had been spun. The schools provided incentives to pupils in the form of prizes and payment for the homespuns. By 1790, spinning classes had been introduced into 500 parish schools, almost 25 percent of all schools in Bohemia.[141] Moreover, these schools were well attended. In the district of Kaurzim, for example, 53 percent (1,224 pupils) of all school-age children attended school. At the seventeen schools in the district that offered spinning classes, however, the atten-

[138]Kindermann, *Einflusse der niederen Schulen,* p. 107.
[139]Anton Weiss, *Geschichte der theresianischen Schulreform in Böhmen,* 2 vols. (Vienna, 1906), 1:411–412.
[140]Quoted in ibid., 1:353.
[141]Friedrich Wiechowski, "Ferdinand Kindermanns Versuch einer Verbindung von Elementar- und Industrieschulen," *Beiträge zur österreichischen Erziehungs- und Schulgeschichte,* 9 (1907), pp. 185–188.

dance ratio was significantly higher: Here 75 percent (1,224 pupils) of the school-age population attended.[142] The relative success of school reform in Bohemia owed much to Kindermann's organizational talents and ability to integrate textile production into primary schooling. In recognition of his efforts, Kindermann was ennobled in 1777 and appointed bishop of Leitmeritz (Bohemia) in 1790.

The uses of Pietist pedagogy

Kindermann's success demonstrates how Pietist pedagogy, incorporated into the moral and political concerns of the German Enlightenment, remained an important force throughout the eighteenth century. In combining spiritual goals with a pronounced work ethic, Pietist pedagogy was able to link the religious concerns of earlier reformers with the economic aims of cameralism. Pietism remained influential pedagogically in no small part because it addressed issues articulated by cameralist writers and officials. As we have seen, cameralists blamed labor shortages in the textile industry on the subsistence ethos of proto-industrial households. Pietist pedagogy, for its part, promised to transform this ethos. The Pietist conception of work as an omnipresent moral obligation gave labor a significance beyond the mere fulfillment of subsistence needs. This moralization of labor removed all limits to self-exploitation, thereby subverting the subsistence ethos by imposing on individuals the moral obligation to produce beyond their immediate needs.

Pietism and cameralism were also similar in their sharp distinction between work time and leisure time. Francke's stress on "free time," like the Pietist revival of the Sabbath as a day of rest and worship, reflected the trend toward the polarization of work and leisure that characterized the eighteenth century.[143] By condemning the disruptive impact of religious festivals and processions on production, cameralist writers sought to abstract a notion of work time from a precapitalist rhythm of production that was discontinuous, intimately tied to "leisure," and broken up by religious festivals, popular entertainment, and the seasons themselves.[144]

---

[142]"Stand der Schulen in kaurzimer Kreises," in J. A. Riegger, ed., *Nachrichten zur alten und neuen Materialien von Böhmen,* 10 (Leipzig and Prague, 1789), pp. 185–198.

[143]See Nahrstedt, *Entstehung der Freizeit,* pp. 26–61.

[144]In peasant-artisanal societies, Jürgen Habermas has written, "the process of production, organized both in accordance with the seasonal rhythm of the year as well as with the festivals growing out of this rhythm, is eventually transformed into the routine of a mechanistically organized work day. In the process, the unity of work and play disap-

Finally, Pietist pedagogy and cameralism both hoped to integrate children of the poor into the production process. Proponents of compulsory schooling often cited the large proportion of children among the mendicant population – in Prussia more than one-third, according to Horst Krüger.[145] These children were frequently orphans, victims of the endemic warfare between 1740 and 1763. In Berlin, Vienna, and other major cities, many were regimental children who roamed the streets freely. For such children, the primary "agent of socialization" was neither the school nor the family, but the street.[146] One of the aims of educational reformers in the eighteenth century was to replace the street with the school and thereby to integrate socially marginal elements into the social order. In Berlin, as noted earlier, Hecker's Pietist elementary schools were aimed at children of soldiers and the urban poor. In Austria, the decision to reform primary schooling was also justified on the grounds that it would remove children of the poor from the street. An insert in the semi-official *Wiener Diarium* asserted:

The main purpose of our comprehensive school reform is to provide the poorest members of society with the enduring capacity to fulfill the duties pertaining to their occupation and station in life. . . . Does not one observe daily how so many youths, left to their own devices, loiter in the streets and grow up into idle, ignorant beggars? How can the church and the state expect them to become anything other than useless and unskilled parasites who plague the human race and the fatherland?[147]

In cities and in the countryside alike, the weakening of patriarchal authority that accompanied the decline of guilds and the expansion of proto-industry further enhanced the role of the school as an agent of socialization. The traditional guild household was distinguished by its decidedly patriarchal character. Family relationships and production were organized according to the principle of the "integral household" (*das ganze Haus*): The patriarchal authority of guildmasters encom-

pears." Habermas, "Soziologische Notizen zum Verhältnis von Arbeit und Freizeit," in G. Funke, ed., *Konkrete Vernunft. Festschrift für Ernst Rothacker* (Bonn, 1958), p. 220. See also Keith Thomas, "Work and Leisure in Pre-Industrial Societies," *Past and Present*, 29 (1964), p. 52. On absolutist ordinances as a reflection of this cameralist tendency see Raeff, *The Well-Ordered Police State*, p. 78.

[145]Krüger, *Manufakturen*, p. 372.

[146]On the "street" as an agent of socialization for lower-class children see Jürgen Schlumbohm, "Socialization and the Family: The Case of the German Lower Middle Classes circa 1800," *International Review of Social History*, 12 (1980).

[147]*Nachricht an das Publikum. Von der Absicht und dem Nutzen des auf allerhöchsten Befehl verbesserten Schulwesens in Österreich unter der Enns* (Vienna, 1771), p. 2.

passed not only their wives and children, but also their apprentices. In his relationship with the apprentice, the master was both employer and *Hausvater*.[148] Hence the master was responsible not only for the vocational training of his apprentice, but also his moral and spiritual welfare. Thus the tailors' guild in Hohenstein (East Prussia) instructed guild masters in 1701 to "ensure that your children and apprentices are exposed to the Word of God, not only on religious holidays, but every Sunday." The supreme master (*Obermeister*) of the masons' guild in the Electoral Mark enjoined each guildmaster to see that his apprentice "fears God and behaves in an honorable and Christian manner, shunning bad company, gambling, whoring, drunkenness, thievery, and other sins." In this regard, the guild household in early modern Central Europe functioned as an important instrument of social control, imposing discipline and controlling the behavior of its members. Absolutist rulers explicitly recognized and approved this function. In the words of a Württemberg guild ordinance from 1750, a master had the duty to ensure that his apprentices were "diligent, loyal, discreet, and obedient. An apprentice should attend church regularly, and never leave his house or city without the permission of his master. He should never be allowed to roam the streets mischievously." In the Prussian General Code (1793), instilling discipline and morality remained the first duty of the guild master toward his apprentice.[149]

Yet it was precisely the moral and educational function of the apprentice system that eighteenth-century critics had begun to question. As seen earlier, the apprentice system had begun to draw bitter criticism from cameralist officials. They charged that guildmasters neglected the moral and vocational training of their charges, using them as household servants instead of giving them moral and vocational training. From the standpoint of these critics, guilds were no longer dependable instruments of moral education.

Moreover, the absolutist assault on guild exclusivity, the exemption of numerous trades from guild control, and the expansion of rural industry – all signaled the growth of a work force that was not subject to guild

---

[148]On this concept see Otto Brunner, "Das 'ganze Haus' und die alteuropäische 'Ökonomik'," in *Neue Wege der Verfassungs- und Sozialgeschichte,* 2d ed. (Göttingen, 1980). On the guild household as integral household see Griessinger, *Das symbolische Kapital der Ehre,* pp. 57–66. When the apprentice moved into his master's household, he customarily brought his bed with him as a symbol of the transfer of authority from his parents to the guildmaster. See Stratmann, *Krise,* p. 18.

[149]These examples are taken from Stratmann, *Krise,* pp. 6–10.

controls or sanctions. In Berlin, for example, the proportion of non-guilded workers exceeded their guilded counterparts by 1805.[150] Even while guilds were under attack as agents of socialization, then, their economic control over the urban labor force was declining

A similar weakening of patriarchal structures took place in the Prussian and Austrian countryside in the eighteenth century. Studies of the peasantry have emphasized the decidedly patriarchal character of the traditional peasant household. Here the "integral household" was even more entrenched: The peasant household functioned as both a social and an economic unit, a family as well as a small firm.[151] Thus the head of the household occupied a powerful position; his authority as head of the family was inseparable from his position as the "boss" of the family farm. Strengthening his paternal authority was his control over land and property inheritance, which enhanced his control over the marriage decisions and mobility of his children.

But in land-poor, proto-industrial households — those that had come to dominate the Prussian and Austrian rural landscape by the eighteenth century — the family head lacked such a firm basis for his authority. To be sure, the proto-industrial household remained a unit of production, since it was still dependent on the labor of its members for subsistence. Indeed, the labor of its children was crucial to the economic survival of the proto-industrial household.[152] Still, the declining importance of land and property inheritance in these households, as well as the availability of nonagricultural sources of income, weakened patriarchal control considerably. The head of the proto-industrial household lacked the sanctions through which his peasant counterpart could enforce his authority. By the time children reached adolescence, little prevented them from leaving the parental household to start their own families.

To be sure, the impact of proto-industry on patterns of patriarchal authority cannot be fully understood without further research. However, the fear of the "masterless" (*herrenlose Gesindel*) expressed in absolutist edicts, as well as complaints about the absence of discipline among children from poor rural households, betrayed a genuine concern about

---

[150]Ibid., p. 143.
[151]For recent discussions of the patriarchal character of peasant households see Rebel, *Peasant Classes*, pp. 142–198, and Alan Macfarlane, *The Origins of English Individualism: The Family, Property, and Social Transition* (New York, 1978), pp. 25–27.
[152]See Medick, "Proto-Industrial Family Economy," pp. 54–62.

social control in the countryside. Frederick II noted disapprovingly that in the Electoral Mark, these households "allow their children to roam about the countryside without any sort of useful employment, and make no attempt to discipline them."[153] The governor of Bohemia in the 1770s, Prince Carl Egon von Fürstenberg, condemned what he perceived as the utter absence of paternal responsibility in poor rural households. Fürstenberg lamented that the heads of these households "know nothing of the duties of fatherhood, for otherwise they would devote more attention to the conduct of their wives, children, and household affairs."[154] Johann Brünn, a Moravian estate manager, blamed widespread theft in the countryside on youths from propertyless households. These families "live in the countryside but own no land. Out of this group there has emerged a class that threatens the peace and security of the countryside. The children of this class grow up idle and unsupervised, which explains the widespread thievery of crops from fields and gardens."[155]

Viewed in this light, the reasons for the appeal of Pietist pedagogy in the eighteenth century become clearer. Criticisms of the apprentice system, the expansion of a nonguilded work force, the growth of a class of rural poor increasingly dependent on nonagricultural sources of income – all point to the changes that had begun to undermine existing forms of patriarchal authority in Prussia and Austria. The century witnessed the expansion of social groups existing outside traditional patriarchal structures. Pietist pedagogy, for its part, offered an instrument for accommodating this expansion. Pietism provided a more internalized matrix of authority, the efficacy of which hinged on self-discipline rather than extraneous coercion. At a time when patriarchal forms of household control were weakening, Pietist education offered an instrument through which the exaction of obedience no longer required the "external" action of patriarchal force.

---

[153]Quoted in Kuczynski and Hoppe, *Kinderarbeit*, 1:92.
[154]*HHStA*, Nachlass Zinzendorf, vol. 158, fol. 17.
[155]*HHStA*, Nachlass Zinzendorf, vol. 148b, fol. 524–525.

6

From compulsory labor to compulsory
schooling: education and the crisis of
seigniorial authority

These peasants have always been coerced; they have never learned to coerce
themselves.

Christian Garve, 1786

Chapter 5 showed how an expanding textile industry helped promote
popular schooling. Yet the rise of rural industry alone cannot account for
the preoccupation with labor so central to pedagogical discourse in eighteenth-century Prussia and Austria. Changing conceptions of the proper
relationship between lord and peasant also played an important role.

The crisis of seigniorial authority in eighteenth-century Prussia and Austria

As historians like Otto Brunner and Robert Berdahl have argued, the
ideology of Central European lordship was informed by profoundly personalized and paternalistic conceptions of authority.[1] The tendency to
define lord–peasant relations in paternalistic terms reflected the fusion of
private and public functions characteristic of seigniorial authority in pre-
industrial Europe. In Prussia and Austria alike, seigniorial authority was
both economic and juridical in nature: The lord not only exacted a part of
his peasants' surplus, but also exercised "public" authority through patrimonial courts and other juridically sanctioned forms of control that
enabled him to intervene in the daily lives of his subjects. Occasional acts

---

[1]Otto Brunner, *Adeliges Landleben und europäischer Geist. Leben und Werk Wolf
Helmhards von Hohberg 1612–1688* (Salzburg, 1949); Robert Berdahl, "Preussischer
Adel: Paternalismus als Herrschaftssystem," in Hans-Jürgen Pühle and Hans-Ulrich
Wehler, eds., *Preussen in Rückblick* (Göttingen, 1981), and idem, "Paternalism, Serfdom,
and Emancipation in Prussia," in Erich Angermann and Marie-Luise Frings, *Oceans
Apart? Comparing Germany and the United States: Studies in Commemoration of the
150th Anniversary of the Birth of Carl Schurz* (Stuttgart, 1981).

of seigniorial charity and beneficence, such as the distribution of grain in times of dearth or the provision of free food and drink at village festivals, contributed further to the paternalistic legitimation of seigniorial authority.

While paternalist conceptualizations of lordship were hardly new, they acquired increasing importance in the wake of seventeenth-century agrarian developments. The rise of large estates oriented toward cash-crop production (*Gutsherrschaft*) in regions like Bohemia, Silesia, and East Elbian Prussia was accompanied by a revival of paternalism as a mode of legitimation.[2] The intensification of seigniorial exploitation and control, far from rendering a paternalistic ideology obsolete, made it all the more natural and necessary as a legitimating device. The enormous popularity of *Hausvaterliteratur* after the late sixteenth century is evidence of the attempt by landlords to restate and refurbish traditional conceptions of seigniorial authority. These manuals on estate management expounded a paternalistic ideology, rooted in Aristotelian conceptions of household authority, that sanctioned the patriarchal authority of the lord as both natural and beneficial. While Otto Brunner viewed the emergence of *Hausvaterliteratur* as the nostalgic reaction of a declining, petty-noble class to the rise of large-scale agriculture,[3] *Hausvaterliteratur* remained enormously popular up to the middle of the eighteenth century. This continued popularity suggests, with due respect to Brunner, that *Hausvaterliteratur* was as much a product of the "second serfdom" as it was a reaction to it.

By the eighteenth century, however, economic changes in the countryside had begun to belie many of the cherished assumptions of seigniorial paternalism. As explained in Chapter 5, the rapid expansion of a land-poor, subpeasant stratum was creating a *herrenlose* class only loosely bound by seigniorial ties. A lack of land made this group less subject to the juridical authority of the lord, while the growing availability of employment in rural industry further increased their independence from seigniorial control. The landless laborer's relationship to seigniorial authority was far more ambigious than that of the peasant, whose plot of land concretely defined his feudal obligations. The day laborer's contacts with his noble employer were likely to be more sporadic, less formalized, and

---

[2]Berdahl, "Preussischer Adel," p. 127; Gotthardt Frühsorge, "Die Gattung der 'Oeconomia' als Spiegel adligen Lebens," in Dieter Lohmeier, ed., *Arte et Marte. Studien zur Adelskultur des Barockzeitalters in Schweden, Dänemark, und Schleswig-Holstein* (Neumünster, 1978), pp. 104–107.

[3]Brunner, *Adeliges Landleben*, pp. 293–312.

mediated by economic subordination to his more prosperous peasant counterparts. A rural laborer often lived under the immediate authority not of a seignior, but a prosperous peasant who employed him as a farm servant. This sometimes worked to the lord's advantage: During peasant uprisings, lords were occasionally able to play on the antagonism between prosperous peasants and the rural poor.[4] In general, however, the sheer numbers of "masterless" persons in eighteenth-century Austria and Prussia raised alarming questions about how authority was to be exercised in the countryside. The ideology of paternalism had traditionally rested on a conception of authority that was personalized, hallowed by tradition, sanctioned by law, and reinforced by contractual relations based on the holding of land. Now, however, the growth of a class that owned little or no land and whose relationship to seigniorial authority was less direct posed a clear challenge to traditional paternalist assumptions.

Rising grain prices, especially after the mid-eighteenth century, also undermined the ideology of seigniorial paternalism.[5] Historians have examined this phenomenon most exhaustively for Prussia, where the resulting increase in the value of estates produced a tremendous speculative boom in land. In some regions of Silesia, the value of estates increased by 90 percent or more between 1700 and 1780, while in areas of East Prussia it was not uncommon for estates to double in value between 1750 and 1770.[6] As estates changed hands with ever-increasing frequency, observers voiced concern about the disruptive impact of land speculation on lord–peasant relations. Critics feared that the "wholeness" of estate life, with its paternalistic relationships and "organic" ties, would disintegrate in the face of the new market in land. Von Reibnitz, a Prussian official in Silesia, noted with dismay that "the condition of the peasantry worsens every year because so many nobles have cast aside the hallowed belief of their ancestors that a lord should be a father to his subjects, and instead prefer to carry on like bankers and usurers."[7] Sur-

---

[4]In eighteenth-century Bohemia, for example, the rural poor sometimes refused to participate in peasant strikes and uprisings. In some cases, such as the peasant rebellion on the lordship of Novy Hrad in the early 1770s, lords were actually able to enlist the aid of poorer peasants in suppressing uprisings led by their more prosperous counterparts. See Jiří Svodoba, *Protifeudálni a sociálni hnuti v Čechách na konci doby Temna (1750–1774)* (Prague, 1967), p. 93.
[5]On this point see Berdahl, "Preussischer Adel," p. 144.
[6]Hanna Schissler, *Preussische Agrargesellschaft im Wandel. Wirtschaftliche, gesellschaftliche und politische Transformationsprozesse von 1763 bis 1847* (Göttingen, 1978), pp. 78–79.
[7]Quoted in Ziekursch, *Hundert Jahre schlesischer Agrargeschichte*, p. 60.

veying the social consequences of estate speculation at the end of the
eighteenth century, the Prussian official Von Cölln concluded that "the
uninterrupted sale and purchase of estates has destroyed the ethical
bonds derived from the mutual respect and veneration that have evolved
over the years between lord and peasant, making them strangers to each
other and uniting them only temporarily by naked economic interest."[8]
A bourgeois observer, the noted *Aufklärer* Christian Garve, warned that
the speculation in landed estates was dissolving the bonds of sentiment
uniting lord and peasant, with class conflict the inevitable result: "Frequent changes in the ownership of an estate are sure to produce a breakdown in discipline and obedience. Unrest and willfulness are the consequences of this market in estates."[9]

The rise in grain prices and estate values undermined a paternalistic
ethos in other ways. The prospect of high agricultural profits was a
growing inducement for enterprising bourgeois investors to purchase
estate leases from noble proprietors. This was especially common in
Brandenburg, where noble proprietors typically leased their estates for
periods ranging from two to six years. Largely as a consequence of the
growth of bourgeois leaseholding, only 25 percent of noble landowners
in Brandenburg resided on their estates by 1780.[10] Although many leaseholders probably managed their estates in an effective and farsighted
manner, some doubtless sought quick returns on their investments without regard for their peasant tenants.[11] Frequent absences by the estate
owner, as well as the undisguised greed of some leaseholders, led critics
like Garve to view the leaseholding system as an impersonal and pernicious form of exploitation.[12]

But the most disruptive change in the relationship between lord and
peasant came in the area of labor obligations. Throughout much of
Prussia and Austria, compulsory labor on the demesne of the lord had
been the predominant form of seigniorial rent since at least the seventeenth century. The essence of labor services, or what was called *corvée*
in France, *Frondienst* in Germany, and *Robot* in parts of Eastern Europe
and Russia, was extra-economic coercion. Where labor services pre-

[8]Ibid., p. 60. This passage is also cited in Berdahl, "Preussischer Adel," p. 144.
[9]Garve, *Über den Charakter der Bauern und ihr Verhältnis gegen die Gutsherrn und gegen
die Regierung* (Breslau, 1786), pp. 150–151.
[10]H. H. Müller, *Märkische Landwirtschaft vor den Agrarreformen von 1807* (Potsdam,
1967), p. 112.
[11]Ibid., p. 119.
[12]Garve, *Über den Charakter der Bauern*, pp. 91–103.

vailed, labor for the peasant household was neither a matter of choice nor a means of meeting its subsistence needs, but a legal obligation. The extent of peasant labor obligations varied widely within the Habsburg and Hohenzollern territories. In general, labor services were heaviest in those regions, such as Bohemia, Silesia, East Prussia, and Pomerania, where noble landlords managed extensive agricultural enterprises. Even within these provinces, the level of labor services required of peasants varied considerably. In Brandenburg and Lower Silesia, peasants with full holdings worked one or two days per week for their lords. In parts of Bohemia, Upper Silesia, and East Prussia, on the other hand, peasant labor obligations could be as high as six days per week. In regions where lords were not involved in large-scale agriculture, such as Upper and Lower Austria, labor services were far less onerous. In Upper Austria, for instance, a peasant worked for his lord no more than two weeks out of the year.[13]

During the first half of the eighteenth century, the increased demand for rural labor that accompanied rising grain prices and expanding proto-industry had produced a general rise in peasant labor services. In Bohemia and Moravia, for example, the labor services of an average peasant household rose from two to three days a week. By the 1770s, peasant labor services in Styria had risen to 165 days per year. Labor services in Silesia also escalated, partly through the efforts of landlords, but also as a result of military requisitions during the Silesian wars.[14]

In numerous regions of Prussia and Austria, the peasantry stubbornly resisted rising labor rents. Aside from the usual forms of passive resistance (e.g., careless work, neglect or abuse of seigniorial farm equipment and cattle), strikes and rebellions increased in number and intensity during the middle decades of the eighteenth century. Rural tensions continued to grow until 1765, when the peasantry of Upper Silesia rose in rebellion. The uprising began on the estates of Count Wilhelm Leopold von Gessler, the cavalry hero of Hohenfriedberg, when the peasantry stopped working in response to the count's efforts to enclose pastureland and raise labor rents. As rumors circulated that Frederick II planned to

[13]Blum, *Rural Europe,* pp. 50–59.
[14]Ibid., pp. 71–73; Gerhard Schilfert, *Deutschland 1648–1789* (East Berlin, 1962), p. 114; Grünberg, *Bauernbefreiung,* 1:83–84; Georg Grüll, *Die Robot in Oberösterreich* (Linz, 1952), p. 250; Ziekursch, *Hundert Jahre schlesischer Agrargeschichte,* pp. 200–201; Stanislaw Michałkiewicz, "Einige Episoden aus der Geschichte der schlesischen Bauernkämpfe im 17. und 18. Jahrhundert," in Ewa Malczyńska, ed., *Beiträge zur Geschichte Schlesiens* (East Berlin, 1958), p. 387.

abolish labor services, the strikes spread into the districts of Pless, Beuthen, and Tost-Gleiwitz, as well as the linen-weaving districts of Glatz and Schweidnitz. In Ratibor, the rebels were led by an unemployed journeyman who claimed to have orders from Frederick II abolishing labor services.[15]

The Habsburg monarchy experienced continual rural unrest during this period. In 1762, peasants in the county of Eisenburg (western Hungary) stopped rendering labor services and in 1765 were joined by the peasants of neighboring counties.[16] In 1766, the peasant uprisings in Prussian Silesia spilled over into Austrian Silesia, where peasants armed themselves and openly defied the authorities.[17] However, the most violent uprisings by far occurred in Bohemia. Although a royal patent in 1738 had attempted to place a ceiling on Bohemian labor services, these continued to rise during the reign of Maria Theresa. As a consequence, tensions between lords and peasants grew steadily, with peasants on lordships like Třebaň, Chebsko, and Chod resorting to strikes and litigation during the 1740s and 1750s.[18] Peasant resistance in Bohemia culminated in the mass uprising of 1775. As in Prussian Silesia, the rebels claimed that the nobility had suppressed a royal patent freeing them of all labor services. The uprising took two years and a force of 40,000 troops to suppress.[19] Maria Theresa was genuinely shaken by the uprising, especially since it had followed on the heels of the Pugachev jacquerie in Russia. Concerned that peasant unrest might spread to other provinces, she warned that "not in Bohemia alone are the peasants to be feared, but also in Moravia, Styria, Austria. At our very doors, here at home, they commit the greatest impudences. The consequences for themselves and for many innocent people are to be feared."[20]

[15]Hubatsch, *Frederick the Great*, pp. 177–181. For a good discussion of other sources of peasant labor unrest during this period, see William W. Hagen, "The Junkers' Faithless Servants: Peasant Insubordination and the Breakdown of Serfdom in Brandenburg-Prussia, 1763–1811," in *The German Peasantry: Conflict and Community in Rural Society from the Eighteenth Century to the Present*, ed. Richard J. Evans and W. R. Lee (London, 1985).

[16]Rudolf Kropf, "Agrargeschichte des Burgenlandes in der Neuzeit," *Zeitschrift für Agrargeschichte und Agrarsoziologie*, 20 (1972), p. 17.

[17]See the report by the Prussian minister Von Schlabrendorff in *A.B.*, 1/13:780.

[18]Svoboda, *Protifeudální a sociální hnuti*, pp. 14–37.

[19]Petran, "Höhepunkt der Bewegungen," pp. 330–334; William Wright, *Serf, Seigneur, and Sovereign: Agrarian Reform in Eighteenth-Century Bohemia* (Minneapolis, 1966), pp. 41–45. Documents relating to the suppression of the uprising are located in the *Kriegsarchiv*, Vienna: Feldakten, 1775, Fasz. 262 (Bauernunruhen in Böhmen), fol. 1–128.

[20]Quoted in Edith Link, *The Emancipation of the Austrian Peasant, 1740–1798* (New York, 1949), p. 56.

The unrest fostered by rising labor services helps to explain why their regulation had become not just a matter of enlightened reform, but an urgent political issue. For proponents of agrarian reform, the most insidious aspect of labor services was their coercive character. Reformers believed it self-evident that peasants who labored freely, for themselves, were more productive than those whose labor was coerced by and for others. Implicit in their arguments was the conviction that *interest* was the mainspring of human action, an idea that Albert Hirschmann has viewed as the primary organizing principle of seventeenth- and eighteenth-century social theory.[21] Within the context of Central European society during the 1760s and 1770s, this critique of labor rent specifically reflected the importation of Physiocratic doctrine from France. The abolition or commutation of feudal obligations as a means of transforming the peasantry into a class of independent producers was a central tenet of Physiocratic theorists like François Quesnay and Dupont de Nemours.[22]

It was the issue of labor services that brought reformers face to face with the central issue posed by the crisis of seigniorial authority. The paternalist ideal of seigniorial control had presumed the physical presence of an external, coercive force. The lord, or at least his immediate representative, the estate steward, exercised control in a direct and personalized fashion.[23] Insofar as labor services embodied the direct and personal control of the lord, efforts to commute them touched at the heart of the paternalist ideal. Like the economic changes described earlier – an expanding underclass of rural poor, the overheated market in estates, the leasing of estates to bourgeois investors – proposals for the commutation of labor services threatened to reduce the immediate control of the seignior. In this respect, the issue of labor services became a metaphor for more fundamental changes in the structure of seigniorial authority during the second half of the eighteenth century. In their efforts to reduce the labor obligations of the peasantry, Prussian and Austrian agrarian reformers grappled with the central dilemma posed by their

21Albert Hirschman, *The Passions and the Interests: Political Arguments for Capitalism before Its Triumph* (Princeton, 1977).
22Heinz Holdack, "Der Physiokratismus und die absolute Monarchie," *Historische Zeitschrift*, 145 (1931) pp. 517–525. The diffusion of Physiocratic ideas in Austria in the 1760s awaits detailed study. Helen Liebel-Weckowicz, "Modernisierungsmotive in der Freihandelspolitik Maria Theresias," in Walter Koschatzky, ed., *Maria Theresia und ihre Zeit* (Salzburg, 1979) pp. 154–155, points to the Physiocratic influence on Theresian proponents of free trade. One such proponent, Count Karl Zinzendorf, met Quesnay and Dupont while visiting the elder Mirabeau's salon in Paris in 1767. Zinzendorf, a Kaunitz protégé who became a leading advisor to Joseph II, would prove to be the most important conduit of Physiocratic thought in Austria.
23On this point see Berdahl, "Paternalism," pp. 32–33.

changing agrarian landscape: How could the lord exact the labor and obedience of his subjects once the coercive mechanisms of seigniorial control had been removed? In the face of economic changes that weakened the direct and personal exercise of seigniorial authority, how could one induce rural subjects to perform their social and economic obligations? Schools were to provide reformers with an answer to these questions.

From agrarian reform to school reform: the case of Prussia

Frederick II was not the first Hohenzollern to concern himself with agrarian reform. In 1719 and 1723 his father had made peasant holdings on royal domains hereditary, hoping that Prussian landlords would follow suit. In a further attempt to guarantee the security of peasant land tenure, he issued a general decree in 1739 forbidding peasant displacement.[24] Here fiscal and military concerns were paramount: Frederick William sought both to prevent the conversion of taxable peasant holdings into nontaxable noble demesne, and to preserve the peasantry as a pool of potential recruits.

Like his father, Frederick II also attempted to prevent peasant displacement.[25] But as Otto Hintze noted, the thrust of Frederick II's agrarian policies differed fundamentally from that of his father. For Frederick II, the main source of imbalance in the lord–peasant relationship was not peasant displacement, but excessive labor services.[26] The most detailed statement of Frederick's agrarian program is found in his 1748 instructions to the General Directory, the central collegial body in Berlin charged with coordinating the administration of the state. Frederick's instructions focused on labor services as the central target of reform. Singling out Pomerania, where he had found peasants forced to work for their lords as many as six days a week, he ordered sizable reductions. On crown lands, Frederick commuted peasant *Spanndienst* (the provision of a horse and a man) into cash payments.[27] Although Frederick's policies

---

[24]R. Stadelmann, ed., *Preussens Könige in ihrer Tätigkeit für die Landeskultur*, 4 vols. (Leipzig, 1878–1887), 2:76–84; Gustavo Corni, *Stato assoluto e società agraria in Prussia nell'età di Federico II* (Bologna, 1982), pp. 48–79, 247–253.

[25]Frederick issued ordinances against peasant displacement in 1749, 1752, 1755, and 1764. See Stadelmann, *Preussens Könige*, 2:117.

[26]Otto Hintze, "Zur Agrarpolitik Friedrichs des Grossen," *Forschungen zur brandenburgischen und preussischen Geschichte*, 10 (1898), p. 276.

[27]Ibid., pp. 275–276; Stadelmann, *Preussens Könige*, 2:101–119.

yielded some success on crown domains, his efforts in Pomerania proved a dismal failure. Pomeranian nobles in the provincial estates skillfully used the vagueness of Frederick's decrees to escape compliance. Frederick's initial efforts in 1753 to regulate Silesian labor services met a similar fate. His edict abolishing "serfdom" in Upper Silesia was couched in such vague terms that landlords effectively evaded its provisions.[28] Only after Ernst Wilhelm von Schlabrendorff became minister of the province did royal policy in Silesia seriously tackle the problem of labor services. Von Schlabrendorff's efforts deserve closer analysis, because they reveal the intimate relationship between agrarian and educational reform in Frederickian Prussia.

Before his appointment as Silesian minister in 1755, Schlabrendorff (1719–69) had studied law at Halle and accumulated over twenty years of administrative experience. He began his career as a protégé of Adam Ludwig von Blumenthal, who as president of the Lithuanian War and Domains Chamber in Gumbinnen had appointed him to a chamber clerkship.[29] Blumenthal had distinguished himself in the 1730s by bluntly advocating limits on labor services and peasant displacement. A camarilla of cabinet officals centered around Frederick von Görne was able to sabotage Blumenthal's efforts, and the king himself reprimanded Blumenthal for occupying himself with "theoretical" speculations.[30] Although Frederick William found Blumenthal's proposals too radical, both he and his son valued his services. Frederick II appointed him to the General Directory in 1745, and as his own career prospered, so did that of his protégé. Schlabrendorff married Blumenthal's daughter in 1742, and in 1745 Blumenthal appointed him to a high post in the Pomeranian War and Domains Chamber. Here Schlabrendorff, like his patron Blumenthal earlier, began to acquire a reputation as an *enfant terrible* in agrarian questions. It was his 1749 memorandum, for example, that provoked Frederick to issue another decree forbidding peasant displacement.[31]

Although Blumenthal continued to recommend Schlabrendorff when-

---

[28]See the instructions published in Lehmann, *Preussen und die katholische Kirche,* 3:390–391.

[29]A.B., 1/5 (pt. 2):467. For Schlabrendorff's biography see Hermann von Petersdorff, "Ernst Wilhelm von Schlabrendorff," *Schlesische Lebensbilder,* 2 vols. (Breslau, 1926), 2:1–14. The War and Domains Chambers (Kriegs- und Domänenkammer) represented the highest tier of royal administration at the provincial level. Except in Silesia, where they reported directly to the King, the Chambers were subordinate to the General Directory.

[30]A.B., 1/5 (pt. 2): 799–803.

[31]A.B., 1/8:492–494.

ever a chamber presidency grew vacant, the ambitious reformer was repeatedly passed over because of his youth. In 1754, finally, Frederick named him to the presidency of the Magdeburg War and Domains Chamber. In accordance with Frederick's decree of that year, Schlabrendorff vigorously promoted and supervised the commutation of labor services into quitrent on royal domains. Schlabrendorff's experience in Magdeburg, where landlords had already begun to commute labor services on their own initiative, served as a blueprint for his later efforts at agrarian reform.[32]

The crowning moment of Schlabrendorff's career came in 1755, when he was appointed minister of Silesia. To become familiar with his province, Schlabrendorff undertook an inspection tour in January, 1756. He found conditions particularly disturbing in Upper Silesia, the rather desolate region lying between the Oder River and Poland. The social and economic position of the Upper Silesian peasant, who often worked as many as six days a week for his lord, was the lowest in the province. Patrimonial courts offered little or no protection against rising labor services, while appeals to higher courts were expensive and often self-defeating. Von Massow, Schlabrendorff's predecessor in Silesia, had reported in 1755 that Upper Silesian landlords "continually burden their peasants with extra labor services and treat them harshly. If a peasant resists, his lord involves him in costly litigation, wearing him down to the point where he finally vacates his holding."[33] The resumption of war in 1756 exacerbated tensions, and peasants now came to resent having to render the same labor obligations in wartime as in peacetime.[34]

Returning to Breslau, Schlabrendorff immediately wrote to the king recommending a partial commutation of the peasantry's labor obligations into quitrent. He also proposed that peasant land tenure be made hereditary to guarantee the security of peasant holdings. Basing his arguments on purely economic grounds, Schlabrendorff assured Frederick that these reforms would make the peasant more diligent. Excessive labor services, he insisted, bred discontent and were a barrier to peasant productivity. Schlabrendorff was convinced that security of tenure and the realization on the part of the peasant that his economic well-being was directly tied to his labor would stimulate initiative: "It is beyond ques-

[32]Ziekursch, *Hundert Jahre schlesischer Agrargeschichte*, p. 164.
[33]A.B., 1/10: 307.
[34]A.B., 1/11 (pt. 1):249–250.

tion that the peasant who works on his own property will labor far more enthusiastically."[35]

Arguments of this sort had become common by the reign of Frederick II, who himself had no doubts as to the destructive effects of high labor rent on the productive capacities of the peasantry. In their remonstrance protesting Frederick's agrarian reform proposals of 1748, Lithuanian nobles from the district of Schlawe had insisted that without high labor services, peasants would simply quit working. Limiting labor services, they warned, would only aggravate existing labor shortages in the countryside. This was indeed the standard argument advanced by opponents of agrarian reform, but Frederick II rejected it categorically. Instead, he insisted that a reduction in labor services would actually improve the economic morale of the peasant: "The nobility groundlessly maintains that the slovenly and lazy peasant will grow even lazier if his labor services are reduced. . . . But it is far more likely that the extra time available to the peasant will encourage him to work his field more efficiently and improve his wretched circumstances."[36] Cameralists like Justi agreed. Justi condemned labor services as a purely extraneous form of coercion that stifled peasant initiative: "The peasant, who always performs such obligations unwillingly and with resentment, works as little as possible and then only perfunctorily and lethargically. The estate manager must stand over him with a whip, something a well-ordered state cannot allow. Labor services are exceedingly harmful to state and landlord alike."[37]

---

[35]Quoted in Ziekursch, *Hundert Jahre schlesischer Agrargeschichte,* pp. 164–165. Here Schlabrendorff was echoing arguments advanced by his patron Blumenthal during the 1730s. Advocating the commutation of peasant labor services in Lithuania, Blumenthal asserted that "these peasants presently have no desire to work or exert themselves in any way, because when they see that even in the best years they reap no rewards from their labor, they lose heart and let their hands drop to their sides." *A.B.,* 1/5 (pt. 2):798.

[36]Quoted in Hintze, "Agrarpolitik," p. 279.

[37]Justi, *Abhandlung von der Vollkommenheit der Landwirtschaft und der höchsten Kultur der Länder* (Ulm, 1761), pp. 26–27. Johann Georg von Dresky, an enterprising Silesian landowner and a member of the Silesian Economic-Patriotic Society, wrote that Upper Silesian peasants "work only because they are forced to do so." Dresky, *Die nach Grundsätzen und Erfahrung abgehandelte schlesische Landwirtschaft.* 2 vols. (Breslau, 1771–72), 2:4. The ethnographer Friedrich Albrecht Zimmermann asserted that because of high labor services, peasants in the Upper Silesian district of Tost "can be moved to hard work neither through benevolence nor through threats, but only with the rod." Peasants in the neighboring district of Oppeln, similarly, obeyed laws and rendered their duties "poorly, grudgingly, and only with the threat of force." Zimmermann, *Beyträge,* 2:289; 3:29. J. P. Süssmilch, the noted Prussian statistician, argued that labor services

But in condemning the coercive character of labor services, reformers faced a dilemma. If decades of coercion had stifled the development of peasant self-discipline, how, as opponents of reform argued, could the peasant be expected to work without coercion? John Gagliardo noted this dilemma in his study of the image of the German peasantry: "The qualities necessary for the implementation of that personal initiative which economists had come to feel was essential to the progress of agriculture – these simply did not exist in the person of the peasant as he was conceived by the overwhelming majority of the educated and politically responsible classes in Germany in the eighteenth century."[38]

For reformers, education became the tool for resolving this contradiction. They attributed peasant lethargy not to qualities inherent in peasant character, but to the existing structure of agrarian relations. They assumed that the character of the peasant was malleable: If existing institutions had made peasants slothful, new ones could make them diligent. This belief in the malleability of the peasant character explains the dialectical relationship between Frederickian agrarian reform and educational reform. Labor services, agrarian reformers argued, had retarded the development of an internalized work ethic in the peasantry. The reduction of these services, or their commutation into quitrent, would in time transform the peasant into a more productive laborer. However, such a transformation required education. Before the peasant's labor obligations were reduced, it was first necessary to reconstitute him as a morally autonomous being. Peasants, as Garve argued, had always been coerced; they had never learned to coerce themselves. The school was to be the place where the peasant was to learn self-coercion.

Schlabrendorff's 1756 tour of Silesia convinced him that a reduction in the level of peasant labor services had to be accompanied by a reform of rural schools. After returning to Breslau, he wrote to Frederick that peasant children in Silesia "grow up like cattle" and had no knowledge of Christianity outside of a *Pater noster* or *Ave Maria*.[39] In Upper Silesia Schlabrendorff found that even communicating with the peasantry was

---

stifled in the peasant any desire to improve his farming techniques. The peasant's response to any attempt at raising his productivity was: "That may well be true, but the more I produce, the higher my obligations." Süssmilch, *Die göttliche Ordnung in den Veränderungen des menschlichen Geschlechts,* 4th ed., 2 vols. (Berlin, 1775), 2:190.

[38] John Gagliardo, *From Pariah to Patriot: The Changing Image of the German Peasant 1770–1840* (Lexington, Ky., 1969), p. 57.

[39] Lehmann, *Preussen und die katholische Kirche,* 4:182.

difficult, since most spoke only Polish.[40] Upper Silesian *Landräte*, who were charged with implementing royal decrees at the district level, complained that Polish-speaking peasants were illiterate and hence could not read royal decrees.[41] Schlabrendorff returned from his tour convinced of the need to train schoolmasters who could teach German to the Polish-speaking peasantry. Accordingly, he ordered that bilingual teachers be hired in Polish-speaking areas. The War and Domains Chambers forwarded his edict to the *Landräte*, who then (presumably) circulated it throughout their districts.[42]

Schlabrendorff's initial efforts on behalf of educational and agrarian reform proved ineffective, since few bilingual schoolmasters could be found. Indeed, subsequent complaints by Felbiger and others suggest that it was difficult enough to find literate schoolmasters, not to mention bilingual ones. Aside from a 1761 prohibition on raising labor services, no steps of any consequence were taken in the direction of agrarian reform. Throughout the Prussian monarchy, the Seven Years War imposed a moratorium on domestic reform. Only after the return of peace in 1763 was Schlabrendorff able to pursue his agrarian policies vigorously. Even then, his success was limited by the opposition his policies aroused among Silesian landlords.[43]

For our purposes, the significance of Schlabrendorff's efforts lies not in their success or failure, but in what they reveal about the relationship between agrarian and school reform. From the 1760s on, the relationship between the reform of peasant obligations and the promotion of popular schooling was expounded in cameralist lecture halls, in the journals of

[40]In Upper Silesia, the area to the east of the Oder River, Polish-speaking peasants predominated.

[41]Alois Kosler, *Die preussische Volksschulpolitik in Oberschlesien, 1742–1848* (Breslau, 1930), p. 49. The Prussian *Landrat* occupied the lowest tier of the Prussian bureaucracy in the countryside. If the War and Domains Chambers were responsible for adapting royal policy to provincial reality, the *Landräte* reconciled provincial policy with local conditions in the countryside. In Silesia, as in other Prussian provinces, the *Landrat* was selected from the ranks of the local nobility. All edicts relating to the administration of his district were sent directly to him. He in turn sent his district "police," the *Landdragonen*, to deliver copies to every landlord and parish priest. The edict was then either read aloud by the parish clergy on Sunday, or posted in a conspicuous place in the village. See the Cabinet order on procedures for the publication of edicts in *A.B.*, 1/6 (pt. 2): 601. On the office of *Landrat* see the fascinating dissertation by Oskar Kutzner, "Das Landratamt in Schlesien 1740–1806," Ph.D. diss., University of Breslau, 1911.

[42]Kosler, *Preussische Volksschulpolitik*, p. 49.

[43]Corni, *Stato assoluto*, pp. 344–355; Ziekursch, *Hundert Jahre schlesischer Agrargeschichte*, pp. 158–355.

agricultural societies, and in manuals on estate management. The *Schlesische Oeconomische Sammlungen* (1755–62), an economic journal to which progressive landowners, estate managers, and agronomists submitted practical articles on estate improvement, proposed creating an economic society devoted to peasant education. The journal assured its readers that the promotion of schools where peasants learned not simply the externals of religion, but also its moral precepts, would raise their productivity: "The inner contentment which the peasant will obtain from such schooling will not only dry the sweat on his brow, but cultivate in him the incentive to work for the good of society. . . . Disloyalty, laziness, idleness, disobedience, disorder, and drudgery would all disappear."[44] Von Dresky, the progressive Silesian landowner mentioned earlier, considered the peasantry's lack of education to be the major barrier to increased agricultural productivity. "Many peasants," he asserted, "are ignorant even of fundamental words like God, man, soul, death, religion, lord, servant, duty, obedience, happiness, or unhappiness." He called upon the state to promote the education of peasants in order to teach them "how best to pursue their profession and fulfill their duties."[45] The journal of the Silesian Economic-Patriotic Society, established in 1763 and later headed by Felbiger, voiced a similar faith in the ability of education to create an internalized work ethic in the peasantry. Journal articles repeatedly stressed the relationship between education and productivity, and addressed in detail the question of how to transform peasant attitudes toward work. One issue offered a prize competition on the question: "Which habits, customs, and practices have a harmful effect on the industry and health of the rural population, and how can these best be abolished?" The peasant had to be educated, answered one reader, "for if the peasant's character is not improved, neither the rod nor the workhouse will induce him to fulfill his duties." The peasantry's loyalty and obedience were best commanded not through force, but through its acceptance of duty out of inner conviction: "Complaints about disobedient subjects will persist until the moral char-

[44]"Vorschlag zu einer oeconomischen Gesellschaft," in *Schlesische oeconomische Sammlung*, 2 (Breslau, 1757), pp. 592–593.
[45]Dresky, *Schlesische Landwirtschaft*, 2:5. Dresky's handbook for estate stewards provides a striking example of how cameralist ideas had begun to filter down to the level of estate management. His manual sought to apply Bielfeld's model of a "well-ordered police state" to the management of a landed estate. Dresky believed that a well-managed estate had to regulate everything from farm wages to the number of hours the peasant slept. His ideal estate was a microcosmic version of Frederickian absolutism, and included grain magazines, schools, numbered houses, poorhouses, spinning schools, and prisons.

acter of the peasantry is improved. Is it not in the best interest of the lord . . . if his subject willingly, out of an inner consciousness of his duties and a love of God, not only fulfills his obligations but even renders services beyond those required by law?"[46]

Agrarian reform and popular schooling in Austria

In the Habsburg monarchy, attempts to regulate labor services dated back to the seventeenth century. Following an outburst of rural disorder in Bohemia, Leopold I issued an edict in 1680 placing a ceiling on peasant labor services. Subsequent edicts, such as that issued by Charles VI in 1738, likewise attempted to regulate peasant labor obligations. These efforts were essentially ad hoc, hastily drafted measures with little impact.[47]

On the surface, the achievements of Theresian agrarian reform were equally modest. Yet the reign of Maria Theresa witnessed the first comprehensive effort to redefine the lord–peasant relationship.[48] The most significant reform phase fell between 1768 and 1775. Peasant uprisings in Austrian Silesia sparked the creation in 1768 of a special agrarian commission to investigate rural conditions in the province. Franz Anton Blanc, a Chancellery official who emerged as one of the most vocal proponents of commutation, proposed abolishing labor services and transforming peasant holdings into private property. Although Blanc's proposals enjoyed the support of Gebler and Kaunitz in the Council of State, Count Rudolf Chotek, the conservative and influential court chancellor, succeeded in blocking the implementation of much of Blanc's program. Hence the resulting patent of 1771 did little more than codify existing obligations.[49] But lurid reports of widespread abuses on the Bohemian estates of Prince Mansfeld, followed in 1771–72 by the devastating effects of a famine in which 16,000 Bohemian peasants were reported to have perished from hunger and disease, helped strengthen the

[46]*Ökonomische Nachrichten der Patriotischen Gesellschaft in Schlesien*, 6 vols. (Breslau, 1773), 1:130; 2:63.

[47]On pre-Theresian agrarian reforms see William Wright, *Serf, Seigneur, and Sovereign*, pp. 22–24.

[48]The best and most recent analysis of Theresian agrarian policy is found in Helen Liebel-Weckowicz and Franz Szabo, "Modernization Forces in Maria Theresia's Peasant Policies," *Histoire sociale – Social History* 15 (1982).

[49]Ibid., pp. 312–313. On Blanc see also Karl Grünberg, *Franz Anton von Blanc. Ein Sozialpolitiker der theresianisch-josefinischer Zeit* (Leipzig, 1921).

hand of reformers.[50] The renewed outbreak of peasant uprisings in 1771 and 1773 made reform an urgent necessity, and on April 7, 1774, a royal decree gave each Bohemian landowner six months to negotiate a fixed level of labor services with his peasants. But it was too late: The Bohemian peasantry, devastated by the effects of the famine, its patience worn thin by dilatory tactics, revolted on January 1, 1775. The Council of State worked feverishly to produce a reform patent before the revolts worsened. In August and September of 1775, Maria Theresa issued patents for Bohemia and Moravia that limited labor services to a maximum of three days a week.[51]

At this point Franz Anton Raab, a councillor in the Court Chancellery with experience in the administration of crown domains, came forward with a plan for the total commutation of all labor services. Raab's scheme proposed carving up noble demesne into plots over which peasants would have full title. The lord had the option either of selling or leasing the land; labor services were to be abolished, but peasant owners were obliged to pay a cash rent equal to the lord's previous level of income. Livestock and farm equipment, formerly provided by the lord, were now to be sold or rented to the peasantry.[52]

Raab's attempt at a general commutation of labor services foundered on the opposition of Kaunitz and Crown Prince Joseph, who feared the plan was too radical and violated noble property rights.[53] Blanc was demoted to a remote Alpine post, while the government limited the implementation of Raab's plan to several crown estates. Although a patent from March 1777 set rates for the commutation of labor services, these provisions were purely voluntary.[54]

But again, we are concerned less with the fate of agrarian reform than with its relationship to school reform. It is no accident that efforts to reform peasant obligations coincided with the establishment of com-

[50]Grünberg, *Bauernbefreiung*, 2:155–186; Liebel-Weckowicz and Szabo, "Modernization Forces," pp. 315–316.
[51]For a more detailed anlaysis of the patents see Liebel-Weckowicz and Szabo, "Modernization Forces," pp. 324–325. They are published in Kropatschek, *Vollständige Sammlung*, 7:16ff.
[52]Grünberg, *Bauernbefreiung*, 1:302; Wright, *Serf, Seigneur, and Sovereign*, pp. 101–106.
[53]In contrast with Joseph, Maria Theresa proved far more willing to enact Raab's proposals, and she abandoned their implementation with reluctance. This leads one to question the traditional contrast between Theresian "conservatism" and Josephinian "radicalism." On this point see Liebel-Weckowicz and Szabo, "Modernization Forces," pp. 320–321.
[54]Grünberg, *Blanc*, p. 161.

pulsory schooling. As in Prussia, the debate over peasant labor obligations evolved dialectically into a pedagogical issue.

Like their Prussian counterparts, Austrian critics of labor rent focused on the insidious nature of external coercion. Field Marshall Franz Moritz von Lacy, who had had ample opportunity to observe rural conditions while reorganizing the system of Bohemian conscription in 1771, described a peasantry demoralized with excessive labor services, starving from famine, and ridden with venereal disease spread by soldiers during the Seven Years War. Lacy argued that labor services conditioned the peasantry to work "purely through coercion and physical force." He proposed commuting labor services in order to "lift peasants out of their indolence and make them diligent."[55] Prince Carl Egon von Fürstenberg, who became Governor of Bohemia in 1771, was convinced that labor services had given many Bohemian peasants such a distaste for work that the idea of acquiring additional property into which they would need to invest their labor was anathema. Landlords should commute labor services into quitrent, he argued, because "ten work days which a peasant devotes to his plot yield more than fifteen spent working for his lord."[56] An anonymous proposal for the abolition of mendicancy (1771) blamed rural poverty on the system of labor services: "Under this system, diligence and a spirit of enterprise are lacking; the peasant works only so long as is necessary for his subsistence and the fulfillment of his obligations."[57] Echoing Fürstenberg, the Moravian estate steward Johann Brünn argued that "six hands which are coerced are worth less than two hands which labor freely." Coercion was ultimately ineffective, he insisted, because it required constant supervision by the lord or estate steward. Because "the lord and his steward each have only two eyes," Brünn concluded that an internalized spirit of acquisitiveness among the peasantry had to replace the external coercion of labor services.[58] Other critics warned that labor services were not only unproductive, but also engendered class hatred. An anonymous pamphlet from 1775, which Raab either authored or plagiarized, flatly stated that peasants rendering labor services displayed "an almost bestial indifference to God and re-

[55]*HHStA*, Kaiser Franz Akten, Fasz. 62, fol. 434.
[56]*HHStA*, Nachlass Zinzendorff, vol. 158, fol. 454.
[57]*Kurzer Unterricht von der Notwendigkeit und Weise die umlaufenden Bettler abzuschaffen, und von der christlichen Schüldigkeit und Mitteln die würdigen Arme zu versorgen* (Vienna, 1770), pp. 151–152.
[58]*HHStA*, Nachlass Zinzendorf, vol. 148b, fol. 513.

ligion, a coldness towards their lords bordering on hate, and a stupid insensitivity to all morality. Neither disgrace nor honor can move their bitter hearts. They manage their households carelessly, perform their work resentfully and reluctantly, and are lazy and disloyal, all because they know that they work not for themselves, but their masters."[59] Raab himself wrote of the social and psychological effects of labor services:

One can see the languor of those peasants forced to labor in the fields of their lords. One sees how much coercion is needed to make them fulfill their duties. Their sullen temperament breeds a contempt for their duties, so that all they desire is to work as little as the presence or absence of their overseer allows. . . . They have lost the desire to work even their own plots. Their miserable circumstances have made them vile and mean, living from day to day, immediately consuming whatever surplus they may have produced for themselves.[60]

Labor services, argued Raab and other critics, were ultimately unproductive because they violated the laws of nature. Raab proclaimed that "in nature, reaping and sowing are inextricably linked; nature repays man's efforts by making him diligent. But if an arbitrary power deprives him of the rewards guaranteed by nature, nature is violated, labor becomes drudgery, and idleness one's sole pleasure."[61]

As in Prussia, then, agrarian reformers in the Habsburg monarchy blamed the peasants' unproductivity on the conditions under which they labored, not on peasants themselves. Reformers could then insist that if institutions had corrupted peasants, institutions could also improve them. Here, again, education became central to proposals for agrarian reform. Raab himself proved a vigorous supporter of compulsory schooling. He kept a vigilant eye on the dominial schools under his jurisdiction and arranged for the transportation of wood from dominial forests to construct and heat school buildings.[62]

Johann Joseph Trnka's handbook for estate stewards (1771) also illustrates the dialectical relationship between agrarian reform and the promotion of peasant education.[63] Trnka, himself a steward on the

[59]*Philosophisch-Politische Abhandlungen von den Naturalfrondiensten und deren Verwandlungen in anderen Leistungen* (Frankfurt am Main, 1775), p. 454. Since this passage is found verbatim in Raab's *Unterricht über die Verwandlung der K.K. böhmischen Domänen in Bauerngüter* (Vienna, 1777), p. 7, he either wrote it or borrowed it.
[60]Raab, *Unterricht*, pp. 7–8.
[61]Ibid., p. 52.
[62]Ignaz Böhm, *Historische Nachricht von der Entstehungsart und Verbreitung des Normalinstituts in Böhmen* (Prague, 1784), p. 20.
[63]Johann Josef Trnka, *Pflicht eines Wirtschaftsbeamter* (Dresden, 1771).

Dietrichstein estates in Proskau (Bohemia),[64] favored commutation. Yet he warned that commutation alone would not make the peasant productive and diligent. Years of forced labor had so demoralized the peasant that immediate commutation would have disastrous consequences for agriculture:

Hardly would the Bohemian peasant gain his freedom before he would begin to abuse it. Immediate freedom would be as destructive to agriculture as serfdom [*Leibeigenschaft*] itself. Fear, which at present is all that motivates the peasant and controls his behavior, would disappear. Where virtue, honor, and the promise of prosperity can motivate a free individual, only the threatening whip of an overseer can motivate a peasant whose labor is coerced.[65]

An edict could abolish a peasant's labor obligations, but "what law is supposed to reform his moral condition?"[66] Hence Trnka favored commutation, but only after education had rendered coercion superfluous. One could free the peasant from coercion only "if he first acquires better morals and a docile outlook, only if he becomes more trusting, sociable, and patriotic."[67]

The Austrian agronomist Johann Wiegand, a tutor in the Liechtenstein household in Vienna, had recommended commutation as early as 1762. Under a system of quitrent, Wiegand asserted, peasants "work and conduct their affairs more freely, happily, and diligently" than those burdened with labor services.[68] But Wiegand also warned that the peasantry had to be educated before its labor services could be commuted. Hence his essay on the peasantry submitted to the Lower Austrian Economic

[64]Little is known about Trnka's life. According to Ignaz de Luca, *Das gelehrte Österreich*, 2 vols. (Vienna, 1776), 1:227, Trnka was a member of the Silesian Economic-Patriotic Society who emigrated to Russia in 1778. He was widely read by agrarian reformers like Raab and Governor Fürstenberg of Bohemia. See Joseph Goldman, "Land, Labor, and Lord: Count Hatzfeld, the Imperial State Council, and Robot Abolition in Austria and Bohemia, 1740–1790," Ph.D. diss., University of Minnesota, 1971, p. 172; and Fürstenberg's reference to Trnka's manual in *HHStA*, Nachlass Zinzendorf, vol. 158, fol. 361. Trnka's handbook, like that of Dresky, revealed the influence of cameralist theory on estate management. In cameralistic fashion, Trnka divided the duties of the estate manager into the categories of agriculture, manufacturing, and police. Trnka compared the estate owner with a king and the estate manager with his bureaucracy: "the head of the household makes the laws, while the housekeeper puts them into practice." Trnka, *Pflicht eines Wirtschaftsbeamter*, p. 120.

[65]Trnka, *Pflicht eines Wirtschaftsbeamter*, p. 120.

[66]Ibid., p. 20.

[67]Ibid., p. 22.

[68]Johann Wiegand, *Der wohlerfahrene Landwirt, oder Anleitung wie die Landwirtschaftsökonomie in einen verbesserten Stand gebracht werden könnte* (Leipzig, 1762), p. 96.

Society proposed a compulsory school ordinance based upon Felbiger's Rural School Ordinance for Prussian Silesia.[69]

Noble landlords and rural schools

The fact that rural schools were promoted on the estates of a number of prominent Austrian and Prussian landlords suggests that nobles were beginning to recognize that changes in the social relations of production required more refined methods of seigniorial control. In Bohemia, the expansion of parish schooling during the 1700s coincided with a period of rapid change in the Bohemian countryside. Not only was there an intensification of proto-industrial activity, as seen in Chapter 5, but this period was also one in which the commutation of labor services was proceeding apace.[70] In Chapter 5 we saw how these two tendencies converged on the estates of Count Johann Buquoi, who fostered proto-industrial activity while commuting the labor services of his peasants. At the same time, he hired Ferdinand Kindermann to reform the parish schools on his estates in accordance with Felbiger's Pietist pedagogy. The reform efforts of Carl Egon von Fürstenberg, governor of Bohemia from 1771 to 1782, also exemplify the connection between educational and agrarian reform.

A scion of one of Bohemia's most powerful and wealthy aristocratic families, Fürstenberg had studied at Leipzig before embarking on his administrative career.[71] When he assumed his duties as governor in 1771, Bohemia was in the midst of a devastating famine. While supervising the implementation of emergency measures to ameliorate the effects of the catastrophe, Fürstenberg submitted to Maria Theresa a series of memoranda providing an analysis of Bohemia's deteriorating social and economic situation. "Every minute," Fürstenberg warned Maria Theresa, "Bohemia approaches one step closer to its utter ruin."[72] Fürstenberg blamed not just the famine, but the system of labor services for the

---

[69]Wiegand, *Versuch den Fleiss unter dem Landvolk einzuführen*, pp. 47 ff.

[70]Already by the middle of the eighteenth century, Bohemian landowners had commuted labor services into wage labor or intermediary forms of rent on 20 percent of all estates. See Klíma, "Agrarian Class Structure," p. 62.

[71]For Fürstenberg's biography see Ernst Münch, *Geschichte des Hauses und Landes Fürstenberg*, 4 vols. (Aachen and Leipzig, 1829–47), 4:297–314; and Hermann von Hermannsdorf, "Versuch einer Biographie Carl Egon Fürsten von Fürstenberg," *Abhandlung der königlichen böhmischen Gesellschaft der Wissenschaften*, 3 (1788): 1–18.

[72]"Wohlgemeinte Gedanken, über die sich täglich und augenscheinlich verschlimmende Umstände des Königreichs Böhmen," *HHStA*, Nachlass Zinzendorf, vol. 158, fol. 129.

impoverishment of Bohemian peasants. Labor services demoralized both full peasants and those dependent on nonagricultural pursuits, who had little time to tend their plots or spin. In these households, a life of idleness and drunkenness became preferable to the cares that accompanied the maintenance of property: "The Bohemian peasant is thoroughly indifferent to property. . . . Indeed, he disdains even its acquisition, for he would rather lead a life of uncertainty as a beggar, chased from one miserable hut to another, than assume the responsibilities of a property owner."[73] Fürstenberg sought to turn the tables on those who objected that "if the peasant's labor services are reduced, he will spend his free time in taverns rather than his fields."[74] For Fürstenberg, the very fact that Bohemian landlords had no other means than coercion to induce their peasants to work testified to the bankruptcy of the entire system of agrarian relations. But like Trnka and Wiegand, Fürstenberg believed one must first improve the moral character of the peasant before reducing his obligations: "The character of the peasant has been so neglected that the will and aptitude necessary for his self-improvement will require long and serious cultivation. In short, we must educate an entirely new generation."[75] For Fürstenberg, the future stability of society depended on peasant education:

As long as the peasant's moral character is not reformed, his indolence and resentment toward his lord will persist. He will continue to consider even the slightest chore too difficult, and will lack any interest in the acquisition of property. But if one improves his character before reducing his excessive labor obligations, this education will muffle his discontent and suppress the dangerous impulses bred by constant maltreatment.[76]

To whom could one entrust the moral education of the peasantry? Not to the clergy alone, insisted Fürstenberg. From the parish priest the peasant acquired little more than formulaic phrases and superficial devotional forms. Because most peasants could not read the Bible, they were ignorant of its moral teachings. Since the church had failed to give the peasantry a moral education, argued Fürstenberg, the state had to take the initiative. Fürstenberg advocated compulsory schooling and state fund-

---

[73] "Beantwortung der kaiserlichen Pro Memoria über die Aufhebung der Robotten," *HHStA*, Nachlass Zinzendorff, vol. 158, fol. 75–76.
[74] "Von dem Robotwesen," *HHStA*, Nachlass Zinzendorf, vol. 158, fol. 443–444.
[75] "Beantwortung der kaiserlichen Pro Memoria," fol. 24.
[76] "Zweyte Abhandlung, wie die Agrikultur und Viehzucht in Böhmen bestellet sey," *HHStA*, Nachlass Zinzendorf, fol. 158, fol. 385.

ing for the training of competent parish schoolmasters. Only after education had enlightened the rural population could other reforms have their desired effect: "The agriculture and commerce of a nation will never flourish until its subjects have acquired diligence, thrift, and other civic virtues."[77]

Fürstenberg ultimately commuted the labor services of his own peasants into quitrent. Before doing so, however, he worked energetically to expand schooling on his estates. In 1772 he paid to send Karl Benda, a young parish priest, to attend Felbiger's teacher-training institute in Sagan. When Benda returned, Fürstenberg hired him to establish a similar institute on his estate in Dobrowitz. Fürstenberg required all parish schoolmasters to attend the Dobrowitz institute, which trained them in accordance with Felbiger's pedagogy. Fürstenberg also contributed sixty florins a month to establish and maintain the Prague orphanage, and was one of the chief financial supporters of the Prague normal school established in 1775.[78] Fürstenberg later paid to have *Der Volkslehrer,* a monthly agricultural journal aimed at the peasantry, translated into Czech and distributed to his peasants.[79]

In Prussia, commutation had also become increasingly common in provinces like Magdeburg, Brandenburg, and East Prussia.[80] The career

[77]"Beantwortung der kaiserlichen Pro Memoria," fol. 124. Fürstenberg's qualified advocacy of free trade closely paralleled his views on agrarian reform and popular schooling. By this time, the empress had abolished internal tolls in numerous provinces, and introduced free trade in grain in Milan and Tuscany. These efforts would culminate in the establishment of a customs union (1775) comprising all Austrian and Bohemian provinces except the Tyrol. In supporting these liberalizing tendencies, Fürstenberg argued that coercion was a poor mainspring for the production of national wealth. Expedients like tolls and tariffs, which were extraneous to production and consumption, did not safeguard national prosperity. It was rather the free circulation of money, a phenomenon intrinsic to production and consumption, that yielded prosperity. But just as Fürstenberg believed that an accumulation of "moral capital" in the Bohemian peasantry was a precondition for its freedom from coercive labor services, so he was convinced that an accumulation of real capital was necessary before Bohemia could be freed from coercive tolls and tariffs. He therefore advocated the creation of rural credit institutions to promote manufacturing and investment. Fürstenberg's position on free trade is elaborated in his "Kurzer Begriff einer ständischen Leih-Bank für das Königreich Böhmen," *HHStA,* Nachlass Zinzendorf, vol. 158, fol. 149–194, and "Beantwortung der kaiserlichen Pro Memoria," fol. 14–58.

[78]Böhm, *Historische Nachricht,* p. 60; Hermannsdorf, "Versuch einer Biographie," p. 15; Münch, *Fürstenberg,* 4:299–313.

[79]I was unable to locate this journal. It is briefly discussed in Gagliardo, *From Pariah to Patriot,* p. 107. For examples of other Bohemian aristocrats who promoted rural schools during this period see Böhm, *Historische Nachricht,* p. 45; Kindermann, *Nachricht von der Landschule zu Kaplitz,* pp. 49, 69; Weiss, *Geschichte der theresianischen Schulreform in Böhmen,* 2:21–23.

[80]See Müller, *Märkische Landwirtschaft,* p. 35. For specific instances of commutation see Ingrid Mittenzwei, *Preussen nach dem siebenjährigen Krieg* (East Berlin, 1979), pp. 181–182.

of Friedrich Eberhard von Rochow, the Brandenburg estate owner and noted pedagogue, illustrates how agrarian concerns were translated into pedagogical activity. Rochow stemmed from solid *Junker* stock: His father was a Prussian minister under Frederick II, and young Rochow attended the Berlin *Ritterakademie* in preparation for a military career. But as a result of wounds he received while serving as an officer in the Seven Years War, he returned to his estates outside Berlin and devoted himself to agricultural improvements. He subsequently founded the Brandenburg Economic Society, was one of the earliest estate owners to transform village common lands into private peasant holdings, and was the first director of the noble credit cooperative established by Frederick II in 1777 to finance estate improvements in Brandenburg. Topping off this pattern of capitalist-oriented reform activity was his commutation of peasant labor services into quitrent.[81]

As with the Bohemian landowners, however, Rochow's commutation of feudal dues followed a period of intense pedagogical activity.[82] With the aid of subsidies provided by Von Zedlitz, head of the Ecclesiastical Department and a proponent of compulsory schooling, Rochow increased the annual salary of the schoolmasters on his estates from 20 to 180 talers. Attendance rose dramatically, since pupils no longer paid school fees. His school in Reckahn, which more than seventy peasant children attended in 1773, soon won wide acclaim throughout Central Europe. Equally famed was his primer, *Der Kinderfreund* (1776), which was to be widely emulated throughout Germany. Written in a brisk, simple style deliberately aimed at rural pupils, *Der Kinderfreund* (*The Children's Friend*) attempted to instill the moral and religious teachings of the Bible on the basis of fables drawn from rural life. The Ecclesiastical Department recommended that it be adopted in Prussian rural schools, and it continued to be used well into the nineteenth century.[83]

Significantly, most of the characters in Rochow's fables were "free"

[81]On Rochow's life see the biographical essay in Fritz Jonas and Friedrich Wienecke, eds., *Friedrich Eberhard von Rochows sämtliche pädagogische Schriften*, 4 vols. (Berlin, 1907–10), 4:387–436. On his pedagogy see Gessinger, *Sprache und Bürgertum*, pp. 57–63, and Peter Lundgreen, "Analyse preussischer Schulbücher als Zugang zum Thema 'Schulbildung und Industrialisierung'," *International Review of Social History*, 15 (1970), pp. 89–94, 103–110.

[82]See Rochow's description of his schools in his "Geschichte meiner Schulen," in *Rochows sämtliche pädagogische Schriften*, 3:9–55.

[83]*Der Kinderfreund*, 2 pts. (Brandenburg and Leipzig, 1776–1779), published in *Rochows sämtliche pädagogische Schriften*, 1:142–301. Engelsing, *Analphabetentum und Lektüre*, p. 59, calculates that in the years immediately following the publication of Rochow's primer, more than 100,000 copies had been sold. In time, *Der Kinderfreund* would go through 200 editions.

day laborers, not peasants with seigniorial obligations. His fables stressed the need for moral autonomy among those less bound by seigniorial ties, and provided examples of wage laborers who freely displayed loyalty and diligence even in the absence of coercion. In "Der Abwendigmacher" (The Dissuader), for example, a day laborer loyally remained in the service of his noble employer although another lord had offered him higher wages and finer clothes.[84] In "Lied eines frommen Tagelöhners" (Song of a pious day laborer), a rural laborer pledged "to look upon any time I may waste as theft."[85] Conversely, Rochow's fables condemned those for whom the observance of duty was limited to outward compliance. "Der Heuchler oder Augendiener" (The hypocrite, or the untrustworthy servant), related the following tale:

Klaus worked for a lord who was preoccupied with business outside the estate, and was rarely around to supervise those he employed. Noting this, Klaus worked furiously when he knew his master would be watching. But as soon as his lord was gone, he dropped his work and did as he wished. In church he comported himself piously, sobbing and shedding tears for all to see. In private, however, his behavior was utterly contemptible. Still, his lord held him to be most loyal, since in his presence Klaus always made a point of criticizing those who were lazy or disloyal. But one day Klaus, unaware that his master was watching, was caught pilfering. The lord afterward learned that Klaus was in truth a deceitful being, and increased his punishment twofold. Moral: Of all vices, hypocrisy is the most shameful. A hypocrite tries to deceive not only humans, but also God. But be not deceived: God will not be mocked.[86]

In contrast to Klaus, the inhabitants of "Das ordentliche Dorf" (The well-ordered village) had fully internalized their duties. Through education they had achieved such a level of moral autonomy that "there was not even a jail in the village. The old one had collapsed, and the lord refused to build a new one. 'Jails are only for the wicked,' said the lord, 'and I have no wicked subjects.' "[87] Rochow himself later claimed that because of the moralizing influence of his schools, he no longer needed to administer corporal punishment or maintain a jail on his estates.[88]

[84] *Der Kinderfreund*, 2:219.
[85] Ibid., p. 309.
[86] Ibid., 1:165–166.
[87] Ibid., 2:254.
[88] Letter to Franz Ludwig von Erthal, prince-bishop of Bamberg-Würzburg, January 20, 1791, in *Rochows sämtliche pädagogische Schriften*, 4:325.

Part III

The limits of reform

7

School reform in Frederickian Prussia

Opposition to this undertaking has been general: Catholics and Protestants, clergy and laity, rich and poor, have all worked to undermine it.

Johann Ignaz Felbiger (1768)

So far this book has focused on the social, economic, and cultural roots of educational reform in Prussia and Austria. We now turn to the reforms themselves and their actual implementation. The two remaining chapters evaluate the achievements of Frederickian and Theresian school reform, as well as the formidable, sometimes insurmountable obstacles that hampered the effectiveness of absolutist educational policy.

The advent of reform

Historians commonly divide the reign of Frederick II into two parts: the period between 1740 and 1763, when he fought three wars to preserve his grip on Silesia, and the relatively peaceful years from 1763 to his death in 1786. It was during the second part of his reign that Frederick was able to devote more of his energies to domestic matters, such as school reform.

Preoccupied with military and diplomatic matters, Frederick and his officials undertook few initiatives on behalf of school reform prior to 1763. Rather, the leading spokesman for reform during the 1740s and 1750s was Hecker, whose appointment to the Supreme Consistory (Oberkonsistorium) in 1750 further enhanced his influence on educational policy.[1] Hecker used that influence in 1752 to obtain a state

[1] The Supreme Consistory possessed authority over every provincial Lutheran consistory outside of those in Silesia and Guelders. Created by the justice minister Samuel Cocceji in 1750, the Supreme Consistory was responsible for the ordination of Lutheran pastors and the supervision of Lutheran churches, schools, and charitable institutions. On the duties of this body see *A.B.*, 1/8:740–741; and Vollmer, *Preussische Volksschulpolitik*, pp. 24–25.

subsidy for his pedagogical institute in Berlin. Although Frederick did give graduates of Hecker's institute preference in all parish school appointments on crown domains in Brandenburg, the pedagogical impact of the institute was slight. A few graduates were able to obtain positions in schools directly under crown patronage, but in most Brandenburg villages nobles held the right of patronage (*Patronenrecht*) and jealously guarded their control over the appointment of schoolmasters and other parish personnel.[2]

Hecker's project for the reform of schools in the western territories of Minden and Ravensberg proved no more successful. Hecker based his Minden–Ravensberg plan (1754) on an earlier proposal drafted by the Pietist theologian Friedrich Wagner in 1727.[3] Although Frederick II formally approved the plan in 1754, the resumption of war in 1756 ended any immediate hope of implementing it.

Indeed, the outbreak of the Seven Years War effectively postponed domestic reform of any kind. In 1756, Frederick ordered his provincial War and Domains Chambers to devote their energies solely to the maintenance of commerce and the collection of taxes. In Silesia, for example, he instructed Minister Schlabrendorff not to bother him with memoranda unless they bore directly on military affairs: "My present occupation," wrote Frederick, "does not permit my being distracted by other matters."[4]

Nevertheless, Frederick's close contact with his soldiers during the next seven years, as well as his opportunity to observe rural conditions in the more remote regions of the monarchy, convinced him that further educational reforms were necessary. According to Hecker, Frederick first resolved to reform Prussian schools in 1759, while he was bivouacked with his troops in Brandenburg: "While camped with his troops in the Electoral Mark in the spring of 1759, His Majesty noticed the lack of education among peasant youths. At that moment he resolved that as soon as God had put an end to the war, he would work tirelessly to improve the pitiable condition of our rural schools."[5]

---

[2]Clausnitzer, "Zur Geschichte der preussischen Volksschule," pp. 345–347; Gloria, *Pietismus als Förderer der Volksbildung*, pp. 64–70; Neugebauer, *Schulwirklichkeit*, p. 333. Neugebauer's exhaustive study is indispensable for any historian of Prussian schooling, although his conclusions are somewhat at variance with my own.
[3]On the Minden-Ravensberg reform see Vollmer, *Preussische Volksschulpolitik*, pp. 26–34.
[4]Quoted in Hubatsch, *Frederick the Great*, p. 114.
[5]Johann Julius Hecker, *Nachrichten an den Schulanstalten der Dreyfältigkeitskirche zu Berlin* (Berlin, 1759), as quoted in Felbiger, *K.S.*, p. 445.

The subsequent history of Frederickian school reform supports Hecker's observation that a concern with rural schools was the chief motive behind the king's decision to reform Prussian education. His edict of 1763, which made primary schooling compulsory for the Protestant population of the monarchy, applied only to schools in the countryside. There were noteworthy exceptions: The provisions of the 1763 edict were later extended to towns in Brandenburg and Pomerania, while the reform of Catholic schools in Silesia (1765) also included the urban population. Still, the fact that Frederick's first major compulsory school edict focused exclusively on rural schools testifies to the agrarian origins of Frederickian school reform.

Some have viewed the king's preoccupation with rural education as proof of the primacy of military concerns in Frederickian educational policy.[6] According to this argument, Frederick's concern with popular education stemmed from his severe shortage of noncommissioned officers during the Seven Years War. Some degree of literacy was necessary for a noncommissioned officer, who, like most recruits, was a peasant. In order to boost the quantity and quality of his noncommissioned officers, then, Frederick directed his efforts solely at rural education.

Although military concerns did circumscribe Frederickian school reform, as we will see shortly, this argument ignores the fact that the Prussian army did not draw its recruits exclusively from the countryside. Towns were also expected to contribute their share of conscripts.[7] Furthermore, Frederick was in the midst of demobilizing his army, not expanding it, when he finally turned his attention to school reform in 1763. In the decade after Hubertusburg, Frederick reduced the size of his army while raising the number of foreign mercenaries to a level roughly equal to that of native recruits.[8] Finally, as already mentioned, towns and cities would also fall under the purview of Frederick's school reforms, although not to the extent of the countryside.

The rural character of Prussian society, not Hohenzollern militarism, explains Frederick's preoccupation with rural schools. Since Prussian society was predominantly agrarian, it is hardly surprising that Frederick assigned priority to the reform of rural schools. Widespread peasant

[6]This argument was originally advanced by J. H. von Wessenberg, *Die Elementarbildung des Volkes im 18. Jahrhundert* (Zurich, 1814), p. 33, and was subsequently elaborated in Vollmer, *Preussische Volksschulpolitik*, p. 47.
[7]Hubatsch, *Frederick the Great*, pp. 130–131.
[8]Schieder, *Friedrich der Grosse*, p. 71.

illiteracy, as well as the critical problems of rural industry and peasant labor described in Chapters 5 and 6, help explain the rural orientation of school reform. Moreover, if additional schools were needed, it made far more sense to establish them in rural areas, where distance often limited access to schooling. Finally, the initial restriction of the reforms to the countryside made sense given the precarious financial situation of the Prussian monarchy. Frederick promulgated the General-Landschul-Reglement of 1763 on the heels of a war that had debased the coinage, reduced revenues, and brought Prussia to the brink of financial collapse. The severe depression of 1763–64, precipitated by the collapse of the speculative boom initiated by the Berlin entrepreneur Johann Ernst Gotzkowsky, had further disrupted the Prussian economy.[9] Given this financial scarcity, then, the initially restricted scope of the reforms is perfectly understandable.

The General-Landschul-Reglement of 1763

At the conclusion of peace in 1763, Frederick and his officials turned their attention to school reform with remarkable speed. Even before the formal signing of the Peace of Hubertusburg in February, the king instructed Hecker and his colleague in the Supreme Consistory, the statistician and theologian Johann Peter Süssmilch, to draft a plan for the general reform of primary schooling in the monarchy. Hecker assumed control of the project, basing his plan on the earlier proposal for Minden and Ravensberg. Hecker completed the plan in June of 1763, and after it was approved by the king, some 6,000 copies were circulated throughout the towns and villages of the monarchy.[10]

The General-Landschul-Reglement of 1763 was a historic decree. Earlier edicts had been issued only for specific provinces or municipalities, never on a national scale. The General-Landschul-Reglement was the first Prussian school edict to apply to the entire monarchy, and its provisions remained in effect well into the nineteenth century. The aim of the edict was to establish a uniform system of compulsory elementary education for all children between the ages of five and thirteen. Only Catholics (who received their own ordinance in 1765) and urban residents were

9 On the economic crisis of 1763 see Henderson, *Studies in the Economic Policy of Frederick the Great,* pp. 45–59.
10 Vollmer, *Preussische Volksschulpolitik,* pp. 63–79.

excluded from its initial provisions. Attendance was to be year-round: Children were to attend six hours a day except in the summer, when the school day was reduced to three hours. Using parish baptismal records, the schoolmaster was to keep a record of all school-age children to ensure that no families were keeping their children at home. Class roll was to be taken daily, and families who refused to send their children to school were to be fined sixteen groschen. To help pay the school fees (six pfennig per week) of children from families too poor to afford the tuition, each parish was to contribute its Sunday offering twice a year.

Although the nomination of schoolmasters remained in the hands of the school patron, the General-Landschul-Reglement made all appointments contingent on the approval of the provincial consistory. Pastors were to inspect schools in their parishes twice a week to monitor religious instruction, while consistorial inspectors were to visit the schools annually to police attendance and evaluate the performance of the schoolmaster. Schoolmasters were forbidden to own or work in taverns, and those who fostered discord in the community, or drank heavily, were to be dismissed.

The pedagogical aims of the General-Landschul-Reglement reflected the Pietist convictions of its author. The edict enjoined the schoolmaster to cultivate diligence and obedience in the pupil by breaking the child's will, but he was to administer corporal punishment only as a last resort. If the schoolmaster found it necessary to administer severe punishment, he was first to consult with the parish pastor. By bringing the pastor into the disciplinary process, the edict sought to bolster the authority of the schoolmaster and forestall parental objections in cases where corporal punishment was necessary.

Religion dominated the curriculum. The three hours of morning instruction opened with a hymn and a prayer, followed by catechistic instruction. Students were to learn not only the doctrinal significance of the catechism, but also how to apply its precepts in daily life. Reading instruction then followed. The class was divided into a beginning and an advanced group so that the schoolmaster could teach pupils collectively rather than individually. Afternoon instruction proceeded in a similar fashion, with further instruction in reading and the catechism.

The General-Landschul-Reglement of 1763 was an ambitious attempt to create a uniform system of compulsory schooling. Yet the goal of uniformity remained elusive as long as the state lacked an adequate supply of trained teachers. The four teaching institutes then in existence

– Berlin, Kloster Berg (near Magdeburg), Stettin (Lithuania), and Königsberg (East Prussia) – produced far too few graduates to meet the goals of the reform. For example, the royal subsidies supporting Hecker's institute, the largest of the four, were sufficient for the training of only twelve candidates each year.[11]

But the lack of teacher-training institutes was only one obstacle to implementation. Even more serious was the failure of the monarchy to provide the necessary financial support. Timing was partly to blame – as mentioned earlier, Frederick promulgated the General-Landschul-Reglement in a period of financial crisis. In the years immediately following Hubertusburg, the monarchy's ambitious educational goals clearly exceeded its fiscal grasp. As a consequence, the burden of building schools and paying schoolmasters fell squarely on the shoulders of the parish community. Forced to bear the costs of the edict, local communities naturally resisted its implementation. Compulsory school fees were a threat to the very subsistence of poorer families, especially those having to pay fees for several children. More prosperous peasant families, for their part, resented having to subsidize school tuition for the village poor. Peasants often refused to contribute in church to the school collection plate, while others tossed in debased coins or worthless tokens. Confronting resistance of this sort, village pastors were reluctant to incur the disapproval of their parishioners through excessive zeal for the reforms. Furthermore, it was simply impossible to enforce the provisions for summer school since summer was the season when rural families were particularly dependent on the labor of their children. Schoolmasters themselves disliked teaching in the summer, since most could earn more working in the fields. In Pomerania, where many schoolmasters were required to perform labor obligations in the summer, the provisions for summer school were especially unrealistic.[12]

The distrust of nobles was yet another obstacle to implementation. Some nobles, it is true, proved cooperative, and actually established or improved schools on their estates. Rochow and Brenckenhoff in the Electoral Mark, Haugwitz and Gessler in Silesia, and Borck and Maltzahn in Pomerania offer examples of such cooperation.[13] But most were either

---

[11]Heppe, *Geschichte des deutschen Volksschulwesens*, 3:31.

[12]Vollmer, *Preussische Volksschulpolitik*, pp. 63–79. A more recent and highly skeptical view of the 1763 reform is found in Leschinsky and Roeder, *Schule im historischen Prozess*, pp. 116–122.

[13]Lehmann, *Preussen und die katholische Kirche*, 4:184.

indifferent or, as Hecker wrote in exasperation, "are convinced that a subject who is stupid will be as docile as a cow."[14] Many balked at the idea of teaching their peasants to read and write. Resistance was especially common among the rustic "cabbage Junkers" (*Krautjunker*) of Pomerania, who themselves were often illiterate and whose sons were routinely denied admission to the elite Berlin Cadet Academy on account of their poor educational background.[15] Many viewed literacy as a potential weapon that peasants might use to draft appeals and petitions to royal courts for the reduction of seigniorial dues.

But on occasion it was the Prussian bureaucracy itself, not just local opposition, that sabotaged school reform. The Prussian bureaucracy, of course, was long viewed as a model of administrative efficiency. Max Weber, among others, viewed the Prussian bureaucracy under Frederick II as the prototype of modern bureaucratic rationality.[16] During the past few decades historians have challenged this stereotype, pointing not only to the nepotism and corruption common to any bureaucracy of the Old Regime, but also to the ways in which the Prussian bureaucracy often pursued contradictory goals. In the end, what was preeminent in the minds of Prussian officials was the preservation of the army and the revenues that supported it, even at the cost of sabotaging other policies.[17]

The War and Domains Chambers, for example, were the royal agents responsible for enforcing the provisions of the General-Landschul-Reglement at the provincial level. Yet they also had recruitment quotas to fill, and the two tasks sometimes clashed. In 1764, for example, the Königsberg War and Domains Chamber found it necessary to hire additional schoolmasters in the province, but even as the chamber was hiring new schoolmasters, its military recruiters were arbitrarily conscripting those already employed. On one notorious occasion, an abducted schoolmaster died en route to his garrison as a result of beatings suffered at the hands of his military captors. Following an official inquiry, the chamber freed all conscripted schoolmasters except one, who, it alleged, was unqualified to teach. Further investigation revealed, however, that it was the schoolmaster's height, not his pedagogical incompetence, that kept him in the army. The schoolmaster was unusually tall, and since Freder-

---

[14]Quoted in Vollmer, *Preussische Volksschulpolitik*, p. 80.
[15]Ibid., p. 113.
[16]On this point see Hubert Johnson, *Frederick the Great and His Officials* (New Haven, 1975), p. 3.
[17]Cf. the example of Frederickian agrarian policy in Corni, *Stato assoluto e società agraria*, p. 323–388.

ick II had inherited his father's fondness for tall soldiers, the chamber
was convinced that its actions conformed with the king's wishes. The
General Directory closed the investigation, and the schoolmaster remained in the army.[18] While the king subsequently granted a blanket
deferment to schoolmasters, he also instructed provincial War and Domains Chambers to discourage the hiring of tall schoolmasters so as not
to deprive the army of its famed "giant brigades."[19]

Finally, inadequate provisions for school inspection also hampered the
effectiveness of the reforms. Consistorial inspectors in larger districts
found their tasks virtually impossible. The consistorial inspector in the
district of Rastenburg (East Prussia), for example, was responsible for
more than 158 schools, some more than thirty miles apart. Equally unrealistic was the requirement that a pastor inspect the schools in his parish
twice a week, since it was common for some pastors to have as many as
fifteen schools in their parishes.[20]

Thus it is not surprising that in Brandenburg, for example, the provincial consistory declared in 1765 that the General-Landschul-Reglement
was simply not enforceable in its existing form. Recognizing that the
present system of inspection was ineffective, the Supreme Consistory
sought to tighten enforcement by requiring schoolmasters to keep annual
records. Three times a year, schoolmasters were to fill out three copies of
a sixteen-page questionnaire that included information on the curriculum, outside employment by the schoolmaster, and the names, ages,
family background, performance, and attendance record of each pupil.
One copy was to be sent to the pastor, another to the school inspector,
and a third to the provincial consistory.[21] The introduction of a standardized questionnaire was an important step toward the centralization
of Prussian education. It represented the first attempt by the Prussian
state to monitor its schools nationally and at regular intervals.

In practice, however, the questionnaires produced a nightmare of paperwork for everyone concerned. Many schoolmasters themselves could
barely write, and submitted catalogues that were incomplete or simply
illegible. Those who conscientiously completed the questionnaires found
the chore intolerably burdensome and time-consuming. A Pomeranian
school inspector complained that some schoolmasters had to cancel school

18Vollmer, *Preussische Volksschulpolitik,* p. 233.
19Such incidents nevertheless continued. Ibid., pp. 234–235.
20Ibid., pp. 63–83; Neugebauer, *Schulwirklichkeit,* pp. 128–129.
21Vollmer, *Preussische Volksschulpolitik,* pp. 100–102.

for two weeks to complete the questionnaire, while others even resigned their positions to protest the tedious paperwork. The Supreme Consistory itself lacked the administrative personnel to process the reports, most of which were never read. In the end, the Supreme Consistory abandoned the cumbersome form in favor of a much shorter and more simplified version. The new questionnaire proved somewhat more successful, although the provincial consistories still lacked the clerical personnel needed to make it genuinely effective in monitoring rural schools.[22]

School financing and teacher training

To those charged with carrying out the 1763 edict, it quickly became clear that school reform would remain a dead letter without direct subsidies from the crown. It was not until the 1770s, after the crown had finally emerged from its postwar financial doldrums, that the crown was able to subsidize school reform on any significant scale. Here the *Régie*, the unpopular French tax farmers hired by Frederick to collect taxes, came to his aid. In 1771 their collection of municipal tax revenues in Brandenburg yielded a surplus of 100,000 talers, which Frederick converted into an endowment for the support of primary schooling in the province. The interest (4 percent) was used to establish additional schools and raise the salaries of Brandenburg schoolmasters.[23] It is difficult to determine exactly where these funds were spent, or how effective they were in improving the financial status of schoolmasters. Although Wolfgang Neugebauer's study of schooling in eighteenth-century Brandenburg is highly skeptical about the efficacy of Hohenzollern educational policy, he does provide figures that show a modest improvement in the income of schoolmasters during the remainder of the century. Neugebauer's statistics reveal that the percentage of schoolmasters earning less than twenty talers annually fell from 37.4 percent in 1774 to 16.7 percent in 1800, while those in the top half of the salary range (sixty talers and above) grew from 16.9 percent to 30 percent.[24] Improvement is further evident in the rising percentage of teachers able to subsist on their salaries alone. In the Neumark, for example, this number rose from 17.9 percent in 1770 to 28.3 percent in 1805.[25]

[22]Ibid., pp. 103–114; Neugebauer, *Schulwirklichkeit*, p. 183.
[23]Vollmer, *Preussische Volksschulpolitik*, pp. 145–147.
[24]See the table in Neugebauer, *Schulwirklichkeit*, p. 347.
[25]Ibid., pp. 326–327.

Other regions showed improvement as well. In 1777 Frederick created a similar fund for schools in Pomerania, where the financial distress of schoolmasters was especially acute. That year, 500 out of a total of 1,200 Pomeranian schoolmasters earned less than ten talers per year. Crown subsidies increased the annual salaries of 85 Pomeranian schoolmasters to eighty talers, built 43 additional schools, and hired 40 trained schoolmasters.[26] In West Prussia, the area of Poland acquired through the partition of 1772, the monarchy took special pains to expand primary education. Between 1774 and 1776, the Prussian crown settled 85 schoolmasters in the new province and paid each an average annual salary of sixty talers. By 1778, a total of 125 schools had been established.[27]

These subsidies, however modest, represented an important milestone in Prussian public schooling. In those schools directly subsidized by the crown, the state paid the salaries of schoolmasters. Hence for the first time in the history of Prussian elementary education, pupils attended parish schools for free. Attendance doubtless improved as a result, although truancy still remained widespread. In West Prussia, where distance and a shortage of Polish-speaking schoolmasters posed special problems, attendance at state-subsidized schools only averaged between 25 percent and 50 percent.[28]

Training the teachers necessary for the expansion of schooling remained a problem. Hecker's death in 1768, as well as the rapid rise in Berlin housing rents after 1763, had brought his institute to the verge of collapse. The Stettin institute had never fully recovered from the war, when it had served as a military hospital.[29] This left only the institutes in Königsberg, Kloster Berg, and Breslau (created in 1767) for the training of teachers. Faced with the need for additional institutes, Frederick increased state support for teacher training. In 1772, he subsidized the establishment of a pedagogical institute on the East Prussian estates of Balthasar Philipp von Genge. Genge, a retired officer of deeply Pietist views, added a spinning school and orphanage to the institute. Genge's school proved a moderate success, training fifty-five schoolmasters between 1773 and 1780.[30] In 1776, C. A. Venator, a Lutheran pastor, opened a normal school in

[26]Vollmer, *Preussische Volksschulpolitik,* pp. 166–173.
[27]Ibid., pp. 177–191.
[28]Ibid., p. 244.
[29]Ibid., p. 133.
[30]Ibid., pp. 138–140.

Minden-Ravensberg along the lines of the Kloster Berg institute.[31] The last institute established under Frederick II was in the principality of Halberstadt, west of Magdeburg. Here Christoph Gottfried Streuensee, a former teacher at Kloster Berg and rector of the Halberstadt Cathedral School, opened a pedagogical institute in 1778.[32]

In 1779, however, proponents of teacher training suffered a setback when Frederick approved a scheme proposed by Franz von Brenckenhoff, one of his finance ministers, to fill teaching positions with disabled or retired army veterans. Schoolmasters were now to be hired from a list of veterans compiled in each province. This quintessentially Prussian scheme sought to alleviate the schoolmaster shortage while providing employment to veterans who would otherwise become wards of the state.[33]

Few besides the king and Brenckenhoff liked the plan. Carl Abraham Freiherr von Zedlitz, who became head of the Ecclesiastical Department in 1771 and hence oversaw Lutheran schools and churches in the monarchy, feared that the plan could destroy Prussian education. Zedlitz complained privately to Rochow that the king "confuses the value of rewarding military service with the duty of educating useful subjects."[34] Zedlitz himself did everything he could to sabotage the plan and succeeded in preventing a number of notoriously unqualified veterans from receiving positions.[35] The Pomeranian Consistory found that none of the disabled veterans in the province were competent to teach. Some were unable to read, others could not write, and one confessed that although he had once known how to add, subtract, divide, and multiply, he had since forgotten.[36] When a veteran actually obtained a position, the consequences were sometimes painfully embarrassing. In the village of Litzengörike (Brandenburg), a veteran begged to be transferred after seeing that his pupils could read better than he. After taking over a school in Friedrichshagen (Brandenburg), a grizzled veteran of the Seven Years War confessed that a schoolroom full of rowdy pupils struck more fear in his heart than the French army he had once faced at the Battle of Rossbach. In other cases, veterans received lucrative positions, while

---

[31]Ibid., pp. 207–211.
[32]Ibid., p. 214.
[33]Neugebauer, *Schulpolitik,* pp. 352–363; Vollmer, *Preussische Volksschulpolitik,* p. 218; Notbohm, *Das evangelische Kirchen- und Schulwesen,* p. 153.
[34]Letter to Rochow, May 26, 1781, in Jonas and Wienecke, eds., *Rochows sämtliche pädagogische Schriften,* 4:287.
[35]Vollmer, *Preussische Volksschulpolitik,* p. 230.
[36]Ibid., p. 222.

more experienced and skilled applicants were passed over.[37] The practice
of hiring veterans to fill teaching positions continued into the nineteenth
century, though never on a significant scale. It reveals, again, how the
military priorities of the Prussian state frequently undermined its pedagogical goals.

Although reformers like Zedlitz opposed the hiring of veterans as
schoolmasters, they were ambivalent about the social effects of pedagogical institutes. On the one hand, the achievements of the institutes
were undeniable. Wherever institute graduates introduced Hecker's
method of collective instruction, pupils acquired literacy far more quickly. In the Duchy of Magdeburg, for example, teachers who adopted
Hecker's method were able to teach their pupils the ABC's in two weeks
– a task that had traditionally required six months under the older
method.[38] On the other hand, reformers feared the potentially disruptive
effect of sending institute graduates into the countryside. Graduates of
Hecker's Berlin institute, for example, had earned an unenviable reputation for arrogance and contentiousness. Having lived in the city, those
who obtained positions in rural schools often treated their fellow villagers with condescension. This sort of a schoolmaster was particularly
prone to conflicts with the local pastor, which often had a divisive effect
on the community.[39] Zedlitz, head of the Ecclesiastical Department from
1771 to 1788, was a prominent critic of the Berlin institute. Zedlitz
enjoyed a reputation as one of Frederick's most enlightened ministers and
had long been a dedicated supporter of compulsory schooling.[40] With
authority over Lutheran schools in the monarchy, Zedlitz was in a strong
position to promote the Berlin institute. Yet he hesitated to do so, less out
of financial constraint than a fear of the social consequences. Like most
reformers of his day, Zedlitz firmly believed that a pupil's education
should not exceed the needs of his future occupation.[41] He warned that

[37]Ibid., pp. 228–231.
[38]Danneil, *Geschichte des evangelischen Dorfschulwesens*, p. 131.
[39]In 1798 Christian Benedict Gloerfeld, a Brandenburg pastor, voiced concern over the
appointment of an institute graduate to a school in the village of Klosterfelde: "I fear the
conflicts that will arise when he assumes his post. When an institute graduate is hired as a
schoolmaster, one can usually expect complaints from the pastor and the parish community." Quoted in Neugebauer, *Schulwirklichkeit*, p. 420. On Berlin institute graduates see
also Vollmer, *Preussische Volksschulpolitik*, pp. 206–207.
[40]On Zedlitz's career and educational work see Conrad Rethwisch, *Der Staatsminister
Freiherr von Zedlitz und Preussens höheres Schulwesen im Zeitalter Friedrichs des
Grossen* (Berlin, 1881).
[41]Writing in the *Berlinische Monatschrift* in 1787, Zedlitz pleaded that "it is madness to
provide a future tailor, cabinetmaker, or shopkeeper with the same education as a future

schoolmasters trained in an urban environment would exercise a pernicious influence on their pupils. Exposed to the urban manners and customs of their schoolmaster, peasant children would become dissatisfied with their social position and migrate to the city.[42] Here Zedlitz echoed the views of his king, who advised that "one must teach the peasants what they need to know, but in such a manner that they will not flee the countryside, but remain there contentedly."[43]

Support for the Berlin institute nevertheless continued, and the institution experienced a renaissance in the last two decades of the century. By 1798, it had graduated more than a thousand schoolmasters.[44] The establishment of pedagogical institutes was one of the most important educational achievements of Frederick's reign. While able to train only a small proportion of the necessary schoolmasters, they nevertheless represented an important step toward the professionalization of the schoolmaster. The number of pedagogical institutes steadily increased after Frederick's reign, so that by 1849 they enrolled more than two thousand students.[45]

The origins of Catholic school reform

The acquisition of Silesia had vastly increased the number of Catholics in the monarchy. One-half of the province was Catholic, and because the General-Landschul-Reglement of 1763 had applied only to Protestants, it was necessary to draft a separate edict for Silesian Catholics.

Frederick II basically distrusted his Catholic subjects in Silesia, and he was especially concerned that their schools train loyal Prussian subjects. His distrust dated back to the Silesian wars, when the king had suspected Silesian Catholics of collaborating with the Austrians. Occasional acts of disloyalty fueled this suspicion. In the fall of 1744, for example, the Prussian authorities arrested a Silesian Catholic priest who had provided information on troop movements to the Austrian generals Keuhl and

school rector or consistory official. The peasant must be educated differently from the future artisan, who must in turn have an education different from the future scholar, or youth destined for higher office." Quoted in Rethwisch, *Zedlitz*, p. 96.

[42] Letter to Rochow, May 6, 1779, in Jonas and Wienecke, eds., *Rochows sämtliche pädagogische Schriften*, 4:170.

[43] Bona-Meyer, ed., *Friedrichs des Grossen pädagogische Schriften*, p. 170.

[44] Neugebauer, *Schulwirklichkeit*, pp. 389–390.

[45] Leschinsky and Roeder, *Schule im historischen Prozess*, p. 146. On the expansion of pedagogical institutes during the first half of the nineteenth century, see also La Vopa, *Prussian Schoolmasters*, pp. 52–79.

Holly.[46] In 1745, Frederick accused Catholic schoolmasters in the districts of Jauer and Schweidnitz of providing the Austrians with lists of prosperous Protestant peasants in the area "so that the enemy knows where it can most profitably plunder."[47] Following the resumption of war in 1756, Schlabrendorff accused Catholic priests of using the privacy of the confessional booth to urge Prussian Catholic soldiers to desert. One deserter testified that after confessing to a Dominican priest that he had deserted, the priest pardoned his action with the excuse that the soldier "could serve the Queen of Hungary as loyally as he could that Brandenburg heretic."[48] After the rout of the Prussian army at the Battle of Kolin in 1757, Frederick's hold on his Catholic subjects became even more tenuous. In Upper Silesia, a heavily Catholic region, most of Frederick's *Landräte* deserted to the Austrians.[49] The treason of Philipp Gotthard Graf von Schaffgotsch, a royal favorite whom Frederick had elevated to prince-bishop of Breslau, further fueled Frederick's distrust of Silesian Catholics.[50]

Frederick's suspicions lingered after the war, when Frederick required a loyalty oath from all Catholic clergy and schoolmasters. While Frederick's ecclesiastical policies were by no means anti-Catholic,[51] he was

---

[46]Lehmann, *Preussen und die katholische Kirche*, 2:513.
[47]Ibid., p. 539.
[48]Ibid., p. 695.
[49]Kutzner, "Landratamt in Schlesien," p. 8.
[50]Shortly after the outbreak of war in 1756, Prince-Bishop Schaffgotsch had assured Frederick that he would "resist Austrian slavery up to the last moment of my life," but after the Prussian defeat at Kolin in August 1757, the opportunistic Schaffgotsch began to see Austrian servitude in a different light. Schaffgotsch now began secretly providing the Austrians with information on Frederick and his troops. During a meeting with the Austrian General Daun in Breslau, he demonstrated his loyalty to Maria Theresa by dramatically tearing from his vestments the Prussian Order of the Black Eagle – awarded to him by Frederick and one of the highest honors given to a Prussian subject – and casting it to the ground. He later fled Silesia after the revival of Frederick's military fortunes. On the Schaffgotsch incident see Colmar Grünhagen, "Die Österreicher in Breslau 1757," *Zeitschrift des Vereins für die Geschichte Schlesiens*, 24 (1890), p. 74; *Schlesische Zustände im ersten Jahrhundert der preussischen Herrschaft* (Breslau, 1840), pp. 294–295.
[51]It is sheer exaggeration to view Frederick's church policies in Silesia as a harbinger of Bismarck's *Kulturkampf*, as some Catholic historians have done. Augustin Theiner, *Zustände der katholischen Kirche in Schlesien von 1740–1758*, 2 vols. (Mainz, 1852), saw Frederickian ecclesiastical policy in Silesia as a naked attempt to destroy the autonomy of the Catholic church. The German-Catholic émigré historian Francis Hanus, *Church and State in Silesia, 1740–1786* (Washington, D.C., 1944), viewed Frederick as a godless forerunner of Hitler whose aim was to eradicate Catholicism.
  This view overlooks the fact that at the very beginning of his reign, Frederick had granted Prussian Catholics complete freedom of worship. In response to Protestant complaints of Catholic proselytization in 1740, Frederick flatly responded that "all religions

concerned with the loyalty of his Catholic subjects. Viewing schools as an important instrument for securing that loyalty, Frederick ordered Schlabrendorff, the Silesian minister, to begin work on a Catholic school edict.

Schlabrendorff, an advocate of compulsory schooling since becoming minister of the province in 1755, needed no urging. In 1764 he requested Hecker, then in the midst of the frustrating task of implementing the General-Landschul-Reglement, to suggest someone capable of supervising the reform of Catholic schools. Hecker recommended Felbiger without hesitation, adding that "his ardor for school reform exceeds even that of our Lutheran clergy."[52] After investigating Felbiger's parish reforms in Sagan, Schlabrendorff entrusted Felbiger with the task. Felbiger spent the summer of 1764 drafting his proposal, which he submitted to Schlabrendorff in October.[53]

Felbiger's proposal attributed the low quality of Catholic schools in Silesia to two causes. The first was the schoolmaster's dependence on outside employment, which prevented him from devoting his full energies to teaching. Hence Felbiger proposed raising the schoolmaster's income to meet his subsistence needs. If he was a church servant, his responsibilities had to be kept sufficiently light so as not to interfere with his teaching duties. The second cause of the poor quality of instruction, argued Felbiger, was the schoolmaster's lack of an effective pedagogical method. As a remedy, Felbiger urged the creation of Catholic teaching seminars on the model of Hecker's Berlin institute.

Felbiger no doubt endeared himself to Frederick and Schlabrendorff by stressing the importance of civic education. Schoolmasters needed to inculcate in their pupils not only a sense of their spiritual duties, but also

---

must be tolerated" (quoted in Hubatsch, *Frederick the Great*, p. 41). He faithfully observed the Peace of Berlin (1742), which guaranteed Silesian Catholics freedom of worship, and even provided the Society of Jesus, which the Pope had abolished in 1773, a Prussian refuge. In tolerating the Jesuits, of course, Frederick was guided by pragmatism rather than any genuine sympathy for the order. Writing to Voltaire, who had criticized Frederick's protection of the Jesuits, Frederick explained that had he expelled the Jesuits from Silesia, the University of Breslau would have closed for a lack of professors. Catholic clerical candidates would then have been forced to study in Prague or Olmütz, where they would have come under the dangerous influence of the House of Habsburg. See Lehmann, *Preussen und die katholische Kirche*, 4:240–241. An exhaustive study of Frederick's relations with the Jesuits is found in Hermann Hoffmann, *Friedrich II. von Preussen und die Aufhebung der Gesellschaft Jesu* (Rome, 1969), pp. 281–310.
[52] Lehmann, *Preussen und die katholische Kirche*, 4:151–152.
[53] Ibid., pp. 16–63, 193–195, for the correspondence between Felbiger and Schlabrendorff. See also the account in Felbiger, *K.S.* pp. 450–454. Felbiger's proposal is published in *K.S.*, pp. 109–124.

secular obligations like "loyalty, obedience, and devotion to the king."[54]
Indicative of Felbiger's stress on loyalty and obedience was his 1768
manual for Catholic schoolmasters, which prescribed that pupils memo-
rize the following catechism:

> Q: Who is subject to the power of the ruler?
> A: Everyone. . . .
> Q: Why must everyone submit to authority?
> A: All power comes from God.
> Q: From whence comes the power held by the ruler?
> A: This power comes from God.
> Q: Whom does God ordain?
> A: Everyone who holds authority. Because all who exercise authority are
> ordained by God, subjects must be submissive, loyal, and obedient, even to a
> ruler not of our religion. This was taught by the Apostle Paul, who himself lived
> under the pagan Roman Emperors.
> Q: What does it mean to resist authority?
> A: To resist authority is to rebel against the divine order.
> Q: What happens to those who do not submit to authority?
> A: They will suffer eternal damnation.[55]

This insistence upon the legitimacy of "heathen" authority was clearly
designed to bolster the authority of a Protestant ruler over his Catholic
subjects.

Felbiger insisted, however, that force was not sufficient for teaching
the child obedience. The pupil must learn to render obedience willingly,
not out of coercion. Anticipating the Kantian belief that no action was
moral that did not orginate in the will, Felbiger wrote that "children do
not act morally merely by doing what they are supposed to do, but only
when they act out of conviction and a consciousness of their duties."[56]
Pupils thus read of their duty to obey their ruler and lord "not only
outwardly, but in their hearts."[57]

Felbiger warned that a schoolmaster's indiscriminate use of corporal
punishment stunted the development of this internalized sense of duty.
Accordingly, he recommended the use of corporal punishment only as a
last resort. Pupils who misbehaved were first to receive a rebuke. If the
misconduct continued, the schoolmaster was to threaten them with

[54]Ibid., p. 12.
[55]Scheveling, ed., *Johann Ignaz Felbiger*, p. 64.
[56]Ibid., pp. 120–121.
[57]*Christliche Grundsätze und Lebensregeln zum Unterricht der Jugend* (Sagan, 1767), p.
  58.

punishment. Only after the pupils failed to heed the threat were they to receive physical punishment. Following Francke, Felbiger believed that the fear of punishment was a far greater deterrent to misconduct than the punishment itself.

Felbiger cited with approval how one schoolmaster exploited this fear. When warnings and threats failed to end a pupil's misconduct, the schoolmaster did not administer corporal punishment immediately. He first ordered the pupil to sit in the back row. The schoolmaster then wrote in block letters, next to the pupil's name, "STRAFWÜRDIG" – deserving of punishment. After informing the pupil that he would receive his punishment at the end of the school day, the schoolmaster continued the lesson while the guilty pupil awaited his punishment. By the end of the day the pupil was in tears, sobbing and begging forgiveness from God as well as his teacher.[58]

The moral of the incident was clear: It was the threat of impending punishment, rather than its actual administration, that was the most effective mechanism of control in the classroom. Felbiger was confident that pupils who obeyed their schoolmaster without the use of force would grow into subjects who performed their duties even in the absence of coercion:

Human beings are by nature moved by kindness and reason rather than force. Despotic methods will not induce pupils to obey. They must be convinced that it is useful and correct to follow the schoolmaster's wishes. Only then will they learn to obey even in situations where force is absent. In this way, the school-master accomplishes his most important task: his pupils will observe their duties not only in school, but throughout their lives.[59]

Above all, Felbiger stressed that primary education had to conform to the social environment of the pupil. Since many children in towns would later earn their living as secretaries or clerks, they needed to learn how to write clearly in both cursive and printed hand. For those destined to enter commercial occupations, a strong background in arithmetic was also desirable. The curriculum of rural schools, on the other hand, was to be more rudimental. Felbiger considered calligraphic instruction for peasants to be superfluous and even harmful, since it encouraged migration from the countryside to the towns. Sufficient for the needs of rural pupils were reading, a little writing, the catechism, and basic arithmetic.

---

[58]Scheveling, ed., *Johann Ignaz Felbiger*, p. 105.
[59]Ibid., p. 96.

Felbiger's belief that schooling must be *standesmässig*, in accordance with the pupil's social position, met with Schlabrendorff's full approval. It reflected a concern with labor supply and social discipline in the countryside which, as we have seen, figured so prominently in the minds of reformers. As with most reformers, Schlabrendorff feared the social and economic consequences of educating rural inhabitants beyond the elementary level. The idea of peasants studying Latin, for example, was anathema to him, since it "only stimulates a desire to enter the priesthood, thereby destroying their natural inclination to practice the occupation of their fathers."[60] Hence in 1763 he prohibited the teaching of Latin in rural schools, emphasizing that "it is not the intention of His Royal Majesty that peasants learn Latin, but only reading, writing, the fundamentals of religion, and loyalty and obedience to their ruler."[61] Schlabrendorff's prohibition was aimed partly at discouraging entry into the priesthood. But Schlabrendorff was also convinced that the study of Latin bred arrogance and disobedience among the peasantry: "Various *Landräte* have assured me that the most good-for-nothing, stubborn peasants in their districts are precisely those who have studied Latin."[62] Johann Moritz von Strachwitz, the prince-bishop of Breslau, agreed with Schlabrendorff about the effects of Latin study: "Those peasants who have learned Latin . . . are in all respects the most disobedient."[63]

The severe measures adopted by Schlabrendorff to exclude plebeian pupils from *Gymnasien* and universities illustrate his firm commitment to a well-defined educational class system. These measures, instituted less than a week after the promulgation of Felbiger's compulsory school edict for Silesian Catholic schools (1765), forbade the children of cotters and day laborers to study beyond the elementary level. After learning the fundamentals of religion, reading, writing, and arithmetic, these children were "to be employed in agriculture, or take up handicrafts or some other trade."[64] In the towns, similarly, Schlabrendorff forbade the children of unskilled laborers to advance beyond the primary level. Even the sons of more prosperous *Bürger* were forbidden to continue their studies unless they could demonstrate unusual talent and sufficient financial

[60]Schlabrendorff to the Breslau War and Domains Chamber, May 18, 1763, in Lehmann, *Preussen und die katholische Kirche,* 4:114.
[61]Published in Felbiger, *K.S.,* p. 12.
[62]Lehmann, *Preussen und die katholische Kirche,* 4:114.
[63]Quoted in Weigelt, "Die Volksschule in Schlesien," p. 44.
[64]Ibid., p. 47.

means.[65] These policies reveal a central paradox of absolutist school reform: Even as one hand expanded schooling, the other restricted it.

The Silesian reform of 1765

Now enjoying the full confidence of Schlabrendorff, Felbiger established his first pedagogical institute in Sagan. Felbiger's institute sought not only to train schoolmasters, but also to prepare priesthood candidates for their future responsibilities as school "administrators." Here Felbiger was able to secure the cooperation of Prince-Bishop Strachwitz, who required newly appointed priests to surrender one-quarter of their first year's income to help defray the expenses of schoolmasters and priesthood candidates attending the institute. Anxious to ensure the survival of Silesian Catholicism now that Protestants enjoyed full toleration, Strachwitz supported school reform as a means of improving the quality of pastoral care in his diocese.[66]

Felbiger added a wing to the cloister of the Sagan monastery in order to house the institute participants, who began arriving in December of 1764. The duration of the training course was four weeks, with a new group arriving at the beginning of every month. The elementary school in Sagan now served as a laboratory school where institute participants could observe Felbiger's pedagogy in practice. In the ensuing years, Fel-

---

[65] "No child of a *Bürger* may continue his studies who does not possess superior talents and whose parents are not sufficiently propertied to support his studies. The children of common artisans and day laborers, on the other hand, are to be fully excluded from the pursuit of further studies." Quoted in ibid., p. 47. After the death of Von Schlabrendorff in 1769, the Prussian minister Johann Casimir von Carmer continued efforts to curtail plebeian access to higher education. Von Carmer, who would later play a leading role in the codification of Prussian law in the 1780s and 1790s, worked on behalf of *Gymnasium* and university reform while justice minister of Silesia (1768–79). Writing in 1777, Von Carmer asserted that "I have long been of the opinion that too many young people – especially among our Catholic population – are admitted to higher studies. . . . As half-educated failures they are useless and even a burden on the state. They would have performed a far greater service to the state as tillers of the soil, laborers in manufacturing, or skilled artisans." Quoted in Lehmann, *Preussen und die katholische Kirche*, 5:240. In 1774, Von Carmer authored a reform placing under direct state control the University of Breslau and all *Gymnasien* formerly run by the Jesuits. University and *Gymnasium* admission, previously ill-defined, was now regulated through examinations. The edict is published in Lehmann, *Preussen und die katholische Kirche*, 4:630–637. On Von Carmer's educational reforms see also Reimann, "Über die Verbesserung des katholischen höheren Schulwesens," pp. 381–385.
[66] See the pastoral letter issued by Strachwitz in 1764, published in Lehmann, *Preussen und die katholische Kirche*, 4:140–143.

biger came to refer to his institute cum laboratory school as a "normal
school" (Normalschule). Felbiger was the first to coin the term, which he
employed to refer to the institute's function as a model, or "norm," for
other Catholic schools in the province.[67]

The institute day began each morning with an hour lecture by Felbiger
on the duties of the parish priest and schoolmaster. Classroom observation and practice teaching took up the rest of the day, while in the
evening participants studied the pedagogical treatises and proposals of
Felbiger and Hecker. These included detailed instructions to participants
on how to reform the schools of their parishes upon their return.[68] By
October of 1765, the Sagan institute had trained 8 normal school direc-
tors, 15 normal school teachers, 47 schoolmasters, and 101 candidates
for the regular and secular clergy. By the end of the year, nine additional
normal schools had opened in Breslau, Ratibor, Habelschwerdt, Leubus,
Grussau, Rauden, Franckenstein, Neisse, and Oppeln. All were staffed
with graduates of the Sagan normal school.[69]

Felbiger had in the meantime returned to Berlin to consult with
Hecker on the adoption of textbooks. Felbiger had already published a
primer based on that of Hecker, as well as a religious manual that summarized the books of the Bible.[70] He now began work on a catechism,
along with textbooks on writing and arithmetic. He also commissioned
Simon Jaschieck, a priest fluent in Polish and German, to translate Felbiger's primer into Polish. Felbiger published this primer the following
year for use in the Polish-speaking regions of Silesia.[71]

Felbiger completed his edict for the reform of Silesian Catholic schools
in October of 1765.[72] Frederick approved it in November, and the Silesian War and Domains Chambers sent thousands of copies to the Steuer-
räte and Landräte of the province. These local officials then distributed
copies to the priests, schoolmasters, and school patrons of their districts
(Polish-speaking towns and villages received translations of the edict).

[67]See Felbiger, Was sollen Normalschulen sein, die man in den K.K. Erbländern errichtet
hat (Vienna, 1776).
[68]Felbiger, K.S., pp. 148–160, 167–198.
[69]Ibid., pp. 481–482; Lehmann, Preussen und die katholische Kirche, 4:254.
[70]I have been unable to locate the primer, entitled Neu eingerichtetes ABC-Buchstabir- und
Lesebuchlein zum Gebrauch der schlesischen Schulen (Sagan, 1764). A copy of Felbiger's
religious manual, the Kurzer Inhalt sämtlicher Bücher, die sich in der Heiligen Schrift
befinden (Sagan, 1764), survives in the library of Wrocław University.
[71]Felbiger, K.S., pp. 471–472.
[72]Published in Lehmann, Preussen und die katholische Kirche, 4:255–273.

Prince-Bishop Strachwitz in turn sent out pastoral letters urging parish priests to comply with the reform.[73]

Felbiger's plan differed from its Protestant predecessor in its provisions for urban education. Urban schools were to include advanced classes in calligraphy and style, with Gottsched's *Kern der deutschen Sprachkunst* serving as a stylistic model. If he possessed the requisite qualifications, the schoolmaster could also teach history, geography, natural science, and French. Far less extensive was the curriculum prescribed for rural schools, which was confined to reading, writing, religion, and basic arithmetic.

Felbiger's plan also established a more effective system of teacher training. With the ten normal schools now operating in Silesia, a trained nucleus of schoolmasters became an attainable goal. *Winkelschulen* were of course forbidden, and private tutors had to be certified by a parish priest or normal school director. The edict required normal school certification for every Catholic schoolmaster, as well as written confirmation from his normal school director as to his piety and character.

Felbiger was the first reformer in the history of Central European schooling to create an effective network of normal schools. These schools linked the training of schoolmasters to formal certification procedures. In seeking to standardize teaching methods and curriculum, Felbiger's aim was to neutralize the personal and pedagogical idiosyncrasies of the schoolmaster. He distinguished between the office and the person of the schoolmaster, seeking to separate the schoolmaster's public role from his private life. Felbiger advised schoolmasters, if possible, not to hold school in their private quarters, since "it is well known that pupils are distracted from learning if the schoolmaster's wife, children, or relatives are scurrying about the classroon."[74] Felbiger's attempt to curb the employment of schoolmasters outside the school also illustrated this trend towards professionalization. He designed a graduated system of school fees (two groschen for the child of a full peasant, eight pfennig for the child of a gardener or cottager, and four pfennig for children from propertyless families) to guarantee that the schoolmaster could gain his subsistence from teaching alone. His plan allowed only those who taught in heavily Protestant areas, where Catholic schoolmasters earned less be-

[73]Eduard Reimann, "Über die Verbesserung des niederen Schulwesens in Schlesien in den Jahren 1763–1769," *Zeitschrift des Vereins für die Geschichte Schlesiens,* 17 (1873), p. 340; Kosler, *Preussische Volksschulpolitik,* p. 150.
[74]Lehmann, *Preussen und die katholische Kirche,* 4:264.

cause of the paucity of pupils, to work at outside chores. He also exempted schoolmasters from a number of parish duties customarily assigned to them, such as the delivery of messages to neighboring parishes.

Felbiger's reform did not secularize Catholic education, any more than the Protestant edict of 1763 secularized Protestant schools. In Prussian elementary schools, both Protestant and Catholic clergy continued to play an important administrative role.[75] Felbiger instituted a system of school administration in which the administrative infrastructures of the Prussian state and the Catholic church complemented each other, with the two institutions pooling their respective resources. The following chart represents the system of school administration established by Felbiger:

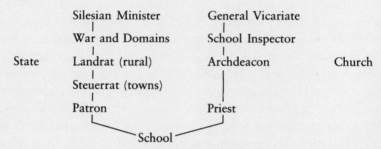

Felbiger entrusted the direct supervision of the schoolmaster to the parish priest, who was required to inspect the school(s) in his parish once a week. The priest could exempt a child from further attendance if the pupil demonstrated sufficient competence. An archpriest, selected from the parish priests in his district, inspected the parishes within his jurisdiction once a year to ensure that priests were performing their supervisory duties. The archpriest was in turn supervised by one of twenty-five school inspectors appointed by Prince-Bishop Strachwitz. Inspectors visited their school districts twice a year, conducting spot checks and inspecting school catalogues. They then reported to the General Vicariate, headed by Prince–Bishop Strachwitz, which functioned both as an ecclesiastical appellate court and as general overseer of Catholic schools in the diocese. The vicariate then reported to the War and Domains Chambers on the general condition of Catholic schools.

Although these procedures formally subordinated the General Vicari-

[75]On the continued role of the Protestant church in school inspection, see Neugebauer, *Schulwirklichkeit*, pp. 64–167.

ate to the War and Domains Chambers, their relationship was a horizontal rather than vertical one. The General Vicariate reported to the chambers on those problems that the relevant ecclesiastical authorities could not remedy. For example, the General Vicariate sought the cooperation of the chambers when, say, the magistrates in a town or the landlords in a district interfered unduly in school affairs. The chambers then referred the matter to the *Steuerrat* or *Landrat,* the respective representatives of royal authority in the towns and the countryside. Hence the relationship between church and state that emerged from the reform was one of cooperation rather than subordination. In Prussian Silesia, as in Austria, the relationship between church and state was far less conflictual than has commonly been supposed.

Obstacles to implementation

Judged solely on the basis of figures provided by Minister Schlabrendorff, Felbiger's reforms appear to have been a success. A week before Felbiger's edict had even been published, Schlabrendorff reported to the king that 251 Protestant and Catholic rural schools had already been established.[76] But the reliability of Schlabrendorff's figures is doubtful, since he was almost surely manipulating figures provided by the Breslau War and Domains Chamber a few months earlier.[77] This kind of behavior was not unusual. Indeed, exaggerating one's administrative accomplishments was crucial to survival in the Prussian bureaucracy. Frederick II was notorious for his harsh treatment of subordinates who failed to meet his expectations, and he took a dislike to ministers who habitually submitted bad news and gloomy reports. Schlabrendorff's predecessor, Joachim Ewald von Massow, had learned this to his great regret.[78] De-

[76]Lehmann, *Preussen und die katholische Kirche,* 4:254.

[77]In July of 1765, the chamber had reported that out of a projected goal of 174 Catholic and 77 Protestant schools, only 91 (62 Catholic and 29 Protestant) had actually been built. Ibid., pp. 248–250. Two years later, the chamber reported that a total of 131 Catholic schools had been established – 43 short of the projected goal. Reimann, "Verbesserung des niederen Schulwesens," p. 343. Thus Schlabrendorff's figure of 251 represents a goal, not an accomplished fact.

[78]After becoming minister in 1753, Massow had made the mistake of sending repeated reports to the king that documented widespread corruption in the bureaucracy. This poisoned his relations with Frederick from the very beginning. By 1755 Massow's position, weakened by his strained relationship with Frederick and undermined by the intrigues of subaltern officials, became so uncomfortable that he suffered a nervous collapse and had to resign. On the circumstances surrounding Massow's collapse see *A.B.,* 1/11:335–338, and Johnson, *Frederick the Great and His Officials,* pp. 150–151.

termined not to share Massow's fate, Schlabrendorff was far more tactful in his dealings with the king. He developed a keen bureaucratic knack for accentuating the positive and glossing over the negative, all the while taking care to place his own administration in the best possible light. This enabled him to survive under Frederick, who spared him the harassment and sarcasm reserved for politically less adroit officials.[79]

Felbiger's own balance sheet on the reforms was far less sanguine. Viewing the results in 1768, Felbiger bitterly observed: "It is almost beyond comprehension that the express commands of such a powerful monarch, commands which a royal minister and two provincial chambers have sought to execute for the past several years, have had so little effect. Opposition to this undertaking has been general: Catholics and Protestants, priests and laity, rich and poor, have all worked to undermine it."[80] Others confirmed Felbiger's judgment. However bouyant his reports to the king, Schlabrendorff privately criticized the administrative lethargy of his War and Domains Chambers, who in turn blamed the *Landräte* for the slow pace of reform. Similar complaints echoed from Prince-Bishop Strachwitz, who rebuked his parish clergy for not fulfilling their supervisory duties.

Felbiger was somewhat more satisfied with the implementation of the reforms in Silesian towns, where every school had been staffed with a normal school graduate by 1767.[81] The success in filling urban school positions is understandable, since these posts were generally more desirable and lucrative. But even if municipal schools were successful in hiring trained schoolmasters, enforcing attendance still proved difficult. The main obstacle was the apprentice system. At Felbiger's request, the War and Domains Chambers had forbidden guildmasters to hire apprentices who had not attended school. Guildmasters who had already hired unschooled apprentices were required to release them for school two hours a day.[82] But Felbiger's inspection tour of Upper Silesia in 1766 revealed that such provisions were all but ignored. Guildmasters continued to hire apprentices who had never attended school, a practice that remained a major cause of urban truancy well into the nineteenth century.[83]

The enforcement of compulsory schooling in the Silesian countryside

---

[79]Ibid., p. 175.
[80]Felbiger, *K.S.*, p. 525.
[81]Lehmann, *Preussen und die katholische Kirche* 4:354–355; Reimann, "Verbesserung des niederen Schulwesens," p. 343.
[82]Felbiger, *K.S.*, p. 214.
[83]Ibid., pp. 510–511; Zimmermann, *Beyträge*, 7:301.

faced even greater difficulties. The picture was not entirely bleak: Strach-witz's inspectors reported that by 1768, 176 rural schools had been established. The training of rural schoolmasters proceeded, albeit slowly: By 1767, Felbiger's normal schools had trained ninety rural schoolmasters, although 629 rural schools remained without certified teachers.[84]

But as always, enforcing attendance proved an obstacle. Many rural families who depended on the field and household labor of their children simply kept them at home. Others refused to provide transportation for inspectors, a service required by the edict. Some peasants resorted to more active forms of resistance. In the district of Neisse, where the ecclesiastical school inspector worked tirelessly against truancy, peasants devised an ingenious way of contravening his zeal. They went to the nearest infantry regiment and informed the recruiting officers that their schoolmaster was eligible for conscription. Prussian recruiting officers, as Voltaire's Candide learned, were not noted for their restrictive conscription policies. They paid a visit to the unsuspecting schoolmaster and immediately drafted him. It was several weeks before he finally obtained his release.[85]

Landlords also had good reason to find the reforms a burden. Many resented having to contribute wood from seigniorial forests to build additional schools, while those accustomed to using parish schoolmasters as personal servants found the edict to be an unwelcome intrusion. In 1766, for example, a Brandenburg lord ordered the schoolmaster of Neu Reetz to do an errand during school hours. When the schoolmaster, Johann Besenius, replied that the lord's order violated the instructions of the Supreme Consistory, the infuriated landlord cursed him profusely and boxed his ears.[86] As in other parts of the monarchy, moreover, some nobles feared the consequences of educating their subjects. These nobles, according to Felbiger, "feared that their subjects would in time learn to use their reason to shirk obligations towards their lords."[87] Reinforcing this fear was the growing tendency on the part of Silesian peasants to appeal cases of seigniorial mistreatment in the *Oberamtsregierungen,* the provincial courts of appeal that had been reorganized under the Prussian jurist Samuel von Cocceji. As an observer noted of Upper Silesian peasants in 1785, "for many years, peasant subjects did not know that

[84]Reimann, "Verbesserung des niederen Schulwesens," p. 343.
[85]Felbiger, *K.S.,* pp. 528–529.
[86]Neugebauer, *Schulwirklichkeit,* p. 151.
[87]Felbiger, *K.S.,* p. 527.

provincial courts existed to which they could bring their grievances. In recent decades, however, many subjects . . . have grown more clever and have learned to use these courts."[88] Litigious peasants doubtless confirmed the worst fears of many nobles regarding an educated peasantry. Thus many simply ignored the edict and continued – in violation of the decree – to require labor services from peasant children (*Waisendienst*) of school age. An observer noted in 1786 that peasant children in Upper Silesia often left school at the age of seven to render their *Waisendienst*.[89]

Although the *Landräte* were charged with enforcing the reforms in the countryside, they often proved uncooperative. The Silesian *Landrat* – like his counterpart elsewhere in Prussia – was invariably a prominent member of the local nobility, whose prejudices he shared and to whom he was bound by ties of class and kinship. The Silesian *Landrat* was himself elected by the nobility of his district, although final confirmation rested with the king. Hence the *Landrat* was reluctant to act against the wishes of those who had elected him. Felbiger, frustrated with the lack of cooperation shown by Silesian *Landräte,* placed the blame for the limited success of rural school reform squarely on their shoulders: "Without the help of the *Landrat*," he sighed, "lords and subjects agree to nothing voluntarily."[90]

The tendency at higher bureaucratic levels to submit false or exaggerated reports was replicated at the local level. Conducting Frederick on an inspection tour of his county in 1779, one Upper Silesian *Landrat* pointed in the distance to what was actually a dilapidated castle and blithely informed the king that it was a school for his peasants. When queried by Frederick about the schools in his district, another Silesian *Landrat* answered with a figure twice as large as the actual number.[91] This sort of deception was not confined to Silesia. In Pomerania, the compliance of local authorities had been worthy of a Potemkin: They concerned themselves with repairing only those schools that lay on the route of the king's inspection tour.[92]

Finally, the Catholic parish clergy in Silesia also proved less than

[88]*Der gegenwärtige Zustand Oberschlesiens* (Dresden, 1786), p. 46. For remarks by Prussian officials that confirm this observation, see *A.B.,* 1/7:509, 1/13:739, and 1/15:383–387.
[89]*Der gegenwärtige Zustand Oberschlesiens*, p. 36. See also Neugebauer, *Schulwirklichkeit*, p. 471.
[90]Felbiger, *K.S.*, p. 412.
[91]Ernst Pfeiffer, *Die Revuereisen Friedrichs des Grossen, besonders die Schlesischen nach 1763, und der Zustand Schlesiens von 1763–1786* (Berlin, 1904), p. 110.
[92]Clausnitzer, "Zur Geschichte der preussischen Volksschule," p. 358.

cooperative. Newly appointed priests naturally resented having to contribute a quarter of their first-years's income, while others disliked the added burden of compiling inspection reports and familiarizing themselves with pedagogical innovations rumored to be Protestant. More conservative clergy, moreover, were suspicious of the reforms, seeing them as a disguised attempt by a Protestant ruler to undermine the Catholic church.[93]

Given the passive or active resistance on the part of lord, subject, *Landrat,* and priest, the economic position of rural schoolmasters showed little immediate improvement. In 1785, schoolmasters in the Upper Silesian countryside still had to spin on the side to make ends meet.[94] An observer noted in 1840 that most rural Silesian schoolmasters continued to practice an outside trade, and he placed their social rank below that of a stable attendant.[95] In Silesian towns, on the other hand, the economic fortunes of schoolmasters did improve. By the end of the eighteenth century, most Silesian towns paid their schoolmasters from a permanent communal fund, thus relieving them of the need to collect tuition from each pupil.[96] Raising a schoolmaster's standard of living did have occasional drawbacks. The Breslau War and Domains Chamber reported in 1768 that, in some cases, schoolmasters refused to admit any more pupils once they earned enough to support themselves and their families.[97]

By 1770, Felbiger had begun to disengage himself from his pedagogical responsibilities. Schlabrendorff, Felbiger's friend and patron, died in 1769, and his successor, Karl Georg Heinrich von Hoym, proved much less responsive to Felbiger's requests for administrative and financial support.[98] After 1772, moreover, the king's attention was primarily devoted to his newly acquired Polish territories, and Silesia and the older Prussian provinces, the focus of Frederick's reform efforts since 1763, were now less important.[99] No longer enjoying the attention he had once received, Felbiger absorbed himself in his scientific and agronomical in-

[93]Felbiger, *K.S.*, pp. 524–525.
[94]*Der gegenwärtige Zustand Oberschlesiens,* pp. 409–411.
[95]*Schlesische Zustände,* p. 331.
[96]Kosler, *Preussische Volksschulpolitik,* p. 70.
[97]Lehmann, *Preussen und die katholische Kirche,* 4:250.
[98]On Hoym see Kosler, *Preussische Volksschulpolitik,* p. 228; Hubatsch, *Frederick the Great,* p. 82.
[99]On the role of West Prussia in Frederickian domestic policy after 1772 see Hubatsch, *Frederick the Great,* pp. 181–189.

terests. He recorded astronomical observations from his observatory in Sagan, conducted experiments on the use of barometric readings to determine altitudes, and wrote a number of treatises on lightning rods and fertilizers. In 1773 the Prussian justice minister, Johann Casimir von Carmer, appointed him director of the Silesian Economic-Patriotic Society.[100]

Although Felbiger had put aside his pedagogical work for the time being, his Silesian reforms had begun to attract the attention of educational reformers throughout Catholic Central Europe. While there was no dearth of pedagogical reformers in Germany, virtually all were Protestants. Felbiger alone offered a pedagogical model to Catholics who, for whatever reason, were dissatisfied with the condition of parish schooling in their territories. In 1768 the Bavarian Academy of Sciences, a center of reform-Catholic sentiment in the empire, had elected Felbiger an honorary member in recognition of his pedagogical contributions. In 1770 Heinrich Braun, a Benedictine member of the academy, had established a normal school in Munich along the lines of Felbiger's Sagan institute. Three years later, Braun modeled his reform of Bavarian parish schooling on the Sagan method.[101] In the bishopric of Bamberg-Würzburg, Prince-Bishop Adam Friedrich Count von Seinsheim based his parish school reform of 1770 on Felbiger's writings. The prince-bishop had learned of the Sagan method through Michael Ignaz Schmidt, the anti-Jesuit church historian and reformer of the University of Würzburg.[102] In the Electorate of Mainz, Elector Emmerich Joseph became familiar with Felbiger's ideas through Joseph Steigentesch, a court official and *Aufklärer*. Steigentesch helped found the College of Education, a teacher-training institute modeled on Felbiger's normal school. Steigentesch would also

[100]Very little is known about the organization of the society or Felbiger's role in it. Although based in Breslau, the society boasted some nine provincial chapters by July of 1773. The society published a weekly magazine between 1773 and 1784, with a circulation totaling five hundred. Since the magazine almost never mentioned contributors by name, it is difficult to assess the extent of Felbiger's contribution. Articles relating to popular education often appeared in the magazine, and it is likely that Felbiger authored some of them. A brief description of the Economic-Patriotic Society can be found in Mittenzwei, *Preussen nach dem siebenjährigen Krieg*, pp. 183–184.
[101]Ludwig Hammermeyer, *Gründungs- und Frühgeschichte der Bayerischen Akademie der Wissenschaften* (Munich, 1959), p. 217; Stanzel, *Schulaufsicht*, p. 300.
[102]See the correspondence between Felbiger and Schmidt in Franz Oberthür, *Michael Ignaz Schmidt's des Geschicht-schreibers des Deutschen Lebensgenschichte* (Hanover, 1802), pp. 302–310. On Schmidt see also Anton Schindling, "Die Julius-Universität im Zeitalter der Aufklärung," in *Vierhundert Jahre Universität Würzburg*, ed. Peter Baumgart (Neustadt an der Aisch, 1982), 91–93.

borrow freely from Felbiger in his 1773 reform of parish schools in the Electorate.[103]

Felbiger's reputation as a Catholic pedagogical reformer explains why, in 1774, he was invited to Austria to supervise the most ambitious school reform of the eighteenth century. Chapter 8 examines that enterprise.

[103]A copy of the Steigentesch plan is located in *AVA*, Nachlass Pergen, 1771. Count Johann Anton Pergen, the Austrian official whose reform proposals are discussed in Chapter 8, received a copy of this plan from Karl Friedrich Willibald Freiherr von Groschlag, his brother-in-law and a chief advisor to the Elector of Mainz. Pergen subsequently passed it along to Maria Theresa. On Steigentesch and school reform in Mainz see Blanning, *Reform and Revolution in Mainz*, pp. 114–121, and F. G. Dreyfus, *Societé et mentalités à Mayence dans la seconde moitié du dix-huitième siècle* (Paris, 1968), pp. 450–458.

8

The Theresian school reform of 1774

Are children . . . now supposed to consult the Scriptures on their own? Are the decrees of the Council of Trent mere paper?

Cardinal Migazzi, 1777

The creation of the Vienna Normal School

On May 30, 1769, Maria Theresa ordered the provincial administrations of Upper and Lower Austria to submit proposals for improving primary schooling in the Habsburg monarchy. Her action came in response to an alarming memorandum from the prince-bishop of Passau, Leopold Ernst Count Firmian. Firmian warned of rampant heresy and unbelief in his diocese, which included Upper Austrian and most Lower Austrian parishes.[1]

As bishop of Seckau from 1739 to 1763, Firmian had worked energetically to halt the spread of crypto-Protestantism in Styria and Carinthia. His countermeasures had been harsh and direct: At one point he recommended simply closing parish schools in the countryside.[2] His efforts to eradicate Protestantism in the Seckau diocese had borne the stamp of his

---

[1]As we have seen, the problem of crypto-Protestantism was not new. The Seven Years War may have encouraged its further spread, however, by bringing the Catholic population into contact with Protestant soldiers and chaplains from the Prussian and Saxon armies. In 1759, a church visitation of Upper Austria blamed the revival of crypto-Protestantism on the spread of Lutheran ideas and books by Protestant chaplains from the Saxon army. *AVA*, Alte Kultus, 68 (Missionen in genere): no. 72, 1759 (visitation report by P. Johann Battista Krämer). On Firmian's memorandum see Helfert, *Gründung*, pp. 121–122. This monumental work, written by a leading historian of the monarchy and the founder of the *Institut für österreichische Geschichtsforschung*, remains an indispensable source. Drawing heavily on archival sources, Helfert's study is unsurpassed in its wealth of detail and acuity of judgment.

[2]See Chapter 3, "The Non-literate Legacy of Habsburg Baroque Catholicism."

notorious uncle, Leopold Anton von Firmian, who as archbishop of Salzburg had exiled thousands of Protestants.[3]

By 1769, however, his methods for fighting heresy had radically changed. By the time he became prince-bishop of Passau in 1763, Leopold Ernst had evolved into a model of reform Catholicism. The reasons for this conversion are unclear. Firmian perhaps realized that his earlier methods against crypto-Protestantism had been ineffective, or he may have been influenced by the growth of Muratorian sentiment among the Habsburg episcopacy. Whatever the causes, Firmian's turnabout is illustrated by the medallion he struck to commemorate his appointment. The inscription on the medallion read "non vi sed amore" – with love, not force.[4]

In Passau, Firmian proceeded to implement a program of reform that included the establishment of hospitals, workhouses, and a theological seminary. Above all, Firmian became a firm advocate of popular schooling and lay literacy. His 1769 memorandum to the empress warned that only schools could rescue the youth of his archdiocese from the dangers of atheism and heresy. But the ecclesiastical authorities alone, he argued, were not powerful enough to carry out this task, and he pleaded for the monarchy's help in reforming those parish schools that lay in the Austrian part of his diocese.[5]

Habsburg officials in the Lower Austrian administration passed along Firmian's proposals to Archbishop Migazzi of Vienna and Bishop Ferdinand von Hallweil of Wiener Neustadt, both representatives of the older generation of reform Catholics. Migazzi and Hallweil applauded his proposals, and specifically recommended improved teacher training, a uniform catechism, and the drafting of a primary school edict.[6] Their recommendations were submitted to the Court Chancellery (*Hofkanzlei*), the central administrative body for the Habsburg hereditary territories. The Court Chancellery, headed by the aging and phlegmatic Count Rudolf Chotek, was a cautious and conservative body not prone to initiating reforms. Chotek referred the matter to another chancellery official, Flo-

---

[3]Weiss, *Bistum Passau*, pp. 311–335. Leopold Ernst was not without traces of his uncle's despotic temperament. A passionate hunter, Leopold Ernst was known to punish poachers by strapping them to a buck, which was then let loose to run wild in the forest. See August Leidl, "Leopold Ernst Kardinal von Firmian (1707–83), ein Kirchenfürst an der Wende vom Barock zur Aufklärung," *Ostbairische Grenzmarken*, Neue Folge, 13 (1971), p. 26.
[4]Helfert, *Gründung*, p. 121.
[5]Ibid., p. 122.
[6]Ibid., pp. 125–126.

rian von Pergenstein, who saw no urgent need for reform. Pergenstein conceded that improvements might be needed in rural education, but insisted that no major changes were necessary in urban schools.[7]

School reform might well have proceeded no further had not the Council of State (*Staatsrat*) intervened. A Kaunitz creation, the Council of State was charged with coordinating domestic policy throughout the monarchy. Dominating the council were *Aufklärer* who looked to Protestant North Germany for inspiration. Three of its six members had been trained at Protestant universities: Kaunitz had studied law at Leipzig, Egid von Borié had attended the lectures of Christian Wolff at Marburg, and Tobias Philip Gebler had matriculated at Halle, Göttingen, and Jena.[8] The Council of State was a dynamic force within the Habsburg bureaucracy and played a key role in most reforms of the Theresian era.

Gebler sarcastically dismissed Pergenstein's lukewarm response to Firmian's urgent request. "On the question as to whether the common man should read and write," he wrote in disgust, "the Chancellery seems to harbor doubts. One might expect to find such doubts in Muscovy on the eve of the accession of Peter I. But one can only marvel to hear them advanced today by our own officials in Vienna."[9] Gebler, with the support of other council members, then proposed creating a special commission within the Lower Austrian administration (whose jurisdiction included Vienna) to draw up a general plan of reform. At the same time he asked Joseph Messmer (no relation to the Viennese physician and magnetist) to submit detailed proposals for reform. Messmer, a Swabian by birth, was rector at the St. Stephan *Stadtschule* in Vienna.[10] A proponent of what by now was known as the "Sagan method," Messmer would play a key role in popularizing Felbiger's ideas in Austria.

Given Felbiger's renown in Catholic Central Europe, it is no surprise that Messmer's proposals reflected his influence. Ignaz Parhammer, head of the Rennweg orphanage in Vienna, had already reorganized the curriculum of the orphanage in accordance with the Sagan method. In 1768 Parhammer had helped to finance a journey to Sagan by Anton Felkel, a former teacher at the St. Stephan *Stadtschule* from whom Messmer most likely learned of Felbiger's reforms.[11] Like Felbiger, Messmer stressed the

[7]Ibid., p. 127.
[8]On the significance of Protestant universities in the training of Austrian state servants see Klingenstein, *Aufstieg des Hauses Kaunitz*, pp. 159–219.
[9]Helfert, *Gründung*, p. 129.
[10]Ibid., pp. 130–132.
[11]Ibid., p. 134.

importance of teacher training. Parish education, charged Messmer, had "no prescribed method of instruction, no norm." Schoolmasters wasted valuable instruction time by teaching pupils individually instead of in a group. The resulting confusion and disorder were compounded, he argued, by the lack of separation between the classroom and the teacher's home or place of work. Hence Messmer, like Felbiger, emphasized the need to professionalize schoolmastering. Messmer not only favored raising the salaries of schoolmasters, but he also insisted on putting them through intensive training and preparation. Accordingly, he recommended transforming the St. Stephan *Stadtschule* into a normal school on the Sagan model.[12]

The Council of State praised Messmer's proposals and forwarded them to Maria Theresa in May of 1770. Additional support for Messmer's normal school came from Franz Karl Hägelin and Philippides von Gaya, two Gebler protégés in the Lower Austrian administration. Hägelin and Gaya were typical examples of the "Protestant connection" in the Habsburg bureaucracy. Both had been classmates at the University of Halle in the early 1750s, where they attended the lectures of Christian Wolff.[13] Hägelin, who had just succeeded Sonnenfels as theater censor in Vienna, had been favorably impressed by the Pietist schools he had visited in Halle.[14] As a proponent of Pietist schooling, Hägelin viewed school reform as a solution to the mendicancy problem: "There will be less misery in the poorhouses and hospitals, the streets will be empty of beggars, and idleness will no longer sap the strength of the commonwealth."[15]

Maria Theresa promptly approved Messmer's plan for a normal school, granting it an annual subsidy of 3,000 florins.[16] The Vienna Normal School opened on January 2, 1771. A flyer in the semiofficial *Wiener Diarium* celebrated the occasion, proclaiming it as but the first step toward a general reform of elementary education in the monarchy.[17]

---

[12]Messmer, "Zustand der hiesigen gemeinen deutschen Schulen," and "Unmassgebliche Gedanken zur Verbesserung der hiesigen deutschen Stadt- und Vorstadtschulen," in *AVA*, Akten der Studienhofkommission, Fasz. 70 (Niederösterreich in genere).

[13]Helfert, *Gründung*, p. 110.

[14]Ibid., p. 143.

[15]Hägelin, "Beschreibung der verbesserten Lehrart in deutschen Schulen, und ihre Folgen für den Staat und die Religion," January 20, 1772, *AVA*, Akten der Studienhofkommission, Fasz. 70 (Niederösterreich in genere).

[16]Helfert, *Gründung*, p. 145.

[17]*Nachricht an das Publikum. Von der Absicht und dem Nutzen des auf allerhöchsten Befehl verbesserten Schulwesens in Österreich unter der Enns* (Vienna, 1771).

With Messmer as director, the Normal School was divided into four classes: the first three gave instruction in reading, writing, arithmetic, and the catechism, and the fourth trained prospective schoolmasters and tutors. The Normal School proved a success in its first year, with a total of 150 pupils and thirty teachers attending.[18]

The Pergen plan

Even before the Vienna Normal School had opened its doors, the Council of State was debating another, more radical project for reform. That the author of this plan was Count Johann Anton Pergen, later notorious as head of the Habsburg secret police under Joseph II, aptly illustrates the role of "social discipline" in Theresian educational reform. Having previously held diplomatic posts in Hanover and Mainz, Pergen, like other advocates of school reform in the Habsburg bureaucracy, had been exposed to intellectual and cultural currents beyond the borders of the monarchy.[19] Pergen first became involved in educational matters in 1769, when Kaunitz charged him with overseeing the administration of the Oriental Academy in Vienna. Kaunitz had established the Oriental Academy as a language school for prospective diplomats in the East. But the previous Jesuit director, Joseph Franz, had so mismanaged the academy that a part of its property had to be sold to cover its debts. When a new director, Father Johann de Deo Negrep, replaced the discredited Franz, Kaunitz and the Council of State instructed Pergen to draft a plan for reforming the finances and curriculum of the academy.[20]

Pergen seized the occasion to outline a far more ambitious plan, one that proposed a complete reorganization of education in the monarchy. Submitted to the Council of State in August 1770, the Pergen plan advocated that the state have control over all educational institutions. The administration of education was to be entrusted to a supreme directory, whose purview was to extend from the universities down to the most

---

[18]Helfert, *Gründung*, pp. 146–147. On the establishment of the Vienna Normal School see also Rudolf Gönner, *Die österreichische Lehrerbildung von der Normalschule bis zur Pädagogischen Akademie* (Vienna, 1967), pp. 24–41.

[19]Helfert, *Gründung*, pp. 190–191. In Mainz he became a close friend and later brother-in-law of Karl Friedrich Willibald Groschlag, chief advisor to the Elector Emmerich Joseph. Educated at Marburg and Göttingen, Groschlag was a chief architect of the Elector's ambitious reform program. On Groschlag see Blanning, *Reform and Revolution in Mainz*, pp. 110–112.

[20]Helfert, *Gründung*, pp. 190–193.

humble village school. "The state," proclaimed Pergen, "must at all times know and determine how, where, why, and by whom instruction is given."[21] He favored complete uniformity at each level, with standardized textbooks, curricula, and normal schools. For the pre-university level, Pergen's plan proposed a three-tiered system comprising universal primary schooling, vocational schools (*Realschulen*) for those entering specialized occupations or professions, and *Gymnasien* for pupils planning to enter the university.[22]

Pergen's system left no room for the regular clergy, whom he favored dismissing from all teaching positions. Pergen argued that religious orders, particularly the Jesuits, were corporations whose particularistic goals were incompatible with the educational needs of the state. Pergen charged that religious orders monopolized secondary schools and universities in order to recruit the most talented and intelligent pupils for themselves. These orders thereby prevented the state from fully exploiting the intellectual resources of its subjects. Their schools, he maintained, educated neither good Christians nor useful subjects. Otherwise "one would not hear so many complaints about the spread of free thought, the decline of religion, morals, honor, and virtue, the lack of proficient and skilled individuals in every class of the population, mediocrity in the arts and sciences, and a general trend toward immoderate luxury and idleness."[23]

The inspiration for Pergen's plan was without question the famous *Essai d'éducation nationale* (Paris, 1763) by Louis-René Caradeuc de La Chalotais, although Pergen never cited the work. Pergen's plan is virtually identical to that published by La Chalotais in the wake of the expulsion of the Jesuits from France in 1762. Like Pergen, La Chalotais bitterly denounced clerical control of education. Both stressed the need to cultivate a "national character" through uniformity of curricula and textbooks. Both were proponents of a class-based educational system that regulated educational advancement.[24] Pergen had most likely become acquainted with the work of La Chalotais through Groschlag, his

---

[21]*HHStA*, Alte Kabinettsakten: Studiensachen, 1736–1773, Fasz. 1, fol. 1087.

[22]Ibid., fol. 1125ff.

[23]Ibid., fol. 1090.

[24]On La Chalotais see R. R. Palmer, *The Improvement of Humanity: Education and the French Revolution* (Princeton, 1985), pp. 52–59; and Chisick, *The Limits of Reform*, pp. 89–92. In France, as in Austria, efforts to expel the Jesuits were accompanied by proposals for school reform. See Jean Morange and Jean François Chassaing, *Le mouvement de réforme de l'enseignement en France 1760–1798* (Paris, 1974), pp. 9–92; and Palmer, *Improvement of Humanity*, pp. 59–70.

brother-in-law in Mainz. A frequent traveler to France, Groschlag was an important conduit for French ideas in Germany.[25] Groschlag had served as ambassador to Versailles from 1758 to 1761, at the very height of anti-Jesuit sentiment in France. He must certainly have been familiar with La Chalotais, who as procurator-general of the Parlement of Rennes had helped precipitate the judicial proceedings that led to the expulsion of the Jesuits.[26]

To some extent, the radicalism of Pergen's proposals derived from his ebullient self-confidence and fierce ambition.[27] But Pergen's radicalism also reveals the depth of anti-Jesuit sentiment that had developed in the Habsburg monarchy by this time. Underlying much of this hostility was the sense of cultural inferiority that afflicted both bureaucratic and ecclesiastical reformers. This feeling had crystallized in the wake of military defeat at the hands of Prussia and helps to explain the urgency of cultural reform in the Theresian era. The conviction that Austria was backward, at least in comparison with her Protestant neighbors, served to legitimate reforms that would have been considered far too radical under any other circumstances.

Although *Aufklärer* in the Council of State, most notably Kaunitz and Gebler, applauded Pergen's bold plan, they nevertheless recognized the enormous obstacles facing its implementation. Under the Pergen plan, schoolmasters would have to be trained on a massive scale. But how was the monarchy to finance the necessary normal schools? Who was to replace the dismissed clerical teachers? Blümegen, a defender of the Jesuits, also warned that depriving religious orders of the right to teach would not only drive those like the Jesuits and Piarists to the verge of

---

[25]Blanning, *Reform and Revolution in Mainz*, p. 110.

[26]Groschlag was himself a harsh critic of monastic orders in Mainz. Indeed, his vigorous advocacy of monastic reform ultimately led to his fall from power in 1774. Ibid., pp. 141–162, for a detailed account.

[27]Pergen's later role in the political reaction of the 1790s has colored his historical reputation. The portrait of Pergen presented in Ernst Wangermann, *From Joseph II to the Jacobin Trials* (Oxford, 1959), pp. 37–45, typifies the standard view of Pergen as an obscurantist opponent of enlightened reform. However, the sweeping nature of his educational project demonstrates that Pergen was no reactionary, at least not in the context of the 1770s. While his advocacy of absolutist centralization had reformist implications in the 1770s, it was equally compatible with reaction once the monarchy abandoned its reformist path in the wake of the French Revolution. In this respect Pergen epitomized the Janus-faced legacy of "Josephism," which, as Fritz Valjevec has noted, was as conducive to reaction as it was to reform. See Fritz Valjevec, "Die josephinischen Wurzeln des österreichischen Konservatismus," *Südostforschungen*, 14 (1955).

bankruptcy, but it would also damage their prestige and destroy the credibility of the Catholic church at the popular level.[28]

Pergen stubbornly defended his plan in another proposal submitted on July 16, 1771.[29] He insisted that the removal of regular clergy from all teaching positions was crucial to the success of his proposal: "The health of a state depends on a coherent system of schools staffed by secular personnel, or at least those who do not belong to religious orders or similar ecclesiastical corporations." Pergen's star appeared to be on the rise when Maria Theresa, impressed by Pergen's spirited defense of his plan, requested that he nominate candidates for his proposed supreme directory. Pergen offered the directorship to Gerhard van Swieten, Maria Theresa's physician, who had earlier led the drive to remove censorship from Jesuit control. Van Swieten, however, declined the post because of age.[30] Other candidates for the directory included the jurist Martini, the Augustinian Müller, and Felbiger.

Convinced as he was of Austrian backwardness, Pergen felt it necessary to look beyond the borders of the monarchy in order to staff the directory. He thus dispatched Johann Melchior Edler von Birkenstock, a young clerk and Kaunitz protégé in the State Chancellery, to recruit potential administrators in Protestant Germany. After an extensive tour of universities in Saxony and Hanover, Birkenstock returned with a list of five candidates. Except for Felbiger, these included four prominent academicians, all young, all Protestant, from the University of Erfurt: Friedrich Justus Riedel, professor of philosophy and belles lettres (*schöne Wissenschaften*); the distinguished poet and writer Christoph Martin Wieland, at that time a professor of philosophy; Carl Friedrich Bahrdt, later to become a radical theologian and enfant terrible of the German Enlightenment; and Johann Georg Meusel, professor of history and literature who later authored the noted lexicon.[31] In effect, Birkenstock proposed placing Habsburg school reform in the hands of Protestant foreigners.

The circumstances surrounding Birkenstock's journey remain obscure. Kaunitz undoubtedly had a hand in it: He warmly supported the candidacies of the four Protestants, arguing in the Council of State that the

[28]Helfert, *Gründung*, pp. 208–214.
[29]*AVA*, Nachlass Pergen, 1771.
[30]Letter from Van Swieten to Pergen, Oct. 7, 1771, in *AVA*, Nachlass Pergen, 1771.
[31]Helfert, *Gründung*, p. 441.

importation of Protestant reformers was necessary given the dearth of qualified Catholics.[32] Whoever was responsible, the attempt to enlist Protestants for the task of school reform backfired. It provoked angry protests from Archbishop Migazzi, and Maria Theresa herself recoiled from the idea of entrusting the education of her Catholic subjects to Protestant *Aufklärer*. She promptly ordered Pergen, who somewhat disingenuously had tried to distance himself from the scheme, to drop the idea. The unfortunate Riedel, who had already arrived in Vienna from Erfurt in eager anticipation of his post, was informed that his pedagogical services were no longer desired. Pergen's opponents in the Council of State now exploited the scandal in order to sabotage his plan. Count Heinrich Blümegen and the recently appointed Count Friedrich Hatzfeld, two of the more conservative council members, recommended shelving the Pergen plan. Even the reform-minded Franz Kressel von Qualtenberg, director of the Vienna law faculty and another recent appointee to the Council of State, expressed deep reservations about the project. Kressel warned that the appointment of Protestant advisors would antagonize the Catholic population and unnecessarily provoke opposition to school reform. Kressel also found the idea of removing the secular clergy from teaching posts to be impractical. A final vote of opposition came from the co-regent, Joseph, who questioned the utility of a supreme directory. Joseph argued – with good reason – that instead of subsidizing lucrative sinecures for foreign scholars and literary critics, the monarchy would be better advised to hire and train elementary schoolmasters.[33]

As a result of misgivings voiced from all quarters, the Pergen plan was quietly shelved in January of 1772.[34] On one level, the rejection of the Pergen plan illustrates how Maria Theresa's deep Catholic piety, her refusal to brook heresy in any form, represented the outer limits of her pragmatic reformism. But the personality of the empress aside, Pergen also failed because his plan was genuinely impractical. Even his supporters in the council recognized the difficulty, if not impossibility, of a purely secular reform. Any reform that sought to dispense with the administrative infrastructure of the Catholic church was doomed to failure.

[32]*HHStA*, Kaunitz Voten, Kart. 2, Fasz. 2, Nov. 3, 1771.
[33]Helfert, *Gründung*, pp. 239–251; A. Ritter von Arneth, *Geschichte Maria Theresias*, 10 vols. (Vienna, 1863–79), 9:235–237.
[34]A copy of the empress's final resolution (January 15, 1772) on the Pergen plan is found in *AVA*, Nachlass Pergen, 1772.

The success of school reform in Austria, as in Prussia, depended not on displacing the church, but on enlisting it as a partner.

Felbiger and the General School Ordinance

Pergen's failure also highlighted another important stumbling block to reform, namely finances. Additional sources of revenue were required to fund normal and elementary schools, textbooks, and teaching salaries. However, the levying of additional taxes to expand education invariably provoked opposition. Gebler's proposal to finance the reforms through a tax on monasteries raised an outcry among the regular clergy, while the conservative Blümegen managed to veto Hägelin's plan to secure funds through additional contributions from the provincial estates.[35]

The prospects for reform continued to dim in July of 1773, when an investigation into the Vienna Normal School revealed a faculty wracked by petty jealousies, intrigue, and widespread dissatisfaction with Messmer's leadership. One faction charged that the Sagan method was being applied too rigidly, whereas the other complained that Messmer had abandoned Felbiger's principles.[36] Symptomatic of the declining prestige of the Normal School was a scathing pamphlet, published anonymously in 1774, that dismissed Messmer as an ineffectual bungler and ridiculed Gebler for having ever placed his trust in him. The author implicitly criticized Felbiger as well, calling the Vienna Normal School "a poor copy of a mediocre original."[37] Banned in Austria and doubtless written by a Protestant, the pamphlet reflected the declining fashionability of traditional Pietist pedagogy among Protestant *Aufklärer*. Enlightened critics such as Friedrich Nicolai considered the methods of Hecker and Felbiger too mechanical and authoritarian, preferring the more "progressive" pedagogy of Rousseau or Basedow.[38]

With the Normal School in disarray and no apparent funds available for schools, Theresian school reform may well have proceeded no further. What saved the reforms was the suppression of the Society of Jesus

[35]Helfert, *Gründung*, p. 164, 261–262.

[36]*AVA*, Studienhofkommission, Fasz. 70 (Niederösterreich in genere), investigation of the Normal School Faculty, July 24, 1773.

[37]*Freymütige Briefe an Herrn Grafen von V. über den gegenwärtigen Zustand der Gelehrsamkeit, der Universität, und der Schulen Wien* (Frankfurt am Main and Leipzig, 1774), p. 13.

[38]See Nicolai's later critique of the Vienna Normal School in his *Beschreibung einer Reise durch Deutschland und die Schweiz*, 4 vols. (Berlin, 1784), 4: 651–661.

by Pope Clement XIV in July of 1773. The significance of this event, both real and symbolic, cannot be overstated. The Jesuits had epitomized the visual, theatrical, and "plastic" qualities associated with the Habsburg baroque and Counter Reformation. More than any other single event, the dissolution of the Jesuits symbolized the end of the Counter Reformation in Austria. In 1740, the year Maria Theresa ascended the throne, the cultural influence of the Jesuits had been at its zenith. Their subsequent abolition illustrates the degree to which the reign of Maria Theresa, perhaps even more than that of Joseph, represented a genuine cultural revolution.

Beyond its broader cultural significance, the dissolution of the Jesuits was a monumental event in the history of Austrian schooling. For the expulsion of the Jesuits left not only an educational and cultural vacuum; it also left wealth. Pope Clement XIV considered the empress a valuable ally, and anxious to preserve the Papacy's cordial relations with the Habsburg dynasty, he ceded to Maria Theresa all Jesuit schools, colleges, houses, and other property remaining in the monarchy. At the accession of Joseph, the total value of ex-Jesuit property was assessed at approximately 13 million florins.[39] The confiscation of Jesuit property proved timely, for it provided a source of property and income for schools. The subsequent reform and expansion of Austrian parish schooling would never have been possible without the wealth left by the Jesuits. It explains above all why school reform proved more successful in Austria than in Prussia, where the Hohenzollern monarchy benefited little from the demise of the Society. The Habsburg monarchy, although far from enjoying fiscal health, had nevertheless derived a small financial boost from the abolition of the Jesuits.

The dissolution of the Jesuits infused new life into Habsburg school reform. After publishing the abolition order in September of 1773, Maria Theresa entrusted its implementation to a commission headed by Kressel. Since the dissolution of the Jesuits also necessitated the reorganization of secondary and university education, she charged the Kressel commission with developing guidelines for a general reform of education in the monarchy. Other members of the commission included Franz Sales von Greiner, a proponent of agrarian reform and religious toleration; the Augustinian abbot Ignaz Müller, confessor to Maria Theresa and a reform Catholic of deep Muratorian convictions; and Karl Anton von

[39]Hanns Leo Mikoletzky, *Österreich: Das grosse 18. Jahrhundert* (Vienna, 1967), p. 250.

Martini, professor of natural law at the University of Vienna and a key figure in the Austrian Enlightenment. The commission symbolized the alliance of *Aufklärer* and reform Catholics that had been so instrumental in efforts to reform censorship, the universities, and popular religion.

Drafted by Martini, the commission's plan of December 1, 1773, recommended that confiscated Jesuit property be used to help finance a system of universal compulsory schooling.[40] Martini's plan called for the creation of normal schools in order to standardize curricula, textbooks, and pedagogical methods. Martini also insisted that schooling be *standesmässig* and made a strict distinction between the curricula of urban and rural schools. Rural schools were to teach only reading, writing, arithmetic, and religion. In town schools, which were to educate future artisans, merchants, and secretaries, a more advanced curriculum was necessary. This was to include German, orthography, mathematics, applied arts and sciences, history, and geography. The commission also recommended transforming many of the smaller Latin schools into elementary schools, thereby expanding primary education while reducing the number of pupils pursuing higher studies.

After approving the recommendations of the Kressel commission, Maria Theresa asked Kaunitz to inquire into the possibility of bringing Felbiger to Vienna to supervise the reforms. Both Kressel and Gebler in the Council of State had been in regular contact with Felbiger ever since the establishment of the Normal School. When the Normal School fell victim to factional strife, Gebler had suggested bringing Felbiger to Vienna to take over the institution.[41] In January of 1774, Kaunitz wrote to Gottfried van Swieten, the Austrian ambassador in Berlin, asking whether Frederick II would grant Felbiger a brief leave of absence from his administrative duties. On February 1, the Prussian minister Finkenstein notified van Swieten of the King's willingness to place Felbiger's talents at the disposal of the empress. The king, assured Finkenstein, "only wishes for more opportunities to be of service to Her Majesty and to offer proof of His genuine friendship."[42]

Felbiger leaped at the chance to supervise what promised to be the most ambitious reform of his century. Once Frederick had released him from his duties in Sagan, Felbiger hastily arranged for his departure to

---

[40]*HHStA*, Alte Kabinettsakten: Studiensachen (1736–1773), Fasz. 1, fol. 602–631.
[41]Helfert, *Gründung,* p. 308.
[42]Informed that her archenemy had acquiesced, Maria Theresa drily replied, "How gallant." Ibid., p. 309.

Vienna. He arrived in the Austrian capital on May 1, 1774, and was immediately given wide-ranging authority over primary education in the monarchy. Maria Theresa, whose confidence in Felbiger's abilities remained unshaken until her death, appointed him to the Commission on Education (*Studienhofkommission*). This agency enjoyed supreme authority over all matters relating to education.[43] She also named him to the Lower Austrian School Commission, where he enjoyed complete authority over the Vienna Normal School and all elementary schools in the city.

Felbiger's prestige as founder of the Sagan method enabled him to end the factionalism that had crippled the Normal School. At the same time, he began work on his main task, the drafting of a compulsory school edict. While working on the edict Felbiger also found time to prepare textbooks and teaching manuals for future use in the schools. By July of 1774, Felbiger had completed the edict. Following revisions by the Lower Austrian School Commission and Court Chancellery, Maria Theresa signed the General School Ordinance (*Allgemeine Schulordnung*) on December 6, 1774.

"The education of youth of both sexes," affirmed the preamble to the ordinance, "is vital to the happiness of a nation."[44] Hence schooling was now compulsory for all children between the ages of six and twelve. Rural schoolmasters were to consult parish registers to ensure that all school-age children were enrolled, while schoolmasters in larger towns and cities were to check attendance against a list compiled twice a year by the local magistrate. Pupils were to attend five days a week, with three hours of instruction in the morning and two in the afternoon. Although school was to be held year-round, pupils in the countryside were excused from school at harvest time to help in the fields. Pupils desiring to leave school before their thirteenth year had to produce a certificate, signed by their priest, attesting to their proficiency in the required subjects. The ordinance prohibited admitting boys into apprenticeships or girls into

---

[43]The Commission on Education had emerged in the late 1750s as a department within the *Directorium in Publicis et Cameralibus,* the central body that coordinated domestic policy. Following the abolition of the *Directorium* in 1760, the Commission became an independent agency directly subordinate to the Court Chancellery. Migazzi, who originally headed the Commission, was succeeded in 1773 by Franz Kressel von Qualtenberg.

[44]The General School Ordinance is published in Anton Weiss, ed., *Die Allgemeine Schulordnung der Kaiserin Maria Theresia und J. I. Felbigers Förderungen an Schulmeister und Lehrer* (Leipzig, 1896). For a detailed discussion see Engelbrecht, *Geschichte des österreichischen Bildungswesens,* 3:135–137.

domestic service who could not produce a similar certificate. Here the edict reflected the belief, common among reformers, that guildmasters were no longer providing their apprentices with an adequate moral and religious education.[45]

The General School Ordinance established three kinds of schools. Every town and every rural parish seat were to have at least one minor school (*Trivialschule*), which was to provide elementary instruction in those subjects deemed necessary for all classes of the population. These included reading, writing, arithmetic, and religion, the last of which was given special emphasis.

The second type of school, the so-called major school (*Hauptschule*), was an urban grammar school designed for middle-class pupils. At least one major school was to exist in each provincial district (Kreis). Major schools were to be attended both by pupils hoping to advance to a *Gymnasium* and by those desiring vocational preparation for careers as merchants, skilled craftsmen, and clerks. The curriculum of major schools included those subjects offered in minor schools, as well as courses in German composition, basic Latin, history, geography, mechanics, trigonometry, and architecture.

Finally, the edict required that a normal school be established in every province. In the future, no schoolmaster was to be hired who had not been certified by the director of a normal school. Even tutors were required to obtain normal school certification.[46] In addition to training teachers, the normal school served as the model for all other schools in the province. Patterned on the Vienna institute, the provincial normal schools served to provide uniformity in curriculum, teaching methods, and textbooks. Uniformity (*Gleichförmigkeit*) was a central theme of the reforms. In theory at least, a pupil in a Lower Austrian minor school was to receive instruction in the same subject, at the same time, using the same textbook, from a teacher using the same methods, as a pupil attending its Tyrolean equivalent.

Like its Prussian counterpart, the General School Ordinance relied on both lay and clerical school inspectors for enforcement. Supervisory duties over a minor school were shared by the local priest and a lay inspector (either a town magistrate or the deputy of the noble patron). The lay

---

[45]See Chapter 2, "Pietist Pedagogy after Francke."
[46]Felbiger later published the *Vorschrift zur Unterweisung der Hauslehrer* (Vienna, 1776), a teaching manual required for all tutors. A copy is to be found in *AVA*, Studienhofkommission, Fasz. 60 (Privatlehrer, 1771–90).

inspector was responsible for keeping the school in good repair and for ensuring that the schoolmaster, if new, was properly certified. The clerical inspector, for his part, made sure that the schoolmaster was teaching the proper subjects and using only those schoolbooks approved by the Vienna Normal School. Both inspectors were required to report annually to their district supervisor, normally an archpriest appointed by the bishop. District supervisors in turn reported to the provincial school commission, whose members were appointed by the provincial administration.

In contrast to minor schools, normal and major schools were supervised solely by lay individuals, except in the case of religious instruction, which was to be provided or supervised by a local priest. The supervisor of a normal school was the director himself, while a designated magistrate periodically inspected the major school in his town or city. Both were to report twice a year to the provincial school commission.[47]

At the peak of the administrative hierarchy was the Commission on Education. Within the commission, Felbiger's favor with the empress gave him de facto control over primary school policy in the monarchy. In 1777, Maria Theresa further extended his authority by appointing him supreme director of all normal schools, major schools, and minor schools in the monarchy. With this appointment, Felbiger became responsible to the empress alone.[48]

Compulsory schooling and educational exclusion

As seen earlier, a revealing paradox lay at the heart of eighteenth-century educational reform: Proponents of compulsory schooling invariably advocated socially restrictive policies at the secondary and university level. A striking example of this paradox was seen in Prussian Silesia, where Schlabrendorff's efforts to expand primary schooling were accompanied by draconian measures that prohibited children of the urban and rural poor from studying beyond the elementary level.

A similar dialectic characterized Theresian educational reform. At the very moment the General School Ordinance was being implemented, reformers were taking steps to curtail plebeian educational advancement

---

[47]On the system of inspection established by the GSO see Stanzel, *Schulaufsicht*, pp. 256–275.
[48]Helfert, *Gründung*, p. 273.

beyond the elementary level.[49] This is not surprising, since virtually all supporters of compulsory schooling in the Habsburg monarchy favored tighter restrictions on entry into *Gymnasien* and universities.[50] Pergen's attempt to "nationalize" education reflected not only a hostility toward the Jesuits, but also an attempt to regulate educational advancement more efficiently. Only in exceptional cases, argued Pergen, should the state allow children of the poor to study beyond the age of twelve: "their occupations require little else, and to do more would merely breed doubt, discontent, and unhappiness."[51] The Kressel commission, to which the empress had entrusted the administration of ex-Jesuit schools and property, shared this view. The commission's educational guidelines issued in December of 1773 advocated reducing the number of Latin schools and *Gymnasien*.

The dissolution of the Jesuits did in fact give the state an excuse to close dozens of *Gymnasien* and *Stadtschulen*. In Bohemia alone, thirty-one *Gymnasien* were closed following the expulsion of the Jesuits. Most of these never reopened, but some were transformed into major, minor, or normal schools.[52] Countless *Stadtschulen*, which occupied an intermediary rung between parish schools and *Gymnasien*, also closed. The larger ones became major schools, while smaller *Stadtschulen* were downgraded to the level of minor schools.[53] The effect of these closings was to further constrict avenues of educational advancement.

The exclusionary implications of Austrian compulsory schooling become even clearer when viewed in conjunction with the *Gymnasium* reforms of the period. Mathes Ignaz von Hess, a Martini protégé who taught universal and literary history at the University of Vienna, submitted the first detailed proposal for *Gymnasium* reform in May of 1774. Its

---

[49]On the problem of "academic overproduction" in eighteenth-century Austria, see Klingenstein, "Akademikerüberschuss."

[50]A notable exception is Kaunitz. With reference to Hungary, Kaunitz favored broadening educational opportunities and increasing scholarships for promising youths, regardless of class. Here Kaunitz's educational program must be viewed in the specific context of his Hungarian policy, which attacked aristocratic particularism and sought to create a more efficient and professionalized bureaucratic infrastructure. Kaunitz's Hungarian policies are discussed in Franz A. J. Szabo, "The Social Revolutionary Conspiracy: The Role of Prince W. A. Kaunitz in the Policies of Enlightened Absolutism towards Hungary, 1760–1780," paper presented at the annual meeting of the Canadian Association of Hungarian Studies, Montreal, P. Q., Canada, 3 June, 1985.

[51]*AVA*, Nachlass Pergen, 1771.

[52]Weiss, *Schulreform in Böhmen*, 1:9.

[53]Helfert, *Gründung*, p. 402.

provisions included reducing the number of plebeian students admitted to secondary schools. "It is no loss to society," assured Hess, "if the state prevents intelligent individuals from pursuing higher studies, and instead guides them into other occupations."[54] Although the Commission on Education ultimately rejected the Hess plan for insufficient stress on vocational subjects,[55] the reforms that were finally adopted in 1776 were equally restrictive in their admission guidelines. This plan, drafted by the Piarist school reformer Gratian Marx,[56] imposed a double standard on *Gymnasium* aspirants. The children of nobles and state officials were to be granted admission automatically, but the reform imposed far more rigorous standards on plebeian applicants. The edict of 1776 affirmed that "the children of noble persons, councillors, and clerks are to be admitted even if they possess only mediocre talent and little proficiency in the necessary subjects. Children from the lower orders, however, are to be admitted only if they possess exceptional talent."[57] Moreover, by their very nature, Marx's admissions guidelines excluded most rural inhabitants. The subjects to be covered on *Gymnasium* entrance examinations included Latin, a subject that the General School Ordinance had confined to urban major schools. The system of inspection for primary schools further reinforced restrictive *Gymasium* policies. In the major and minor schools under their charge, school inspectors were required to examine pupils twice a year in order to screen those hoping to pursue further study.[58]

Felbiger himself was careful to allay any fears that compulsory schooling might encourage the educational aspirations of lower-class pupils. He published a sequel to his primer in 1777 specifically for this purpose:

The second part of my primer proves that happiness is possible for all classes of society as long as one is pure of heart, free of unhealthy desires, and content with one's station in life. By instilling this profound truth in our pupils, we hope to

---

[54]Ignaz von Hess, *Entwurf zur Einrichtung der Gymnasien in K. K. Erbländern* (Vienna, 1775), pp. 9–10.
[55]See Klingenstein, "Bildungskrise," pp. 220–221.
[56]Published in Wotke, *Das österreichische Gymnasium*, pp. 255ff.
[57]Ibid., p. 271.
[58]GSO, article 22. Joseph II would place further restrictions on plebeian educational advancement in 1784. He abolished all *Gymnasium* stipends in order, as the edict stated, "to prevent a horde of useless creatures from burdening society." Those unable to pay their tuition fees were to leave school immediately. This measure, combined with Joseph's abolition of numerous *Gymnasien,* led to a 25 percent decline in *Gymnasium* enrollment – a drop of more than 2,200 pupils – in the following school year. See Wotke, *Das österreichische Gymnasium*, p. lxxiii.

stifle any inclination to pursue further studies, thereby making them content with the station into which they are born.[59]

Ferdinand Kindermann likewise instructed Bohemian school inspectors to discourage peasant youths from reading too much, since "the welfare of society requires that the education of the common man reach no higher than his occupation. Otherwise he will no longer wish to fulfill his duties."[60] Felbiger's *Namenbuchlein,* a speller for beginning pupils, contained a song entitled "Contentment with My Station" (*Zufriedenheit mit meinem Stand*).[61] Elsewhere, Felbiger's schoolbooks mustered biblical citations to discourage aspirations for social advancement. Felbiger's primer cited *Corinthians* to prove that "each has an obligation to live in accordance with the duties and conditions proper to his station. . . . One should not frivolously aspire to a higher social position."[62] Pupils also read that Jesus listened obediently to his teachers, ate and drank moderately, and "never complained about the hardships that went with his station in life."[63] As Kindermann told an audience at the Prague Normal School, "It is more virtuous to be skilled in a humble occupation than incompetent in a higher one."[64]

The implementation of the General School Ordinance

By February 1775, each of the Habsburg hereditary provinces had established a school commission to implement the General School Ordinance. These included Upper and Lower Austria, Austrian Silesia, Moravia, Bohemia, Outer Austria, Carniola, Tyrol, Styria, Carinthia, Gorizia, and Istria. The edict affected neither the Austrian Netherlands nor the Italian duchies of Milan and Mantua, since their viceregal administrations were virtually independent of Vienna. Nor did it apply to Hungary and the Banat (today southern Hungary and northern Yugoslavia), where ethnic and religious variations required separate school edicts. In the Banat, where Orthodox Serbs and Rumanians dominated, the court issued a variant of the edict in 1776. The Hungarian version of the ordinance

---

[59]Felbiger, *Nachricht von dem für die K. K. Staaten vorgeschriebenen Katechismus* (Vienna, 1777), p. 26.
[60]Quoted in Weiss, *Geschichte der theresianischen Schulreform in Böhmen,* 1:261.
[61]I was unable to locate this work, which is cited in Helfert, *Gründung,* pp. 510–511.
[62]Felbiger, *Zweyter Theil des Lesebuches für die Landschulen* (Vienna, 1777), p. 58.
[63]Ibid., p. 58.
[64]Kindermann, *Von dem Einflusse der niederen Schulen auf das gemeine Leben,* p. 15.

Table 4 *Sources of primary school financing in the Habsburg monarchy, 1781*

Source	Amount (florins)
Ex-Jesuit fund	28,711
Capital interest	15,600
Taxes on masked balls and comedies	11,616
Subsidies from the Court Treasury	9,243
Sale of textbooks	6,265
Contributions from provincial estates (Stände)	6,038
Ecclesiastical contributions	5,759
Inheritance taxes	4,117
Taxes on benefice recipients	3,420
Municipal contributions	679
Miscellaneous	4,007

Source: Ernst Wangermann, *Aufklärung und staatsbürgerliche Erziehung. Gottfried van Swieten als Reformator des österreichischen Unterrichtswesens 1781–1791* (Vienna, 1978), pp. 50–61.

appeared in 1777 with the promulgation of the *Ratio Educationis*. An exception was the Military Frontier, the strip extending along the Turkish border from the Adriatic to Transylvania. In this area, which was under the direct administration of the Court War Council (*Hofkriegsrat*), the General School Ordinance took effect immediately.[65]

After the creation of provincial school commissions, the most pressing need was to train teachers. By 1776, normal schools existed in Innsbruck (Tyrol), Linz (Upper Austria), Freiburg im Breisgau (Outer Austria), Brünn (Moravia), Prague (Bohemia), Graz (Styria), Klagenfurt (Carinthia), Troppau (Austrian Silesia), Laibach (Carniola), Lemberg (Galicia), Gorizia (the Duchy of Gorizia), and the City of Trieste. The creation of a normal school network, one of the most important achievements of

[65] On the adaptation of the GSO to Hungary and the Banat see Domokos Kosáry, "Die ungarische Unterrichtsreform von 1777," in *Ungarn und Österreich unter Maria Theresia und Joseph II: Neue Aspekte im Verhältnis der beiden Länder,* ed. Anna Drabek et al. (Vienna, 1982), pp. 91–100; Moritz Csáky, *Von der Aufklärung zum Liberalismus. Studien zum Frühliberalismus in Ungarn* (Vienna, 1981), pp. 174–175; Philip J. Adler, "Habsburg School Reform among the Orthodox Minorities, 1770–1780," in *Slavic Review,* 33 (1974), p. 34; Strahinja K. Kostić, "Kulturorientierung und Volksschule der Serben in der Donaumonarchie zur Zeit Maria Theresias," in Plaschka and Klingenstein, *Österreich im Europa der Aufklärung,* 2:855–866; Hans Wolf, *Das Schulwesen des Temesvarer Banats im 18. Jahrhundert* (Baden, 1935), pp. 178–181.

Theresian school reform, was greatly facilitated by the use of ex-Jesuit property. Most normal schools were located in Jesuit *Gymnasien,* while interest from the sale of confiscated Jesuit property helped pay salaries of normal school teachers and supply books and teaching materials.[66] Table 4, which is based on figures from the beginning of Joseph's reign, demonstrates that ex-Jesuit property constituted the major source of school funding in the Habsburg monarchy. Other sources included a tax on masked balls and theater comedies. In 1775, for example, the Moravian school commission was able to collect 1,480 florins during carnival season.[67] This amount alone sufficed to subsidize more than half the annual budget of the Brünn Normal School.[68]

This investment in normal schools began to show impressive results by the end of the decade. By 1779, 546 normal school graduates were teaching in Viennese and Lower Austrian primary schools.[69] In Moravia, the Brünn Normal School had trained 344 teachers by this time, and the Prague Normal School graduated 253 schoolmasters by 1780.[70] The head of the Bohemian School Commission, Ferdinand Kindermann, also encouraged parish priests and clerical candidates to attend the Prague Normal School in order to fulfill their supervisory duties more effectively. The archbishop of Prague, Anton Peter Count Přichovský, supported Kindermann's promotion of normal school training among the Bohemian clergy. Přichovský decreed in 1776 that parish appointments were to be awarded only to those who had attended a normal school.[71] As a consequence, 179 candidates for the Bohemian priesthood had attended the Prague Normal School by 1780.[72]

The normal schools also functioned as publishing houses for the distribution of textbooks. This arrangement provided provincial school commissions with additional income, and facilitated the diffusion of inexpensive textbooks. Vienna was the first normal school to have a printing press; the empress subsequently granted publication licenses to normal schools in Prague, Brünn, Innsbruck, Freiburg im Breisgau, Linz, Graz, Laibach, and Lemberg. Textbooks were relatively inexpensive: A

[66]Helfert, *Gründung,* pp. 384–385.
[67]Ibid., pp. 396–397.
[68]Ibid., p. 386.
[69]"Einladung zu der öffentlichen Prüfung der zwei und achtzig Schüler in der kaiserlichen-königlichen Normalschule bei St. Anna in Wien, nach geendigtem Winterkurs, 1778," in *AVA,* Studenhofkommission (Niederösterreich in genere), Fasz. 70.
[70]Helfert, *Gründung,* p. 408.
[71]Ibid., 410–411.
[72]Weiss, *Geschichte der theresianischen Schulreform in Böhmen,* 1:15–24, 391–393.

first-year pupil in an urban elementary school paid about eighteen
kreuzer for his or her schoolbooks, roughly twice the daily wages of a
nonguilded laborer in a textile manufactory.[73] The volume of sales was
so great, however, that normal school presses still operated at a substantial profit. Indeed, profits were so high that school commissions began
distributing one-quarter of their textbooks free to the poor of their parishes.[74] This measure doubtless improved attendance by easing the financial burden on poorer households.

Statistical evidence, though scattered and not always reliable, does
show a rise in elementary school attendance. In Vienna, the number of
elementary schools rose from sixty-four in 1771 to seventy-nine in 1779.
More significantly, the number of children between six and thirteen who
attended school increased from 4,665 to 8,039 during the same period.
However, the fact that a substantial number (5,400) still received their
schooling from tutors, suggests that public schools had yet to shed their
unsavory reputation.[75]

School attendance also increased in the provinces. The surveys just
cited showed that in Lower Austria, the percentage of children attending
elementary schools rose from 16 percent in 1771 to 34 percent in 1779.
In Graz, attendance among school-age children increased from 17 percent to 30 percent between 1772 and 1780.[76] In the Salzkammergut, the
mountainous royal domain in Upper Austria, Maria Theresa took a
strong personal interest in school reform. The Salzkammergut was a
notorious center of crypto-Protestantism. Determined to eradicate heresy
in the region, she founded a special fund for the creation of schools. Her
efforts yielded substantial results: In 1773 only 378 out of a total of
1,580 school-age children attended a parish school, but by 1778 the
number had grown to 1,044.[77] Her campaign against heresy in the Salzkammergut further illustrates the continuity between Theresian school
reform and earlier Counter-Reform traditions.

Bohemia was another region in which reform proved relatively suc-

[73]On the price of schoolbooks see Helfert, *Gründung*, p. 495. Wage estimates are taken
from the appendix in Bodi, *Tauwetter*, pp. 441–444.
[74]Helfert, *Gründung*, p. 495.
[75]"Tabellarisches Verzeichnis sämmtlicher von 5. bis 12. und 13. Jahren Schulfähigen,"
AVA, Nachlass Pergen, 1771; and "Formular zu den ferneren halbjährigen Nach-
weisen," AVA, Studienhofkommission (Niederösterreich in genere), Fasz. 70.
[76]"Zustand der gratzerischen Schulen," AVA, Studienhofkommission, Fasz. 70 (for 1772
figures). The figures from 1780 are provided in the useful study by Walter Pietsch, *Die
theresianische Schulreform in der Steiermark (1775–1805)* (Graz, 1977), p. 47.
[77]Helfert, *Gründung*, pp. 409–410.

cessful. With a ratio of roughly one school per thousand inhabitants in 1780, Bohemia had the most extensive network of elementary schools in the entire monarchy.[78] Bohemia boasted 1,700 elementary schools in 1776; the number had risen to 2,400 by 1790, when two-thirds of all school-age children in the province were attending Bohemian elementary schools.[79]

An important reason for the success of the reforms in Bohemia was the support they enjoyed among traditional ecclesiastical and aristocratic elites. Ecclesiastical support for the reforms in Bohemia reflected the extent to which reform Catholicism had taken root in the ecclesiastical hierarchy. Archbishop Přichovský of Prague was an energetic supporter, establishing an endowment of 40,000 florins to support elementary education in the province. By requiring all priesthood candidates to attend a normal school, Přichovský also helped to integrate the Bohemian clergy into the new system of public education.

Supplementing this endowment was an annual grant of two thousand florins from the Bohemian estates, an amount matched by the monarchy through contributions from the Ex-Jesuit Fund (*Exjesuitenkasse*).[80] The financial assistance provided by the Bohemian estates indicates the degree of aristocratic support for the reforms. As seen earlier, influential aristocrats like Count Buquoi and Governor Fürstenberg actively promoted school reform on their estates. Count Klamm-Gallas, who hired a young normal school graduate to reform parish education on his estates in Reichenberg, Friedland, Grafenstein, and Lamberg, was also a noted patron.[81] Other Bohemian aristocrats sympathetic to the reform included scions of such powerful families as the Czernins, Kollowrats, Kinskys, Lobkowitzes, and Schwarzenbergs.[82]

Much of the credit for mobilizing aristocratic support goes to Kindermann, who headed the Bohemian School Commission. By introducing spinning into Bohemian schools, Kindermann helped meet the labor needs of Bohemian landowners. Kindermann introduced spinning classes into the Prague Normal School in 1776, and spinning was soon incorporated into more than 500 Bohemian schools. The introduction of spin-

[78]Pietsch, *Schulreform in der Steiermark*, p. 47.
[79]Weiss, *Geschichte der theresianischen Schulreform in Böhmen*, 1:17–29; Wangermann, *Aufklärung und staatsbürgerliche Erziehung*, p. 59.
[80]Böhm, *Historische Nachricht*, p. 19.
[81]Ibid., p. 45.
[82]Kindermann, *Landschule zu Kaplitz*, p. 49; Weiss, *Geschichte der theresianischen Schulreform in Böhmen*, 2:21–23.

ning, as mentioned earlier, also improved attendance by providing economic incentives to rural families. The relatively high attendance rate (75 percent) in schools with spinning classes points to Kindermann's success in linking elementary schooling with rural industry.[83]

Obstacles to reform

As in Prussia, there was resistance to compulsory schooling.[84] The salary of the schoolmaster remained the responsibility of the parish community, and although the free distribution of textbooks somewhat reduced the financial burden, school fees remained a source of hardship for poorer families. In general, families were less inclined to send their daughters to school than their sons, although the General School Ordinance applied equally to both sexes. Theodor Janković, head of the Banat School Commission, reported in 1781 that half of all school-age boys went to school regularly, whereas only one-quarter of their female counterparts attended.[85] Attendance records from Styria, where the reforms have been studied most thoroughly, reveal that more than three times as many boys as girls attended school. This gap would narrow, however, so that by 1800, school attendance by boys exceeded that of girls by only three to two.[86]

Although compulsory schooling enjoyed widespread support among clergy of reform-Catholic persuasion, many of their more conservative colleagues distrusted the reforms. Charging that the reforms were a Protestant plot, numerous Tyrolean priests refused to cooperate. Clerical discontent in turn gave sanction to popular opposition. Riots erupted in Innsbruck in 1774, when rumors circulated that a school census being compiled by archducal authorities was actually a list of those eligible for conscription. In some Tyrolean villages, opposition to the reforms was so intense that schoolmasters and their families were physically assaulted.[87] In Bohemia, similarly, Archbishop Přichovský occasionally had to reprimand priests who condemned the reforms from the pulpit. One Bohe-

---

[83]See Chapter 5, "From Spinning Bee to Spinning School."
[84]For a general account see Engelbrecht, *Geschichte des österreichischen Bildungswesens*, 3:112–118.
[85]Adler, "Orthodox Minorities," p. 44.
[86]Pietsch, *Schulreform in der Steiermark*, p. 125.
[87]Sebastian Hölzl, "Das Pflichtschulwesen in Tyrol ab der theresianischen Schulreform bis zur politischen Schulverfassung," Ph.D. diss., University of Innsbruck, 1972, pp. 380–389.

mian priest caused a stir by charging that Felbiger's textbooks contained heretical Hussite doctrines.[88]

A particularly delicate issue among the clergy was Felbiger's "documented" catechism. Before Felbiger, the most popular catechism in Catholic Central Europe had been that of Peter Canisius, the sixteenth-century Jesuit. By Felbiger's day, the Canisius catechism was under attack for its dry, scholastic language. Catholic critics of the Canisius catechism turned to France for models, translating the catechisms of Jacques Bossuet and Claude Fleury.[89] Felbiger modeled his own catechisms on those of Fleury. Arguing that catechistic instruction must take into account the child's age and developmental level, Fleury had divided his catechism into levels of difficulty.[90] Following Fleury, Felbiger composed three catechisms, one for each school class.[91]

What was new about Felbiger's catechistic approach was the use of *Beweisstellen,* lengthy scriptural passages that provided documentary support for Catholic doctrine. Felbiger's incorporation of biblical passages into his advanced catechism reflected the move among reform Catholics to reform popular devotion by rooting it more firmly in the Scriptures. Felbiger argued that the rampant progress of unbelief among the laity required the church to rely more heavily on direct scriptural evidence: "In the present day, when unbelief waxes rife and so many show so little regard for religion, we must take care to acquaint pupils with the Scriptural foundations of faith."[92]

When Felbiger first proposed incorporating scriptural passages into his advanced catechism in 1777, he sparked immediate controversy. Previously a supporter of Felbiger, Archbishop Migazzi now protested that Felbiger's proposed use of lengthy biblical passages violated the Bull Unigenitus: "Are children or uneducated adults now supposed to consult the Scriptures on their own? Are the decrees of the Council of Trent mere

[88]Helfert, *Gründung*, pp. 427–428.
[89]Translations of Bossuet's catechism appeared in Vienna in 1758 and 1771, while versions of Fleury were published in Vienna (1766 and 1777), Strassburg (1771), and Breslau (1776). On these catechisms see Johann Schmitt, *Der Kampf um den Katechismus in der Aufklärungsperiode Deutschlands* (Munich, 1935), p. 286.
[90]Ibid., p. 287.
[91]In Prussian Silesia, *Römisch-Katholischer Katechismus für die erste Classe* (Sagan, 1766); *Römisch-Katholischer Katechismus für die II. Classe* (Sagan, 1765); *Romisch-Katholischer Katechismus für die III. Classe* (Sagan, 1766). In Austria, catechisms designed by Felbiger would include *Der kleine Katechismus* (appendix to the *Namenbuchlein*, Vienna, 1774); *Auszug aus dem grossen Katechismus* (Vienna, 1777); and *Der grosse Katechismus* (Vienna, 1777).
[92]Felbiger, *Nachricht von dem für die K. K. Staaten vorgeschriebenen Katechismus*, p. 24.

paper? Then why, in this century, did the Church condemn Quesnel's proposition that 'the reading of Scripture is for all'?"[93] Although Migazzi had long advocated greater emphasis on scriptural study in the training of clergy, he feared that placing even a fraction of the Scriptures in the hands of the laity threatened the authority of the church.

Other Catholic bishops joined Migazzi, charging that the catechism itself contained heretical propositions. Maria Theresa suspended publication of the catechism while Migazzi, aided by a panel of theologians, investigated the alleged doctrinal errors.[94] Although Felbiger accepted the corrections of Migazzi and his panel, he pleaded with Maria Theresa not to expurgate the scriptural passages. Hägelin and the Lower Austrian School Commission joined in Felbiger's defense, arguing that the use of scriptural passages in the catechism would help inoculate the population against Protestantism:

Because Protestants read the Bible, they charge Catholics with ignorance of the Holy Scriptures. Hence it would be useful to provide the peasantry with sufficient Scriptural evidence to confute opponents of the Church. Such a measure would in no way violate the teachings of the Church; on the contrary, it would enhance the influence of Catholic doctrine if the peasantry gained more insight into its sources, while the charge leveled by heretics, namely that our religion is little more than the teachings of men and cannot be proven through the Word of God, would be refuted.[95]

Hägelin's defense, cleverly couched in anti-Protestant language, helped sway the empress. Maria Theresa sided with Felbiger and urged Migazzi to consent to the publication of the catechism, scriptural passages and all. Migazzi grudgingly agreed, and by 1778, 135,000 copies of the catechism had been published and circulated throughout the monarchy.[96] Felbiger's catechisms replaced that of Canisius as the most popular in Catholic Central Europe, where they continued to be used well into the nineteenth century.[97]

School reform in the non-German territories

Not surprisingly, the most serious impediment to reform was the multiethnic character of the monarchy. In an empire comprising Czechs, Slov-

[93]Quoted in Wolfsgruber, *Migazzi,* p. 303.
[94]On the controversy surrounding the *Beweisstellen* see Johannes Hofinger, *Geschichte des Katechismus in Österreich* (Innsbruck, 1937), pp. 74–106.
[95]Quoted in Helfert, *Gründung,* p. 520.
[96]Hofinger, *Katechismus in Österreich,* p. 104.
[97]Friedrich Bürgel, *Geschichte der Methodik des Religionsunterricht in der katholischen Volksschule* (Gotha, 1890), p. 255.

aks, Italians, Hungarians, Poles, Rumanians, Serbs, Slovenes, Croatians, Armenians, and Ruthenes, only the most rigid and unrealistic centralist could expect the reforms to be applied in a uniform fashion. Ethnic and religious minorities naturally viewed the reforms with a mixture of fear and suspicion. Distrust was especially prevalent in Hungary and the Banat, where religious divisions among Catholics, Protestants, Orthodox, and Uniates served to exacerbate ethnic differences. Not surprisingly, then, some have viewed Theresian school reform among the non-German population of the monarchy as a thinly disguised attempt at Germanization.[98]

However, a closer look reveals that Theresian school reform was surprisingly moderate on the language question. It is true that German-speaking bureaucrats in Vienna favored the diffusion of German throughout the monarchy. Their motives, more political than national, rested on the assumption that the effective exercise of power depended on the ability of the state and its subjects to communicate with each other. Efforts to diffuse the German language were pursued most vigorously in Bohemia, where the state prohibited the hiring of schoolmasters who were not proficient in German.[99] A knowledge of German was also required for teachers in schools on the military frontier, where military efficiency was the paramount issue. On the southwestern frontier, for example, German-speaking officers sometimes had to rely on Franciscan missionaries to translate orders into Slovenian.[100]

Although Theresian school reform encouraged the study of German in non-German areas, it never actually required the use of German as the language of instruction. Even where vigorously promoted, the teaching of German was designed to supplement, not replace, instruction in the native language. The Habsburg court explicitly rejected coercive measures in its promotion of German. In reference to Galicia, a Polish-speaking region, the Court Chancellery affirmed in 1780 that it would be "destructive and unreasonable to impose the German language on the Galician population. The Polish language can instill religion and morality just as effectively as German."[101] In the same conciliatory spirit, Maria

[98]See, for example, C. A. McCartney, *The Habsburg Empire 1790–1918* (New York, 1969), pp. 112–114.

[99]Helfert, *Gründung*, pp. 469–471.

[100]Felbiger, *Die Beschaffenheit und Grosse der Wohlthat welche Maria Theresia durch die Verbesserung der deutschen Schulen Ihren Unterthanen dem Staate und der Kirche erwiesen hat* (Prague, 1781), p. 83; Kostić, "Kulturorientierung," p. 852.

[101]Helfert, *Gründung*, p. 483.

Theresa exempted Slovenes on the Military Frontier from those taxes
that went to support German schools.[102] This kind of ethnic pluralism
was also implicit in the Hungarian version of the General School Ordinance, the *Ratio educationis* of 1777, which allowed each of the seven
linguistic groups represented in the province (Magyars, Germans, Slov-
aks, Croatians, Ruthenians, Serbs, and Rumanians) to establish schools
providing instruction in its own language.[103]

Although the reforms eschewed the goal of linguistic uniformity, they
did aim for uniformity of teaching methods, curricula, and textbooks.
This goal could not be achieved without translations of teaching manuals
and textbooks. Thus numerous Italian translations were commissioned
for the Italian-speaking population of the South Tyrol, Gorizia, and Istria, while in Bohemia the normal schools in Prague and Brünn translated
catechisms and primers for the Czech population.[104]

A striking example of successful translation policy was the Banat,
where the Serbian reformer Theodor Janković translated many of Felbiger's works into Serbian. Up until this time, Serbo-Croatian had not
existed as a literary vehicle. The most literate segment of society in the
Banat was the Orthodox clergy, who used a variant of Church Slavonic
rather than their own vernacular. In this respect, Theresian school reform
constituted a major step in the emergence of Serbo-Croatian as a literary
language. Efforts to diffuse the written vernacular began in 1770, when
the court sanctioned the establishment of a Cyrillic press by the Viennese
publishing firm of Joseph von Kurzböck. Schoolbooks were also translated for the Rumanian population, which was concentrated in the south-
eastern Banat. A Rumanian version of Felbiger's *Nothwendiges Handbuch für den Gebrauch der Schullehrer in den deutschen Trivial-Schulen*
appeared in 1777.[105]

In Hungary, the obstacles to reform proved all but insurmountable.
Hungary's traditional position as a buffer against the Turks had forced
Habsburg rulers to concede a degree of administrative autonomy and
religious toleration unknown in most regions of the monarchy. Hence the
Ratio Educationis allowed each confession to use its own religious in-
structors and catechisms. Any intrusion by Vienna into the educational

---

[102]Ibid., p. 479.
[103]Ibid., p. 441; Engelbrecht, *Geschichte des österreichischen Bildungswesens*, 3:130–134.
[104]Helfert, *Gründung*, pp. 549–551.
[105]Adler, "Orthodox Minorities," p. 36; Wolf, *Schulwesen*, pp. 192–194; Kostić,
    "Kulturorientierung," pp. 862–864.

and cultural life of the province provoked the immediate distrust of the Protestant and Orthodox clergy. This distrust, combined with the plethora of languages in the province, greatly impeded the implementation of Theresian school reform.[106]

Religious pluralism posed similar problems in the Banat. The Orthodox religion had enjoyed statutory autonomy since the late seventeenth century, when Leopold I granted ecclesiastical self-government in exchange for military assistance against the Turks. Both lay and clerical education of the Orthodox population was in the hands of the Metropolitanate in Karlowitz.[107] Hence the success of Theresian reform in the Banat hinged upon the ability of Vienna to reach a modus vivendi with the Orthodox hierarchy. That such a compromise was achieved was largely the work of Janković, who had close ties with both absolutist reformers and the Orthodox clergy. Janković had not only studied under Sonnenfels at Vienna and attended the normal school, but also served under the Orthodox bishop of Temesvar before his appointment as school director for the Banat in 1773.[108] Janković was thereby able to win the trust both of the court and of the Orthodox clergy.

The school ordinance for the Banat (1776) reflected the resulting compromise. School instruction was to be in Serbian or Rumanian, although higher salaries were offered to those schoolmasters capable of providing German instruction. Although Orthodox children were required to attend a Catholic school if no Orthodox school existed, they "are not to be given the slightest injury, or compulsion in their religious belief; at the time for religious instruction they are to be released forthwith from attendance; and also, in these mixed schools, no book is to be used with confessional content."[109] Supervision of the schools was to be divided between the state (i.e., the Banat School Commission in Temesvar) and the Orthodox clergy. The state and the Orthodox church also shared

---

[106]Helfert, *Gründung,* pp. 440–444; Csáky, *Von der Aufklärung zum Liberalismus,* pp. 174–175.

[107]Adler, "Orthodox Minorities," pp. 24–25.

[108]On Janković's activities in the Banat, see Peter Polz, "Theodor Janković de Mirijevo: Der erste serbische Pädagoge, oder, Die Theresianische Schulreform bei den Serben und in Russland," Ph.D. diss., University of Graz, 1969, pp. 33–157. Janković later journeyed to St. Petersburg in 1782 at the behest of Catherine II, where he helped supervise reforms in Russian primary education. See Peter Polz, "Theodor Janković und die Schulreform in Russland," in Erna Lesky et al., eds., *Die Aufklärung in Ost- und Südosteuropa* (Cologne, 1972), pp. 119–174.

[109]*Regulae directive für die Verbesserung der illyrischen und wallachischen nicht-unierten Elementar- oder Trivialschulen,* paragraph 4, as cited in Adler, "Orthodox Minorities," p. 33.

financial responsibility for the building and maintenance of the schools. The Court Treasury in Vienna provided free building materials, subsidized the distribution of textbooks and teaching manuals, and paid the salaries of administrative personnel in the Temesvar School Commission. The Court Treasury also subsidized the training of seventeen Serbian schoolmasters at the Vienna Normal School, and established three-month seminars in Sombor and Osijek where Orthodox schoolmasters were instructed in the fundamentals of the Sagan method.[110] The Metropolitanate in Karlowitz, for its part, also contributed funds for the training of schoolmasters and the distribution of catechisms. The Metropolitanate was chiefly interested in reform as a way of defending the Orthodox religion against the competing influence of the Catholic church, whose adherents included most of the Hungarian and Croatian population of the Banat.[111] Ironically, then, it was hostility to Catholic influence that induced the Orthodox hierarchy to cooperate with Theresian school reformers.

The result was a considerable expansion of primary schooling in the Banat. Janković claimed that the number of Orthodox schools in the Banat had almost doubled to 183 by 1776; the number had grown to 205 by 1778, and 452 in 1781.[112] The Hungarian Court Chancellery, which took over administration of the Banat in 1778, estimated in 1780 that most Serbian villages and more than half of all Rumanian villages had Orthodox elementary schools.[113]

In short, Theresian school reform had a significant impact on the educational level of the Banat. At the very least, as mentioned earlier, the reforms promoted the rise of Serbian and Rumanian as literary vernaculars. It is no accident in this regard that the noted Serbian playwright Joakim Vujić and the poet and translator Alexsije Vezelić, both pioneers in the rise of Serbian literature, had graduated from schools established by the reforms in the 1770s. Similarly, three of the earliest Rumanian writers to publish in the vernacular – Michael Rosu, Dmitrie Tischindeal, and Paul Iorgovici – taught in schools created by the reforms. The rise of literary

[110] Ibid., p. 38. Adler claims that in the ensuing years, the majority of Serbian and Rumanian schoolmasters were introduced to the Sagan method.

[111] Ibid., pp. 25–26, 40–41.

[112] Ibid., pp. 31, 36.

[113] The higher concentration of schools among the Serbs reflected the fact that the Serbian population tended to be concentrated in the southern and central Banat, a region of market towns and agrarian villages. In the eastern Banat, where most Rumanians lived, a more rural, pastoral economy prevailed. Ibid., p. 24.

vernaculars in turn helped bring about a fundamental reorientation of the Banat away from the Russo-Byzantine East, and toward the Germanic West. By promoting the vernacular, Theresian school reform hastened the decline of Church Slavonic and thereby severed an important cultural link with the East.[114] At the same time, of course, the promotion of the vernacular would contribute to the emergence of the national, anti-Habsburg movements of the subsequent century.

The fall of Felbiger

In 1781, Felbiger estimated that the Habsburg monarchy had a total of 6,197 schools below the level of the *Gymnasium*. More than half of this number, claimed Felbiger, had been reformed in accordance with the provisions of the General School Ordinance. These included 15 normal schools, 83 major schools, 47 special cloister schools for girls, and 3,848 minor schools. These were attended by a total of 208,508 pupils, more than 20,000 of whom were poor pupils who paid no school fees.[115]

Despite his successes, however, Felbiger had made enemies. This enmity was partly due to the jealousy of those who resented his influence with the empress. Felbiger's enormous salary (6,000 florins per year!) doubtless aroused resentment as well. Maria Theresa's unfailing support had also bred a certain arrogance in Felbiger, who grew ever more convinced of his rectitude and administrative invulnerability. His critics frequently complained that Felbiger too often took personal credit for the achievements of others.[116]

Felbiger's attempt to extend school reform to the army was the issue that precipitated his downfall. Already in the 1760s, the upbringing of soldier children had become a deep source of concern to civil and military authorities alike. Barracks were a notorious breeding ground for prostitution and juvenile crime. In an attempt to counter the corrupting influence of the barracks, field marshalls Daun and Laudon had ordered their field chaplains to provide religious instruction to regimental children. In Vienna, the co-regent Joseph instituted a new system in 1772 whereby regimental children were marched daily to the nearest parish school. This arrangement soon became common in provincial cities as well.[117]

---

[114]Ibid.; Kostić, "Kulturorientierung," pp. 848–849, 866; Wolf, *Schulwesen*, pp. 192–194.
[115]Felbiger, *Beschaffenheit*, p. 35.
[116]Helfert, *Gründung*, pp. 562–563.
[117]Ibid., pp. 604–605.

In 1780, Felbiger proposed changes in this system. Instead of attending schools outside the barracks, the children of soldiers were now to attend special schools of their own. In addition, schooling was to be extended to soldiers themselves. Weekly visits by a normal school graduate were to provide instruction in reading, writing, and religion. Maria Theresa strongly endorsed the proposal, and forwarded it to the Court War Council (*Hofkriegsrat*).[118]

Infuriated by Felbiger's meddling in military affairs, the Court War Council enlisted Joseph's support in opposing the plan. Joseph considered Felbiger's proposal a harebrained scheme that, if implemented, would have disastrous effects on military morale. To introduce an additional source of authority in the barracks, argued Joseph, would be to undermine military discipline and encourage disobedience. As usual, however, Maria Theresa stood firmly behind Felbiger. The issue soon mushroomed into another one of those conflicts between Joseph and his mother that had become so common by the last decade of Maria Theresa's reign.[119]

By opposing Joseph, Felbiger had overreached himself. The death of Maria Theresa later that year left him completely vulnerable to the attacks of his enemies. His rivals included Joseph Anton Gall, a former teacher at the Vienna Normal School whose pedagogical influence had begun to rival that of Felbiger. Heavily influenced by the Rousseauean pedagogy of Johann Bernhard Basedow, Gall was critical of Felbiger's continued emphasis upon memorization. Gall was an advocate of the so-called Socratic method, in which instruction took the form of a conversation between teacher and pupil.[120] Out of favor with the emperor, his pedagogical methods under attack, and his patroness dead, Felbiger accepted the inevitable and resigned. Felbiger's replacement was Joseph Sucher, a close associate, but Sucher was now tightly subordinated to the Commission on Education. Sucher's replacement by Gall in 1784 excluded Felbiger completely from educational affairs. Felbiger retired to Pressburg with a comfortable pension, where he remained until his death in 1788.

[118]Ibid., pp. 609–610.
[119]Ibid., pp. 611–612.
[120]On Gall see Wangermann, *Aufklärung und staatsbürgerliche Erziehung*, pp. 62–68.

Conclusion

<hr/>

As should be clear from the previous two chapters, the compulsory school movement in eighteenth-century Prussia and Austria had to contend with a variety of obstacles that conspired against success. Historians who write about the Old Regime often underestimate the impediments to state action and too often accept at face value the testimony of absolutist administrators naturally more prone to advertise success than to publicize failure. Although administrative sources may shed valuable light on the intentions of administrators, they are less useful for determining the extent to which those intentions were actually realized. As we have seen, the geographical and cultural distance between Sans Souci and the marshes of Pomerania, or the Vienna Hofburg and the alpine villages of Upper Styria, posed problems of implementation and enforcement that were often insurmountable. Inadequate systems of transportation and communication, a shortage of trained administrative personnel, language differences, passive or active resistance at the local level – all conspired to frustrate even the best-laid plans of reformers. In both states, the clash between absolutist goals and local conditions limited the effectiveness of absolutist school policy.

This was particularly true in the economic realm, where the very conditions that gave rise to reform also stymied it. In the countryside, the expansion of rural industry and a desire to commute peasant labor services led reformers to focus on education as a way of inculcating labor discipline. Yet the policies designed to instill this discipline in children were often resisted by both landlords and peasants precisely because they disrupted household production. It was not simply the hostility of "traditional" social groups toward "modernization" that induced peasants to keep their children at home, or landlords to send peasant children into the fields rather than to school. This sort of resistance instead reflected an understandable resentment toward policies which, though seeking to promote work discipline, would have removed children from the labor force. Only in Bohemia, where Kindermann was able to integrate compulsory schooling into the structure of rural industry, did the demands of state policy mesh with the labor needs of noble landlords and rural households. Elsewhere, there remained a sharp contradiction between the rather abstract goals of absolutist policy on the one hand, and social and economic realities on the other.

Above all, the incessant financial difficulties that plagued every government of the Old Regime were an obstacle. The maintenance of large standing armies, the drive to obtain or regain territory through warfare, the expense of rebuilding or repopulating areas devastated by war, the fiscal constraints imposed by societies rooted in corporate privilege – all of these help to explain the chasm that often separated a decree from its enforcement.

In the case of Prussia, where the unfavorable fiscal condition of the monarchy after 1763 posed objective limits to reform, these constraints were particularly severe. Beyond finances, however, the reasons for the limited success of Prussian school reform also have to do with the very nature of Hohenzollern absolutism. Financial and administrative weaknesses aside, the military and fiscal priorities of Prussian absolutism often collided with social and economic policy. However concerned with the social and economic behavior of its subjects, the Prussian state was in the last analysis a *Militärstaat* dependent on the army for its external and internal security. We have seen some of the mundane yet revealing ways in which military and pedagogical aims often clashed. Frederick II's estimate of state revenues and expenditures for 1768 provides a telling example of royal priorities. That year, according to the king, state revenues totaled some 13.8 million talers. Of that amount, approximately 10.4 million, or 75 percent of all state revenues, went to the army.[1] When we compare this percentage with Frederick's paltry subsidies for elementary schooling in Brandenburg – four thousand talers per year after 1771 – the king's priorities become clear.

In comparison, school reform in the Habsburg territories was better funded and on the whole more successful. The expansion of popular education under Maria Theresa was an impressive achievement, all the more so given the tremendous heterogeneity of the monarchy's popula-

[1]Mittenzwei, *Preussen nach dem siebenjährigen Krieg,* pp. 105–106.

tion. Here the financial resources that became available following the abolition of the Jesuits in 1773 were crucial to the successes achieved by reformers. Ex-Jesuit property and capital enabled the monarchy to establish normal schools in virtually every province, an achievement that helped create the most advanced system of teacher training in Europe. Ex-Jesuit wealth also enabled normal schools to operate printing presses that not only allowed provincial school commissions to standardize textbooks on an unprecedented scale, but also yielded profits that helped pay the school fees of children from poorer families.

However, finances alone cannot explain the achievements of Theresian school reform. That the reform was pursued more vigorously and successfully in Austria than in Prussia reflected the sense of urgency that motivated Habsburg reformers. The jolting experience of military defeat and the loss of Silesia produced an atmosphere of crisis in which absolutist reformers — especially those educated in Protestant universities — grew convinced of Austrian "backwardness." For them, far-reaching reforms in social, economic, and cultural life were the monarchy's only hope of competing with its more advanced European neighbors. Ecclesiastical reformers, for their part, were driven by a similar awareness of crisis. Threatened by Protestantism on one side and a rising tide of unbelief on the other, these reformers looked to schooling as a means of preserving the dominion of their faith.

Felbiger's dismissal by Joseph II in 1782 by no means signified the abandonment of the monarchy's commitment to school reform. On the contrary, Joseph's reign witnessed a massive increase in school expenditures (see Table 5). Under Maria Theresa, the monarchy had devoted the bulk of its primary school budget to the creation and maintenance of normal schools. Under Joseph, the monarchy began to funnel funds directly to parish schools, and elementary schooling expanded further through Joseph's confiscation of monastic property and expropriation of revenues previously earmarked for processions and pilgrimages.[2]

Granted, the array of obstacles and contradictions that thwarted school reform meant that in both states, compulsory schooling was never firmly established until later in the nineteenth century. However, one appraises the success of any reform not only by its immediate, quantitatively measurable results, but also by the traditions it supersedes and

[2]Wangermann, *Aufklärung und staatsbürgerliche Erziehung*, pp. 62–68; Engelbrecht, *Geschichte des österreichischen Bildungswesens*, 3:125.

Table 5 *Primary school expenditures in the Habsburg monarchy,*
1781–89 (florins)

Province	1781	1789
Lower Austria	18,942	241,935
Upper Austria	6,390	22,267
Styria	7,093	33,489
Carinthia	3,697	36,883
Carniola	2,330	23,794
Tyrol	n.a.	25,913
Outer Austria	6,397	19,777
Bohemia	12,499	146,771
Moravia/Silesia	15,582	78,010
Gorizia/Gradiska	3,450	6,598
Galicia	3,969	65,046

n.a. Not available.
Source: Wangermann, *Aufklärung und staatsbürgerliche Erziehung*, p. 53.

the precedents it establishes. A reform, in other words, may have a historical significance that transcends the success or failure of initial efforts to
implement it.[3] Whatever its limits, school reform in eighteenth-century
Prussia and Austria created a foundation on which the rapid expansion
of public education in the nineteenth century could build. For one thing,
school reform marked the culmination of a process whereby universal
literacy was established as a desirable social goal. For another, rulers
now assumed direct (though limited) financial responsibility for public
education. Although subsidies for education comprised only a small proportion of state expenditures under Frederick II and Maria Theresa, the
reforms nevertheless established a firm precedent for state-supported
schools. Equally significant for the subsequent development of public
schooling were the new types of educational institutions arising in the
eighteenth century. One, the normal school, in time served to professionalize the occupation of schoolmaster, giving elementary school teachers a professional identity and a heightened sense of their value to state
and society. Industrial schools, another institution to emerge in the eigh-

[3]It is on these grounds, for example, that Reinhardt Koselleck's *Preussen zwischen Reform
und Revolution: Allgemeines Landrecht, Verwaltung, und soziale Bewegung von 1791 bis
1848*, 2d ed. (Stuttgart, 1975), argues for the innovative features of the Prussian General
Code of 1793.

teenth century, were also to figure prominently in nineteenth-century education.

Finally, the reforms marked the beginning of state efforts to regulate educational advancement. Ironically, the pedagogical economy articulated in the eighteenth-century compulsory school movement aimed at constricting avenues of educational mobility for the lower classes. A paradoxical feature of the reforms, in other words, was the attempt to limit plebeian educational advancement by making education compulsory. In this respect, the introduction of compulsory schooling helped to establish the contours of an educational class system by defining the parameters within which the vast majority of the rural and urban lower classes were to be educated.

What of the effects of the reforms on the mentality of Prussian and Austrian subjects? Did school reform succeed in making subjects any more loyal, hard-working, and obedient? Partisans of compulsory schooling naturally tended to emphasize its psychological efficacy. One such advocate was Johann Peter Süssmilch, the Prussian clergyman and statistician who wrote confidently in 1756 about the expansion of East Prussian schooling under Frederick William I: "The stubborn Lithuanian has become a completely different human being in civil society. He now understands and fulfills his duties toward his lord. This is especially true of the younger generation, who have had the opportunity to attend schools. What a splendid return on the king's investment!"[4]

However, reform often has consequences that its original architects had not anticipated, and there is evidence to suggest that the legacy of eighteenth-century school reform was far more ambiguous than Süssmilch's assurances would indicate. In the case of Austria, the unforeseen consequences of reform manifested themselves in a number of ways. By encouraging the rise of literary vernaculars among the non-German population of the monarchy, Theresian school reform hastened the emergence of the nationalistic, anti-Habsburg movements of the following century. A similar irony underlay the promotion of German literary culture that accompanied the reforms, a phenomenon that contributed to the extraordinary effervescence of German literary production during the Josephinian thaw. By 1781, when Joseph II decreed that "every common man should have a copy of the Bible," the idea of universal literacy had clearly triumphed.[5]

---

[4]Quoted in Leschinsky and Roeder, *Schule im historischen Prozess*, p. 92.
[5]See the decree published in Jaksch, *Gesetzeslexikon*, 2:296–297.

Joseph also relaxed literary censorship that year, another sign of the monarchy's faith in the political utility of literate culture. Joseph's liberal censorship policy represented a shrewd and calculated effort to enlist literary support for his policies. Through discreet government sponsorship, writers sympathetic to Joseph were encouraged to publish cheap pamphlets in support of his reforms. In the end, however, six years of relaxed censorship ultimately helped foster an autonomous literary culture that condemned Joseph's "despotism" even as it applauded many of his reforms. Alarmed by the increasingly radical tone of his literary opponents, Joseph finally abandoned his cultural experiment and reimposed strict literary censorship.[6]

If absolutist efforts to co-opt literate culture in Austria failed, so did attempts at reforming nonliterate culture. As the popular resistance to Joseph's religious reforms demonstrates, baroque piety remained deeply entrenched in Austrian culture. Nor was the Viennese popular stage ever entirely domesticated. After 1770 it migrated to suburban working-class districts, where censorship was more intermittent and less effective.[7] In the nineteenth century, extemporaneous comedy returned to the Viennese stage with a vengeance in the bitterly satirical performances of Johann Nestroy. In short, although I have focused on absolutist and reform Catholic efforts to promote literate culture in the Habsburg monarchy, one must neither exaggerate their efficacy nor overlook the survival of a nonliterate, baroque cultural tradition into the nineteenth century. Indeed, the stubborn persistence of this tradition into the twentieth century — here Hugo von Hoffmannsthal can serve as an example — was to be a distinctive feature of Austrian culture.

In the case of Prussia, school reform would appear to have bolstered the authority of Hohenzollern absolutism. After all, it served to popularize Pietist attitudes toward authority, with their stress on the virtues of obedience and deference. At the same time, Pietist *Innerlichkeit* is often credited with having fostered a fundamental indifference to politics among the educated strata of the German bourgeoisie. If Pietist schooling did contribute to what Thomas Mann called "subjectivism in things of the mind, therefore, a type of culture that might be called pietistic, given to autobiographical confession and deeply personal, one in which the

---

[6]Bodi, *Tauwetter in Wien*, p. 57; Wangermann, *From Joseph II to the Jacobin Trials*, pp. 25–50.
[7]Emil Blümml and Gustav Gugitz, *Alt-Wiener Thespiskarren: Die Frühzeit der Wiener Vorstadtbühnen* (Vienna, 1925), pp. 21–23.

world of the *objective*, the political world, is felt to be profane and is thrust aside with indifference" – then the legacy of Pietist reform was indeed conservative.[8] Moreover, historians like Koppel Pinson and Gerhard Kaiser have both pointed to the Pietist roots of German nationalism, finding antecedents in Pietist subjectivity, "enthusiasm," and a missionary concern with the larger Christian community.[9] To the extent that German nationalism offered the monarchy a new source of legitimacy, and to the degree that eighteenth-century school reform served to popularize the Pietist attitudes that went into creating that nationalism, then the reforms of the eighteenth century did ultimately serve the political interests of Hohenzollern absolutism.

However, there is also compelling evidence that eighteenth-century school reform was by no means successful in creating reliable and effective mechanisms of social control. As Kenneth Barkin has argued, continued attempts by Prussian ministers in the nineteenth century to foster docility through schooling "may have been due to their recognition that prior attempts had failed."[10] In fact, as Barkin points out, the numerous foreigners who visited Prussian schools in the nineteenth century were impressed by the broad education provided both teachers and pupils. Returning from a tour of Silesia, John Quincy Adams wrote in 1804 that the aim of Prussian schools was "not merely to load the memory of their scholars with words, but to make things intelligible to their understanding." The American educational reformer Horace Mann was an unabashed admirer of Prussian schooling. Mann found that in contrast to Massachusetts schools, where "the child was taught NOT TO THINK" (his emphasis), Prussian school children were "taught to think for themselves." Another observer, the American school reformer Alexander Bache, reported in 1839 that Prussian schools "would apply as perfectly in a republic as in a monarchy."[11] One cannot know, of course, whether this kind of testimony accurately reflected the condition of Prussian schools in general. But it does clash with the stereotypical image of *Kadavergehorsam* that modern historians, zealous in searching out the roots of National Socialism, often associate with Prussian schooling.

[8]Quoted in W. R. Bruford, *The German Tradition of Self-Cultivation: "Bildung" from Humboldt to Thomas Mann* (Cambridge, 1975), vii.
[9]Pinson, *Pietism as a Factor in the Rise of German Nationalism;* Kaiser, *Pietismus und Patriotismus.*
[10]Kenneth Barkin, "Social Control and the Volksschule in Vormärz Prussia," *Central European History*, 16 (1983), p. 35.
[11]Citations are from ibid., pp. 41, 47.

Less equivocal evidence for the ambiguous legacy of eighteenth-century school reform was the role played by schoolmasters in the democratic movements of the *Vormärz*. In this respect, Zedlitz's concern that teachers trained in pedagogical institutes might be a socially disruptive force (see Chapter 7, "School Financing and Teacher Training") was not unfounded. His arguments foreshadowed those of conservatives in the nineteenth century, who blamed schoolmasters for subverting traditional bonds of loyalty and solidarity. The conservative publicist Wilhelm Heinrich Riehl, for example, condemned the village schoolmaster of his day as a corrosive force in rural society. The village schoolmaster, he argued, was often himself the product of a rural upbringing, but once he had attended a normal school in the city, he returned to the countryside alienated from his roots and dissatisfied with his low pay. His presence in the village was divisive: while older villagers resented his arrogance and newfangled ideas, village youth were awed by his relative sophistication. By exposing rural youth to alien values, the schoolmaster encouraged them to disparage the occupation of their fathers and rural life in general.[12]

Riehl's polemic typified the attitude of conservatives after 1848, many of whom specifically blamed the revolution on subversive schoolmasters. The Prussian king Frederick William IV told a group of schoolmasters that "you alone are guilty of all the misery that has befallen Prussia during the past year," and he accused them of "destroying in my subjects all sentiments of loyalty and faith, thereby turning their hearts against me."[13] In 1851 the Prussian conservative Ludwig Häusser wrote in the same vein: "One part of this society displayed a dangerous and undermining activity, namely, the schoolteachers. They fostered in the proletariat discontent with their status and their position, and approved of their inclination to undermine the moral and religious foundations of society."[14]

Accusations of this sort were more than the pique of reactionaries in search of scapegoats. In Austria and Prussia alike, large numbers of schoolmasters actively participated in the revolutions of 1848.[15] An-

---

[12]For Riehl's critique see his *Die bürgerliche Gesellschaft,* ed. Peter Steinbach (Frankfurt am Main, 1976), pp. 85–86.
[13]Quoted in Thomas Nipperdey, "Volksschule und Revolution in Vormärz," in K. Kluxen and W. J. Mommsen, eds., *Politische Ideologien und nationalstaatliche Ordnung. Festschrift für Theodor Schieder* (Munich and Vienna, 1968), p. 117.
[14]Quoted in Barkin, "Social Control," p. 36.
[15]On the role of schoolmasters in the Viennese Revolution of 1848 see Gönner, *Österreichische Lehrerbildung,* p. 110.

thony La Vopa and Thomas Nipperdey have traced the emergence of a revolutionary consciousness among this group to the establishment of normal schools in the eighteenth century.[16] Although pedagogical training gave schoolmasters a professional identity and heightened their self-esteem, their economic situation remained precarious throughout the *Vormärz*. Thus, even though schoolmasters considered themselves civil servants, their economic circumstances placed them among the proletariat. As La Vopa has shown, the resulting discrepancy between the schoolmaster's heightened sense of status on the one hand, and his objective class position on the other, helps to explain the dissatisfaction and radicalization of Prussian schoolmasters during the *Vormärz*. It was an irony of eighteenth-century school reform that schoolmasters, originally trained to be an arm of the state, were by 1848 among its most vocal critics.

This irony points to the obvious failure of what I have argued was a central aim of Prussian and Austrian "enlightened absolutism": namely, the attempt to reconstitute authority on a less coercive basis. Had Austrian absolutism achieved this goal, Joseph II would have died a popular ruler, Austrian "Jacobins" would have been unthinkable, Metternich's police unnecessary, and the year 1848 uneventful. In Prussia, similarly, the army would not have disintegrated at Jena, nor would the Hohenzollern crown have ever been tarnished in the gutters of 1848. Above all, in both states the social question – early capitalism's reserve army of landless peasants, jobless journeymen, and factory proletariat – would not have been a question at all. Driven by an inner compulsion to work, pray, and obey, rural and urban laborers in Prussia and Austria would have remained quietly in their rooms. Far from creating a stable social and political order, however, the absolutist policies examined here merely contributed to the disorder they sought to prevent. The typical product of eighteenth-century agrarian reform was not to be the contented rural proprietor, but the proletarianized, potentially revolutionary, rural day laborer. The legacy of absolutism's promotion of rural industry was not the disciplined cottage laborer, but the pauperized spinners and weavers in Silesia and Bohemia who revolted in the 1840s. And the heritage of school reform was less the docile pupil than it was the defiant schoolmaster.

This was to be the true legacy of eighteenth-century absolutism – the dialectic of reforms that, in the long run, would undermine the social balance they sought to preserve.

---

[16]La Vopa, *Prussian Schoolteachers*, pp. 3–77; Nipperdey, "Volksschule und Revolution," pp. 138–141.

Selected bibliography

Note: I have made no attempt to list every source I have consulted in the course of writing this book; instead, I have generally included only those that are cited more than once in the text.

I. ARCHIVAL SOURCES

Preussisches Geheimes Staatsarchiv, Dahlem
  Staatsarchiv Königsberg, Königsberger Kammer
    Tit. 38a, 39a/1, 42a/4, 43c/45
  Staatsarchiv Königsberg, Gumbinnen Kammer, Rep. 8
    Abt. VI: Nr. 1, Bd. 3
  Provinz Brandenburg, Rep. 40
    Nr. 796, 819, 1115, 1773
Allgemeines Verwaltungsarchiv, Vienna
  Akten der Studienhofkommission
    Fasz. 1 and 70
    Nachlass Pergen
  Alte Kultus, Rubrik 68
    Cassa Salis
    Missionen
Haus-, Hof-, und Staatsarchiv, Vienna
  Alte Kabinettsakten
    Studiensachen, Kart. 1 and 74
  Kaiser Franz Akten
    Fasz. 62, 63, 75c, and 148b
  Nachlass Zinzendorf
    Vols. 30b, 148b, and 158
Hofkammerarchiv, Vienna
  Kommerz Niederösterreich
    Nr. 24 and 207
  Kommerz Böhmen
    Nr. 794
Hausarchiv des regierenden Fürstens von Liechtenstein, Vienna
  Karton 650
Archiv des Erzbischöflichen Ordinariats, Vienna
  Schulakten, Mappe 120, fasz. 3

Visitationen D.D. Dechanten (1664–1760), Passau
Archiv des österreichischen Bundesverlags, Vienna
Textbook Collection

2. PRINTED SOURCES

Acta Borussica. Denkmäler der preussischen Staatsverwaltung im 18. Jahrhundert. Abteilung 1: *Die Behördensorganisation und die allgemeine Staatsverwaltung Preussens im 18. Jahrhundert.* Ed. Preussische Akademie der Wissenschaften. Berlin, 1894–1936.

Becher, Johann Joachim. *Politische Diskurs.* Frankfurt am Main, 1673.

Bergius, Johann Heinrich Ludwig, ed. *Sammlung auserlesener teutschen Landesgesetze welche das Policey- und Cameralwesen zum Gegenstand haben.* 7 vols. Frankfurt am Main, 1780–87.

Bernoulli, Johann, ed. *Johann Heinrich Lambert's deutscher gelehrten Briefwechsel.* 4 vols. Berlin, 1781–84.

Bielfeld, Baron de. *Institutions politiques.* 2 vols. The Hague, 1760.

Böhm, Ignaz. *Historische Nachrichten von der Entstehungsart und der Verbreitung des Normalinstituts in Böhmen.* Prague, 1784.

Bona-Meyer, Justus, ed. *Friedrichs des Grossen pädagogische Schriften und Äusserungen.* Langensalza, 1885.

Burney, Charles. *The Present State of Music in Germany, the Netherlands, and United Provinces.* Ed. Percy A. Scholes. London, 1959.

Codex Austriacus. 6 vols. Vienna, 1704–77.

Darjes, Joachim Georg. *Erste Gründe der Kameralwissenschaften.* 2d ed. Leipzig, 1768.

Der gegenwärtige Zustand Oberschlesiens. Dresden, 1786.

Dresky, Johann Georg. *Die nach Grundsätzen und Erfahrung abgehandelte schlesische Landwirtschaft.* 2 vols. Breslau, 1771–72.

Engelschall, Carl Gottfried. *Zufällige Gedanken über die deutsche Schaubühne.* Vienna, 1760.

Felbiger, Johann Ignaz. *Anekdoten zur Geschichte des Angriffes und der Verteidigung der Normalschulen in den K.K. Staaten.* Frankfurt am Main and Leipzig, 1784.

Anleitung für diejenigen, welche von der Beschaffenheit der Verbesserten deutschen Schulen in den K.K. Staaten Kenntnisse zu erlangen begehren. Vienna, 1782.

"Ausführliche Nachricht von der erst zu Sagan, dann aber in ganz Schlesien und in der Grafschaft Glatz unternommenen Verbesserung der katholischen Schulen." In *K.S. Christliche Grundsätze und Lebensregeln zum Unterricht der Jugend.* Sagan, 1767.

Die allgemeine Schulordnung der Kaiserin Maria Theresias und J. I. Felbigers Förderungen an Schulmeister und Lehrer. Ed. Anton Weiss. Leipzig, 1896.

Die Beschaffenheit und Grosse der Wohlthat welche Maria Theresia durch die Verbesserung der deutschen Schulen Ihren Unterthanen dem Staat und der Kirche erwiesen hat. Prague, 1781.

Einladungen zu öffentlichen Prüfungen der Wiener Normalschulen. Vienna, 1777–81.

General-Land-Schulreglement. Eigenschaften, Wissenschaften, und Bezeigen rechtschaffener Schulleute. Ed. Julius Scheveling. Paderborn, 1958.

Kleine Schulschriften nebst einer ausführlichen Nachricht von den Umständen und dem Erfolge der Verbesserung der katholischen Land- und Stadt-Trivialschulen in Schlesien und Glatz. Sagan, 1768.

Lesebuch für Schüler der deutschen Schulen in K.K. Staaten. Erster Theil: Gegenstände, welche die Religion betreffen. Vienna, 1774.

Johann Ignaz von Felbigers Methodenbuch. Mit einer geschichtlichen Einleitung über das deutsche Volksschulwesen von Felbiger und das Leben und Wirken Felbigers und seinen Zeitgenossen Ferdinand Kindermann und Alexius Vinzenz Parzizek. Ed. Johann Panholzer. Freiburg im Breisgau, 1892.

Was sind Trivialschulen? Ist es nützlich, Schulen auf dem Lande besser einzurichten? Vienna, 1782.

Was sollen Normalschulen sein, die man in den K.K. Erbländern errichtet hat? Vienna, 1776.

Zweiter Theil des Lesebuches für die Landschulen ohne Fragen, zum Gebrauch der Schüler. Vienna, 1777.

Francke, August Hermann. *Schriften über Erziehung und Unterricht.* Ed. Karl Richter. Berlin, 1871.

Pädagogische Schriften. Ed. Hermann Lorenzen. Paderborn, 1957.

Garve, Christian. *Über den Charakter der Bauern und ihr Verhältnis gegen die Gutsherrn und gegen die Regierung.* Breslau, 1786.

Gottsched, Johann Gottfried. *Beobachtung über den Gebrauch und Missbrauch vieler deutschen Wörter und Redensarten.* Strassburg, 1758.

Kern der deutschen Sprachkunst, aus der ausführlichen Sprachkunst des Herrn Professor Gottscheds. Vienna, 1765.

Versuch einer critischen Dichtkunst. 3d ed. Leipzig, 1742.

Hess, Mathes Ignaz von. *Entwurf zur Einrichtung der Gymnasium in K.K. Erbländern.* Vienna, 1775.

Jaksch, P. K., ed. *Gesetzeslexikon im geistlichen, Religions- und Toleranzfache, wie auch in Güter-, Stiftungs-, Studien-, und Zensursachen für das Königreich Böhmen von 1601 bis 1800.* 5 vols. Prague, 1828.

Jonas, Fritz, and Wienecke, Friedrich, eds. *Friedrich Eberhard von Rochows sämtliche pädagogische Schriften.* 4 vols. Berlin, 1907–10.

Justi, Johann Heinrich Gottlob von. *Abhandlung von der Vollkommenheit der Landwirtschaft und der höchsten Kultur der Länder.* Ulm, 1761.

Moralische und philosophische Schriften. Berlin, 1760.

Oeconomische Schriften über die wichtigsten Gegenstände der Stadt- und Landwirtschaft. Berlin and Leipzig, 1760.

Politische und Finanzschriften über wichtige Gegenstände der Staatskunst, der Kriegswissenschaften, und des Cameral- und Finanzwesens. 3 vols. Copenhagen, 1761–1764.

Kropatschek, J., ed. *Handbuch aller unter der Regierung Kaiser Joseph des II. ergangenen Verordnungen.* 3d ed. 9 vols. Vienna, 1789.

Kundmann, Johann Christian. *Die hohen und niederen Schulen Teutschenlandes, insbesonderheit des Herzogthum Schlesiens.* Breslau, 1741.

"Kurze Übersicht des teutschen Schulwesens seit der Einführung der verbesserten Lehrart bis Ende März, 1790." In J. A. Riegger, ed., *Materialien zur alten und neuen Statistik von Böhmen.* Vol. 10. Leipzig and Prague, 1790.

Ladogórski, Tadeusz. *Generalne Tabele Statystyczne Śląska 1787 Roky.* Wrocław, 1955.

Lehmann, Max, ed. *Preussen und die katholische Kirche seit 1640.* 9 vols. Leipzig, 1878–85.

Meusel, Johann. *Lexikon der vom Jahr 1750 bis 1800 verstorbenen teutschen Schriftsteller.* 15 vols. Leipzig, 1802.

Migazzi, Christoph Anton Graf von. *Unterricht von der Verehrung der Bilder.* Vienna, 1761.

Muratori, Ludovico Antonio. *Die wahre Andacht des Christen.* 3d ed. Vienna, 1762.

Nachricht an das Publikum. Von der Absicht und dem Nutzen des auf allerhöchsten Befehl verbesserten Schulwesens in Österreich unter der Enns. Vienna, 1771.

Nicolai, Friedrich. *Beschreibung der Königlichen Residenzstädte Berlin und Potsdam, aller daselbst befindlichen Merkwürdigkeiten und der umliegenden Gegend.* 3 vols. 3d. ed. Berlin, 1786.

Beschreibung einer Reise durch Deutschland und die Schweiz. Berlin, 1784.

Ökonomische Nachrichten der Patriotischen Gesellschaft in Schlesien. 6 vols. Breslau, 1773–84.

Parhammer, Ignaz. *Vollkommener Bericht über den Zustand des Waisenhauses auf dem Rennweg.* Vienna, 1776.

Philosophisch-Politische Abhandlungen von den Naturalfrondiensten und von deren Verwandlung in anderen Leistungen. Frankfurt am Main, 1775.

Pirker, Max, ed. *Teutsche Arien, welche auf dem Kayserlich-privilegirten Wienerischen Theatro in unterschiedlich producirten Comoedien . . . gesungen worden.* Vienna, 1929.

Raab, Franz Anton. *Unterricht über die Verwandlung der K.K. boehmischen Domaenen in Bauerngueter.* Vienna, 1777.

Sammlung aller in dem souveränen Herzogthum Schlesien . . . ergangenen Ordnungen, Edikte, und Mandate. 19 vols. Breslau, 1759–90.

Schlesische Oeconomische Sammlungen. 3 vols. Breslau, 1755–1762.

Schlesische Zustände im ersten Jahrhundert der preussischen Herrschaft. Breslau, 1840.

Seckendorff, Veit Ludwig von. *Christen-Stat.* 2 vols. Leipzig, 1685.

Teutscher Fürsten-Stat, 3d ed. Frankfurt am Main, 1665.

Seibt, Karl Heinrich. *Von dem Einflusse der Erziehung auf die Glückseligkeit des Staates.* Prague, 1771.

Von dem Unterschiede des zierlichen, des Hof- und Curialstyls. Prague, 1768; republished in Wotke, "Seibt," pp. 91–121.

Sonnenfels, Joseph. *Der Mann ohne Vorurteil.* 3 vols. Vienna, 1765–67.

Sätze aus der Polizey-, Handlungs-, und Finanzwissenschaften. Vienna, 1765.

Über die Liebe des Vaterlandes. Vienna, 1771.

Gesammelte Schriften. Vols. 5–6. Vienna, 1784 (contains his *Briefe über die wienerische Schaubühne*).

Spener, Philipp Jacob. *Die evangelische Lebenspflichten.* 2 vols. 3d ed. Frankfurt am Main, 1715.

Pia Desideria. Ed. Kurt Aland. Berlin, 1955.

Stadelmann, Rudolf, ed. *Preussens Könige in ihrer Tätigkeit für die Landeskultur.* 4 vols. Leipzig, 1876–87.

"Stand der Schulen des kaurzimer Kreises." In J. A. Riegger, ed. *Materialien zur alten und neuen Statistik von Böhmen.* Vol. 10. Leipzig and Prague, 1790.

Streit, Carl Conrad. *Alphabetischer Verzeichnis aller 1774 in Schlesien lebenden Schriftsteller.* Breslau, 1776.

Süssmilch, Johann Peter. *Die göttliche Ordnung in den Veränderungen des menschlichen Geschlechts.* 2 vols. 3d ed. Berlin, 1765.

Thurn, Rudolf Payer von, ed. *Wiener Haupt- und Staatsaktionen.* 2 vols. Vienna, 1908.

Trnka, Johann Josef. *Pflicht eines Wirtschaftsbeamter.* Dresden, 1771.

Walter, Friedrich, ed. *Die Geschichte der österreichischen Zentralverwaltung.* Vol. 1, pt. 1. Vienna, 1938.

Wiegand, Johann. *Oekonomische Betrachtungen von der Roboth oder den Frondiensten überhaupt.* Vienna, 1776.

Versuch den Fleiss unter dem Landvolk einzuführen. Vienna, 1772.

Der wohlerfahrene Landwirt, oder Anleitung wie die Landwirtschaftsökonomie in einen verbesserten Stand gebracht werden könnte. Leipzig, 1762.

Wotke, Karl. ed. *Das österreichische Gymnasium im Zeitalter Maria Theresias.* Berlin, 1905.

Zimmermann, Friedrich Albrecht. *Beyträge zur Beschreibung von Schlesien.* 13 vols. Brieg, 1783–96.

3. SECONDARY WORKS

Adel, Kurt. *Das Wiener Jesuitentheater und die europäische Barockdramatik.* Vienna, 1960.
Adler, Philip, "Habsburg School Reform among the Orthodox Minorities, 1770–1780." *Slavic Review,* 33 (1974).
Aigner, Josef. *Der Volks- und Industrieschulen-Reformator Bischof Ferdinand Kindermann.* Vienna, 1867.
Appolis, E. *Entre jansenistes et zelanti. Le "tiers parti" catholique au XVIIIe. siècle.* Paris, 1960.
Aretin, Karl Otmar Freiherr von. "Der aufgeklärte Absolutismus als europäisches Problem." *Der aufgeklärte Absolutismus.* Cologne, 1975.
Ariès, Philippe. *Centuries of Childhood: A Social History of Family Life.* Trans. Robert Baldick. New York, 1962.
Arneth, Alfred von. *Geschichte Maria Theresias.* 10 vols. Vienna, 1863–79.
Baar-de Zwaan, Monica. "Gottfried Prehauser und seine Zeit." Vienna: Ph.D. diss., 1968.
Barkin, Kenneth. "Social Control and the Volksschule in Vormärz Prussia." *Central European History,* 16 (1983).
Beck, August. *Ernst der Fromme, Herzog zu Sachsen-Gotha.* Weimar, 1865.
Benjamin, Walter. *Ursprung des deutschen Trauerspiels.* Frankfurt am Main, 1955.
Berk, Janet Wolf. "The Elementary School Reforms of Maria Theresa and Joseph II in Bohemia." Columbia: Ph.D. diss., 1970.
Berkner, Lutz Karl. "Family, Social Structure, and Rural Industry: A Comparative Study of the Waldviertel and the Pays de Caux in the Eighteenth Century." Harvard: Ph.D. diss., 1973.
Biedermann, Karl. *Deutschland im 18. Jahrhundert.* 2 vols. 2d ed. Leipzig, 1880.
Blanning, T. C. W. *Reform and Revolution in Mainz, 1743–1803.* Cambridge, 1974.
Bloth, Hugo. "Johann Julius Hecker (1707–1768). Seine Stellung zum Pietismus und Absolutismus." *Jahrbuch des Vereins für westfälische Kirchengeschichte,* 61 (1968).
Blum, Jerome. *The End of the Old Order in Rural Europe.* Princeton, 1978.
Bodi, Leslie. *Tauwetter in Wien. Zur Prosa der österreichischen Aufklärung 1781–1795.* Frankfurt am Main, 1977.
Boelcke, Willi. "Wandlungen der dörflichen Sozialstruktur während Mittelalter und Neuzeit." In Heinz Haushofer and Willi Boelcke, eds., *Wege und Forschungen der Agrargeschichte. Festschrift zum 65. Geburtstag von Günther Franz.* Frankfurt am Main, 1967.
Böhne, Hermann. *Die pädagogischen Bestrebungen Ernst des Frommen von Gotha.* Gotha, 1888.
Bourdieu, Pierre. *Entwurf einer Theorie der Praxis.* Trans. Cordula Pialoux and Bernd Schwibs. Frankfurt am Main, 1976.
Bourdieu, Pierre, and Passeron, Jean-Claude. *Reproduction in Education, Society and Culture.* Trans. Richard Nice. London and Beverly Hills, 1970.
Braem, Andreas. *Der Gothaische Schulmethodus. Untersuchung über die ersten Spuren des Pietismus in der Pädagogik.* Berlin, 1877.
Breunlich, Maria. "Die Jugend des Grafen Karl von Zinzendorf und Pottendorf." *Mitteilungen des österreichischen Staatsarchivs,* 37 (1984).
Brunner, Otto. "Das 'ganze Haus' und die alteuropäische 'Ökonomik'." *Neue Wege der Verfassungs- und Sozialgeschichte.* 2nd ed. Göttingen, 1980.

Adeliges Landleben und europäischer Geist. Leben und Werk Wolf Helmhards von Hohberg 1612–1688. Salzburg, 1949.

Brunschwig, Henri. *Enlightenment and Romanticism in 18th Century Prussia.* Trans. Frank Jellinek. Chicago, 1975.

Burke, Peter. *Popular Culture in Early Modern Europe.* London, 1978.

Chayanov, A. V. "Peasant Farm Organization." In D. Thorner et al., *A.V. Chayanov on the Theory of Peasant Economy.* Trans. R. E. F. Smith. Homewood, 1965.

Chisick, Harvey. *The Limits of Reform in the Enlightenment: Attitudes towards the Education of the Lower Classes in Eighteenth-Century France.* Princeton, 1981.

Clausnitzer, E. "Zur Geschichte der preussichen Volksschule unter Friedrich den Grossen." *Die deutsche Schule,* 5 (1901).

Coreth, Anna. *Pietas Austriaca. Ursprung und Entwicklung barocker Frömmigkeit in Österreich.* Munich, 1959.

Corni, Gustavo. *Stato assoluto e società agraria in Prussia nell'età di Federico II.* Bologna, 1982.

Csáky, Moritz. *Von der Aufklärung zum Liberalismus. Studien zum Frühliberalismus in Ungarn.* Vienna, 1981.

Czimeg, Johann Georg. "Die Entwicklung der Pfarrschulen im heutigen Schulbezirk Liezen." Graz: Ph.D. diss., 1965.

Danneil, Friedrich. *Geschichte des evangelischen Dorfschulwesens im Herzogthum Magdeburg.* Halle, 1876.

Dedic, Paul. *Der Geheimprotestantismus in den Vikariaten Schladming und Kulm-Ramsau in den Jahren 1753–60.* Vienna, 1941.

Delumeau, Jean. *Catholicism between Luther and Voltaire.* London, 1977.

D'Elvert, Christian. *Geschichte der Studien-, Schul- und Erziehungs-Anstalten in Mähren und österreichischen Schlesien.* Brünn, 1857.

Deppermann, Klaus. *Der hallesche Pietismus und der preussische Staat unter Friedrich III (I).* Göttingen, 1961.

Dittrich, Erhard. *Die deutschen und österreichischen Kameralisten.* Darmstadt, 1974.

Dorwart, Reinhold. *The Prussian Welfare State before 1740.* Cambridge, Mass., 1971.

Dreyfus, F. G. *Société et mentalités à Mayence dans la seconde moitié du dix-huitième siècle.* Paris, 1968.

Drozd, Kurt. *Schul- und Ordenstheater am Collegium S.J. Klagenfurt (1604–1773).* Klagenfurt, 1965.

Dülmen, Richard van. "Die Prälaten Franz Töpsl aus Polling und Johann Ignaz von Felbiger aus Sagan. Zwei Repräsentanten der katholischen Aufklärung." *Zeitschrift für bayerische Landesgeschichte,* 30 (1967).

Duesterhaus, Gerhard. *Das ländliche Schulwesen im Herzogthum Preussen im 16. und 17. Jahrhundert.* Bonn, 1975.

Duhr, B. *Geschichte der Jesuiten in den Ländern deutscher Zunge.* 4 vols. Freiburg im Breisgau, 1921.

Ehalt, Hubert Christian. *Ausdrucksformen absolutistischer Herrschaft. Der Wiener Hof im 17. und 18. Jahrhundert.* Vienna, 1980.

Eichler, H. "Zucht- und Arbeitshäuser in den mittleren und östlichen Provinzen Brandenburg-Preussens." *Jahrbuch für Wirtschaftsgeschichte,* 1 (1970).

Eisenstein, Elizabeth. *The Printing Press As an Agent of Change,* 2 vols. Cambridge, 1979.

Elias, Norbert. *Über den Prozess der Zivilisation.* 2 vols. Bern, 1969.
Die höfische Gesellschaft. Neuwied, 1969.

Endres, Rudolf. "Das Armenproblem im Zeitalter des Absolutismus." In Franklin Kopitzsch, ed., *Aufklärung, Absolutismus, und Bürgertum in Deutschland.* Munich, 1976.

Engelbrecht, Helmut. *Geschichte des österreichischen Bildungswesens.* 3 vols. Vienna, 1982–84.

Engelsing, Rolf. *Analphabetentum und Lektüre. Zur Sozialgeschichte des Lesens in Deutschland zwischen feudaler und industrieller Gesellschaft.* Stuttgart, 1973.

Enzinger, Moriz. *Die Entwicklung des Wiener Theaters vom. 16. zum 19. Jahrhunderts.* 2 vols. Berlin, 1918.

Evans, R. J. W. *The Making of the Habsburg Monarchy 1559–1700.* Oxford, 1979.

Fechner, Hermann. *Wirtschaftsgeschichte der Provinz Schlesien in der Zeit ihrer provinziellen Selbständigkeit 1741–1806.* Breslau, 1907.

Feigl, Helmuth. *Die niederösterreichische Grundherrschaft.* Vienna, 1964.

Fischer, Konrad. *Geschichte des deutschen Volksschullehrerstandes.* Hanover, 1898.

Flemming, Willi. *Geschichte des Jesuitentheaters in den Ländern deutscher Zunge.* Berlin, 1923.

Fooken, Enno. *Die geistliche Schulaufsicht und ihre Kritiker im 18. Jahrhundert.* Wiesbaden-Dotzheim, 1967.

Foucault, Michel. *Discipline and Punish. The Birth of the Prison.* New York, 1977.

Frauenstadt, Paul. "Das Bettel- und Vagabundenwesen in Schlesien vom 16.–18. Jahrhundert." *Preussische Jahrbücher,* 89 (1897).

Freudenberger, Herman. "Zur Linzer Wollzeugfabrik." In Herbert Knittler, ed., *Wirtschafts- und sozialhistorische Beiträge. Festschrift für Alfred Hoffmann zum 75. Geburtstag.* Vienna, 1979.

"The Woolen Goods Industry of the Habsburg Monarchy in the 18th Century." *Journal of Economic History,* 20 (1960).

The Waldstein Woolen Mill. Noble Entrepreneurship in 18th Century Bohemia. Boston, 1963.

Friedrichs, Christopher. "Whose House of Learning? Some Thoughts on German Schools in Post-Reformation Germany." *History of Education Quarterly,* 22 (1982).

Frijhoff, Willem. "Surplus ou déficit? Hypothesen sur le nombre réel des étudiants en Allemagne a l'époque moderne (1576–1815)." *Francia,* 7 (1979).

Fröhler, Josef. "Von der Klosterschule zum Gymnasium. Das höhere Schulwesen in Steyr von 1500 bis 1773." Manfred Brandl, ed., *500 Jahre Dominikaner und Jesuiten in Steyr 1478–1978.* Steyr, 1978.

Fulbrook, Mary. *Piety and Politics: Religion and the Rise of Absolutism in England, Württemberg, and Prussia.* Cambridge, 1983.

Gagliardo, John G. *From Pariah to Patriot: The Changing Image of the German Peasant 1770–1840.* Lexington, Ky., 1969.

Gawthrop, Richard, and Strauss, Gerald. "Protestantism and Literacy in Early Modern Germany." *Past and Present,* 104 (1984).

Gerth, Hans. *Bürgerliche Intelligenz um 1800. Zur Soziologie des deutschen Frühliberalismus.* Göttingen, 1976.

Gessinger, Joachim. *Sprache und Bürgertum. Zur Sozialgeschichte sprachlicher Verkehrsformen in Deutschland des 18. Jahrhunderts.* Stuttgart, 1980.

Gloria, Elisabeth. *Der Pietismus als Förderer der Volksbildung und sein Einfluss auf die preussische Volksschule.* Osterwieck, 1933.

Glossy, C. "Zur Geschichte der Wiener Threaterzensur." *Jahrbuch der Grillparzergesellschaft,* 7 (1897).

Godelier, Maurice. *Rationality and Irrationality in Economics.* Trans. Brian Pearce. New York, 1972.

Goldman, Joseph. "Land, Labor, and Lord: Count Hatzfeld, the Imperial State Council, and Robot Abolition in Austria and Bohemia, 1740–1790." University of Minnesota: Ph.D. diss., 1971.

Gönner, Rudolf. *Die österreichische Lehrerbildung von der Normalschule bis zur Pädagogische Akademie.* Vienna, 1967.

Good, David F. *The Economic Rise of the Habsburg Empire 1750–1914.* Berkeley, 1984.

Görner, Karl. *Der Hanswurst-Streit in Wien.* Vienna, 1884.

Griessinger, Andreas. *Das symbolische Kapital der Ehre. Streikbewegungen und kollektives Bewusstsein deutscher Handwerksgesellen im 18. Jahrhundert.* Frankfurt am Main, 1981.

Grüll, Georg. *Die Robot in Oberösterreich.* Linz, 1952.

Grünberg, Karl. *Die Bauernbefreiung und die Auflösung des gutsherrlich-bäuerlichen Verhältnissen in Böhmen, Mähren, und Schlesien.* 2 vols. Leipzig, 1893–94.

Franz Anton von Blanc. Munich and Leipzig, 1921.

Grünberg, P. *Philipp Jakob Spener,* 3 vols. Göttingen, 1893–1906.

Grünhagen, Colmar. *Schlesien unter Friedrich dem Grossen.* 2 vols. Breslau, 1890–92.

Gugitz, G. *Das Jahr und seine Feste im Volksbrauch Österreichs.* 2 vols. Vienna, 1949–50.

Österreichs Gnadenstätten in Kult und Brauch. 5 vols. Vienna, 1955–58.

Günther, Karl-Heinz, et al. *Geschichte der Erziehung.* East Berlin, 1960.

Haase, Theodore. "Das evangelische Schulwesen in Bielitz bis zum Toleranzpatent." *Jahrbuch für die Geschichte des Protestantismus in Österreich,* 53 (1932).

Haass, R. *Die geistige Haltung der katholischen Universitäten Deutschlands im 18. Jahrhundert.* Freiburg im Breisgau, 1952.

Habermas, Jürgen. "Soziologische Notizen zum Verhältnis von Arbeit und Freizeit." In G. Funke, ed., *Konkrete Vernunft. Festschrift für E. Rothacker.* Bonn, 1958.

Strukturwandel der Öffentlichkeit. Darmstadt, 1962.

Haider-Pregler, Hilde. *Des sittlichen Bürgers Abendschule. Bildungsanspruch und Bildungsauftrag des Berufstheaters im 18. Jahrhundert.* Vienna, 1980.

Hammerstein, Notker. *Aufklärung und katholisches Reich. Untersuchung zur Universitätsreform und Politik in den katholischen Territorien des Heiligen Römischen Reiches der deutschen Nation im 18. Jahrhundert.* West Berlin, 1977.

Hanus, Francis. *Church and State in Silesia, 1740–1786.* Washington, D.C., 1944.

Hanzal, Josef. "K dějinám nižšího školství před rokem 1775." *Acta Universitatis Carolinae-Historiae Universitatis Carolinae Pragensis,* 6 (1965).

"Vzdělanost a lidová osvěta v počátcich národního obrozeni." *Sbonrík historický,* 18 (1971).

Hassinger, Herbert. "Der Stand der Manufaktur in den deutschen Erbländern der Habsburgermonarchie am Ende des 18. Jahrhundert." In Friedrich Lütge, ed., *Die wirtschaftliche Situation in Deutschland und Österreich um die Wende vom 18. zum 19. Jahrhundert.* Stuttgart, 1964.

Heinemann, Manfred. *Schule im Vorfeld der Verwaltung. Die Entwicklung der preussischen Unterrichtsverwaltung von 1771–1800.* Göttingen, 1974.

Heiss, Gernot. "Erziehung der Waisen zur Manufakturarbeit. Pädagogische Zielvorstellungen und ökonomische Interessen der maria-theresianischen Verwaltung." *Mitteilungen des Instituts für österreichische Geschichtsforschung,* 85 (1977).

Helfert, Joseph Alexander Freiherr von. *Die Gründung der österreichischen Volksschule durch Maria Theresia.* Prague, 1860.

Henderson, W. O. *Studies in the Economic Policy of Frederick the Great.* London, 1963.

Henning, Friedrich-Wilhelm. *Dienste und Abgaben der Bauern im 18. Jahrhundert.* Stuttgart, 1969.

Heppe, Heinrich. *Geschichte des deutschen Volksschulwesens.* 3 vols. Gotha, 1858.

Heubaum, Alfred. *Das Zeitalter der Standes- und Berufserziehung.* Berlin, 1905.

Herrlitz, Hans-Georg. *Studium als Standesprivileg. Die Entstehung des Maturitätsproblems im 18. Jahrhundert.* Frankfurt am Main, 1973.

Hersche, Peter. *Der Spätjansenismus in Österreich.* Vienna, 1977.

——— ed. *Der aufgeklärte Reformkatholizismus in Österreich.* Bern, 1976.

Hinrichs, Carl. *Die Wollindustrie in Preussen unter Friedrich Wilhelm I.* Berlin, 1933.

——— *Preussentum und Pietismus. Der Pietismus in Brandenburg-Preussen als religiös-soziale Reformbewegung.* Göttingen, 1971.

Hintze, Otto. "Zur Agrarpolitik Friedrichs des Grossen." *Forschungen zur brandenburgischen und preussischen Geschichte,* 10 (1898).

Hinze, Kurt. *Die Arbeiterfrage in Brandenburg-Preussen zu Beginn des modernen Kapitalismus.* Berlin, 1927.

Hirschman, Albert. *The Passions and the Interests: Political Arguments for Capitalism before Its Triumph.* Princeton, 1977.

Hoffmann, Alfred. *Wirtschaftsgeschichte des Landes Oberösterreich.* Salzburg, 1952.

——— "Österreichs Wirtschaft im Zeitalter des Absolutismus." *Festschrift für K. Eder.* Innsbruck, 1959.

Hoffmann, Hermann. "Zur Vorgeschichte der Breslauer Jesuiten-Universität." *Zeitschrift des Vereins für die Geschichte Schlesiens,* 68 (1934).

Hoffmann, V. "Die Anfänge der österreichischen Baumwollwarenindustrie in den österreichischen Alpenländern im 18. Jahrhundert." *Archiv für österreichische Geschichte,* 110 (1926).

Houston, Rab. "Literacy and Society in the West, 1500–1850." *Social History,* 8 (1983).

——— *Scottish Literacy and the Scottish Identity: Illiteracy and Society in Scotland and Northern England.* New York, 1986.

Hubatsch, Walter. *Geschichte der evangelischen Kirche Ostpreussens.* 3 vols. Göttingen, 1968.

Hubel, J. "Das Schulwesen Niederösterreichs im Reformationszeitalter." *Jahrbuch für die Geschichte des Protestantismus in Österreich,* 51 (1930).

Hübl, Albert. "Die Schulen." In Anton Mayer, ed., *Geschichte der Stadt Wien,* Vol. 5. Vienna, 1914.

Jacobi, Leonard. *Ländliche Zustände in Schlesien während des vorigen Jahrhunderts.* Breslau, 1884.

Johnson, Hubert. *Frederick the Great and His Officials.* New Haven, 1975.

Jordan, S. *Die kaiserliche Wirtschaftspolitik im Banat im 18. Jahrhundert.* Vienna, 1967.

Kaiser, Gerhard. *Pietismus und Patriotismus im literarischen Deutschland.* Wiesbaden, 1961.

Kapner, Gerhardt. *Barocker Heiligenkult in Wien und seine Träger.* Munich, 1978.

Kisch, Herbert. "The Textile Industries in Silesia and the Rhineland: A Comparative Study in Industrialization (with a postscriptum)." In Peter Kriedte, Hans Medick, and Jürgen Schlumbohm, eds., *Industrialization before Industrialization: Rural Industry in the Genesis of Capitalism.* Cambridge, 1981.

Klamminger, Karl. "Leopold III. Ernst Graf Firmian." In Karl Amon, ed., *Die Bischöfe von Graz-Seckau 1218–1968.* Graz, 1969.

Klíma, A. "Industrial Development in Bohemia, 1648–1781." *Past and Present,* 11 (1957).

——— "Agrarian Class Structure and Economic Development in Pre-Industrial Bohemia." *Past and Present,* 85 (1979).

"The Role of Rural Domestic Industry in Bohemia in the 18th Century." *Economic History Review*, 2d ser., 27 (1974).

Klingenstein, Grete. "Vorstufen der theresianischen Schulreform in der Regierungszeit Karls VI." *Mitteilungen des Instituts für österreichische Geschichtsforschung,*" 76 (1968).

Staatsverwaltung und kirchliche Autorität im 18. Jahrhundert. Das Problem der Zensur in der theresianischen Reform. Munich, 1970.

Der Aufstieg des Hauses Kaunitz: Studien zur Herkunft und Bildung des Staatskanzlers Wenzel Anton Kaunitz. Göttingen, 1975.

"Akademikerüberschuss als soziales Problem im aufgeklärten Absolutismus. Bemerkungen über eine Rede Joseph von Sonnenfels aus dem Jahre 1771." In *Bildung, Politik, und Gesellschaft.* Vienna, 1979.

"Bildungskrise. Gymnasium und Universitäten im Spannungsfeld theresianischer Aufklärung." In Walter Koschatzky, ed., *Maria Theresia und ihre Zeit.* Salzburg, 1979.

König, Helmut. *Zur Geschichte der Nationalerziehung in Deutschland im letzten Drittel des 18. Jahrhunderts.* East Berlin, 1960.

Koser, Reinhold. *Geschichte Friedrichs des Grossen.* 4 vols. Stuttgart, 1912.

Kosler, Alois. *Die preussische Volksschulpolitik in Oberschlesien.* Breslau, 1930.

Kostić, Strahinja. "Kulturorientierung und Volksschule der Serben in der Donaumonarchie zur Zeit Maria Theresias." In Richard Plaschka and Grete Klingenstein, eds. *Österreich im Europa der Aufklärung.* Vol. 2. Vienna, 1985.

Kriedte, Peter, Medick, Hans, and Schlumbohm, Jürgen. *Industrialization before Industrialization: Rural Industry in the Genesis of Capitalism.* Trans. Beate Schempp. Cambridge, 1981.

Krieger, Leonard. *The German Idea of Freedom.* Chicago, 1957.

An Essay on the Theory of Enlightened Despotism. Chicago, 1975.

Krienke, Gerhard. "Das Berliner Elementarschulwesen von 1696 bis 1739." *Bär von Berlin,* 32 (1983).

Kromer, Ulrich. *Johann Ignaz Felbiger. Leben und Werk.* Freiburg im Breisgau, 1966.

Krüger, Horst. *Zur Geschichte der Manufakturen und der Manufakturarbeiter in Preussen. Die mittleren Provinzen in der zweiten Hälfte des 18. Jahrhunderts.* East Berlin, 1958.

Kuczynski, Jürgen. *Geschichte des Alltags des deutschen Volkes.* Vol. 2. Cologne, 1981.

Kuczynski, Jürgen, and Hoppe, Ruth. *Geschichte der Kinderarbeit in Deutschland, 1750–1939.* 2 vols. East Berlin, 1958.

Küther, Carsten. *Menschen auf der Strasse. Vagierende Unterschichten in Bayern, Franken, und Schwaben in der zweiten Hälfte des 18. Jahrhunderts.* Göttingen, 1983.

Kutzner, Oskar. "Das Landratamt in Schlesien." Breslau: Ph.D. diss., 1911.

La Vopa, Anthony J. *Prussian Schoolteachers: Profession and Office, 1763–1848.* Chapel Hill, 1980.

"Vocations, Careers, and Talent: Lutheran Pietism and Sponsored Mobility in Eighteenth-Century Germany." *Comparative Studies in Society and History,* 28 (1986).

Lehmann, Hartmut. "Der Pietismus im alten Reich." *Historische Zeitschrift,* 214 (1972).

Leidl, August. "Leopold Ernst Kardinal von Firmian (1708–83), ein Kirchenfürst an der Wende vom Barock zur Aufklärung." *Ostbairische Grenzmarken,* N.F., 13 (1971).

"Die religiöse und seelsorgerliche Situation zur Zeit Maria Theresias (1740–80) im Gebiet des heutigen Österreichs." *Ostbairische Grenzmarken,* N.F., 16 (1974).

Leschinsky, Achim, and Roeder, Peter. *Schule im historischen Prozess. Zum Wechselverhältnis von institutioneller Erziehung und gesellschaftlicher Entwicklung.* Stuttgart, 1976.

Leube, Hans. *Orthodoxie und Pietismus*. Bielefeld, 1975.

Lewin, Heinrich. *Geschichte der Entwicklung der preussischen Volksschule und die För-derung der Volksbildung durch die Hohenzollern*. Leipzig, 1910.

Liebel-Weckowicz, Helen. "Modernisierungsmotive in der Freihandelspolitik Maria There-sias." In Walter Koschatzky, ed., *Maria Theresia und ihre Zeit*. Salzburg, 1979.

Liebel-Weckowicz, Helen, and Szabo, Franz J. "Modernization Forces in Maria Theresia's Peasant Policies, 1740–1780." *Histoire sociale—Social History*, 15 (1982).

Link, Edith. *The Emancipation of the Austrian Peasant, 1740–1798*. New York, 1949.

Loserth, Johann, *Die protestantischen Schulen der Steiermark im sechzehnten Jahrhundert*. Berlin, 1916.

McClelland, Charles E. *State, Society, and University in Germany, 1700–1914*. Cambridge, 1980.

Maynes, Mary Jo. *Schooling for the People: Comparative Local Studies of Schooling History in France and Germany, 1750–1850*. New York, 1985.

Schooling in Western Europe: A Social History. Albany, 1985.

Medick, Hans. "Spinnstuben auf dem Dorf. Jugendliche Sexualkultur und Feiera-bendbrauch in der ländlichen Gesellschaft der frühen Neuzeit." In Gerhard Huck, ed., *Sozialgeschichte der Freizeit. Untersuchungen zum Wandel der Alltagskultur in Deutschland*. Wuppertal, 1980.

Melton, James Van Horn. "Pedagogues and Princes: Reform Absolutism, Popular Educa-tion, and the Dialectics of Authority in Eighteenth-Century Prussia and Austria." University of Chicago: Ph.D. diss., 1982.

"Arbeitsprobleme des aufgeklärten Absolutismus in Preussen und Österreich." *Mit-teilungen des Instituts für österreichische Geschichtsforschung*, 90 (1982).

"Absolutism and 'Modernity' in Early Modern Central Europe." *German Studies Re-view*, 8 (1985).

"From Image to Word: Cultural Reform and the Rise of Literate Culture in Eighteenth-Century Austria." *Journal of Modern History*, 58 (1986).

Mertineit, Fritz. *Die friderizianische Verwaltung in Ostpreussen*. Heidelberg, 1958.

Michael, Edmund. "Die schlesische Dorfschule im 16. Jahrhundert." *Zeitschrift des Ver-eins für die Geschichte Schlesiens*, 63 (1929).

Mikoletzky, Hanns Leo. *Österreich. Das grosse Jahrhundert*. Vienna, 1967.

Mittenzwei, Ingrid. *Preussen nach dem siebenjährigen Krieg*. East Berlin, 1979.

Moeller, Bernd, et al., eds. *Studien zum städtischen Bildungswesen des späten Mittelalters und der frühen Neuzeit*. Göttingen, 1983.

Müller, Detlef. *Sozialstruktur und Schulsystem. Aspekte zum Strukturwandel des Schul-wesens im 19. Jahrhundert*. Göttingen, 1977.

Müller, Hans-Heinrich. *Märkische Landwirtschaft vor den Agrarreformen von 1807*. Pots-dam, 1967.

Nahrstedt, Wolfgang. *Die Entstehung der Freizeit. Dargestellt am Beispiel Hamburgs. Ein Beitrag zur Strukturgeschichte und zur strukturgeschichtlichen Grundlegung der Freizeitspädagogik*. Göttingen, 1972.

Neugebauer, Wolfgang. "Bemerkungen zum preussischen Schuledikt von 1717." *Jahrbuch für die Geschichte Mittel- und Osteuropas*, 31 (1982).

Absolutistischer Staat und Schulwirklichkeit in Brandenburg-Preussen. West Berlin, 1985.

Neuss, Erich. "Entstehung und Entwicklung der Klasse der besitzlosen Lohnarbeiter in Halle." *Abhandlungen der sächsischen Akademie der Wissenschaften zu Leipzig*, Philosophisch-historische Klasse, 51 (1958).

Notbohm, H. *Das evangelische Kirchen- und Schulwesen in Ostpreussen während der Regierung Friedrichs des Grossen*. Heidelberg, 1959.

Oestreich, Gerhard. "The Structure of the Absolutist State." In Brigitta Oestreich and H. G. Koenigsberger, eds., *Neostoicism and the Early Modern State*. Trans. David McLintock. Cambridge, 1982.

Oschlies, Wolf. *Die Arbeits- und Berufspädagogik August Hermann Franckes (1663–1727)*. Witten-Ruhr, 1969.

Osterloh, K. H. *Joseph von Sonnenfels und die österreichische Reformbewegung im Zeitalter des aufgeklärten Absolutismus. Eine Studie zum Zusammenhang von Kameralwissenschaft und Verwaltungspraxis*. Lübeck, 1970.

Ostrowski, Wincentz. *Wiejskie szkolnictwo parafialne na Śląsku drugiej 17. Wieku*. Wrocław, 1971.

Payne, Harry. *The Philosophes and the People*. New Haven, 1976.

Peschke, E. "August Hermann Francke und die Bibel." In Kurt Aland, ed. *Pietismus und Bibel*. Witten-Ruhr, 1970.

Peters, Jan. "Ostelbische Landarmut—Sozioökonomisches über landarme und landlose Agrarproduzenten im Spätfeudalismus." *Jahrbuch für Wirtschaftsgeschichte*, 3 (1967).

Petersdorf, Hermann von. "Schlabrendorff." In *Schlesische Lebensbilder*, 2 (1926).

Panholzer, Johann, ed., *Johann Ignaz von Felbigers Methodenbuch. Mit einer geschichtlichen Einleitung über das deutsche Volksschulwesen vor Felbiger und das Leben und Wirken Felbigers und seinen Zeitgenossen Ferdinand Kindermann und Alexius Vinzenz Parzizek*. Freiburg im Breisgau, 1892.

Petran, Josef. "Der Höhepunkt der Bewegungen der untertänigen Bauern in Böhmen." In Winfried Schulze, ed., *Europäische Bauernrevolten der frühen Neuzeit*. Frankfurt am Main, 1982.

Petrỳ, Ludwig, and Menzel, Joachim. *Geschichte Schlesiens*. Vol. 2: *Die Habsburgerzeit, 1526–1740*. Darmstadt, 1973.

Pfeiffer, Ernst. *Die Revuereisen Friedrichs des Grossen, besonders die Schlesischen nach 1763 und der Zustand Schlesiens von 1763–1786*. Berlin, 1904.

Pietsch, Walter. *Die theresianische Schulreform in der Steiermark (1775–1805)*. Graz, 1977.

Pinson, Koppel S. *Pietism as a Factor in the Rise of German Nationalism*. New York, 1934.

Polz, Peter. "Theodor Jaković de Mirijevo: Der erste serbische Pädagoge, oder, Die Theresianische Schulreform bei den Serben und in Russland." Graz: Ph.D. diss., 1969.

"Theodor Janković und die Schulreform in Russland." In E. Lesky et al., *Die Aufklärung in Ost- und Südosteuropa*. Cologne, 1972.

Raab, Fritz. *Johann Joseph Felix von Kurz genannt Bernardon. Ein Beitrag zur Geschichte des deutschen Theaters im XVIII. Jahrhundert*. Frankfurt am Main, 1899.

Raeff, Marc. *The Well-Ordered Police State. Social and Institutional Change through Law in the Germanies and Russia, 1600–1800*. New Haven, 1983.

Rebel, Hermann. *Peasant Classes: The Bureaucratization of Property and Family Relations under Early Habsburg Absolutism*. Princeton, 1983.

Reimann, Eduard. "Über die Verbesserung des niederen Schulwesens in Schlesien in den Jahren 1763–1769." *Zeitschrift des Vereins für die Geschichte Schlesiens*, 17 (1883).

"Über die Verbesserung des katholischen Schulwesens in Schlesien durch Friedrich den Grossen." *Zeitschrift des Vereins für die Geschichte Schlesiens*, 19 (1885).

Rethwisch, Conrad. *Der Staatsminister Freiherr von Zedlitz und Preussens höheres Schulwesen im Zeitalter Friedrichs des Grossen*. Berlin, 1881.

Richter, Jochen. "Zur Schriftkundigkeit mecklenburgischer Bauern im 17. Jahrhundert." *Jahrbuch für Wirtschaftsgeschichte*, 3 (1981).

Rittershausen, Dietrich. "Beiträge zur Geschichte des Berliner Elementarschulwesens von der Reformation bis 1836." *Märkische Forschungen*, 9 (1865).

Rommel, Otto. *Die Alt-Wiener Volkskomödie.* Vienna, 1952.

Rusiński, Wladyslaw. "Das Bauernlegen in Mitteleuropa im 16.–18. Jahrhundert." *Studia Historiae Oeconomicae,* 11 (1976).

Sabean, David. *Power in the Blood: Popular Culture and Village Discourse in Early Modern Germany.* Cambridge, 1984.

Schenk, Eleonore. "Die Anfänge des Wiener Kärtnertortheaters (1710–1748)." Vienna: Ph.D. diss., 1969.

Schieder, Theodor. *Friedrich der Grosse: ein Königtum der Widersprüche.* Franfurt am Main, 1983.

Schiel, Adelbert. *Ignaz von Felbiger und Ferdinand Kindermann. Ihr Leben und ihre Schriften.* Halle, 1902.

Schilfert, Gerhard. *Deutschland 1648–1789.* East Berlin, 1962.

Schissler, Hanna. *Preussische Agrargesellschaft im Wandel. Wirtschaftliche, gesellschaftliche und politische Transformationsprozesse von 1763 bis 1847.* Göttingen, 1978.

Schlesinger, L. "Zur Geschichte der Industrie in Oberleutensdorf." *Mitteilungen des Vereins für die Geschichte der Deutschen in Böhmen,* 3 (1865).

Schlumbohn, Jürgen. "Sozialization and the Family: The Case of the German Lower Middle Classes circa 1800." *International Review of Social History,* 12 (1980).

Schmidt, K. A. *Geschichte der Erziehung.* 4 vols. Stuttgart, 1896.

Schmidt, M. "Philipp Jakob Spener und die Bibel." In Kurt Aland, ed., *Pietismus und Bibel.* Witten-Ruhr, 1970.

Schmidt. R. *Volksschule und Volksschulbau von den Anfängen des niederen Schulwesens bis in die Gegenwart.* Dotzheim, 1967.

Schmitt, Johann. *Der Kampf um den Katechismus in der Aufklärungsperiode Deutschlands.* Munich, 1935.

Schmut, Johann. "Erstes Eingreifen des Staates zur Hebung des niederen Schulwesens in der Steiermark unter Maria Theresa." *Beiträge zur österreichischen Erziehungs- und Schulgeschichte,* 11 (1909).

Schöffler, Herbert. *Deutsches Geistesleben zwischen Reformation und Aufklärung. Von Martin Opitz zu Christian Wolff.* 2d ed. Frankfurt am Main, 1956.

Schrötter, Friedrich Freiherr von. "Die schlesische Wollindustrie im 18. Jahrhundert." *Forschungen zur brandenburgischen und preussischen Geschichte,* 11 (1898).

Sombart, Werner. *Der moderne Kapitalismus.* 4th ed. 3 vols. Munich, 1921–28.

Sommer, Luise. *Die österreichischen Kameralisten in dogmengeschichtlicher Entwicklung.* 2 vols. Vienna, 1920–25.

Stanzel, Josef. *Die Schulaufsicht im Reformwerk des J. I. Felbiger.* Paderborn, 1976.

Stekl, Hannes. *Österreichs Zucht- und Arbeitshäuser 1671–1920.* Vienna, 1978.

Stephan, Gustav. *Die häusliche Erziehung im 18. Jahrhundert.* Wiesbaden, 1898.

Stoeffler, F. Ernest. *German Pietism during the Eighteenth Century.* Leiden, 1973.

Stoll, Andreas. *Geschichte der Lehrerbildung in Tirol.* Weinheim and Berlin, 1968.

Stolze, Wilhelm. "Friedrich Wilehlm I. und die Volksschule." *Historische Zeitschrift,* 107 (1911).

Strakosch-Grassmann, Gustav. *Geschichte des österreichischen Unterrichtswesens.* Vienna, 1905.

Stratmann, Karl Wilhelm. *Die Krise der Berufserziehung im 18. Jahrhundert als Ursprungsfeld pädagogisches Denkens.* Ratingen, 1967.

Strauss, Gerald. *Luther's House of Learning: Indoctrination of the Young in the German Reformation.* Baltimore, 1978.

Svodoba, Jiří. *Protifeudálni a sociálni hnuti v Čechách na konci doby Temna* (1750–1774). Prague, 1967.

Terveen, Fritz. *Gesamtstaat und Rétablissement. Der Wiederaufbau des nördlichen Ostpreussens unter Friedrich Wilhelm I. 1714–1740.* Göttingen, 1954.

Theiner, A. *Zustände der katholischen Kirche in Schlesien von 1740–1758.* Mainz, 1852.

Thomas, Keith. "Work and Leisure in Pre-Industrial Societies." *Past and Present,* 29 (1964).

Tibitanzl, Josef. *Die Bedeutung Ferdinand Kindermanns für das Schulwesen.* Munich, 1905.

Tröger, H. *Die kurmärkischen Spinnerdörfer.* Leipzig, 1936.

Veit, L. A., and Lenhart, L. *Kirche und Volksfrömmigkeit im Zeitalter des Barock.* Freiburg im Breisgau, 1956.

Vierhaus, Rudolf. "Deutschland im 18. Jahrhundert: soziales Gefüge, politische Verfassung, geistige Bewegung." In F. Kopitzsch, ed., *Aufklärung, Absolutismus, Bürgertum.* Munich, 1976.

Volkmer, J. *Johann Ignaz von Felbiger und seine Schulreform.* Habelschwerdt, 1890.

Vollmer, Ferdinand. *Friedrich Wilhelm I. und die Volksschule.* Göttingen, 1909.
Die preussische Volksschulpolitik unter Friedrich dem Grossen. Berlin, 1918.

Walker, Mack. *German Home Towns: Community, State, and General Estate, 1648–1871.* Ithaca, 1971.

"Rights and Functions: The Social Categories of Eighteenth Century Jurists and Cameralists." *Journal of Modern History,* 15 (1978).

Wallmann, Johannes. *Philipp Jakob Spener und die Anfänge des Pietismus.* Tübingen, 1970.

Wandruszka, Adam. "Geheimprotestantismus, Josephinismus, und Volksliturgie in Österreich." *Zeitschrift für Kirchengeschichte,* 78 (1967).

Wangermann, Ernst. *From Joseph II to the Jacobin Trials: Government Policy and Public Opinion in the Habsburg Dominions in the Period of the French Revolution.* Oxford, 1959.

"Reform Catholicism and Political Radicalism in the Austrian Enlightenment." Roy Porter and Mikuláš Teich, eds. *The Enlightenment in National Context.* Cambridge, 1981.

Aufklärung und staatsbürgerliche Erziehung. Gottfried van Swieten als Reformator des österreichischen Unterrichtswesens 1781–1791. Vienna, 1978.

Wehrl, F. " 'Neue Geist.' Eine Untersuchung der Geistesrichtungen des Klerus in Wien von 1750–1790." *Mitteilungen des österreichischen Staatsarchivs,* 19 (1967).

Weigelt, Carl. "Die Volksschule in Preussen nach der preussischen Besitzergreifung." *Zeitschrfit des Vereins für die Geschichte Schlesiens,* 24 (1890).

Weilen, Alexander von. "Das Theater." In Anton Mayer, ed., *Geschichte der Stadt Wien.* Vol. 6. Vienna, 1918.

Weiss, Anton. "Ferdinand Kindermann und die Landschule zu Kaplitz. Ein Beitrag zur Schulgeschichte Böhmens." *Beiträge zur österreichischen Erziehungs- und Schulgeschichte,* 6 (1905).
Geschichte der theresianischen Schulreform in Böhmen. 2 vols. Vienna, 1906.

Weiss, Rudolf. *Das Bistum Passau unter Kardinal Joseph Dominikus von Lamberg (1723–1761). Zugleich ein Beitrag zur Geschichte des Kryptoprotestantismus in Oberösterreich.* St. Ottilien, 1979.

Werner, Richard Maria, ed. *Der Wiener Hanswurst: Stranitzky und seine Nachfolger. Ausgewählte Schriften.* 2 vols. Vienna, 1881–1886.

Wiechowski, Friedrich. "Ferdinand Kindermanns Versuch einer Verbindung von Elementar-

und Industrieschule." *Beiträge zur österreichischen Erziehungs- und Schulgeschichte,* 9 (1907).

Wiedermann, Theodor. *Geschichte der Reformation und Gegenreformation im Lande unter der Enns.* 5 vols. Prague, 1879–82.

Wienecke, F. "Die Begründung der evangelischen Volksschule in der Kurmark und ihre Entwicklung bis zum Tode König Friedrichs I. 1540–1713." *Zeitschrift für die Geschichte der Erziehung und des Unterrichts,* 3 (1913).

Wlczek, Hermann. "Das Schuldrama der Jesuiten zu Krems 1616–1763." Vienna: Ph.D. diss., 1952.

Wolf, Hans. *Das Schulwesen des Temesvarer Banats im 18. Jahrhundert.* Baden bei Wien, 1935.

Wolff, Hans M. *Die Weltanschauung der deutschen Aufklärung in geschichtlicher Entwicklung.* 2d ed. Bern and Munich, 1963.

Wolfsgruber, Coelestin. *Christoph Anton Kardinal Migazzi.* Regensburg, 1897.

Wotke, Karl. "Karl Heinrich Seibt. Der erste Universitätsprofessor der deutschen Sprache in Prag, ein Schuler Gellerts und Gottscheds. Ein Beitrag zur Geschichte des Deutschunterrichts in Österreich." *Beitrage zur österreichischen Erziehungs- und Schulgeschichte,* 9 (1907).

Wright, William. *Serf, Seigneur, and Sovereign: Agrarian Reform in Eighteenth-Century Bohemia.* Minneapolis, 1966.

Wurzbach, Constant von. *Biographisches Lexicon des Kaisertums Österreich (1750–1850).* 60 vols. Vienna, 1856–91.

Zechmeister, Gustav. *Die Wiener Theater nächst der Burg und nächst dem Kärntnertor von 1747 bis 1776.* Vienna, 1971.

Ziekursch, Johannes. *Beiträge zur Charakteristik der preussischen Verwaltungsbeamten in Schlesien bis zum Untergang des friderizianischen Staates.* Breslau, 1907.

Hundert Jahre schlesischer Agrargeschichte. Breslau, 1927.

Zlabinger, E. *Ludovico Antonio Muratori und Österreich.* Innsbruck, 1970.

Zwiedineck-Südenhorst, Hans von. *Dorfleben im achtzehnten Jahrhundert. Culturhistorische Skizzen aus Innerösterreich.* Vienna, 1877.

Index